T0183646

Lecture Notes in Computer Science   11193

Commenced Publication in 1973
Founding and Former Series Editors:
Gerhard Goos, Juris Hartmanis, and Jan van Leeuwen

Editorial Board

David Hutchison
  Lancaster University, Lancaster, UK
Takeo Kanade
  Carnegie Mellon University, Pittsburgh, PA, USA
Josef Kittler
  University of Surrey, Guildford, UK
Jon M. Kleinberg
  Cornell University, Ithaca, NY, USA
Friedemann Mattern
  ETH Zurich, Zurich, Switzerland
John C. Mitchell
  Stanford University, Stanford, CA, USA
Moni Naor
  Weizmann Institute of Science, Rehovot, Israel
C. Pandu Rangan
  Indian Institute of Technology Madras, Chennai, India
Bernhard Steffen
  TU Dortmund University, Dortmund, Germany
Demetri Terzopoulos
  University of California, Los Angeles, CA, USA
Doug Tygar
  University of California, Berkeley, CA, USA
Gerhard Weikum
  Max Planck Institute for Informatics, Saarbrücken, Germany

More information about this series at http://www.springer.com/series/7409

Svetlana S. Bodrunova (Ed.)

Internet Science

5th International Conference, INSCI 2018
St. Petersburg, Russia, October 24–26, 2018
Proceedings

 Springer

Editor
Svetlana S. Bodrunova ⓘ
School of Journalism and Mass
 Communications
Saint Petersburg State University
St. Petersburg, Russia

ISSN 0302-9743   ISSN 1611-3349 (electronic)
Lecture Notes in Computer Science
ISBN 978-3-030-01436-0   ISBN 978-3-030-01437-7 (eBook)
https://doi.org/10.1007/978-3-030-01437-7

Library of Congress Control Number: 2018955708

LNCS Sublibrary: SL3 – Information Systems and Applications, incl. Internet/Web, and HCI

© Springer Nature Switzerland AG 2018
This work is subject to copyright. All rights are reserved by the Publisher, whether the whole or part of the material is concerned, specifically the rights of translation, reprinting, reuse of illustrations, recitation, broadcasting, reproduction on microfilms or in any other physical way, and transmission or information storage and retrieval, electronic adaptation, computer software, or by similar or dissimilar methodology now known or hereafter developed.
The use of general descriptive names, registered names, trademarks, service marks, etc. in this publication does not imply, even in the absence of a specific statement, that such names are exempt from the relevant protective laws and regulations and therefore free for general use.
The publisher, the authors and the editors are safe to assume that the advice and information in this book are believed to be true and accurate at the date of publication. Neither the publisher nor the authors or the editors give a warranty, express or implied, with respect to the material contained herein or for any errors or omissions that may have been made. The publisher remains neutral with regard to jurisdictional claims in published maps and institutional affiliations.

This Springer imprint is published by the registered company Springer Nature Switzerland AG
The registered company address is: Gewerbestrasse 11, 6330 Cham, Switzerland

Preface

The 5th International Conference on Internet Science (INSCI 2018) took place during October 24–26, 2018, in St. Petersburg, Russia, and was organized by the School of Journalism and Mass Communications and the Faculty of Applied Mathematics and Control Processes, St. Petersburg State University. This conference built on the success of the First and Second International Conference on Internet Science that took place in Brussels, Belgium, that were organized by the FP7 European Network of Excellence in Internet Science (EINS) project, with the support of the European Commission. In its third year, the conference moved to Florence, Italy, with support from the Collective Awareness Platforms for Sustainability and Social Innovation (CAPS) initiative. In 2017, the conference was organized by CERTH Information Technology Institute in Thessaloniki, Greece.

Internet Science is a conference with a unique and precise scope; despite its wide-encompassing title, it focuses on interdisciplinary views on the Internet and Internet platforms as tools for people's engagement, opportunities, and better quality of life. In 2018, the sub-theme of the conference was "User Empowerment in World Regions," with a focus on post-Soviet spaces. During the conference, a podium discussion, several keynote speeches, as well as four workshops were organized (see Vol. 2 of the INSCI 2018 proceedings).

In the current volume, the best conference papers are published. Of 73 submissions, 23 were selected for publication in the first volume. They are organized into three thematic chapters.

The first part deals with risks, harm, and challenges for users and the ways to study them via online content. The first contributions are dedicated to the detection of risks linked to health issues, including anorexia and HIV/AIDS, and hate speech elimination from user comments. These are followed by papers on the detection of Islamic extremism in online media; this theme further continues in the papers on regulation of extremism in Russia and the EU and on the topic of international migration (mostly from post-Soviet Islamic Central Asia) in Russian online media.

The second part of the volume focuses on online audiences and methods of defining and detecting them. This more technical part of the volume contains the papers that link network studies to online platforms and user behavior and experience. The variety of platforms being researched ranges from classic websites (university portals and movie recommender systems) to Tumblr and YouTube.

The third part links computational methodologies to communication and media studies. The first three papers here deal with various aspects of users' emotions and concerns, with mixed methodologies used for measuring discovered agendas and user sentiment. The next few papers deal with online tools for certain audience segments, either professional (in public relations and education) or those of the general public. The last paper of the volume describes the Russian cybersports community as a platform for intercultural dialogue.

Along with these papers, the conference hosted keynote speeches by Olessia Koltsova, head of the Laboratory for Internet Studies (LINIS) at the Higher School of Economics (St. Petersburg, Russia), Cornelius Puschmann, senior researcher at the Hans-Bredow-Institut (Hamburg, Germany), Elena Scherstoboeva, an expert on Internet regulation at the Higher School of Economics (Moscow, Russia) and other scholars from Russia and Europe. Also, on October 26, four workshops were held. Two more tech-oriented workshop were dedicated to chatbot research and design as well as to detecting social problems via texts on online platforms. The two other workshops focused on the role of distributed technologies in decentralization of governance and to government and media narratives on the Internet itself.

This focused and intense program would not be possible if not for the support from representatives of various academic, governmental, and industrial institutions around Europe and Russia. We express our gratitude to our international Steering and Program Committees, as well as to the reviewers and local organizers, panel and workshop chairs, for their commitment and hard work. We are grateful to all the submitters, authors of published papers, and conference participants for their continuous effort to make this volume a decent contribution to the field of Internet science. We are happy to see the conference expanding in its scope and coverage of world regions, and hope for INSCI's future success.

October 2018   Svetlana S. Bodrunova

Organization

Steering Committee

Thanassis Tiropanis	University of Southampton, UK
Anna Satsiou	Centre for Research and Technology Hellas, Greece
Jonathan Cave	University of Warwick, UK
Olessia Koltsova	National Research University - Higher School of Economics, Russia
Fabrizio Sestini	European Commission DG CONNECT, Belgium
Franco Bagnoli	University of Florence, Italy

Local Organizing Committee

Svetlana Bodrunova	St. Petersburg State University, Russia
Heiko Niedermayer	Technical University of Munich, Germany
Anna Smoliarova	St. Petersburg State University, Russia
Ivan Blekanov	St. Petersburg State University, Russia
Ovanes Petrosyan	St. Petersburg State University, Russia

Program Committee

Svetlana Alexeeva	St. Petersburg State University, Russia
Nora Alrajebah	King Saud University, Saudi Arabia
Gregory Asmolov	King's College London, UK
Ruslan Bekurov	St. Petersburg State University, Russia
Natalia Belyakova	ITMO University, Russia
Ivan Blekanov	St. Petersburg State University, Russia
Svetlana Bodrunova	St. Petersburg State University, Russia
Ekaterina Bogomoletc	North Carolina State University, USA
Ilia Bykov	St. Petersburg State University, Russia
Jonathan Cave	University of Warwick and Regulatory Policy Committee, UK
Yulia Danilova	St. Petersburg State University, Russia
Sergey Davydov	National Research University Higher School of Economics, Russia
Sotiris Diplaris	Information Technologies Institute, Centre for Research and Technology Hellas, Greece
Olga Dovbysh	St. Petersburg State University, Russia
Ksenia Eltsova	Russian State University for the Humanities, Russia
Anastasia Folts	Lomonosov Moscow State University, Russia
Anna Gladkova	Lomonosov Moscow State University, Russia
Margarita Gladkova	St. Petersburg State University, Russia

Anna Golovkina	St. Petersburg State University, Russia
Maria Gourieva	St. Petersburg State University, Russia
Jens Grossklags	Technical University of Munich, Germany
Aliaksandr Herasimenka	University of Westminster, UK
Yury Kabanov	National Research University Higher School of Economics, Russia
Konstantinos Kafetsios	University of Crete, Greece
Aikaterini Katmada	Information Technologies Institute, Centre for Research and Technology Hellas, Greece
Anastasia Kazun	National Research University Higher School of Economics, Russia
Nora Kirkizh	City University of New York, USA
Hanna Klimpe	Hamburg University of Applied Sciences, Germany
Polina Kolozaridi	National Research University Higher School of Economics, Russia
Olessia Koltsova	National Research University Higher School of Economics, Russia
Efstratios Kontopoulos	Information Technologies Institute, Centre for Research and Technology Hellas, Greece
Suriya Kumacheva	St. Petersburg State University, Russia
Yanina Ledovaya	St. Petersburg State University, Russia
Elena Lezhnina	St. Petersburg State University, Russia
Anna Litvinenko	Free University of Berlin, Germany
Alexandra Lukina	St. Petersburg State University, Russia
Yuri Misnikov	ITMO University, Russia
Oleg Nagornyy	National Research University Higher School of Economics, Russia
Alexandra Nenko	National Research University Higher School of Economics, Russia
Heiko Niedermayer	Technical University of Munich, Germany
Kamilla Nigmatullina	St. Petersburg State University, Russia
Yaroslavna B. Pankratova	St. Petersburg State University, International Banking Institute, Russia
Miguel Pardal	University of Lisbon, Portugal
Andrey Parfenov	St. Petersburg State University, Russia
Sergey Pashakhin	National Research University Higher School of Economics, Russia
Ovanes Petrosian	St. Petersburg State University, Russia
Sergey Pogozhev	St. Petersburg State University, Russia
Tatiana Romashko	University of Jyväskylä, Finland
Mark Rouncefield	Lancaster University, UK
Yuri Rykov	National Research University Higher School of Economics, Russia
Laura Sartori	University of Bologna
Anna Satsiou	Information Technologies Institute, Centre for Research and Technology Hellas, Greece

Galina Selivanova	Scuola Normale Superiore, Italy
Elena Sherstoboeva	National Research University Higher School of Economics, Russia
Yadviga Sinyavskaya	National Research University Higher School of Economics, Russia
Paul Smith	Austrian Institute of Technology, Austria
Anna Smoliarova	St. Petersburg State University, Russia
Federico Subervi	University of Leeds, UK
Gabriella Szabó	Centre for Social Sciences, Hungarian Academy of Sciences, Hungary
Thanassis Tiropanis	University of Southampton, UK
Florian Toepfl	Free University of Berlin, Germany
Dirk-Claas Ulrich	Technical University of Dortmund, Germany
Ilya Utekhin	St. Petersburg State University, Russia
Leonid Yuldashev	Internet and Society Club, Russia
Andrei Zavadski	Free University of Berlin, Germany
Nina Zhuravleva	St. Petersburg State University, Russia

Contents

Risks on the Internet: Detecting Harmful Content and Discussing Regulation

Early Risk Detection of Anorexia on Social Media

Diana Ramírez-Cifuentes, Marc Mayans, and Ana Freire(✉)

Web Science and Social Computing Research Group,
Universitat Pompeu Fabra, Barcelona, Carrer Tanger, 122-140,
08018 Barcelona, Spain
{diana.ramirez,ana.freire}@upf.edu
marc.mayans01@estudiant.upf.edu

Abstract. This paper proposes an approach for the early detection of anorexia nervosa (AN) on social media. We present a machine learning approach that processes the texts written by social media users. This method relies on a set of features based on domain-specific vocabulary, topics, psychological processes, and linguistic information extracted from the users' writings. This approach penalizes the delay in detecting positive cases in order to classify the users in risk as early as possible. Identifying anorexia early, along with an appropriate treatment, improves the speed of recovery and the likelihood of staying free of the illness. The results of this work showed that our proposal is suitable for the early detection of AN symptoms.

Keywords: Early risk detection · Eating disorders · Social media
Anorexia · Machine learning

1 Introduction

Eating Disorders (ED) are characterized by abnormal attitudes towards food and unusual eating habits [3]. Every 62 min, at least one person dies as a direct result from an eating disorder [8]. Anorexia Nervosa is an ED defined by the restriction in eating to keep a low weight [3]. With a mortality rate of 5% per decade, AN has the highest mortality rate of all mental disorders [8]. Due to the fact that the symptoms associated with mental illnesses have been proved to be observable on social media [21], different automated methods to detect them have been designed. The review made by Guntuku's et al. [16] shows that most of these methods are based on the analysis of user-generated data on online social networks, Web forums and blogs.

Early intervention for eating disorders is essential. According to the findings of Treasure et al. [29], when adolescents with AN are given family-based treatment within the first three years of the illness onset, they have a much greater likelihood of recovery. The current automated methods to detect mental illnesses, and eating disorders within them, are based on machine learning approaches that

© Springer Nature Switzerland AG 2018
S. S. Bodrunova (Ed.): INSCI 2018, LNCS 11193, pp. 3–14, 2018.
https://doi.org/10.1007/978-3-030-01437-7_1

do not consider the delay in detecting positive cases. This issue is addressed by the work of Losada et al. [19], where the proposal of a temporal-aware risk detection benchmark, complements the evaluation of the accuracy of the decisions taken by the algorithms.

We develop an approach suitable for the early detection of AN symptoms using a labeled dataset corresponding to the eRisk 2018[1] research collection [19], which contains writings posted in Reddit[2]. This approach does not aim to be a complete system for the AN detection, but an algorithm that could be used for the development of a platform for detecting users in risk.

This paper is structured as follows: Sect. 2 reports the related work in detecting eating disorders on social media and the application of early risk measures. Section 3 shows our research proposal, describing mainly the feature extraction process and the learning algorithms used for both tasks. Our experimental setup is reported in Sect. 4, followed by our results and findings in Sect. 5. Finally, Sect. 6 summarises our conclusions.

2   Related Work

In 2003, eating disorders represented the third most common chronic illness in adolescent females worldwide. The prevalence of AN was about 0.3%, whereas Bulimia Nervosa (BN) was more common, with a prevalence of about 1% in young women and 0.1% in men [32]. In Europe, according to a more recent study conducted in 2016, AN was reported by 1–4% of women, and 0.3–0.7% of men. Among these people, only about one-third was detected by health-care [17]. Moreover, young people with ages between 15 to 24 years old with anorexia have 10 times the risk of dying compared to their same age peers [20].

If left untreated, eating disorders tend to become more severe and less receptive to treatment [20]. This can provide an insight on how important is to detect their symptoms as early as possible. In the Web, Pro-eating disorder sites usage is prevalent among adolescents with these conditions [33]. Moreover, their engagement with this type of content has recently been suggested as a screening factor for these kind of illnesses [6]. On social media, people with eating disorders, such as anorexia and bulimia, can be identified by the usage of certain keywords that characterise and promote these conditions [2,31]. In these sense, features or variables that have been extracted from labeled user-generated data [16] are used to generate predictive models capable of doing an automated analysis of social media data. Based on the related work done for detecting mental illnesses in online social platforms, the analysed data is obtained either by diagnosing participants with the usage of surveys [14,26,30], or by crawling directly the data from public online sources like Reddit, Twitter or Facebook [2,11,24].

In order to build predictive models, the most common features extracted for analysing and predicting mental illnesses are those related to the texts written by the users, such as: topics [23,28,30], frequencies of words or combinations of

---

[1] http://early.irlab.org/.
[2] http://www.reddit.com/.

words (N-grams) [28,30], and features obtained using dictionaries like LIWC[3], which can provide an insight on the usage of self references, social words and emotions [13,14]. Related works have studied the users' posting frequency in different periods of the day and year [2,10,13], and have also obtained features from the relationships between users, taking into account the number of friends, or followers [2,14]. Additionally, some studies use features based on sentiment analysis, considering the subjectivity or polarity of a phrase [13,14,30].

To the extent of our knowledge, building predictive models to detect early risk of ED is not a widely explored task yet. For detecting other mental illnesses, such as depression, some works have attempted to do their analysis with data prior to the diagnosis [14,30]. In particular, the work of Losada et al. [19] proposes a new metric to measure the effectiveness of early alert systems. This metric, known as Early Risk Detection Error (ERDE) penalizes the delay in detecting positive cases, and is suitable to evaluate our proposal.

3   Proposal

The main objective of our proposal is to detect positive cases of anorexia as soon as possible, minimizing the ERDE and maximizing the F1 Score. We use machine learning techniques that combine a set of features extracted from the concatenated writings of users on social media. An approach based on the *dynamic strategy* proposed in [19] is used. This method consists in building incrementally, writing per writing, a representation of each user, and applying a classifier, which was previously trained with all the users texts. Following this approach, depending on the algorithm used, a decision is made if the classifier outputs a confidence value above a given threshold.

Our approach modifies the dynamic strategy of [19] by defining a minimum amount of information that should be seen by the system before applying the classifier and emitting a positive decision. We include this threshold to avoid false positives when the posts contain very few words. For instance, if the first post of a user is read and it contains five words with the word *laxative* mentioned twice, our classifier might give it a high score and classify the user as anorexic having seen only one short post. The threshold -number of words- is defined by the *text length threshold TLT* (see Eq. 1). To define the TLT we first assume that each user has a fixed number of words per post, denoted as *maxPostLenght*. To calculate this number we plotted a histogram to visualise the distribution of the number of words per post of all the users with anorexia (see Fig. 1). We could observe that 80% of the users wrote up to 90 words per post. Based on Pareto's principle we chose this number of words for the *maxPostLenght* value. We asumed that seeing just one post of a fixed size was not enough, we considered that exploring more posts would reduce the amount of false positives. This number of posts, was defined by a percentage *selectionPercentage* of the *average number of posts per user*, 372.6 in our case, which was denoted as *avgPosts*. For our

---

[3] http://liwc.wpengine.com/.

experiments we chose to work with 10% for the value of *selectionPercentage*. For the analysed dataset the TLT value resulted in 3330 words.

$$TLT = maxPostLenght \times avgPosts \times selectionPercentage \qquad (1)$$

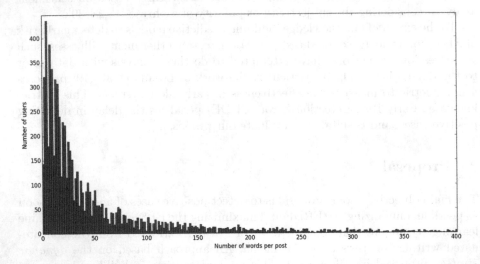

Fig. 1. Histogram of the number of words per post.

3.1 Feature Extraction

We fed our models with features that characterise the content of the writings. Further details are explained below and summarised in Table 1.

Psychological and Linguistic Processes: We calculate features to characterise the users' writings. These features were calculated by taking into account the frequency of words belonging to the categories of the LIWC2007 dictionary [22], which has been previously used in detecting mental health issues [9,10]. In this sense, scores that consider linguistic and psychological processes, as well as personal concerns and spoken categories were obtained. We consider a new feature value for each category defined in the LIWC2007 dictionary. The list and description of these categories can be found in [22]. The scores were calculated normalising the frequencies of words by the total number of words in the writings of a user. Given that certain words could belong to multiple categories, the normalization value was augmented in one each time a word was part of more than one category.

Domain-Related Vocabulary: 9 features were defined by creating categories of words that belong to domains related with anorexia. The vocabulary for these categories was obtained from the codebook's domains and sample key-words defined in [2]. The domains are: anorexia, body image, food and meals, eating, caloric restriction, binge, compensatory behavior, and exercises. These features were calculated in the same way as the psychological and linguistic processes features.

N-Grams: They consist of sets of co-occuring words within a given window (N). Studies have extensively used them in text mining and natural language processing tasks [15]. Considering that previous works have considered them as features for detecting depression and eating disorders [28,30], we did a $tf \cdot idf$ vectorization of the unigrams and bigrams of the training set writings. For this step, we used the *TfIdfVectorizer* from the *scikit-learn* Python library[4], with a stop-words list and the removal of the n-grams that appeared in less than 20 documents. The content of a document was defined by the concatenation of all the writings of a user.

Topic Modelling: Topic Modeling consists on automatically extracting and identifying topics that are present in documents in order to obtain hidden patterns of a corpus. A known method proposed by Blei et al. [4] is the Latent Dirichlet Allocation (LDA), which is an unsupervised generative statistical model in which the topics are represented by a set of terms or words. Many authors evidence that, in tasks of prediction and classification, the use of this method is significant and relevant. For instance, the authors in [27,30,34] conclude that features based on topic modeling are useful in tasks for recognising depressive, and suicidal users. Also, this technique has been used in [7], combined with other features, to quantify and predict the mental illnesses severity in online pro-eating disorder communities.

To define the topics we used English stopwords and only considered the words that appeared at least in 10% of the training documents. The 50 features used by the model are given by the probabilistic distribution of 50 topics for each analyzed text. The *LatentDirichletAllocation* module from the *scikit-learn* Python library(see footnote 4) was used to do this implementation.

3.2   Learning Algorithms

We explored four different prediction methods, i.e., Logistic Regression, Random Forest, Support Vector Machine (SVM), and Multilayer Perceptron (MLP) since they have been used previously as classifiers for similar tasks [18,19,23]. They are briefly explained below:

---

[4] http://scikit-learn.org/.

Table 1. Features considered

Feature type	Details and resources	Number of features
Linguistic and psychological processes	LIWC	64
Domain-related vocabulary	Anorexia vocabulary	9
N-grams	Unigrams	4303
N-grams	Bigrams	667
Topic modeling	Topics using LDA	50

Logistic Regression (LR): it stands as a statistical method used to predict a binary outcome given a set of independent variables. This algorithm fits data to a logit function in order to predict the probability of occurrence of an event [1].

Random Forest (RF): this is a classification method that works by building many decision trees at training time. For the classification tasks, its output is the class that is the mode of the classes of the individual trees [5].

Support Vector Machine (SVM): algorithm that finds a decision plane that maximizes the distance between the different data classes to classify [12]. We have used a linear kernel and balanced class weights.

Multilayer Perceptron (MLP): this algorithm is a feed-forward artificial neural network [25]. We implemented an MLP with one hidden layer of 200 neurons and a logistic activation function. The solver for weight optimization is the Limited-memory BFGS, which is an optimization algorithm in the family of quasi-Newton methods that approximates the Broyden–Fletcher–Goldfarb–Shanno algorithm.

4   Experimental Setup

Our experiments are conducted over the eRisk 2018 research collection [19], which contains a labeled dataset with writings of a control group and of people diagnosed with anorexia as detailed in Sect. 4.1. *Python 3.6.5* [5] and, in particular, the *scikit-learn Python* library was used for the implementation of the proposed methods.

Using the provided data we defined training and test sets. To train our models we applied 10-fold cross validation and optimized the parameters through grid search. Each instance for our training task represented a user, and was defined by the features mentioned in Sect. 3.1. These features were extracted from all the sequentially-concatenated writings of each user. The test set allowed us to evaluate the behavior of the dynamic method, where the classifiers were applied

---

[5] https://docs.python.org/3/.

each time a new writing was read. Also, this set was used to define a threshold that represented the minimum probability value required by an instance to be classified as positive. After having tested different values for the LR and RF classifiers, this threshold was set as 0.75 and 0.55 respectively. Moreover, a minimum number of words (3330) defined by the TLT (1), had to be processed before emitting a positive decision.

4.1 Dataset Description

Our method analysed a collection composed by chronologically ordered writings (posts or comments) from a set of Reddit users [19]. Users were labeled as anorexic and non-anorexic. The dataset statistics are detailed in Table 2.

Table 2. Main statistics of the train and test collections

	Train		Test	
	Anorexia	Control	Anorexia	Control
Num. subjects	20	132	41	279
Num. writings	7,452	77,514	17,422	151,364
Avg num. writings	372.6	587.2	424.9	542.5
Avg num. words per submission	41.2	20.9	35.7	20.9

4.2 Evaluation

For the evaluation of the performance of our methods we report the Precision, Recall and F1-Score. In addition to this commonly known measures, we evaluate our proposal in terms of the ERDE [19], which gives a cost c to each binary decision d taken by the system at a number k of textual items seen before making a decision. This error is defined in our case as:

$$ERDE_o(d, k) = \begin{cases} c_{fp} & \text{if } d = \text{ False Positive (FP)} \\ c_{fn} & \text{if } d = \text{ False Negative (FN)} \\ lc_o(k) \cdot c_{tp} & \text{if } d = \text{ True Positive (TP)} \\ 0 & \text{if } d = \text{ True Negative (TN)} \end{cases} \qquad (2)$$

where $c_{fp} = 0.13$, $c_{fn} = 1$, $c_{tp} = 1$, and the cost function $lc_o(k)$ is a sigmoid function to penalize the late emissions:

$$lc_o(k) = 1 - \frac{1}{1 + e^{k-o}} \qquad (3)$$

Notice that the c_{fp} value was set according to the proportion of positive cases in the data and o is a parameter of (3) which defines the point at which the cost grows more quickly [19].

4.3   Baselines

In order to test our approach we set four different baselines based on Losada et al. [19] since they have a similar objective and a dataset extracted from Reddit as well. The baselines are described as follows:

Random: This is a naïve strategy that makes a random decision after seeing the first message. This decision could be positive ("anorexic") or negative ("non anorexic"). This strategy is fast but we assume its effectiveness will be poor.

Minority: This is another naïve strategy that predicts a positive decision ("anorexic") for each user right after processing the first message. Again, this strategy makes a quick decision but it is expected to have poor effectiveness.

First n: This strategy consists on concatenating the first n submissions from each user and getting the prediction provided by our model. If the user has less than n posts, all the data available for that user is used.

Dynamic: This strategy consists on analyzing and building incrementally a representation of each user. Messages are concatenated one per one, and a prediction is made by our model each time a new message is added. This is done until a positive decision is reached. The system can emit a positive decision ("anorexic") only if the classifier outputs a confidence value above a given threshold (0.75). This method does not work with a fixed number of messages. If the stream of texts is over, the method concludes with a negative decision ("non anorexic").

For the *Dynamic* and the *First n* baselines we have employed a quite simple model, which consisted in a Logistic Regression classifier trained and tested with features extracted from the posts. These features were based on the *tf-idf* vectorization considering unigrams.

5   Results

The evaluation of the proposed baselines can be found in Table 3. The best results are obtained by the *Dynamic* strategy with a confidence threshold of 0.75. In terms of precision, the *First n* strategy offers better results. As we expect, the *Random* and *Minority* strategies have a poor performance. Also we can see clearly that the best results of the ERDE metric are obtained by the *Dynamic* strategy, which is why we choose its results as our baseline to be compared with the models of our proposal.

In Table 4 we report the results obtained after running the learning algorithms described in Sect. 3.2 in combination with the features described in Sect. 3.1. We can see that the usage of features based in the LIWC dictionary, the TLT value and the LDA features have improved the results of the baseline, in terms of the F1 score and ERDE100, using the same learning algorithm (LR).

Table 3. Baselines (Linear Regression). In bold, the best result for each evaluation metric.

	F1	P	R	ERDE5	ERDE10	ERDE50	ERDE100
Random	0.18	0.11	0.44	13.05%	12.95%	12.95%	12.95%
Minority	0.23	0.13	**1.00**	11.40%	11.17%	11.17%	11.17%
First 10	0.46	**0.81**	0.32	12.87%	11.17%	9.46%	9.46%
First 100	0.72	0.73	0.71	13.17%	13.15%	11.53%	8.80%
First 500	0.72	0.64	0.83	13.29%	13.27%	11.65%	11.42%
Dynamic	**0.72**	0.67	0.78	**9.89%**	**8.76%**	**6.97%**	**5.80%**

For the Support Vector Machine classifier, we can see that the algorithm improves significantly the baseline in terms of the F1 score (0.85), and ERDE100 (4.22%). We consider this as our best model.

In the case of the Random Forest algorithm, the results have worsened in terms of the F1 score having a low Recall value but the best precision of all our models (0.94). In terms of the ERDE it does not get better results compared to our baseline.

With the Multilayer Perceptron algorithm, the F1 score has improved, with a higher precision, but the Recall value has decreased compared to the dynamic strategy of the baseline.

Referring to our results, we can see that for all our models the ERDE5 and ERDE10 scores are high due to the TLT value that we have defined in order to decrease the number of false positives. In this sense we have tested the best algorithm (SVM) results, with the same features but without the TLT restriction. Table 5 reports these results. The most remarkable thing is the improvement in the ERDE metric, which is important considering our attempt to detect positive cases as early as possible.

Table 4. Proposed classifiers with the modified Dynamic strategy. In bold, the best result for each evaluation metric.

	F1	P	R	ERDE5	ERDE10	ERDE50	ERDE100
LR + LDA + TFIDF + LIWC	0.76	0.72	0.80	13.33%	13.31%	7.86%	5.05%
SVM + LDA + TFIDF + LIWC	**0.85**	0.85	**0.85**	**13.05%**	**13.04%**	**7.26%**	**4.22%**
RF + LDA + TFIDF + LIWC	0.53	**0.94**	0.37	12.85%	12.85%	11.90%	10.43%
MLP + LDA + TFIDF + LIWC	0.77	0.81	0.73	13.09%	13.09%	8.01%	5.90%

Table 5. Comparision between the best model (SVM + LDA + TFIDF + LIWC) with TLT and without TLT. In bold, the best result for each evaluation metric.

	F1	P	R	ERDE5	ERDE10	ERDE50	ERDE100
SVM + LDA + TFIDF + LIWC	**0.85**	0.85	**0.85**	13.05%	13.04%	7.26%	4.22%
SVM (NO TLT)	0.80	0.73	**0.88**	8.38%	7.41%	4.43%	3.80%

6   Conclusions and Future Work

In this paper we have proposed models for the early detection of cases of anorexia on social media. We present a temporal-aware approach, which aims to reduce the penalisation of the delay for detecting positive cases. Different machine learning models were built and tested. These models were fed with features based on linguistic information, domain-specific vocabulary, topics and psychological processes. In terms of the F1 Score and ERDE of our best models, the results have shown that the proposed approaches are suitable for the early detection of anorexia as they clearly improve our baselines.

As a future work, new features and learning algorithms will be tested. We will study in depth the introduction of voting methods, as they have been previously applied with success in similar cases [18]. Finally, we will investigate how to overcome the trade-off between avoiding the prediction of false positives and reducing the time needed to do the prediction. This means that we will explore a way to get a better precision without getting a high ERDE.

Acknowledgements. This work was supported by the Spanish Ministry of Economy and Competitiveness under the Maria de Maeztu Units of Excellence Programme (MDM-2015-0502).

References

1. Agresti, A.: Categorical Data Analysis. Wiley Series in Probability and Statistics. Wiley, Hoboken (2013). https://books.google.es/books?id=UOrr47-2oisC
2. Arseniev-Koehler, A., Lee, H., McCormick, T., Moreno, M.: #proana: pro-eating disorder socialization on twitter, vol. 58, April 2016
3. American Psychiatric Association: Diagnostic and Statistical Manual of Mental Disorders: DSM-5, 5th edn. American Psychiatric Association, Arlington (2013)
4. Blei, D.M., Ng, A.Y., Jordan, M.I.: Latent dirichlet allocation. J. Mach. Learn. Res. **3**, 993–1022 (2003). http://dl.acm.org/citation.cfm?id=944919.944937
5. Breiman, L.: Random forests. Mach. Learn. **45**(1), 5–32 (2001). https://doi.org/10.1023/A:1010933404324
6. Campbell, K., Peebles, R.: Eating disorders in children and adolescents: state of the art review. https://doi.org/10.1542/peds.2014-0194
7. Chancellor, S., Lin, Z., Goodman, E.L., Zerwas, S., De Choudhury, M.: Quantifying and predicting mental illness severity in online pro-eating disorder communities. In: Proceedings of the 19th ACM Conference on Computer-Supported Cooperative Work & Social Computing, CSCW 2016, pp. 1171–1184. ACM, New York (2016). https://doi.org/10.1145/2818048.2819973
8. Coalition, E.D.: Facts about eating disorders: what the research shows (2016)
9. Coppersmith, G., Harman, C., Dredze, M.: Measuring post traumatic stress disorder in Twitter, pp. 579–582, January 2014
10. Coppersmith, G., Dredze, M., Harman, C.: Quantifying mental health signals in Twitter (2014)
11. Coppersmith, G., Dredze, M., Harman, C., Hollingshead, K., Mitchell, M.: CLPsych 2015 shared task: depression and PTSD on twitter. In: CLPsych@HLT-NAACL (2015)

12. Cortes, C., Vapnik, V.: Support-vector networks. Mach. Learn. **20**(3), 273–297 (1995). https://doi.org/10.1007/BF00994018
13. De Choudhury, M., Counts, S., Horvitz, E.J., Hoff, A.: Characterizing and predicting postpartum depression from shared facebook data. In: Proceedings of the 17th ACM Conference on Computer Supported Cooperative Work & Social Computing, CSCW 2014, pp. 626–638. ACM, New York (2014). https://doi.org/10.1145/2531602.2531675
14. De Choudhury, M., Gamon, M., Counts, S., Horvitz, E.: Predicting depression via social media. In: AAAI, July 2013. https://www.microsoft.com/en-us/research/publication/predicting-depression-via-social-media/
15. Elberrichi, Z.: Text mining using n-grams, January 2006
16. Guntuku, S.C., Yaden, D.B., Kern, M.L., Ungar, L.H., Eichstaedt, J.C.: Detecting depression and mental illness on social media: an integrative review. Curr. Opin. Behav. Sci. **18**, 43–49 (2017). https://doi.org/10.1016/j.cobeha.2017.07.005. Big data in the behavioural sciences
17. Keski-Rahkonen, A., Mustelin, L.: Epidemiology of eating disorders in Europe: prevalence, incidence, comorbidity, course, consequences, and risk factors, vol. 29, September 2016
18. Leiva, Victor, Freire, Ana: Towards suicide prevention: early detection of depression on social media. In: Kompatsiaris, Ioannis, et al. (eds.) INSCI 2017. LNCS, vol. 10673, pp. 428–436. Springer, Cham (2017). https://doi.org/10.1007/978-3-319-70284-1_34
19. Losada, David E., Crestani, Fabio: A test collection for research on depression and language use. In: Fuhr, Norbert, et al. (eds.) CLEF 2016. LNCS, vol. 9822, pp. 28–39. Springer, Cham (2016). https://doi.org/10.1007/978-3-319-44564-9_3
20. Maximilian, F.M., Norbert, Q.: Mortality in eating disorders - results of a large prospective clinical longitudinal study. Int. J. Eat. Disord. **49**(4), pp. 391–401. https://doi.org/10.1002/eat.22501
21. Park, M., Cha, C., Cha, M.: Depressive moods of users portrayed in Twitter, pp. 1–8, January 2012
22. Pennebaker, J.W., Chung, C.K., Ireland, M., Gonzales, A., Booth, R.J.: The Development and Psychometric Properties of LIWC2007. This article is published by LIWC Inc., Austin, Texas 78703 USA in conjunction with the LIWC2007 software program. http://www.liwc.net/LIWC2007LanguageManual.pdf
23. PreoȚiuc-Pietro, D., et al.: The role of personality, age, and gender in tweeting about mental illness. In: Proceedings of the 2nd Workshop on Computational Linguistics and Clinical Psychology: From Linguistic Signal to Clinical Reality, pp. 21–30. Association for Computational Linguistics (2015). https://doi.org/10.3115/v1/W15-1203
24. Prieto, V.M., Matos, S., Alvarez, M., Cacheda, F., Oliveira, J.L.: Twitter: a good place to detect health conditions. PloS one **9**, e86191 (2014)
25. Ramchoun, H., Amine, M., Idrissi, J., Ghanou, Y., Ettaouil, M.: Multilayer perceptron: architecture optimization and training. IJIMAI **4**(1), 26–30 (2016)
26. Reece, A.G., Reagan, A.J., Lix, K.L.M., Dodds, P.S., Danforth, C.M., Langer, E.J.: Forecasting the onset and course of mental illness with twitter data. Sci. Rep. **7**, 13006 (2017)
27. Resnik, P., Garron, A., Resnik, R.: Using topic modeling to improve prediction of neuroticism and depression in college students, pp. 1348–1353, January 2013
28. Schwartz, H.A., et al.: Towards assessing changes in degree of depression through Facebook (2014)

29. Treasure, J., Russell, G.: The case for early intervention in anorexia nervosa: theoretical exploration of maintaining factors. Br. J. Psychiatry **199**(1), 5–7 (2011). https://doi.org/10.1192/bjp.bp.110.087585
30. Tsugawa, S., Kikuchi, Y., Kishino, F., Nakajima, K., Itoh, Y., Ohsaki, H.: Recognizing depression from twitter activity. In: Proceedings of the 33rd Annual ACM Conference on Human Factors in Computing Systems, CHI 2015, pp. 3187–3196. ACM, New York (2015). https://doi.org/10.1145/2702123.2702280
31. Wang, T., Brede, M., Ianni, A., Mentzakis, E.: Detecting and characterizing eating-disorder communities on social media. In: WSDM (2017)
32. Wijbrand, H.H., van Hoeken, D.: Review of the prevalence and incidence of eating disorders. Int. J. Eat. Disord. **34**(4), 383–396. https://doi.org/10.1002/eat.10222
33. Wilson, J.L., Peebles, R., Hardy, K.K., Litt, I.F.: Surfing for thinness: a pilot study of pro-eating disorder web site usage in adolescents with eating disorders. Pediatrics **118**(6), e1635-43 (2006)
34. Zhang, L., Huang, X., Liu, T., Chen, Z., Zhu, T.: Using linguistic features to estimate suicide probability of Chinese microblog users. CoRR abs/1411.0861 (2014). http://arxiv.org/abs/1411.0861

Studying Stigmatization and Status Disclosure Among People Living with HIV/AIDS in Russia Through Online Health Communities

Victoria Dudina[✉] and Anna Tsareva

St. Petersburg State University, Universitetskaya nab., 7-9,
199034 St. Petersburg, Russia
viktoria_dudina@mail.ru, art-comm05@yandex.ru

Abstract. Taking into account that HIV/AIDS is highly stigmatized in Russia, online health communities play an important role in providing emotional and informational support to people living with HIV/AIDS. Online health communities can also be considered as an important way of data collection. The purpose of the study was to examine how people living with HIV/AIDS discuss in Internet disclosure of their HIV-status in the context of stigmatization. Data were collected through the web site "Forum for people living with HIV/AIDS". The processing and analysis of data was carried out in QDAS NVivo. Interpretations of the disease, reported by forum users, vary from total rejection to attempts to justify themselves in front of others. The most negative response to disease reported by users is the concealment of one's status from sexual partners. There are clearly manifested differences between people who have recently learned about their illness and those who have lived with HIV/AIDS for a long time and have developed some strategies for resistance to stigma and for coping with the disease. Based on the data analyzed, we can hypothesize that the more user perceive the illness as a "punishment" for inappropriate behavior the more difficulties she or he experiences with the disclosure of HIV status. The peer support plays an important role in the acceptance of status and in the reduction of internalized stigma.

Keywords: Online health community ·
Stigmatization of people living with HIV/AIDS · Status disclosure

1 Introduction

Giving that HIV/AIDS is still a highly stigmatized disease in Russia, the qualitative research of people living with HIV/AIDS faces some difficulties related to limited access to respondents who suffer stigmatization and refusal of enrolled respondents to talk openly and frankly about their condition. In an attempt to study the topic of stigma, researchers are not always able to obtain data meeting the quality criteria. For example, there is a high probability that less stigmatized respondents are more willing to agree to participate in the research than those who refuse to answer. Another critical factor is the influence of the interviewer. As stigmatized people do not often tend to talk frankly about their problems, some respondents may downplay the effects of stigmatization,

© Springer Nature Switzerland AG 2018
S. S. Bodrunova (Ed.): INSCI 2018, LNCS 11193, pp. 15–24, 2018.
https://doi.org/10.1007/978-3-030-01437-7_2

while others, on the contrary, may overstate the events of their own lives and exaggerate the impact of stigma under the influence of the interviewer's inquiries.

Under the circumstances, unobtrusive methods of data collection could be a good solution. At present, there are many online resources and communities on the Internet where people living with HIV/AIDS can discuss problems with those who are in the similar situation. These online resources can play an important role of the support facility that people living with HIV/AIDS lack in everyday life. Relative anonymity and impersonality of online communication let people speak in public about problems that seem oversensitive to discuss offline with friends, relatives, and, thus, compensates for the lack of communication and contributes to overcoming isolation. Consequently, different kinds of Internet sites, from social networks to thematic forums, where people with HIV-diagnosis communicate and exchange information, became an essential source of information that social researchers can use. Communication on such resources is stimulated not by research questions, as it happens in an interview, but by replicas of participants who bring their concerns to the agenda. Although such data could be unstructured and incomplete, but anonymity and voluntariness of participation in online communities undoubtedly facilitates the process of studying groups vulnerable to stigmatization and makes research of sensitive topics more effective.

The purpose of the research was to examine how people living with HIV/AIDS in Russia discuss disclosure of their HIV-status in the context of stigmatization. The most wide research question that guided the data collection was to understand how people living with HIV/AIDS experience stigmatization, how it affects the perception of the disease and HIV status disclosure. We also had an additional task to consider the functions of online communication concerning opportunities to overcome stigma.

2 Theory

Stigmatization of people with various diseases attracts the interest of researchers in terms of how certain biological conditions are being subjected to negative social categorization. The consequences of stigmatization for people with certain disease are the other aspect of this problem. Although a lot of research has been devoted to the stigmatization of people living with HIV/AIDS, there are many discussed issues remain.

Researchers identify six dimensions of stigma associated with HIV: enacted stigma - discriminating behavior, actions or attitudes of other people; perceived or internalized stigma - the stigma experienced because of having a disease; marginalization; disclosure of status; moral norms and values; visible manifestations of a disease. These six dimensions are all interrelated. They reveal complex dynamics of marginalization, the status disclosure, ethical aspects and visible signs of illness through an enacted and internalized stigma [2, p. 5]. Herek identified four characteristics of HIV/AIDS, which can explain the high stigmatization of this disease. The first characteristic is related to the representation about personal responsibility for the illness, when illness is treated as a result of inappropriate behavior. The second characteristic is connected with the idea of the fatalities of the disease and its incurability, although this view has noticeably changed with the emergence of antiretroviral therapy. Another characteristic is the infectiousness of the disease, which is of particular importance in the context of insufficient medical literacy and awareness of the ways of virus transmission. The forth characteristic is a perception of the visible signs of the disease, the more visible and severe symptoms of the disease people can observe, the more they tend to stigmatize a person with HIV [12, p. 1112]. The same goes for close persons, relatives, and neighbors who are living with HIV-patients. The level of their internalized stigma increases in situations when the signs of the disease become visible to outsiders [3, p. 316].

At present, there are quite a few studies on the stigmatization of people living with HIV/AIDS. Most researchers consider the stigma of people living with HIV in terms of discrimination and overcoming [15, 16], or analyze stigmatization in the context of racial and ethnic inequality [9]. The others treat stigma as a mechanism of deteriorating the quality of life of people living with HIV [10, 11]. Characteristics and conditions of stigmatization of people with HIV demonstrate some contradictions. For example, some researchers suggest that stigmatization occurs as a result of the psychological stress that people experience when they come into contact with a person with HIV. Until now, it remains unclear whether stigma derived from stress and a negative sense of self or stigma itself sets this negative effect [14, p. 317]. Contradictory results are offered in different studies of the topic how the internalized stigma is related to seeking approval or support for a group. The research [7, p. 211] demonstrates that a high level of stigma, especially HIV-stigma, is highly associated with seeking support. However, the other research demonstrates the opposite tendency; the more persons are stigma-tized the less they inclined to seek support from others and to share their experiences [14, p. 316]. Results show that people living with HIV differ in the degree of inter-nalized stigma. Respondents with a high level of internalized stigma received less support, help, understanding, and approval from members of their own family, what had a negative impact on the course of the disease [14, p. 316].

Recently, a relatively new topic of using online communication and participating in online communities for people living with HIV/AIDS had revealed a heightened interest. There are studies of abilities and power of online communities in overcoming the stigmatization of people living with HIV due to different types of social support [1, 5, 6]. Online communities of people living with HIV/AIDS give users possibilities to discuss most important and silent issues. There are researches devoted to the problem of how users negotiate fears related with antiretroviral therapy [8], stigma of HIV testing [13]. Authors of systematic review analyzed 35 recent original research studies of uses of social media in HIV communication mentioned that "the anonymity on social media platforms helped to decrease stigma, fear, and discrimination around HIV and allowed participants to tell personal stories about their sexual orientation and HIV status in a manner they would not with friends, family members, or sexual partners offline" [17].

HIV status disclosure is a very important aspect of living with HIV and HIV treatment which is actively discussed in online communities for people living with HIV/AIDS. HIV status disclosure is closely connected with stigmatization and has both benefits and risks. Online communication gives people living with HIV a possibility to discuss problems associated with status disclosure anonymously and may facilitate decision making about status disclosure in real life. Chaudoir defines disclosure event as "the verbal communication that occurs between a discloser and a confidant regarding the discloser's HIV-positive status" [4]. Unlike many theoretical models of disclosure, the Disclosure Processes Model [3] describes not only disclosure likelihood but disclosure outcomes or consequences of disclosure, what usually is being the main focus of online discussions. The model conceptualizes disclosure "as a single process that necessarily involves decision-making and outcome processes. It highlights the impact of antecedent goals, the disclosure event itself, mediating processes and outcomes, and a feedback loop" [4]. In accordance with this model the disclosure is determined by approach goals and avoidance goals. Approach goals focus on obtaining positive outcomes such as receiving support, improving relations with partner, stopping hiding and keeping secrets. Avoidance goals might focus on obtaining negative outcomes such as breaking relations, rejection, and increased stigma. The qualitative research of discussions focused on the connection between stigmatization and status disclosure gives an opportunity to reveal main themes arising in the process of online communication instead of identify and prescribe to the users some predetermined goals.

3   Methods

At the first stage of the study, we applied Google and Yandex search engines for selection relevant Internet sites. The search query was a set of words "HIV AIDS forum" used in different combinations. As a result of the search we received the list of most popular Internet sites, including the resources on the first top position: Forum for people living with HIV/AIDS; Modern forum about HIV; HIV | AIDS: Personal stories - The Modern Portal on HIV; HIV + Dating | A dating system for people with HIV/AIDS; Forum - HIV.RF. The final choice of research field was made in favor of thematic forums, rather than social networks. Online forums provide the required anonymity of users and create the more favorable conditions for the participation of stigmatized respondents. For the purposes of the research, we chose the Internet resource "Forum for People Living with HIV/AIDS" (http://hivlife.info). This site is the first result issued on the request of the "HIV AIDS forum". Regarding this, we can assume that most people, who are interested in this topic, find this resource first of all. According to the online rating system rankw.ru (http://rankw.ru), the site hivlife.info contains 52,200 pages indexed by Google, and about 594 unique users visit it every day.

Facing that people living with HIV/AIDS prefer not to discuss their stigma in public, we supposed to find the explicit markers that indicate the presence of enacted or internalized stigma. Based on previous studies, we preliminarily identified set of aspects that were directly related to stigmatization: the problem of accepting own HIV/AIDS status; attitude towards oneself and other HIV/AIDS-infected people; the challenge of disclosing the status to partners, relatives and friends; maintaining relationship with partners, relatives and friends after the status disclosure and so on. Further, we selected the sections within the information structure of the forum, where users expressed their personal feelings about an experience of living with stigma and told how it determines their behavior and treatment, and how "others" perceive them. Building on this, we defined the sections of the forum with thematically corresponding headings and topics in which the research issues were somehow affected. However, paying attention to a suitable title is not enough therefore content verification procedure was carried out in two stages. After finding a relevant heading, we checked the information content of its posts. As a result of the formulation and the refinement of the research question and verification of the title and content of the studied sections of the forum, we manually selected a series of the forum's posts with the relevant content and drew up a table of links for further analysis. The final volume of data included 13 sections with the content relevant to the research issues: discussion about the experience of living with HIV/AIDS, the reactions of others to the fact of HIV/AIDS diagnosis and the relationship with people in the context of HIV/AIDS-status.

Data processing and analysis were carried out using the NVivo program. We defined specific groups of issues, contained fragments of texts related to the headings of these groups. Pieces of the text coded as widely as possible for not missing essential details. Therefore, in addition to codes directly related to stigmatization of people living with HIV/AIDS, we added more general codes related to the context of the forum's discussion. A total of 6 basic and 6 additional codes were created. Basic codes (directly related to the subject of research): manifestations of stigma; ethical aspects; attitudes towards stigmatization; relation to the illness; reasons for concealing status; despair and depression. Additional codes (related to the context of the forum's discussion): tips and advices; attitude towards doctors; intimidation/motivation of users; manifestations of the disease; intentions to remedy the situation; help and support.

4 Results

Categories of Forum Users. Users of the forum can be divided into two categories. The first one includes the newcomers - users, who are looking for answers to most difficult questions about HIV/AIDS, trying to build a personal sense of their illness and looking for answers to the question *"how to live with all this at the moment?"*, *"why me?"*, etc. The experienced users of the forum constitute the second category. Their attitude towards the disease is significantly different and based on the personal experience how to live with the diagnosis. Also, they are willing to share advices with others. Members of latter group compare HIV/AIDS with the usual flu, a *"common infection"*, which *"does not need to be ashamed"*, but *"to take pills and to keep living on"*. Thus, the attitude towards the disease tends to change from the negative, including unwillingness to live, fear of the future and refusal to status disclose, to the more positive, when people living with HIV/AIDS do not perceive the disease so negative (*"HIV is no longer a fatal diagnosis! This is just a chronic disease and provided adequate therapy you can live happily ever after"*). In spite of the fact, that the internalized stigma is reduced with "habitualization" of the disease, there are some forum users living with HIV/AIDS for a long time, but still not accepting their status and continuing to experience difficulties in overcoming stigma.

Process of HIV Status Acceptance. The problem of accepting HIV status arises for everyone who has just encountered this diagnosis. The issues of HIV status acceptance are reflected in the following comments: *"I cannot believe that it has happened to me"*;

"It's not long to live"; *"Maybe you should stop this life on your own?"*; *"You have to learn to live with it"*. These cues manifest the painful attempts of users to accept their HIV status. These attempts are accompanied with laments and self-justification: *"the same question all the time: why did it happen to me? I do not smoke, I do not drink, I do yoga, I do not use drugs"*; *"I know for sure that I am not guilty of anything"*.

In the situation when users refuse to accept their own HIV status, they choose a behavioral strategy to ignore the problem, which is usually accompanied by refusal to disclose HIV status even to their sexual partners. Analyzing forum statements, we noticed an alarming tendency of some users to hide their status from sexual partners. Among the stated reasons for concealment, the forum users mentioned shame, fear of losing a loved one, and men's reluctance to use a condom. At the same time the closest relatives usually aware of the condition of the infected person.

Surprisingly that among HIV-positive users of the forum there is the attitude to stigmatize HIV/AIDS, from the latent negation (*"Damn, for 10 years, I could not pronounce the word "HIV"*), to condemnation, dislike (*"You would not believe me, I am HIV-positive too, but I think people living with HIV are dirty"*) and fear of other HIV-positive people (*"I'm a "plus", but I'm also afraid of HIV-infected people, and I cannot overcome this feeling"*).

Status Disclosure and Keeping Relationships. In the case of the status disclosure, forum users discuss two types of possible and actual reactions: breaking or keeping of relationships. Some reported about breaking up relationship with an HIV-positive person: *"they avoid me like the plague"*; *"she said that when guys find out about HIV, they immediately run away from her"*; *"he immediately stopped the relationship, in one second"*; *"they do not want to communicate, and sometimes the closest ones leave us"*. But in many cases, users report that partners of people living with HIV/AIDS decide to stay in the relationship. *"The period of my doubts amounted to an hour and a half, I do not regret a second"*; *"I do not see any obstacles in my diagnosis for my feelings"*; *"But he takes care of me"*; *"I said the guy, he was shocked, of course, but calmly passed the tests, and he is healthy. And now everything is fine with us: we live together and plan to have children."* Based on similar statements, we can assume that a break up in relations provokes an increase in internalized stigma, and on the contrary, the keeping of relations contributes to weakening of internalized stigma.

In the case of the supportive behavior of partners, their altruistic behavior and compassion are brought to the fore: *"I will be with him as long as he wants it"*; *"I sympathize with him so much."* At the same time, this compassion can be hidden: *"I really feel sorry for him, but I understand that I cannot show that"*. All these feelings are accompanied by the fear of being infected, the anger at fate and the inability to believe and reconcile with the diagnosis of a partner.

Internalized Stigma and Relationships. The paradoxical reaction provoked by the fear to be different from the other people and to become stigmatized is manifested in the desire expressed by some users living with HIV/AIDS to make their partners get infected too. *"The result is in 10 days, I want him to have a diagnosis too and I am ashamed of these thoughts"*; *"It's a shame to admit, but I wanted my husband to be HIV-positive when it turned out that I have HIV"*. It is unlikely that respondent could make such confession in a research interview. Adapting to a new status and understanding the difficulties accompanied it, users write about their desire to be together with someone close, but at the same time, they realize that the wishes of HIV for the close ones and relatives are connected with additional problems. Such cases can be seen as an attempt to overcome their stigma by combining efforts with close ones to combat a common problem. Who, if not the HIV-positive partner, is able to share all the emotional stress and worries of this condition? Thus, there is a non-obvious picture of the means by which HIV-positive users cope with internalized stigma: from the one hand there is a fear of harming their partners and from the other hand a paradoxical desire that the partner to be infected too.

Another topic that is actively discussed by forum users is the theme of friendly, romantic and sexual relations between people living with HIV/AIDS and healthy ones. *"Friendship with HIV-positive one did not work out, and I'm no longer looking for such friends <...> constant veiled and direct offers to have sex"*. Disclosure of HIV/AIDS status has important consequences for both HIV-negative and HIV-positive partner. For both of them, these consequences lie between the choice of *"continuing relationship"* and *"concern for the wellbeing of the healthy partner"*. A healthy partner experiences difficulties in accepting the status of partner, living with HIV/AIDS and her or his behavior depends on choosing between own health and relations with the partner. On the forum pages HIV-negative users unfold the discussion within the dichotomy: the safety of one's health versus the keeping of sexual relations with the HIV-positive partner. Although sexual relations with a HIV-positive partner with proper use of condom allow a healthy partner to avoid infection, in statements of healthy users we revealed the dilemma between "to remain uninfected" and "to be in a relationship". These users often describe the situation of "to stay in a relationship" as a "sacrifice" on their part.

Building on reviewed statements we revealed some essential aspects of stigma manifested by healthy and HIV/AIDS-infected partners. On the one hand, the healthy people tend to attribute their attempts to remain "just friends" with HIV-positive partner and search for an excuse for parting, as a result of the uncertainty of these kinds of relations. In some cases, a healthy one tries to shift responsibility for personal choice to an HIV-positive partner. For person living with HIV/AIDS breaking of relationships is equivalent to loss of self-esteem. Self-respect is repeatedly mentioned in discussions at the forum in the context of personal problems, and it is an important condition to combat internalized stigma. We can assume that the solving a problem of accepting the HIV status is largely determined by the possibility of keeping and supporting relations with partners. If healthy partner after status disclosure decides to stays in a relationship, then person living with HIV/AIDS perceives stigmatization not so acutely. Otherwise, protective mechanisms of psychological self-defense of HIV-people are triggered. As a rule, this process of personal self-protection and compensation is accompanied by the self-justification in comparison with the partner (*"he is not better than me"*), arguments in favor of maintaining relations (*"she is happy with me"*). In some cases, HIV-positive users write about breaking up with healthy partner, as a way not to lose self-esteem. This situation, as a rule, occurs when a healthy partner plays a role of a source of stigmatization.

Online Community as a Source of Social Support. The online forum is a kind of support tool for people living with HIV/AIDS, which helps them to cope with stigmatization in the real offline world. Users share links to biographies of people who have experienced HIV/AIDS, references to documentary films and some other supportive materials. These links provide an essential help and support to people who have decided to disclose their status. One user writes: *"Immediately I wanted to show this film to my family and friends (who do not yet know) as a confession in my status."* Thus, the forum helps to accept HIV/AIDS status and in some cases, to talk about their disease to others.

The forum is also a support resource for those who recently encountered HIV/AIDS: the main controversy on its pages unfolds among "newcomers" and "experienced users". HIV-positive "newcomers" can be described as persons interested in accepting their status, and their active use of Internet resources can be seen as manifestation of a strategy for coping with the disease. The online community also includes users trying to help their relatives and friends who chose the strategy of ignoring the disease. Opportunities of the forum are used as a way to awake the "sleeping" - those who are ignoring the treatment and prefer not to notice their HIV-positive status: *"You give him some time to read this forum, maybe it will help him ..."*; *"You will really get scared when you see how anyone dies who does not want to be treated. I think there are plenty of stories on the forum"*; *"We need to set it up and somehow give it to read such posts. Maybe he will go to see a doctor"*. Another function of the forum is related to consulting in personal matters, such as safe sex, excluding the possibility of infection, the birth of healthy children, making informed decision in relationships, etc.

5 Conclusion

The status disclosure is closely connected to stigmatization and has both benefits and risks. The process of disclosure is negotiated and such negotiation is possible when the stigmatized persons have a possibility to keep their anonymity. Therefore such online community as internet forum could be considered as an important possibility for discussing such issues as concealment or disclosure of HIV status.

Online health community is a particular social and communicative space that performs important functions for people living with HIV/AIDS and for their partners. In the study, we focused attention on such aspect of stigma as the attitude towards HIV status disclosure. Based on the data analyzed, we can conclude that the most clearly manifested differences are between people who have a long time experience of living with HIV/AIDS, formed their personal strategies for resistance to stigma and coping with the disease, and the beginners who recently found out about their disease. For the last group, the main problem is acceptance of their status and the building of a new identity. The most challenging aspect of HIV status acceptance is the perception of HIV/AIDS as "punishment" for misbehavior and the awareness of the fatal consequence of the disease. At the same time, the support of people who are in the similar situation plays a key role in adaptation to the disease and, accordingly, in reducing the internalized stigma. As we can see from the data analysis, response of infected people to the disease ranges from the total rejection to the attempts of self-justifying. The most dangerous reaction is the concealment of one's status from the other people, especially if it concerns sexual partners. The leading motives of this concealing behavior are a shame and a fear of breaking up relations. Breaking or maintaining relationship with a healthy partner also determines the perception of stigma. A break up contributes to increasing the perceived stigma, while the supportive behavior of close people with the keeping of relations helps to overcome the stigmatized condition. We revealed some paradoxical aspects of the attitude of users living with HIV/AIDS: a desire of some people living with HIV/AIDS that their healthy partner would be HIV-infected and stigmatization of HIV-positive people by users living with HIV/AIDS. Perhaps, such reactions can be treated as a kind of protective mechanism of psychological self-defense in conditions of high stigmatization of the disease.

As a result of the research, we succeeded to gather information much broader than the original research question suggested. At the same time, collected data was less detailed than it would be in in-depth interviews. Analytical work developed in the directions defined by the collected data. In the process of analysis of statements posted by users without influence of the interviewer, we were able to identify some essential aspects that informants were unlikely reporting in interviews or discussing in public on focus group.

As internet communication is increasingly spread, studying sensitive topics and stigmatized groups through analyses of online discussions could be considered as a perspective development of not only internet studies but methods of sociological research of real-life settings.

Acknowledgements. This work was supported by the Russian Fund for Basic Research [Grant Number 18-013-00726 A].

References

1. Bar-Lev, S.: "We are here to give you emotional support": performing emotions in an online HIV/AIDS support group. Qual. Health Res. **18**(4), 509–521 (2008). https://doi.org/10.1177/1049732307311680
2. Chambers, L., et al., The Stigma Review Team: Stigma: HIV and health: a qualitative synthesis. BMC Public Health **15**(1), 1–17 (2015). https://doi.org/10.1186/s12889-015-2197-0
3. Chaudoir, S.R., Fisher, J.D.: The disclosure processes model: understanding disclosure decision-making and post-disclosure outcomes among people living with a concealable stigmatized identity. Psychol. Bull. **136**(2), 236–256 (2010). https://doi.org/10.1037/a0018193
4. Chaudoir, S.R., Fisher, J.D., Simoni, J.M.: Understanding HIV disclosure: a review and application of the Disclosure Processes Model. Soc. Sci. Med. **72**(10), 1618–1629 (2011). https://doi.org/10.1016/j.socscimed.2011.03.028
5. Chen, L., Shi, J.: Social support exchanges in a social media community for people living with HIV/AIDS in China. AIDS Care **27**, 693–696 (2015). https://doi.org/10.1080/09540121.2014.991678

6. Coursaris, C.K., Liu, M.: An analysis of social support exchanges in online HIV/AIDS self-help groups. Comput. Hum. Behav. **25**, 911–918 (2009). https://doi.org/10.1016/j.chb.2009.03.006
7. Davison, K.P., Pennebaker, J.W., Dickerson, S.S.: Who talks? The social psychology of illness support groups. Am. Psychol. **55**, 205–217 (2000). https://doi.org/10.1037/0003-066X.55.2.205
8. Dudina, V., Judina, D., King, E.: Fears about antiretroviral therapy among users of the internet forum for people living with HIV/AIDS in Russia. AIDS Care **29**(2), 268–270 (2017). https://doi.org/10.1080/09540121.2016.1211607
9. Earnshaw, V., Bogart, L., Dovidio, J., Williams, D.: Stigma and racial/ethnic HIV disparities: moving toward resilience. Am. Psychol. **68**, 225–236 (2013). https://doi.org/10.1037/a0032705
10. Earnshaw, V., Smith, L., Chaudoir, S., Amico, K., Copenhaver, M.: HIV stigma mechanisms and well-being among PLWH: a test of the HIV stigma framework. AIDS Behav. **17**, 1785–1795 (2013). https://doi.org/10.1007/s10461-013-0437-9
11. Fuster-Ruizdeapodaca, M., Molero, F., Holgado, F., Mayordomo, S.: Enacted and internalized stigma and quality of life among people with HIV: the role of group identity. Qual. Life Res. **23**(7), 1967–1975 (2014). https://doi.org/10.1007/s11136-014-0653-4
12. Herek, G.M.: AIDS and stigma. Am. Behav. Sci. **42**(7), 1106–1116 (1999). https://doi.org/10.1177/0002764299042007004
13. Ho, C.L., Pan, W., Taylor, L.D.: Stigma of HIV testing on online HIV forums: self-stigma and the unspoken. J. Psychosoc. Nurs. Ment. Health Serv. **55**(12), 34–43 (2017). https://doi.org/10.3928/02793695-20170905-01
14. Lee, R.S., Kochman, A., Sikkema, K.J.: Internalized stigma among people living with HIV-AIDS. AIDS Behav. **6**(4), 309–319 (2002). https://doi.org/10.1023/A:1021144511957
15. Mahajan, A., Sayles, J., Patel, V., et al.: Stigma in the HIV/AIDS epidemic: a review of the literature and recommendations for the way forward. AIDS **22**, 67–79 (2008). https://doi.org/10.1097/01.aids.0000327438.13291.62
16. Parker, R., Aggleton, P.: HIV and AIDS-related stigma and discrimination: a conceptual framework and implications for action. Soc. Sci. Med. **57**, 13–24 (2003). https://doi.org/10.1016/S0277-9536(02)00304-0
17. Taggart, T., Grewe, M.E., Conserve, D.F., Gliwa, C., RomanIsler, M.: Social media and HIV: a systematic review of uses of social media in HIV communication. J. Med. Internet Res. **17**(11), e248 (2015). https://doi.org/10.2196/jmir.4387

Neural Network Hate Deletion: Developing a Machine Learning Model to Eliminate Hate from Online Comments

Joni Salminen[1,2(✉)], Juhani Luotolahti[2], Hind Almerekhi[1],
Bernard J. Jansen[1], and Soon-gyo Jung[1]

[1] Qatar Computing Research Institute, Hamad Bin Khalifa University,
Doha, Qatar
{jsalminen,hialmerekhi,bjansen,sjung}@hbku.edu.qa
[2] University of Turku, Turku, Finland
mjluot@utu.fi

Abstract. We propose a method for modifying hateful online comments to non-hateful comments without losing the understandability and original meaning of the comments. To accomplish this, we retrieve and classify 301,153 hateful and 1,041,490 non-hateful comments from Facebook and YouTube channels of a large international media organization that is a target of considerable online hate. We supplement this dataset by 10,000 Reddit comments manually labeled for hatefulness. Using these two datasets, we train a neural network to distinguish linguistic patterns. The model we develop, Neural Network Hate Deletion (NNHD), computes how hateful the sentences of a social media comment are and if they are above a given threshold, it deletes them using a language dependency tree. We evaluate the results by comparing crowd workers' perceptions of hatefulness and understandability before and after transformation and find that our method reduces hatefulness without resulting in a significant loss of understandability. In some cases, removing hateful elements improves understandability by reducing the linguistic complexity of the comment. In addition, we find that NNHD can satisfactorily retain the original meaning on average but is not perfect in this regard. In terms of practical implications, NNHD could be used in social media platforms to suggest more neutral use of language to agitated online users.

Keywords: Online hate · Toxic comments · Hate deletion · Neural networks

1 Introduction

Hateful remarks and comments are prevalent in online communities, including YouTube, Reddit, Facebook, Instagram and various other social networks and online discussion forums [1]. But why is hate so prevalent? One reason is due to its contagious nature, spreading from one individual to another [2, 3]. Following this logic of previous research, the more we can reduce the initiation of hate, the more we can reduce the overall hate taking place online. Reducing hate, however, is to a large degree sociological problem, dealing with manners, upbringing, culture, patience, and non-

© Springer Nature Switzerland AG 2018
S. S. Bodrunova (Ed.): INSCI 2018, LNCS 11193, pp. 25–39, 2018.
https://doi.org/10.1007/978-3-030-01437-7_3

provocative behavior [5]. While these principles are well-known and often considered as common sense, they are not to be taken for granted in the online environment. Following the proper netiquette [6] and acting politely would be ideal, but unfortunately, people do not behave in an idealistic manner, as illustrated by the high degree of online hate taking place in social media [7]. Even if we acknowledge the proposition that the ultimate solution to online hate warrants a non-technical solution, it may be possible to combine social and computational techniques as hybrid solutions that reduce the number of hateful comments.

More particularly, sociological theory can be used here to evoke two principles: (1) giving individuals choices for different actions, and (2) urging them to consider their harmful behavior [8]. In the context of online hate, a social network could recommend ways to modify a detected hateful comment before posting it online. The decision remains with the human, but the machine can give options – a digital analogy advising an angry person to wait 10 s before speaking up. While the detection algorithms for online hate have developed rapidly [4, 9–11], there is almost no extant work on suggesting such alterations to hateful comments.

In this research, we tackle the problem of online hate, defined as offensive use of language, by modifying hatefulness of social media comments. We formulate the research objective as follows: *Remove hateful elements from a comment without eliminating the understandability or meaning of the comment.* To achieve this objective, we propose a methodology called Neural Network Hate Deletion (NNHD). This research represents exploratory and experimental work, and we note that rewriting hateful comments is a part of larger research effort, requiring more research. The purpose of this work is to provide a "minimum viable product" [12] and to show that further research on this problem is feasible from a technical point of view. In the following sections, we briefly review the related literature, the present our proposed solution, and evaluate the results with crowd experiments and manual ratings. Finally, we discuss the findings and future avenues for research.

2 Related Literature

We searched for related literature in academic databases, including Google Scholar and Science Direct. The search phrases included ["online hate"], [+hateful "social media"], ["toxic comments"], and other relevant key phrases. We then manually evaluated if the found articles match our research objective. Overall, we found several thousand papers covering this topic. For example, "online hate" alone brings 2,120 results in Google Scholar. To narrow down the scope, we focus on studies that introduce computational solutions to offensive or hateful commenting in online environments. Overall, social media platforms, such as Twitter, Facebook, Reddit, and YouTube have been the most common source for data collection of online hate studies [7, 10, 13–15].

In one of the earlier studies, Sood et al. [16] focused on separating off-topic negative comments from on-topic negative comments. They collected 1,655,131 comments from Yahoo! Buzz, a news website, labeled 6,500 of them according to the presence or absence of insults and profanity, along with topics of hate. The topics were world, business, entertainment, politics, news, and general, and the target was either an author of a previous comment or a third party. The comments were labeled using Amazon Mechanical Turk, instructing the workers to focus on the intention of the comment writer to successfully label clear profanity as well as a disguised one.

The approach by Mondal et al. [10] was based on created a sentence structure that reveals hate, target, and intensity: "I <intensity> <userintent> <hatetarget>". This allowed them to identify a number of explicit hate targets, e.g. minority groups and women. Intent is the emotion of the user; intensity is the level of emotion, and a hate target is the group receiving the emotion of dislike, animosity or hate [15]. To determine hate targets, Mondal et al. [10] placed a specific word before people in order to specify hate targets – black people, Mexican people, stupid people, and used targets from the Hatebase, a dictionary with 1,078 hate words. The most common hate categories they found were race, behavior, and physical.

Much of the previous work utilizes keyword dictionaries to detect hateful comments. However, one shortcoming of the dictionary-based models is that a keyword used as a hate indicator in one community may not represent hate in another community. The same concern has been raised by Sood et al. [17] whose model, using the profanity list from no-swearing.com, was able to detect 40.2% of profanity terms, the conclusion is that even the best list could not achieve good performance at detection of profanity. Keywords may also miss sarcasm, negations, and humor, as these forms of language are particularly challenging to classify [18]. Moreover, Nobata et al. [11] note that blacklists (collections of hateful words and insults) require constant updates. Sood et al. [17] point out new terminology of profane terms as a major challenge.

To overcome these challenges, Saleem et al. [14] used Labeled Latent Dirichlet Allocation (LLDA) to learn the community-specific hate topics, which were compared to baseline language from Reddit. Saleem et al. [14] achieved good performance with Naïve Bayes and Logistic Regression. The classifier trained on the community-based data achieved a better performance than a keyword-based classifier, being 10–20% more accurate on hate detection. Another finding from the literature is that combining several features tends to improve classification accuracy of online hate. For example, Nobata et al. [11] detected abusive language consisting of profanity and derogatory phrases, using four types of features: N-grams, Linguistic, Syntactic, and Distributional Semantics. The combined application provided the best performance [11]. Similar results were obtained by Salminen et al. [4] using the same feature types.

There is also a nascent line of work utilizes neural networks. For example, Djuric et al. [9] detected hateful comments using a two-step approach: (1) Paragraph2vec with a bag-of-words (BOW) neural language model, and (2) embeddings-based a binary classifier distinguishing hateful and non-hateful comments. Paragraph2vec appeared as very useful and precise, discovering some non-obvious swearing words. This method also obtained the higher area under the curve (AUC) than BOW models [9]. Badjatiya et al. [19] classified tweets into three categories: racist, sexist, neither, using deep neural networks. Benchmark dataset of 16,000 tweets was analyzed, and 3,383 were labeled as sexist, 1,972 as racist, and the remaining were labeled as neither. The proposed methods (CNN, LSTM, FastText) were better than the baseline methods (Character n-grams, TF-IDF, Bag of Words). The best accuracy was obtained when deep neural networks were combined with Gradient Boosted Decision Trees [19]. In a similar vein, Park and Fung [20] detected abusive language using three convolutional neural network (CNN) models: CharCNN, WordCNN, and HybridCNN, with character and word features. The best performance was achieved with HybridCNN and the worst with CharCNN.

Overall, there is a substantial number of previous work focusing on the detection and classification of online hate. However, there is almost no extant work on *changing the hateful comments* from the state of hateful to neutral or positive. In fact, we could not locate any prior study solely focusing on this. In previous studies, the objective is detecting and/or deleting the whole comment. However, at the same time, limiting the freedom of speech is noted as a concern in this approach [7, 16], especially when automatic moderation is applied without giving the end user a chance to take corrective action in reformulating his message. Our study aims to improve this condition by *not deleting the whole comment but only the hateful elements within it*. In other words, the social challenge is to balance moderating offensive language with the freedom of speech, while the computational challenge is altering the sentences without losing their understandability and meaning.

3   Methodology

3.1   Data Collection and Validation

We collect data from a major news and media company with an international audience from over 200 countries. This media organization has several channels on several platforms. For this research, we retrieve all the comments from two channels for two platforms. By using Facebook and YouTube application programming interfaces (APIs), we pull comments from videos posted on YouTube and Facebook, including 1,342,597 comments from the period of December, 2013 to January, 2018. The comments originate from all the Facebook posts and YouTube videos of the two channels in the two platforms (several thousands of content pieces). They are written by social media followers of the respective channels. Some posts or videos did not have comments since adding comments was disabled or the comments were deleted. Nevertheless, this provides both longitudinal spectrum (close to five years of commenting) and breadth (more than a million comments). Table 1 shows the breakdown of comments by platform.

Table 1. Number of retrieved comments by platform and channel.

Source	Number of retrieved comments
Channel 1 (YouTube)	780,138
Channel 2 (YouTube)	235,315
Channel 1 (Facebook)	75,002
Channel 2 (Facebook)	252,142
Total	1,342,597

In the dataset of 1,342,597 comments, 327,144 (24%) are from Facebook, 1,015,453 (76%) from YouTube. Initially, while exploring this large dataset, we observed that it contains many hateful comments. This prompted us to find ways to detect and classify them, for automated or computer-aided moderation. Overall, these comments make a useful dataset for dealing with online hate using computational means, and demonstrate a real problem touching online media producers. To make the dataset useful for classification, we automatically label these comments for hate content. To accomplish this, we first build a hateful keyword dictionary. We use a combination of two techniques to generate the dictionary of hateful phrases: (1) open coding, i.e., reading the comments and noting down phrases that are frequently used in a hateful sense [21], and (2) manually screening existing online hate dictionaries[1] for additional hateful words. Using these sources, we collected 1,098 hateful phrases. However, not all of them are present in the dataset based on mining the comments. In addition, the use of hateful expressions has been found to vary by the community using them [14]. Here, the context of the videos is diverse, but most hate, based on our open coding, revolves around political topics (e.g., Israel-Palestine, Police brutality, US presidential elections, etc.). That is why we must adjust the dictionary using open coding, i.e. manually finding hateful expressions that are typical for this dataset. Table 2 includes examples of hateful phrases and their appearance in the comments.

Table 2. Examples from the created hate dictionary. Dictionary includes 203 phrases.

Example key phrase	Example comment (hateful expressions bolded)
Stupid	"Because Denmark is getting smart and Sweden is still **stupid**"
Should be killed	"however the rapist's **should be killed**…. lets give them a bit of their sharia law they so long for. the **fucking pigs**…."
Fuck	"All the libs making a big deal of it. When in reality if it was Hillary's **bitch ass**, you **cowards** would be almost certain you had been shot. Right away blaming the 2nd amendment. Soft **pussy fucks**"
Zionist	"The **zionist scumbags** are losing the battle. #FreePalestine"

Second, we apply this dictionary to social media datasets to retrieve hateful comments. Keyword matching and keyword-based features have been utilized in a similar fashion in several previous works to detect hateful comments [15, 17]. For example, Salminen et al. [4] found that simple term-level features were among the best predictors when detecting hateful online comments. As mentioned, the keyword list was compiled using a combination of open coding and existing hate keywords lists. After retrieving the hateful comments via keyword matching, we label 301,153 hateful comments and 1,041,490 non-hateful comments.

---

[1] We compiled the list of hate words by combining open coding done on our dataset and lists of profanity or swear words available online: http://www.bannedwordlist.com/lists/swearWords.txt; https://github.com/LDNOOBW/List-of-Dirty-Naughty-Obscene-and-Otherwise-Bad-Words/blob/master/en; https://www.frontgatemedia.com/a-list-of-723-bad-words-to-blacklist-and-how-to-use-facebooks-moderation-tool/; http://onlineslangdictionary.com/lists/most-vulgar-words/.

Hateful comments are automatically labeled as 1, non-hateful as 0, corresponding to a classical binary classification task. To ensure that this labeling approach works, we conduct a "sanity check" on a sample of 300 comments we expect to be hateful based on our automatic coding, and 300 comments we expect to be non-hateful. In the sanity check, we use crowd workers, asking them if the comment was hateful or not (options given: 'hateful', 'not hateful'). We provide the workers with examples of both categories through using test questions that also protect against unethical workers [22]. Each comment in each sample is evaluated by three crowd workers, and we use majority voting to assign the final label (e.g., the label with the highest number of ratings is chosen as the final label). The results are shown in Table 3.

Table 3. Validation of training data using crowd ratings.

	Hateful (*observed*)	Non-hateful (*observed*)
Hateful (*expected*)	84.47%	15.53%
Non-hateful (*expected*)	19.80%	80.20%

The sanity check yields 84.47% of the automatically coded hateful comments as hateful (using majority voting, where 2/3 raters agree), and 80.20% of the non-hateful as non-hateful. The observed sentiment of the comments is thus in line with the expected sentiment. However, because the ratings show some number of false positives and negatives (diagonals in Table 3), we also utilize another dataset that contains 10 k manually labeled Reddit comments, to train the network. This dataset was obtained by retrieving comments from AskReddit (a sub-group of Reddit, the popular online social network) covering all the posts between January 2008 and August 2017, and then asking the crowd workers to label if a comment is hateful or not. The 10 k comments from the Reddit corpus were randomly selected from a total of 16 M Reddit comments. By using a combination of the above data containing hateful and non-hateful online comments, we proceed to the next step, which is training and model development.

3.2   Model Development

We develop a model dubbed Neural Network Hate Deletion (NNHD). A simple example of hate deletion is as follows: "you fail once again stupid" (high hatefulness) → "you fail once again" (decreased hatefulness). We thus aim to reduce the hatefulness of the comments while retaining their understandability.

Figure 1 describes the network built for this research. In this model, we are most interested in the network activations after the time-distributed dense layer that correspond to the final classification and should correspond to the hatefulness of the tokens in the input. These will be used to score the tokens in the comments by their hatefulness'. Using this approach, each token in the tree is scored by the neural model. Before pruning the tree, we set a threshold for pruning the tree. From the tree, we remove all tokens with a score above the threshold and all tokens which depend on it or are part of a subtree with the removed token as its head.

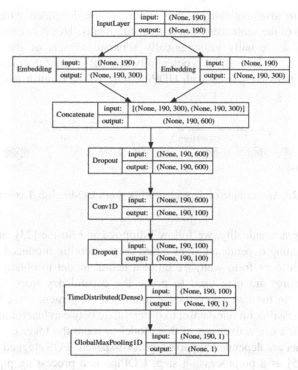

Fig. 1. Description of NNHD.

The aim of the scoring in the ordinary text simplification task is to score the tokens by their meaning [23]. In this research, however, we score them by their hatefulness and compress the sentence to reduce its degree of hatefulness. We follow an approach in which tokens of the comment texts are scored using a neural model trained on a mixture of hand-annotated and automatically generated online comment data. The model is trained on 10,000 comments of hand-annotated Reddit comments and 10,000 of automatically keyword matched news comments. The preloaded embeddings used were 300-dimensional fastText vectors trained on wiki- and news-texts and distributed by Facebook research.[2] We set dropouts at 0.5 to reduce model overfitting.

Overall, we approach the problem as a text simplification task. In a text simplification task, the aim is to compress text so that it keeps its meaning as much as possible, while the output text is compressed in length while remaining grammatically intact. A widely used approach to text simplification is extractive text compression [24]. Extractive text compression achieves the aim of compression by extracting parts of the original text that contain its core meaning. The grammaticality of the output is often maximized using a language model, or dependency trees [23].

---

[2] fastText is a library for learning of word embeddings and sentence classification created by Facebook.

To improve the grammaticality of the output, we use dependency tree pruning, i.e. removing subsets of the sentences from hateful comments. This is because subtrees of a dependency tree are usually grammatically separate subsets of the sentence. For example, in Fig. 2, "In Ramadi" is a potentially prunable part of the example sentence. The dependency trees are parsed with UDPipe with UDv2 English model.

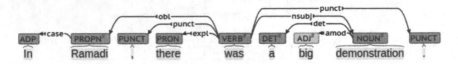

Fig. 2. An example of dependency tree from UD-English Treebank

To improve grammaticality, we follow Filippova and Strube [23] and produce the result text by pruning dependency trees based on the scoring produced by the model. For this approach to perform well, we build a neural model to obtain scores for the tokens. These scores are then used to prune the dependency trees for maintaining grammar. To obtain the hate score for the tokens in the sentence, we build a simple neural network classifier on our dataset to differentiate between hateful and non-hateful comments and then use activations of this model to score the tokens.

The comments are dependency parsed, part-of-speech (POS) tagged and tokenized with UDPipe [25] as a preprocessing step. UDPipe is a processing pipeline for tokenization, morphological analysis and dependency parsing with pretrained models trained on Universal Dependencies data. The network takes as its input a sequence of token indices, fetches two embeddings, one pre-trained and frozen and one trained during the model training. They are concatenated and fed through one-dimensional convolution with a window size of one. This sequence is then fed to a time-distributed dense neural network layer with sigmoid activation and its result is max-pooled to give the final prediction. Because of the max-pooling layer at the end of the network, the network predictions are based on the maximum scoring token, and as such, the model is not meant to give predictions on the comments themselves, but the model creates token weights indicating hatefulness.

4   Evaluation of Results

4.1   Manual Evaluation

We conduct a three-staged evaluation: (a) manual evaluation, (b) quantitative analysis of variance (ANOVA), and (c) rating of original meaning retention. First, we manually check the results of the transformation. We can see that the results vary. While not perfect, the network performs surprisingly well. This leads us to believe our method is providing satisfactory results. Table 4 contains examples from our manual evaluation.

Table 4. Examples of transformed comments. Threshold score in parentheses.

Hateful comment	Transformed comment
"another narrow minded offensive point of view from an ignorant jerk who wants to spread hate wants to make people feel low as he is garbage"	"another narrow minded offensive point of view" [0.5]
"without killing most americans in asia it's hard to achieve peace"	"it's hard to achieve peace" [0.7]
"fucking america why america is trying to have an impact in europe"	"why america is trying to have an impact in europe" [0.9]

In addition, we review the hate scores of the words and find that they seem indeed highly toxic. Table 5 shows the ten most hateful words learned by the network. It is worth noting that these words were learned from the training data without any other supervision than the general label "hateful". The algorithm also deleted some comments completely – we call such comments 'beyond repair' because the comment has no other meaning to retain but hate. On average, the share of completely removed comments was 8.52% for the 0.5, 6.03% for the 0.7, and 4.96% for the 0.9 thresholds.

Table 5. Hateful words learned by the network without supervision. Showing top 10.

Hate Score	Term	Type (based on POS-tagging)
0.99793506	'scum'	noun
0.9974718	'coward'	noun
0.9974164	'fuckin'	adposition
0.99735606	'cunts'	noun
0.9971541	'dumbass'	noun
0.9971535	'fuckers'	noun
0.9969387	'greedy'	adjective
0.9955591	'bastards'	noun
0.9946931	'motherfucker'	noun
0.99336666	'bitch'	verb

4.2 Crowd Experiments

Second, to evaluate, we want to know how many comments will keep their meaning after applying neural network hate deletion. This measures the successfulness of fixing the hateful comments. We opt for crowd evaluation, as done in prior literature dealing with online hate ratings [10, 15]. Here, we use CrowdFlower, a platform that offers good options for crowdsourced tasks. We measure two types of perceptions of crowd workers: (1) hatefulness (*"How hateful is this comment?"*) and (2) understandability (*"Is this comment easy to understand?"*). Figure 3 illustrates the created tasks.

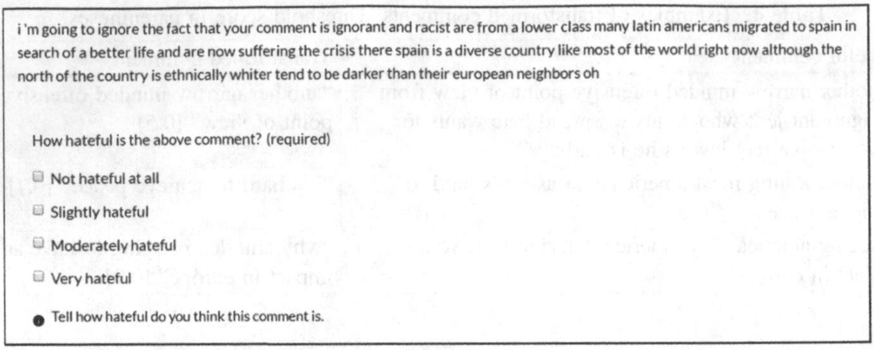

> i 'm going to ignore the fact that your comment is ignorant and racist are from a lower class many latin americans migrated to spain in search of a better life and are now suffering the crisis there spain is a diverse country like most of the world right now although the north of the country is ethnically whiter tend to be darker than their european neighbors oh
>
> How hateful is the above comment? (required)
>
> ☐ Not hateful at all
> ☐ Slightly hateful
> ☐ Moderately hateful
> ☐ Very hateful
>
> ● Tell how hateful do you think this comment is.

Fig. 3. Example question asked from the crowd labelers on hatefulness of the comments.

We evaluate both the original hateful comments and the manipulated comments with three different thresholds of hate scoring (0.5, 0.7, and 0.9). Overall, we carry out eight data collection tasks: *Baseline Hateful* (original hateful comments), *Baseful Senseful* (original hateful comments), *Hateful_05*, *Hateful_07*, *Hateful_09* (each measuring hatefulness with transformation at a given threshold of hate score), *Senseful_05*, *Senseful_07*, and *Senseful_09* (each measuring understandability with transformation at a given threshold of hate score). The tested comments were randomly sampled from the transformed comments, pairing the original comments with their transformed versions at each threshold level. For both tasks, we use a 4-point scale, so that a comment is 'Very hateful' (4), 'Moderately hateful' (3), 'Slightly hateful' (2), or 'Not hateful at all' (1); and 'Very easy to understand' (4), 'Quite easy to understand' (3), 'Slightly difficult to understand' (2) or 'Difficult to understand' (1).

We undertook several measures to ensure the quality of crowd ratings:

- **Test questions:** We created 8 test questions with known values for each task, according to the recommendation of the platform. Test questions quiz the raters randomly; answering correctly makes workers eligible for the job, whereas failing to answer them correctly removes a worker from the task.
- **Max Judgments /Rater:** We chose 50, so that with $300 \times 5 = 1500$ ratings, there is $50/1500 = 3.33\%$ maximum impact per rater, thus avoiding individual bias affecting the results.
- **Minimum time for a rater to complete a page of work:** 25 s; a page has 5 comments and we expect it would take a rater at least 5 s to read and rate each ($5 \times 5 = 25$ s).
- **Quality Level:** Level 2 ("Higher Quality"), consisting of a smaller group of more experienced, higher accuracy raters.
- **Judgments per Row:** 5, to get more information on the preferences, as is suggested for more subjective classification tasks [26].
- **Price per Judgment:** 4 cents (USD), a 33% increase in the price suggested by the crowdsourcing platform.

4.3 Statistical Analysis

We then compare if the perceptions are significantly different between the group that saw the original comment and the group that saw the comment modified by the algorithm. The purpose is to evaluate if the neural network changed the comment successfully to remove hate while retaining the understandability of the comment. In other words, the threshold is the hate score of the algorithm we want to test (experimental condition), comparing to comments that received no transformation.

Testing with a multivariate analysis of variance (MANOVA) model, we find that understandability does not have significant changes between transformed and non-transformed comments, or between the threshold levels. However, for hatefulness, applying transformation results in a very significant decrease in perceived hatefulness. The 0.7 and 0.9 thresholds are statistically similar, with the 0.5 threshold showing the largest decrease in terms of hatefulness. In other words, lowering the threshold for transformation yields a significant decrease of hatefulness without resulting in discernible changes to the understandability of the comment.

The dataset was analyzed using ANOVA tests to determine which questions had statistical different responses by group, followed by Tukey's HSD post-hoc tests to determine which groups significantly differed from the others [27]. Although the dependent variables only have a range of 4 points, research has shown that it is acceptable to use parametric methods in these scenarios [28]. The omnibus test indicated that significant differences between levels could be found for at least one variable (Roy's Largest Root = 0.271, $F(3, 1048) = 94.500$, $p < 0.001$). As such, this was followed-up by individual analysis for both sense-making and hatefulness. These are presented in Table 6, which compares the baseline to the various thresholds.

Table 6. Effects of transformation on understandability and hatefulness.

Level	Sense-making	Hatefulness
Threshold = 0.5	−0.011	−1.631***
	(0.070)	(0.103)
Threshold = 0.7	−0.015	−1.461***
	(0.070)	(0.103)
Threshold = 0.9	−0.038	−1.417***
	(0.070)	(0.103)
Baseline (no transformation)	−	−
R^2	0.000	0.213

Note: Standard errors are in parenthesis. *$p < 0.05$; **$p < 0.01$; ***$p < 0.001$

First, it becomes evident that transformation has no impact on the degree of sense-making ($F(3, 1048) = 0.128$, $p = 0.944$). On the other hand, hatefulness presents a substantial decrease once transformation is applied ($F(3, 1048) = 94.350$, $p < 0.001$). This effect becomes more pronounced as the threshold is lowered; at a 0.9, hatefulness is 1.417 points lower on average than the baseline, which becomes 1.461 points lower at a 0.7 threshold, and finally 1.631 points lower at a 0.5 threshold. Post-hoc tests, using Tukey's HSD, were conducted to ascertain if these differences were statistically significant. The results are reported in Table 7.

Table 7. Comparison of effect by level.

Threshold (i)	Threshold (j)	Mean difference (i − j)
Threshold = 0.5	Threshold = 0.7	−0.170
	Threshold = 0.9	−0.213
	Baseline	−1.630***
Threshold = 0.7	Threshold = 0.5	0.170
	Threshold = 0.9	−0.043
	Baseline	−1.460***
Threshold = 0.9	Threshold = 0.5	0.213
	Threshold = 0.7	0.043
	Baseline	−1.417***
Baseline (no transformation)	Threshold = 0.5	1.630***
	Threshold = 0.7	1.460***
	Threshold = 0.9	1.417***

Note: *$p < 0.05$; **$p < 0.01$; ***$p < 0.001$

Based on these results, it is possible to observe that although all levels of threshold differ from the baseline ($p < 0.001$), they do not statistically differ among themselves, despite some numerical differences being noted. As such, we can conclude that transformation does not impact sense-making, and only minimal transformation needs to be conducted to obtain optimal hatefulness reduction.

Finally, we evaluate how well the modified comments retain the original meaning. This is done by three trusted raters each independently coding a sample of 100 comment pairs (modified–non-modified) for each threshold, in total 300 comment pairs per rater. For each pair, the raters read the original and modified comment and rate it on a scale of 1 to 5, as explained below:

- 1 = Not at all the same meaning
- 2 = Very different meaning
- 3 = Moderately the same meaning
- 4 = Very similar meaning
- 5 = Exactly the same meaning

The raters were explained the purpose of the task, namely that of evaluating if automatically changed comments have their original meaning. They were instructed to give their objective evaluation of each comment pair. In the borderline cases, raters were advised to choose conservatively, that is, if they hesitate, then rate the meaning to have changed. For each comment pair, we calculate the average original meaning rating given by the three raters. Figure 4 shows the average scores by threshold. We can see that as the threshold for deleting the hateful parts decreases, the comments start to lose their original meaning (3.73 for 0.9 threshold versus 3.29 for 0.5 threshold). The reason for this is logical since, on one hand, the number of false positives increases, and, on the other hand, as more hateful content is deleted it is not simultaneously replaced by a more neutral text, leaving some of the comments "crippled". As such, the result shows the limits of the current approach, although even at the lowest threshold, the comments retain "moderately the same meaning" on average.

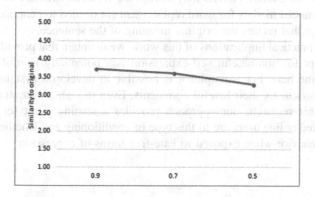

Fig. 4. Evaluation of original meaning retention.

5 Conclusion and Discussion

We have demonstrated an approach of neural network modeling to remove the hateful elements from comments. The approach significantly reduces the hatefulness of the comments while not significantly resulting in the loss of their understandability. The results on the loss of meaning are mixed: there seems to be a certain trade-off between removing hateful elements and losing the meaning, but on average the comments seem to keep their original meaning when applying the NNHD algorithm.

The positive results on understandability can be explained in different ways. First, it may be that the human understanding is robust to simple deletion of parts of comments, so that when one sentence of the comment gets reduced or deleted, the other sentences are used as context to fill in the gaps. Second, we speculated that if the network removes mostly adjectives and adverbs from the sentences, it is logical that the sentence will remain understandable because these word types are used to enhance a point, unlike verbs and nouns that are central for the understandability. However, a POS analysis revealed that the network, in fact, removes most often nouns (5,870 deletions) and verbs (2,785), while adjectives rank only on third place (1,790). Thus, this explanation, although logical, cannot be seen valid. Thus, we postulate that, as a side effect, removing hateful elements from online comments can reduce the linguistic complexity of the comments and thus make them more understandable.

Regarding the limitations of our work, we found three types of comments when looking at the results our algorithm: (1) **beyond repair**, i.e., comments that cannot be transformed without losing everything, (2) **doable but hard**, i.e., comments that a human can alter but that are difficult for machine to transform, and (3) **easy fix**, i.e., comments that can be transformed by simple removal of hateful expressions. The algorithm works well for the last type, but some comments it completely deletes, and some comments may lose their original meaning. Thus, more work is needed to develop automatic hate correction algorithms, especially utilizing more sophisticated methods for language generation, not only removal of hateful elements. This is needed because, as our findings show, sometimes the removal results in the loss of meaning. For example, in some cases, NNHD may disrupt the syntactic structure of the sentence. Thus, more advanced models for word replacement are needed to generate fluent, non-hateful language that retains the original meaning of the sentence.

In terms of practical implications of this work, we maintain that providing choice to end users to opt for non-hateful self-expression is a potentially fruitful approach in decreasing online hate. For example, it is possible to develop a system that recommends users ways to fix their hateful comments. Even though a user study is beyond the scope of this research, our approach provides a starting point for testing how receptive agitated online users are to this type of conditioning and whether they would change their behavior when exposed to hate-free forms of expression.

References

1. Burnap, P., Williams, M.L.: Us and them: identifying cyber hate on Twitter across multiple protected characteristics. EPJ Data Sci. **5**, 11 (2016)
2. Del Vicario, M., et al.: Echo chambers: emotional contagion and group polarization on facebook. Sci. Rep. **6**, 37825 (2016)
3. Kramer, A.D.I., Guillory, J.E., Hancock, J.T.: Experimental evidence of massive-scale emotional contagion through social networks. PNAS **111**, 8788–8790 (2014)
4. Salminen, J., et al.: Anatomy of online hate: developing a taxonomy and machine learning models for identifying and classifying hate in online news media. In: Proceeding of the International AAAI Conference on Web and Social Media (ICWSM 2018), San Francisco, California, USA (2018)
5. Wright, L., Ruths, D., Dillon, K.P., Saleem, H.M., Benesch, S.: Vectors for counterspeech on Twitter. In: Proceedings of the First Workshop on Abusive Language Online, pp. 57–62 (2017)
6. Scheuermann, L., Taylor, G.: Netiquette. Internet Res. **7**, 269–273 (1997)
7. Davidson, T., Warmsley, D., Macy, M., Weber, I.: Automated hate speech detection and the problem of offensive language. In: Proceedings of Eleventh International AAAI Conference on Web and Social Media, Québec, Canada (2017)
8. Bamberg, S.: Changing environmentally harmful behaviors: a stage model of self-regulated behavioral change. J. Environ. Psychol. **34**, 151–159 (2013)
9. Djuric, N., Zhou, J., Morris, R., Grbovic, M., Radosavljevic, V., Bhamidipati, N.: Hate speech detection with comment embeddings. In: Proceedings of the 24th International Conference on World Wide Web, pp. 29–30. ACM, New York (2015)
10. Mondal, M., Silva, L.A., Benevenuto, F.: A Measurement study of hate speech in social media. In: Proceedings of the 28th ACM Conference on Hypertext and Social Media, pp. 85–94. ACM, New York (2017)

11. Nobata, C., Tetreault, J., Thomas, A., Mehdad, Y., Chang, Y.: Abusive language detection in online user content. In: Proceedings of the 25th International Conference on World Wide Web, pp. 145–153. International World Wide Web Conferences Steering Committee, Republic and Canton of Geneva, Switzerland (2016)
12. Ries, E.: The Lean Startup. Penguin Books Ltd, London (2011)
13. Mohan, S., Guha, A., Harris, M., Popowich, F., Schuster, A., Priebe, C.: The impact of toxic language on the health of Reddit communities. In: Mouhoub, M., Langlais, P. (eds.) AI 2017. LNCS (LNAI), vol. 10233, pp. 51–56. Springer, Cham (2017). https://doi.org/10.1007/978-3-319-57351-9_6
14. Saleem, H.M., Dillon, K.P., Benesch, S., Ruths, D.: A web of hate: tackling hateful speech in online social spaces (2017). arXiv:1709.10159 [cs]
15. Silva, L., Mondal, M., Correa, D., Benevenuto, F., Weber, I.: Analyzing the targets of hate in online social media. In: Proceedings of Tenth International AAAI Conference on Web and Social Media, Palo Alto, CA (2016)
16. Sood, S., Antin, J., Churchill, E.: Profanity use in online communities. In: Proceedings of the SIGCHI Conference on Human Factors in Computing Systems, pp. 1481–1490. ACM, New York (2012)
17. Sood, S.O., Churchill, E.F., Antin, J.: Automatic identification of personal insults on social news sites. J. Am. Soc. Inf. Sci. 63, 270–285 (2012)
18. Rajadesingan, A., Zafarani, R., Liu, H.: Sarcasm detection on Twitter: a behavioral modeling approach. In: Proceedings of the Eighth ACM International Conference on Web Search and Data Mining, pp. 97–106. ACM (2015)
19. Badjatiya, P., Gupta, S., Gupta, M., Varma, V.: Deep learning for hate speech detection in tweets. In: Proceedings of the 26th International Conference on World Wide Web Companion, pp. 759–760. International World Wide Web Conferences Steering Committee, Republic and Canton of Geneva, Switzerland (2017)
20. Park, J.H., Fung, P.: One-step and two-step classification for abusive language detection on Twitter (2017). arXiv preprint arXiv:1706.01206
21. Strauss, A., Corbin, J.: Grounded theory methodology. In: Denzin, N.K., Lincoln, Y.S. (eds.) Handbook of Qualitative Research, pp. 273–285. Sage, Thousand Oaks (1994)
22. Geiger, D., Seedorf, S., Schulze, T., Nickerson, R., Schader, M.: Managing the crowd: towards a taxonomy of crowdsourcing processes. In: AMCIS 2011 Proceedings, pp. 1–11 (2011)
23. Filippova, K., Strube, M.: Dependency tree based sentence compression. In: Proceedings of the Fifth International Natural Language Generation Conference, pp. 25–32. Association for Computational Linguistics, Stroudsburg (2008)
24. Alguliev, R., Aliguliyev, R.: Evolutionary algorithm for extractive text summarization. Intell. Inf. Manag. 1, 128 (2009)
25. Straka, M., Hajic, J., Strakova, J.: UDPipe: trainable pipeline for processing CoNLL-U files performing tokenization, morphological analysis, POS tagging and parsing. Presented at the Proceedings of the Tenth International Conference on Language Resources and Evaluation (LREC 2016), Portorož, Slovenia (2016)
26. Alonso, O., Marshall, C.C., Najork, M.: Debugging a crowdsourced task with low inter-rater agreement. In: Proceedings of the 15th ACM/IEEE-CS Joint Conference on Digital Libraries, pp. 101–110. ACM, New York (2015)
27. Norušis, M.J.: IBM SPSS Statistics 19 Statistical Procedures Companion. Prentice Hall, Upper Saddle River (2011)
28. Norman, G.: Likert scales, levels of measurement and the "laws" of statistics. Adv Health Sci. Educ. Theory Pract. 15, 625–632 (2010)

Adaptive Focused Crawling Using Online Learning
A Study on Content Related to Islamic Extremism

Christos Iliou[✉], Theodora Tsikrika, George Kalpakis, Stefanos Vrochidis, and Ioannis Kompatsiaris

Information Technologies Institute, CERTH, Thessaloniki, Greece
{iliouchristos,theodora.tsikrika,kalpakis,stefanos,ikom}@iti.gr

Abstract. Focused crawlers aim to automatically discover online content resources relevant to a domain of interest by automatically navigating through the Web link structure and selecting which hyperlinks to follow based on an estimation of their relevance to the topic of interest; to this end, classifier-guided approaches are typically employed for identifying hyperlinks having the higher likelihood of leading to relevant content. However, the training data used for building these classifiers might not be entirely representative of the domain of interest, or the domain of interest might change over time. To meet these challenges, this work proposes a novel adaptive focused crawling framework that allows the classifiers that underlie the hyperlink selection policy to be adapted based on the evidence they encounter during their crawls. Our framework uses two different approaches to retrain its models: (i) *Interactive Adaptation*, where a user manually evaluates the discovered resources, and (ii) *Automatic Adaptation*, where the framework uses the already trained classifiers to assess the relevance of newly discovered resources. The evaluation experiments in the domain of Islamic extremism indicate the effectiveness of online learning in focused crawling.

Keywords: Focused crawling · Adaptive learning · Online learning
Islamic extremism

1 Introduction

The proliferation of the use of the Web and social media has greatly facilitated the open diffusion of knowledge and the uninterrupted communication of thoughts, ideas, and interests, thus resulting in a significant increase in the information being shared globally. These new opportunities have also proven very useful for terrorists and extremists for advertising their subversive intentions to broader audiences, cutting across different nationalities, cultures, religions, and residences. Several terrorist organisations and extremist groups have exploited the popularity and broad reach of the Web and social media for supporting their

© Springer Nature Switzerland AG 2018
S. S. Bodrunova (Ed.): INSCI 2018, LNCS 11193, pp. 40–53, 2018.
https://doi.org/10.1007/978-3-030-01437-7_4

goals of dispersing their propaganda, orchestrating action plans, recruiting new members, and disseminating material targeting potential perpetrators of future attacks.

In this context, the challenge for governments and Law Enforcement Agencies (LEAs) is to better understand and counter potential threats by discovering information related to terrorist and extremist activity on the Internet. To this end, sophisticated Web search and discovery tools are typically employed, such as Web crawlers, which are capable of systematically traversing the Web for the efficient discovery and collection of online content. Starting from a set of predefined (seed) Web pages, Web crawlers fetch (i.e., download) these pages, parse their content for extracting the hyperlinks they contain, and place the extracted hyperlinks in a queue containing the Web pages to be fetched at later stages of the crawl. This process is iteratively repeated until a termination criterion is applied (e.g., a desired number of pages are fetched).

This work aims at presenting a crawler able to discover Web resources on any given topic, with particular focus on topics of interest to LEAs. To this end, we develop a crawler capable of gathering content focused on a given topic by employing a classifier-guided hyperlink selection strategy based on supervised machine learning techniques, that aims to identify the hyperlinks that most likely lead to relevant content. Given the inherently volatile nature of the Web which forms a continuously evolving environment necessitating the employment of dynamically (re)trained classifiers for supporting the hyperlink selection policy and the potential sparsity of appropriate training data for building these classifiers, the focused crawling approach can benefit by incorporating a mechanism allowing for the automatic adjustment of the employed classifiers to new evidence encountered during its crawls. This way, we can ensure that the focused crawler will take into consideration and adapt to any new knowledge emerging about any given topic.

To meet these challenges, we propose a novel adaptive focused crawling framework using online learning that (i) uses a classifier-guided approach for identifying (during the crawling process) hyperlinks having the higher likelihood of leading to relevant content, and (ii) allows these classifiers that underlie the hyperlink selection policy to be adapted based on the evidence they encounter during their crawls. This allows to address the sparsity of appropriate training data, as well as the need to consider the constantly changing landscape. This adaptive focused crawler is able to retrain its hyperlink selection classifiers online either in an automatic or in an interactive manner based on the users' feedback; this has the potential to significantly increase the effectiveness of the static classifiers previously employed for hyperlink selection. The main contribution of our work is thus the development of a generic adaptive focused crawling framework using online learning, which is configured and demonstrated for a specific topic of interest to LEAs: the discovery of Web resources related to Islamic extremism. Our experimental results indicate the significant potential of the proposed approaches on the targeted domain both for the interactive and automatic adaptation settings; the proposed framework thus forms a solid baseline upon which we can further build adaptive focused crawling methods.

The remainder of this paper is structured as follows: Sect. 2 discusses related work. Section 3 describes the proposed adaptive focused crawling approach. Section 4 presents the results of the evaluation experiments. Finally, Sect. 5 concludes this work.

2   Related Work

This section first presents state-of-the-art approaches for focused crawling and its application to the terrorism and extremism domain. Subsequently, it discusses the benefits of employing adaptation techniques to the hyperlink selection algorithms of the focused crawling process.

Focused crawlers are used for the automatic discovery of online resources related to a domain of interest by automatically navigating through the Web link structure and selecting the hyperlinks to follow by estimating their relevance to the topic of interest. Focused crawling techniques have been researched for many years [4] and take advantage of the 'topical locality' phenomenon, i.e., that most Web pages link to other pages with similar content [3]. State-of-the-art focused crawlers use classifier-guided approaches based on supervised machine learning techniques for the identification of hyperlinks that have higher likelihood of leading to relevant content [10]. More specifically, a feature vector is calculated for each training sample by typically considering as features the most important terms included in the textual content of the Web pages encountered during the crawls and by estimating the importance of these terms using the tf-idf metric. Each training sample may consist of the anchor text related to the hyperlink of interest, the full content of the parent Web page (i.e., the Web page containing the hyperlink), the text appearing in the vicinity of the hyperlink in the parent Web page (referred to as "surrounding text") or any combination of the above [12]. To this end, state-of-the art approaches typically combine (i) the anchor text of the hyperlink of interest, (ii) a text window of x (e.g., $x = 50$) characters surrounding the anchor text that does not overlap with the anchor text of adjacent hyperlinks, and (iii) the terms extracted from the URL [7,12].

Focused crawling is a common approach employed for the identification of potentially suspicious online Web content related to the domain of terrorism and extremism. The Dark Web project at the University of Arizona created a suite for Web mining that performs link and content analysis on the Web [1]. Furthermore, researchers have also mentioned that such content is often published on forums, where traditional crawling techniques might fail [5]. To this end, they propose systems that are able to crawl such content from forums [5] and authenticate themselves when needed, provided that a valid username-password combination are provided [7]. To further improve the understanding of terrorist activities, researchers have also focused on collecting and analysing information of Jihad Web sites and develop visualization of their site content, relationships, and activity levels [2]. Furthermore, hybrid focused crawlers have been proposed that are able to traverse both the Surface Web and some of the most popular darknets of the Dark Web (such as Tor); these have been deployed and evaluated for the collection of homemade explosive recipes [7].

All the aforementioned approaches employ models that are trained "statically" based on a fixed set of training samples which cannot be adapted over time. However, two main challenges arise when using pre-trained "static" focused crawlers: (i) the availability of sufficient and appropriate training data for representing the domain of interest and (ii) changes in the domain of interest over time. The latter encompasses the notions of feature-evolution, concept-evolution, and concept-drift [9], where the initially trained classification models may become obsolete over time. To meet these challenges, research has proposed the use of focused crawlers that automatically adapt to the domain of interest.

One of the proposed techniques in the literature, which considers that initially the knowledge about the environment is incomplete, is the use of learning automata, an adaptive decision-making unit [14]. Focused crawlers that use learning automation learn how to choose the optimal actions from a finite set of allowed actions through repeated interactions with a random environment. Such focused crawlers adapt their behaviour based on the feedback they receive (i.e., pages gathered) from the environment. Other approaches perform adaptation by extracting ontologies through an unsupervised adaptive way [6] using a cyclic "maintenance scheme", triggered based on changes in the input data stream, to constantly update their models.

Given the performance gains acquired by employing focused crawling approaches which adapt over time, we propose an adaptive classifier-based focused crawler that shares this advantage. More specifically, this work proposes a novel adaptive focused crawling framework using online learning in two different modes: (i) the *Interactive Adaptation* mode, which takes as input the end user feedback to identify whether a newly discovered Web page was correctly identified as relevant or irrelevant to the domain of interest, and (ii) the *Automatic Adaptation* mode which uses the already trained classifiers for assessing the relevance of newly discovered pages. These newly discovered Web pages are used as input for updating the classification models. The main contribution of this paper is the proposal of an effective technique based on online learning which exploits the advantages of online adaptation and applies it to a classifier-guided focused crawler.

3   Adaptive Focused Crawler

This work proposes a novel adaptive classifier-guided focused crawling approach for the discovery of Web resources about a given topic that estimates the relevance of hyperlinks to unvisited resources. The adaptive focused crawler uses state-of-the-art focused crawling approaches and goes one step further by introducing the adaptiveness in the hyperlink selection process based on the evidence encountered during crawling.

The general steps of focused crawling are depicted in Fig. 1. Initially, the seed entry points (i.e., the list of Web resources to be crawled) are added to the "frontier", i.e., the list of URLs of the resources not visited yet. In each iteration, a URL is picked from the list and the Web resource corresponding to this

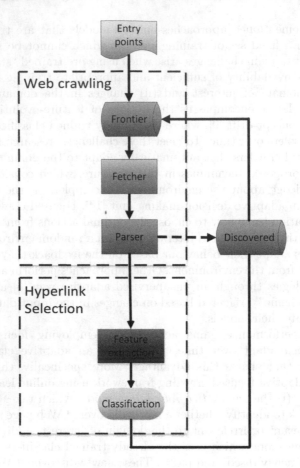

Fig. 1. Classifier-guided focused crawling.

URL is fetched (i.e., downloaded), scraped, and parsed to extract its hyperlinks. Then, the focused crawler estimates the relevance of each hyperlink pointing to an unvisited resource based on the hyperlink's local and global context within its parent Web page. The decision whether a new unvisited hyperlink from a fetched Web resource is relevant to the domain of interest relies on supervised machine learning techniques which train models based on annotated positive and negative samples of online Web content on the domain of interest. Based on these trained classification models, the hyperlink selection process is as follows: each new hyperlink is assigned a confidence score and if this is greater than a threshold, the resource will be considered as relevant and will also be added to the frontier.

Given though that (i) the data to be used for training the classifiers might not be representative of the entire domain, and (ii) changes might occur to the domain of interest over time (e.g., in our case, this could be the introduction of a new terrorist organisation) which might not be covered by the current classifiers, we propose to adapt the classifiers by training them online using the newly discovered data. Next, the hyperlink selection process (Sect. 3.1) and the online learning approach (Sect. 3.2) are described in more detail.

3.1 Hyperlink Selection

The hyperlink selection is performed by estimating the relevance of a hyperlink pointing to an unvisited resource with content relevant to the domain of interest. Research has indicated that the combination of the local context of the hyperlink and the global (i.e., full) text of the parent Web resource can effectively predict the relevance of a hyperlink during the selection process [7]. To this end, the current implementation of the hyperlink selection process is performed in a hybrid mode by combining the outcome of a link-based classifier that classifies the hyperlinks based on their local context (i.e., the anchor and surrounding text) and a Web page classifier that classifies the hyperlinks based on their global context (i.e., the entire content of their parent page). This hybrid approach is presented in Fig. 2.

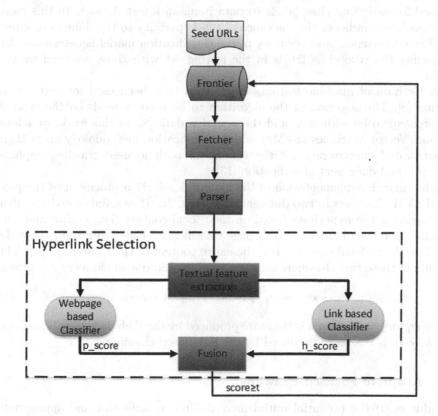

Fig. 2. Hybrid classification architecture.

The first step in the hyperlink selection process is to define a set of features which will most efficiently and meaningfully represent the information that is important for analysis and classification. To this end, our feature extraction relies on textual data. More specifically, each feature corresponds to textual structural components (e.g., words, stems, etc.) found in the context of each resource following a series of processing steps. In particular, given a training set (i.e., a set of Web resources annotated with respect to their relevance to the domain of interest), a lexicon of all terms (features) present in the training set is created by performing the following steps: tokenisation, elimination of stopwords (i.e., non-informative terms that do not facilitate the distinction between dissimilar resources), and stemming, i.e., reducing the extracted terms to their root form (e.g., "islam", "islamic", "islamism", and "islamist" should all be reduced to the same root form). Once the lexicon is created, each resource can be represented in this feature (vector) space by estimating the term frequency-inverse document frequency (tf-idf) of each of its terms.

Generally, hyperlink classification is a two-step process consisting of a *Training* step, where the classification model is build using the aforementioned training data, and a *Prediction* step, where the generated classification model can be used for assigning class labels to data items in a test dataset. In this case, the class labels indicate the relevance of the hyperlinks to the domain of interest. The effectiveness and accuracy of the classification model is determined by comparing the true class labels in the testing set with those assigned by the model.

A plethora of machine learning approaches have been used for text classification [8]. The selection of the algorithm to be used depends on the type of the problem to be addressed and the available data [8]. In this work, we adopt Support Vector Machines (SVMs) as our classification methodology given their demonstrated effectiveness int the context of both focused crawling applications [11] and document classification [13].

The current implementation of the hyperlink selection process uses the proposed SVM classifiers in two different ways (Fig. 2): (i) as a link-based classifier for classifying the hyperlinks based on their local context (i.e., anchor and surrounding text), and (ii) as a Web page classifier for classifying the hyperlinks based on their global context (i.e., the entire content of their parent page). The outputs of these two classifiers are then combined into a single score as follows:

$$score = w_1 \cdot p\_score + w_2 \cdot h\_score \tag{1}$$

where $w_1 + w_2 = 1$, p_score is the score produced by the Web page based classifier, and h_score is the score produced by the link-based classifier.

3.2   Adaptive Focused Crawling

To address (i) the potential initial unavailability of sufficient and appropriate training data for representing the domain of interest, and (ii) the changes occurring in the domain of interest over time, this work proposes a novel adaptive

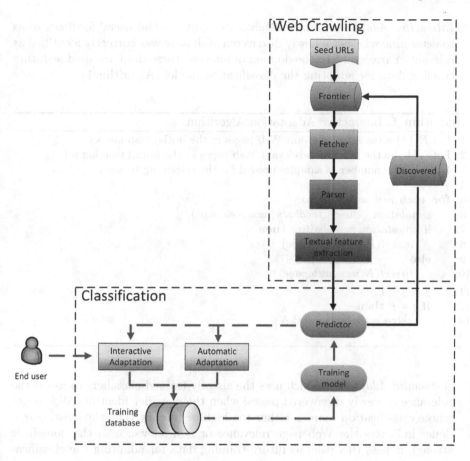

Fig. 3. Adaptive focused crawling.

focused crawling approach, where classifiers are retrained periodically by incorporating the newly found samples. The relevance of the new discovered samples can be assessed either automatically or by enabling the direct user feedback. The retraining frequency of the framework is based on the number of available data for training. If the newly discovered and annotated data surpass a threshold, the retraining process is initiated. When choosing the threshold value, we should consider that the retraining based only on a small number of newly discovered Web pages will have a minimal effect on the models; on the other hand, retraining the classifiers very rarely would reduce the adaptiveness of the focused crawler to any domain changes. Therefore, the adaptive strategy should keep a balance between performing the retraining process rarely and too frequently, without having a sufficient number of new samples.

To achieve the adaptiveness in our framework, we consider two alternatives of online learning (see Fig. 3):

– *Interactive Adaptation* which receives as input the end users' feedback so as to determine whether a newly discovered Web page was correctly identified as relevant or irrelevant to the domain of interest; these data are used as future training data for adapting the classification model (Algorithm 1).

Algorithm 1. Interactive Adaptation Algorithm

1: Let $P\{\}$ be the set of relevant Web pages in the initial training set
2: Let $N\{\}$ be the set of non-relevant Web pages in the initial training set
3: Let k be the number of samples needed for the retraining to start
4: $j \leftarrow 0$
5: **for** each *new_web_page* **do**
6:     $annotation \leftarrow user\_feedback(new\_web\_page)$
7:     **if** *annotation* == *positive* **then**
8:         $insert(P, new\_web\_page)$
9:     **else**
10:         $insert(N, new\_web\_page)$
11:     $j \leftarrow j + 1$
12:     **if** $j = k$ **then**
13:         $retrain\_classifiers(P, N)$
14:         $j \leftarrow 0$

– *Automatic Adaptation* which uses the already trained classifiers to assess the relevance of newly discovered pages; when the classifier identifies Web pages whose classification score is either too high or too low (i.e., the existing evidence indicates the Web page relevance or non-relevance to the domain is strong), it uses this page as future training data for adapting the classification model (Algorithm 2).

Algorithm 2. Automatic Adaptation Algorithm

1: Let $P\{\}$ be the set of relevant Web pages in the initial training set
2: Let $N\{\}$ be the set of non-relevant Web pages in the initial training set
3: Let k be the number of samples needed for the retraining to start
4: Let t_1, t_2 be the threshold values strongly indicating relevance, non-relevance
5: $j \leftarrow 0$
6: **for** each *new_web_page* **do**
7:     $score \leftarrow classification\_probability(new\_web\_page)$
8:     **if** $score \geq t_1$ **then**
9:         $insert(P, new\_web\_page)$
10:     **else if** $score \leq t_2$ **then**
11:         $insert(N, new\_web\_page)$
12:     $j \leftarrow j + 1$
13:     **if** $j = k$ **then**
14:         $retrain\_classifiers(P, N)$
15:         $j \leftarrow 0$

---

4   Evaluation

To assess the effectiveness of the proposed adaptive focused crawling approach, a series of experiments were performed in the domain of Islamic extremism. An initial investigation of online content related to Islamic extremism has shown that this type of content is very diverse. Therefore, when employing focused crawlers in this particular case, the data used for training the classifiers might not be sufficiently representative of all the characteristics of the pages of interest. Thus, models need to be retrained periodically, incorporating new pages that are identified as relevant or non-relevant either in an interactive or in an automatic manner. This section describes the experimental setup (Sect. 4.1) the employed performance metrics (Sect. 4.2), and the results of the experiments (Sect. 4.3).

4.1   Experimental Setup

A set of 15 seed URLs was used for the experiments; these seed URLs have been provided as Web entry points by experts on the terrorism domain. The content of the selected URLs is relevant to Islamic extremism and the focused crawling experiments that employ them as their seed set aim to discover additional online content relevant to Islamic extremism. The seed set was further split into two subsets, the training set, consisting of 11 URLs, and the testing set consisting of the remaining 4 URLs[1].

Starting from these seeds, a crawl at depth $= 1$ (where depth is the maximum distance allowed between seed and crawled pages) was performed and the discovered Web pages, along with their content, were stored locally. The total number of Web pages collected during the crawl was 179 Web pages: 138 Web pages were discovered from the training seed set and 41 from the testing seed set. The collected URLs were annotated based on their relevance to the domain of Islamic extremism; this resulted in having a training set with 80 positive and 58 negative samples, and a test set with 23 positive and 18 negative samples.

Starting from the four seeds in the test set, the hyperlink selection process estimated the relevance of the encountered hyperlinks by combining two classifiers: (i) a link-based classifier that takes advantage of the local context (i.e., anchor text and surrounding text) of the hyperlinks in the parent page, and (ii) a Web page classifier that exploits the content of the parent Web page; see Sect. 3.1 for further details. The total score was calculated using a combination of the scores produced by the Web page and the link-based classifiers, with $w_1 = 0.1$ and $w_2 = 0.9$, respectively (see Sect. 3.1). If the estimated score was greater than $t = 0.5$, the hyperlinks were considered as relevant.

The effectiveness of the proposed adaptive focused crawling approach was evaluated in three stages. The first stage represents the initial point of the focused crawl where the classifier employed is built using a training set consisting of the 80% of the total training samples (i.e., the initial classifier is already built before

---

[1] The actual URLs are not provided so as to avoid the inclusion of potentially sensitive information, but can be made available upon request.

the beginning of the crawl process). The second and the third stage represent the points where the adaptive online training takes place (i.e., at some point during the focused crawl after discovering new pages). In these two stages, an additional 10% of the remaining samples on the original training dataset, respectively, is employed for retraining the initial classifier; the new samples provided simulate the new Web pages discovered during the course of the crawl. Our experiments simulate an online training process where the data are periodically imported to the training set after $k = 14$ new pages are encountered (i.e., 14 additional Web pages were used for retraining the classifiers at each of the second and the third stages, respectively). Furthermore, the classifiers from each stage were tested on the same data. The number of samples employed for training at each stage of our experiments and the number of samples used for testing is illustrated in Table 1.

Table 1. Number of positive and negative samples in the training and test datasets.

	Training data			Test data
	80%	90%	100%	
Positive	64	72	80	23
Negative	46	52	58	18
Total	110	124	138	41

We tested the two online learning approaches implemented in our work (i.e., the Interactive Adaptation and the Automatic Adaptation). In both cases, the first stage of our experiments included the training of the initial classification models (the link-based and Web page classifiers, respectively) on 80% of the available training data. During the second and third stages, the training set was further enriched with an additional 10% of the remaining training data, respectively (i.e., 90% and 100% of the total training samples were used for the second and third stage, respectively).

In the Interactive Adaptation mode, our goal was to simulate the end user feedback provided during the second and third stage of our experiments; therefore, the adaptive models were produced based on the annotation performed by domain experts for all the new pages discovered during the second and the third stages. On the other hand, given that the Automatic Adaptation mode is based on the already trained classifiers for evaluating the relevance of newly discovered pages, it performs the retraining during the second and the third stage by adding new entries for which the estimated relevance or non-relevance to the domain of Islamic extremism is strong enough. Specifically, the newly discovered samples are used as positive samples in the retraining only when their estimated score is greater that a value t_1, or as negatives when their score is lower than a value t_2, indicating strong confidence of the classifiers; these values were set as $t_1 = 0.8$ and $t_2 = 0.2$.

Finally, the classifiers were implemented using the LIBSVM package of the Weka machine learning software[2], with the text-based classification scores corresponding to its probabilistic outputs; their parameters are presented in Table 2.

Table 2. Parameters used for the SVM classifiers.

SVM parameters	
SVM type	C-SVM
Kernel	Radical basis function
Penalty parameter	1
Gamma	1/n, where n is the number of features
Tolerance	0.001
Shrinking heuristics	Enabled

4.2 Evaluation Metrics

To assess the effectiveness of our approach we calculated the precision and recall metrics as well as their harmonic mean, F-measure. Precision is the fraction of relevant pages among all the fetched pages, while recall is the fraction of relevant pages fetched over the total amount of relevant pages. The latter requires knowledge of all relevant pages on a given topic which is a practically infeasible task in the context of the Web. To address this limitation, two recall-oriented evaluation techniques have been proposed [10]: (i) manually designate a few representative pages on the topic and measure the fraction of them discovered by the crawler and (ii) measure the overlap among independent crawls initiated from different seeds to see whether they converge on the same set of pages; only the former could be applied to our experimental set-up.

4.3 Results

Table 3 presents the results for the Interactive Adaptation for the three evaluation stages, when the 80%, 90% and 100% of the training set was used, respectively. As the number of the training data increases, the overall precision also increases, reaching over 90% when all available training samples are used (i.e., in the third stage). This is accompanied by a small decrease in recall, indicating that a few relevant Web pages are missed in the effort to reach a high precision. Nevertheless, the overall performance in terms of the F-measure also improves.

Contrary to the Interactive Adaptation, the Automatic Adaptation does not use all the discovered data for training but only the data whose classification score entails strong confidence (i.e. when the score is either too high or too low). Specifically, we only use as positive samples, data with classification scores greater than 0.8, and as negative samples, data with classification scores less than

---

[2] http://www.cs.waikato.ac.nz/ml/weka/.

Table 3. Evaluation results for Interactive Adaptation of the hyperlink selection classifiers.

	Data for online training		
	80%	90%	100%
# Positive	64	72 (+8)	80 (+8)
# Negative	46	52 (+6)	58 (+6)
# Total	110	124 (+14)	138 (+14)
Precision	0.61	0.70	0.91
Recall	1.00	1.00	0.95
F-measure	0.76	0.82	0.93

Table 4. Evaluation results for Automatic Adaptation of the hyperlink selection classifiers.

	Data for online training		
	80%	90%	100%
# Positive	64	68 (+4 out of 8)	69 (+1 out of 8)
# Negative	46	47 (+1 out of 6)	48 (+1 out of 6)
# Total	110	115 (+5 out of 14)	117 (+2 out of 14)
Precision	0.61	0.70	0.78
Recall	1.00	0.94	0.95
F-measure	0.76	0.80	0.86

0.2 (the values between 0.2 and 0.8 are not considered to provide strong evidence, and hence the respective Web pages are not used for retraining purposes). The total amount of data considered as positive and negative samples (out of all the available data) at each retraining stage are shown in Table 4, together with the results of the evaluation experiments.

Similarly to the above, as the number of the training data increases, the overall precision and F-measure also increase, while recall slightly drops. The achieved results indicate the potential benefits of considering automatically identified training samples; however, additional large-scale experiments are needed so as to reliably assess the potential effectiveness of the proposed approaches.

5   Conclusions

This work proposed a novel adaptive focused crawling framework using online learning that (i) uses a classifier-guided approach for identifying (during the crawling process) hyperlinks having the higher likelihood of leading to relevant content, and (ii) allows these classifiers that underlie the hyperlink selection policy to be adapted based on the evidence they encounter during their crawls.

This adaptive focused crawler is able to retrain its hyperlink selection classifiers online either in an automatic or in an interactive manner based on user's feedback. Experiments in the domain of Islamic extremism indicate the significant potential of the adopted approaches on the targeted domain, given that our framework has demonstrated satisfactory performance, both for the interactive and automatic adaptation settings. Our future work will investigate strategies for the selection of the optimal subset of all available Web pages for online training for further increasing our framework's effectiveness and efficiency.

Acknowledgements. This work was supported by the TENSOR project (H2020-700024), funded by the European Commission.

References

1. Chen, H.: Dark Web: Exploring and Data Mining the Dark Side of the Web, vol. 30. Springer, Heidelberg (2011). https://doi.org/10.1007/978-1-4614-1557-2
2. Chen, H., Chung, W., Qin, J., Reid, E., Sageman, M., Weimann, G.: Uncovering the dark web: a case study of Jihad on the web. J. Assoc. Inf. Sci. Technol. **59**(8), 1347–1359 (2008)
3. Davison, B.D.: Topical locality in the web. In: Proceedings of the 23rd Annual International ACM SIGIR Conference on Research and Development in Information Retrieval, pp. 272–279. ACM (2000)
4. De Bra, P.M., Post, R.: Information retrieval in the world-wide web: making client-based searching feasible. Comput. Netw. ISDN Syst. **27**(2), 183–192 (1994)
5. Fu, T., Abbasi, A., Chen, H.: A focused crawler for dark web forums. J. Assoc. Inf. Sci. Technol. **61**(6), 1213–1231 (2010)
6. Hassan, T., Cruz, C., Bertaux, A.: Ontology-based approach for unsupervised and adaptive focused crawling. In: Proceedings of The International Workshop on Semantic Big Data, p. 2. ACM (2017)
7. Iliou, C., Kalpakis, G., Tsikrika, T., Vrochidis, S., Kompatsiaris, I.: Hybrid focused crawling for homemade explosives discovery on surface and dark web. In: 2016 11th International Conference on Availability, Reliability and Security (ARES), pp. 229–234. IEEE (2016)
8. Khan, A., Baharudin, B., Lee, L.H., Khan, K.: A review of machine learning algorithms for text-documents classification. J. Adv. Inf. Technol. **1**(1), 4–20 (2010)
9. Masud, M.M., et al.: Addressing concept-evolution in concept-drifting data streams. In: 2010 IEEE 10th International Conference on Data Mining (ICDM), pp. 929–934. IEEE (2010)
10. Olston, C., Najork, M.: Web crawling. Found. Trends Inf. Retrieval **4**(3), 175–246 (2010)
11. Pant, G., Srinivasan, P.: Learning to crawl: comparing classification schemes. ACM Trans. Inf. Syst. (TOIS) **23**(4), 430–462 (2005)
12. Pant, G., Srinivasan, P.: Link contexts in classifier-guided topical crawlers. IEEE Trans. Knowl. Data Eng. **18**(1), 107–122 (2006)
13. Sebastiani, F.: Machine learning in automated text categorization. ACM Comput. Surv. (CSUR) **34**(1), 1–47 (2002)
14. Torkestani, J.A.: An adaptive focused web crawling algorithm based on learning automata. Appl. Intell. **37**(4), 586–601 (2012)

Using Corpus Linguistics Tools to Analyze a Russian-Language Islamic Extremist Forum

Tatiana Litvinova[1]([⊠])[iD], Olga Litvinova[1][iD], Polina Panicheva[2][iD], and Elizaveta Biryukova[1]

[1] RusProfiling Lab, Voronezh State Pedagogical University, 86 ul. Lenina,
Voronezh 394043, Russia
centr_rus_yaz@mail.ru
[2] Saint Petersburg State University, Saint Petersburg,
13B Universitetskaya Emb., St. Petersburg 199034, Russia

Abstract. The Internet plays an important role in the continued functioning of extremist and terrorist groups. Studying extremist ideology based on linguistic analysis using methods of corpus and computer linguistics to help supplement and make qualitative analysis more objective is crucial. However, corpus-based linguistic research into the ideology of extremists remains scarce. This is due to a limited access to such texts. The Dark Web Project of the University of Arizona AI Lab that contains gigabytes of texts of private extremist and terrorist forums is a valuable source for corpus-based studies of extremist discourse. The aim of the research is a corpus-based study of Russian-language posts of Caucasian extremists from KavkazChat forum (included on the RF Federal list of extremist materials) where The 2010 Moscow Metro bombings are discussed. WordSmith Tools software package was used to identify most frequent words and word clusters, build concordances, find collocates, etc. A comparative corpus analysis of texts by Islamic extremists and those by common Internet users on the same topic (comments on relevant newsfeeds) allowed us to identify a number of features of Islamic extremist rhetoric.

Keywords: Extremist forum · Dark Web Project · WordSmith tool
KavkazChat

1 Introduction

The Internet has now become a powerful tool of manipulating young people's mind and behavior as well as public opinion. It is giving extremist movements for young people a whole range of new opportunities to form isolated communities. Agitation and propaganda are commonly used on Internet terrorist groups to spread materials and information in favour of terrorism to promote terrorist activities: "Terrorists across different jurisdictions heavily utilize modern transportation and communication systems for relocation, propaganda, recruitment, and communication purposes. Thus, addressing issues such as how to trace the dynamic evolution, communication, and movement of terrorist groups across different jurisdictions and how to analyze and

© Springer Nature Switzerland AG 2018
S. S. Bodrunova (Ed.): INSCI 2018, LNCS 11193, pp. 54–65, 2018.
https://doi.org/10.1007/978-3-030-01437-7_5

predict terrorists' activities, associations, and threats becomes an urgent and challenging issue" [1, p. 333].

To develop effective counter terrorism methods, it is important to analyze and understand terrorist ideology reflected in texts. Previous research into extremist and terrorist ideology has been mainly qualitative in nature and/or was performed on publicly available data around [10]. Linguistic research into the ideology of extremist and terrorist based on quantitative analysis of language remains scarce [8].

This paper considers identifying the ideology expressed in Islamic extremist texts using posts from Russian-language forum of North Caucasian extremists KavkazChat on one particular topic, namely The 2010 Moscow Metro bombing discussion, using automated corpus-linguistic techniques.

KavkazChat is included on the RF Federal list of extremist materials and access to the site is blocked. We accessed KavkazChat due to Dark Web Project.[1] We also compiled a corpus of comments of Internet users on the news about bombings for comparison.

This section of the forum was chosen as its topic and its discussion in KavkazChat where the attacks are justified and approved resonates with media. The importance of the analysis of extremist rhetoric produced immediately after a terrorist attack is due to the fact that following a high-profile attack not only does the character of terrorist propaganda change but it also reaches its peak [14, p. 27]. This is in a way because of the society becoming increasingly sensitive to any information regarding terrorism.

Stepin [14, p. 27] reports a significant increase in the number of queries related to KavkazChat on the search engine Yandex following a terrorist attack. There is a particularly disturbing tendency when there is a new influx of users on these forums who share extremist ideology and thus make the mission of the propaganda accomplished.

We used a range of corpus linguistics techniques to order to identify patterns in the usage of words as well as to analyze word clusters and find word collocates that are unique to the text corpora under examination. We believe that interpreting these patterns affords insights into Islamic extremist ideology, beliefs and justifications. To the best of our knowledge, this is the first corpus-based study of Russian-language Islamic extremist forum. In addition, as far as we know, this is the first study aimed at corpus-based comparison of two "views" on same event (by extremist and non-extremists) expressed immediately after the event.

2 State of the Art

Understand individuals' motivations for terrorism and extremism through content analysis is a promising area of research. But previous studies used mostly qualitative methodology (see [8, 13] for review) which implies manual analysis using techniques of content analysis, discourse analysis, report analysis. In recent years, there has been a rapid growth of research making use of automated approaches to the analysis of

---

[1] https://ai.arizona.edu/research/dark-web-geo-web.

extremist texts (sentiment analysis, social network analysis, methods of corpus linguistics, automated psycholinguistics, etc.) [9].

Corpus linguistics is the study of language patterns in large body of language data referred to as corpora [9, p. 160] which represent the verbal behavior of target population (in our case this is extremists). Corpus linguists often use different type of software to analyze corpora (WordSmith,[2] WMatrix,[3] AntConc,[4] etc.) and reveal patterns of language use typical of a target population. Often, different methods of analysis are combined.

For example, Salama [11] uses WordSmith tool and critical discourse analysis for exploring how clashing ideologies have been actualized at a collocation level across opposing discourses on Wahhabi-Saudi Islam/Wahhabism since 9/11. Analysis of collocations allows one to examine words which are strongly associated with each other. Salama found out that "collocational relations can ideologically contribute to the recontexualization of one discourse topic across clashing texts and statistically significant collocations can precisely reveal opposing discursive voices or textual tones towards the same or similar topics" [11, p. 315].

Prentice et al. [8] applied three corpus-linguistic techniques to extremist statements promoting terrorist violence to get insights into their ideology. Using the software tool WMatrix, they submitted these data to frequency count, key word and key concept, and concordance analyses. Results showed that extremists centre their rhetoric on themes of morality, social proof, inspiration and appeals to religion, and refer to the world via contrasting concepts, suggesting a polarized way of thinking compared to a general population usage.

Another line of research in this direction implies the study of extremist and terrorist texts with the use of Linguistic Inquiry and Word Count (LIWC), content analysis software[5] which calculates the percentage of words in the entire text that match the words in the predefined grammatical (function words, other parts of speech) and semantic categories (affect words, social words, relativity, personal concerns, etc.). For example, Pennebaker and Chung [7] analyzed Al-Qaeda transcripts from Bin Laden and Al-Zawahiri to indicate the authors' psychological state and how it developed over time. Vergani and Bliuc [15] used LIWC to analyze the dynamics of language of the IS internet magazine Dabiq. They discovered increasing references to females and internet jargon words which, according to the authors, is related to the IS desire to recruit females and teens into terrorist activity.

The above mentioned studies as well as many others demonstrate the usefulness of automated approaches applied to the analysis of extremist texts, although, as Prentice et al. argue, a combination of manual and automated approaches "can give one a more rounded understanding of terrorist behavior within a particular online space" [9, p. 166].

---

[2] http://www.lexically.net/wordsmith/.

[3] http://ucrel.lancs.ac.uk/wmatrix/.

[4] http://www.laurenceanthony.net/software.html.

[5] https://liwc.wpengine.com/.

It should be noted that most of the above studies were performed using publicly available sources designed by individual authors (books, extremist media, etc.), however it is also important to analyze forums where people immediately involved in extremist ideology interact with one another.

Access to this kind of forums is limited. In order to obtain access to extremist texts and thus develop methods for identifying extremist materials on the Web, an Artificial Intelligence (AI) Lab run by Chen (University of Arizona, USA) has been working for several years in collaboration with a number of anti-terrorist organizations collecting content of extremist and terrorist forums, blogs, etc. as part of a large-scale Dark Web Project [2]. According to the authors, their Dark Web collection is the largest open-source extremist and terrorist collection in the academic world. Dark Web forums is a part of Dark Web collection.[6] The twenty-eight forums were collected up through 2012. Each collection contains up to millions of postings written by thousands of forum members. Postings are organized into threads which generally indicate the topic under discussion. Each posting includes detailed metadata such as date, member name, etc. Each forum is provided as a downloadable compressed text file which may then be opened in any CSV-compatible text processing program. Forums are organized by primary language: English, Arabic, French, German, and Russian.

Dark Web Project paved the way for a multidisciplinary field – terrorism informatics that studies terrorism using intellectual methods of data analysis. Authorship analysis, sentiment analysis and thematic modeling of texts of extremist forums have been performed (see [2] for review). However, to the best of our knowledge, there have been no studies investigating Russian-language part of this collection. We believe that it is necessary to investigate Islamic extremist texts in different languages in order to get a better insight into extremism and thus to develop more effective ways of identifying extremist content.

3 Materials and Methods

The material of the study are posts extracted from the KavkazChat forum (included on the RF Federal list of extremist materials).[7] This is a Russian-language forum with focus on jihad in the North Caucasus. KavkazChat contains 699,981 posts written by 7,125 members in the period 3/21/2003–5/21/2012. These posts are organized into 16,854 "threads" (topics).

For the ongoing study a thread called "Bombings in Moscow" was chosen where the 2010 Moscow Metro bombings were discussed (http://www.kavkazchat.com/showthread.php?t=34800). The 2010 Moscow Metro bombings were suicide bombings carried out by two women during the morning rush hour of March 29, 2010, at two stations of the Moscow Metro (Lubyanka and Park Kultury), with a roughly 40-min interval between them. At least 40 people were killed and over 100 injured. Russian

---

[6] http://www.azsecure-data.org/dark-web-forums.html.

[7] KavkazChat Forum Dataset. University of Arizona Artificial Intelligence Lab. Retrieved on February 20, 2018, from within https://www.azsecure-data.org/dark-web-forums.html.

officials called the incident 'the deadliest and most sophisticated terrorist attack in the Russian capital in six years'.[8] Two women from Dagestan, the so-called 'black widows' of slain terrorists, were said to have carried out the attacks.[9] On March 31, Caucasus Emirate leader Doku Umarov claimed responsibility for ordering the attacks in a video released on the Internet. He also stated that such attacks in Russia would continue unless Russia grants independence to Muslim states in the North Caucasus region.[10]

Messages on the forum in this topic were posted from March 29, 2010 (the day of the attack) to April 17, 2010. Discussions started on the day of the attack (42 messages on March 29) and continued on March 30 (11 messages) followed by a decline due to temporary closure caused by a rocketing number of users and technical issues. The discussions resumed from April 3 and continued onto April 8 followed by a decreased interest (only 4 messages from April 9 to April 17).

Forum participants are open about approving the attacks: *I really hope these were our people. Looking at those faces of kafirs, that should be true. Allah, let these special operations be of any help! And hopefully they (special operations) continue for the profit of Islam and Muslims! Allahu Akbar! I am happy that the female shahids attacked the Moscow subway, THIS IS FOR VOSHA AND DADA!!!!!! For all the Muslims who lost their lives!* (translations are ours).

There are also threats for new attacks and attempts to hold Russians responsible for what happened:

Inshallah must enter their homes and bring fear and terror so that they can understand what it is like.
There are no innocents. The country's population along with the government should be held accountable for their policies. If what the government does daily is to kill people in the Caucasus, they should expect unrests in Moscow.
Inshallah what happened in Moscow is just a beginning. You will be revenged for these atrocities in the Caucasus before you know it!
You will be blown up, killed and made use of as you don't deserve any better until you start respecting yourselves and put a stop to the continuing massacre in the Caucasus.

Note that there is a persisting opinion on the forum that terrorist acts are acceptable according to religious norms. Any message questioning pseudoreligious ideas favoring terrorism is removed: *Be warned! Any attempts to lead Muslims astray saying that these acts [terrorist acts] are not acceptable for Shariat will be cut short! ...We provide you with a platform for feedback but there will be no leading people astray with fatwas from failed scientists ... Of course, the truth is that only blood and violence will lead to a better, righteous and beautiful world.*

---

[8] Russia braces for terrorism's return as 38 die in subway bombings. Washington Post Foreign Service, March 30, 2010. The Washington Post. Retrieved March 29, 2018 from http://www.washingtonpost.com/wp-dyn/content/article/2010/03/29/AR2010032900007_pf.html?tid=a_mcntx.

[9] Deadliest terrorist attacks on Russia's transportation systems in recent years. Retrieved on March 29, 2018 from https://www.rt.com/news/383323-terrorist-attacks-russia-transport/.

[10] Chechen Rebel Leader Umarov Claims Moscow Metro Blasts. Retrieved on March 31, 2018, from https://www.rferl.org/a/Umarov_On_Video_Says_He_Ordered_Moscow_Attacks/1999257.html.

Russia is called "small stupid Russia", "blood empire", "damned state" with saying such as "a good Russian is a dead Russian".

In addition, these posts drew the public attention and raised a number of discussions on the Internet. Common reactions were: *my jaw dropped. I am shocked. Look at you, you are not even humans* (on the KavkazChat forum – *authors*) *you all think you know better; ah, dear God! Look at what they are writing, they are nuts, etc.* (readers' comments from the online newspaper "The Village").

All the posts in this topic were split into one txt file which made up the extremist corpus (EC).

Two resources were used for compilation of the corpus for comparison. The first one were the readers' comments on the material "There have been explosions on the Moscow metro" posted by online newspaper "The Village" http://www.the-village.ru/village/people/people/88720-v-moskovskom-metro-proizoshel-vzryv#comments. The comments were posted from March 29 to 31 with the total of 816. The corpus contains 127045 characters without spaces, or 22641 words. The number of participants in the discussion was 62. The second source for comparison corpus were the comments on material "Moscow metro bombings: A Chronicle of Tragedy" posted by Radio Svoboda https://www.svoboda.org/a/1996131.html, with the total of 497. The textual data contained 134829 characters without spaces, or 20237 words. The comments were posted from March 30 to April 6, 2010. The number of participants was 81.

We have chosen those two resources since they are rather different in terms of their audience. The online edition "The Village" is the first city newspaper in Russia whose readership includes "young professionals who do care and are willing to make changes in their lifestyle and the world around them"[11] [http://discourseanalysis.org/ada15/st102.shtml]. The website of the Radio Svoboda (www.svoboda.org) is a multimedia portal visited by 6.5–7 million people monthly in 2015—2016 and funded by the grants by the U.S. Congress. This media was listed as a foreign agent by the Russian Ministry of Justice in 2017. According to Media scope, it is daily visited by 42,200 to 109,000 Russians aged from 12 to 64 (depending on the month).[12]

The texts from the two sources were merged into one and made up a corpus for comparison (we called it a reference corpus, or RC). The rationale behind combining texts into one document for analysis was our interest in obtaining a general overview of Internet users on the 2010 Moscow Metro bombings opposite to Islamic extremist rhetoric and to test the use of corpus techniques in the assessment of extremist material.

Therefore the analyzed text corpora that are comparable in terms of the number of texts they contain and dealt with the same topic (discussions of the explosions on the subway produced immediately following the event) were compiled to make it convenient to employ them in comparative analysis using corpus tools.

General statistics on the corpora are presented in Table 1.

---

[11] New Environment of Social Discourse: City Internet-Newspaper (on the Example of the Village). Retrieved on March 29, 2018 from http://discourseanalysis.org/ada15/st102.shtml [in Russian].

[12] Federation Council included Radio Svoboda and CNN to the list of foreign agents, retrieved on March 29, 2018 from https://www.rbc.ru/politics/17/10/2017/59e5e4829a794799d3e26b94 [in Russian].

Table 1. Statistics of the corpora used for the study

Corpus	No. of authors	No. of comments	Dates of posting	Corpus size
Extremist corpus (EC)	67	466	29/03/2010–17/04/2010	274209 characters (without spaces), or 50447 words
Reference corpus (RC)	143	1313	30/03/2010–06/04/2010	261874 characters (without spaces), or 42878 words

It should be noted that the corpora are different in the average length of posts (108 words in EC vs. 32 in RC) as well as the number of people leaving comments (see Table 1). We argue that the differences in the length of texts are due to the fact that extremist forum participants are involved in active propaganda and make references to religious literature, etc. to justify the attack perpetrated by deadly terrorists. The differences in the number of users can be caused by the difficulties in logging in KavkazChat forum.

The corpora of texts underwent preliminary processing. All the metadata (date, name of the author, etc.) was removed. The quotes were removed if they were responses to the previous messages. The quotes from the media, etc. were not removed. Typos were corrected. The texts of the corpus were written in Russian. The materials of the extremist forum contain occasional Chechen words written in the Cyrillic alphabet and they were not removed. All the texts were saved in the.txt format suitable for corpus analysis with the use of Oxford WordSmith Tools [12]. This is an integrated suite of programs which identifies patterns in texts which are widely used for the work based on corpus-linguistic methodology. We used the version 4.0[13] as it is free of charge and its functional is sufficient for the current task.

4   Results and Discussion

4.1   Wordlist Comparison

We have designed two frequency lists individually for each text corpus. There was no lemmatization of text as well as exclusion of stop words. Then the lists were compared using a command *Comparing Wordlists*. The procedure compares all the words in both lists and will report on all those which appear significantly more often in one than the other, including those which appear more than a minimum number of times in one even if they do not appear at all in the other. We used log-likelihood as a test procedure for comparison. The minimum word frequency was set to 10, which means that the comparison will ignore words which do appear at least 10 times in at least one of the two lists. This value of the minimum word frequency was chosen arbitrary to exclude infrequent words.

---

[13] http://www.lexically.net/wordsmith/version4/.

Based on the findings by Pennebaker and Chung about the importance of analyzing function words in examining extremist discourse [7], we deliberately did not exclude such words from our analysis.

The analysis of the obtained data as well as general frequency lists (command *Consistency Analysis (Detailed)*) allowed us to make the following conclusions. In their rhetoric extremists make use of contrasts (*we – you, they; Muslims, Chechens – Russians, stupid Russians, kafirs*). It should be noted that the us-versus-them dichotomy is typical, for example, for Al-Qaeda narrative [6].

Extremists build up a war discourse (frequently used words are *war, enemy, revenge, weapon, against, killing, killed, death*) for land (*land, territory*) on a religious basis (*Allah, Islam, religion, Shariat*). This is similar to previous research which have shown that "a terrorist's mind-set is consistently characterized by a perception of moral superiority—which in religious orientated terrorism is naturally derived from religion—and by violent aggression towards out-groups" [16, p. 2].

For the reference corpus a tragedy discourse is typical (*panic, victim, the dead, casualties, terror, scared, tragedy*) as well as discussions of power (*authorities, the FSB* "The Federal Security Service of the Russian Federation", *Putin*) and causes of the attack (*benefit*).

The analysis of the corpora allowed another observation to be made. In EC there are almost (as we are only working with the words with the frequency of over 10) no lemmas such as *террор* "terror", *терроризм* "terrorism", *теракт/терракт* "a terrorist attack" (lemmatization was made manually for frequency lists), with the lemma *террорист* "a terrorist" far less frequent than in RC (20 occurrences in EC vs. 84 in RC).

For a more detailed analysis of the use of the word *террористы* "terrorists" we employed a tool of the module Wordlist *Compute Concordance*. A more detailed analysis of the concordances allowed us to conclude that this lexeme is seen negatively by extremists and they do not see themselves as such: *according to the Russian kafirs, mujāhids are terrorists; they start screaming that the terrorists blew up innocent people, look at them, they are barbarians, terrorists.*

In the reference corpus the word *terrorists* is widely used to refer to those who perpetrated the attack: *why are terrorists doing this; Muslim territories; terrorists are dreaming of waging war;* etc. A "terrorist" in this sense is equivalent to a criminal.

4.2   Word Cluster

The analysis performed using a tool of the modulus Wordlist *Word Clusters* (cluster size = 3, min frequency = 5) showed that among the most frequent trigrams of words of both corpora there is a trigram *на самом деле* "really" (14 in EC and 11 in RC). As the analysis shows, in the extremist corpus this trigram is related to the intention of the speaker to persuade those participants who are in doubt about the justification of the attack and can be considered as a part of Islamic extremist rhetoric. In the reference corpus, this trigram is related to the real state of affairs which is in contrast (in commentators' views) to what is described in media sources.

As the analysis shows, the extremist corpus is dominated by trigrams related to religion (*may Allah bless him, in Allah's path, live by Quran, and his messenger, no sin*) and the reference corpus mainly contains trigrams for location (*on the Moscow subway, in Park Kultury* – the subway station where the explosion took place, *in our country* vs. *in their land* in the EC) as well as the trigram *Кто это сделал* "Who did this?" and the trigrams associated with the President Putin (*Путин должен уйти* "Putin must resign" – a precedent expression, allusion to the public campaign of the same name where signatures were collected from the Russian citizens in support of the resignation of the RF President V. Putin that was launched online on March 10, 2010 by activists of a number of opposition public organizations as well as a few well-known public personas in Russia; *мочить в сортире* "drown terrorists in the toilet" is an expression that was publicly used by V.V. Putin, the Head of the Government of the Russian Federation at the time, on September 24, 1999 at a press conference in Astana while commenting on the bombing of Grozniy by the Russian aviation forces. This is what Putin literally said: *We will be chasing terrorists wherever they are. If they are at an airport, we will be there. If pardon, we catch them in a toilet, we will drown them in a toilet after all*).

As we can see, the word cluster analysis reflects patterns similar to those obtained in the analysis of wordlists.

4.3   Collocates

Another interesting tool of the modulus Wordlist is a tool *Relationship* that allows collocations to be identified using mutual information (MI) score. The procedure for calculating mutual information takes into account not just the most frequent words found near the word in question, but also whether each word is often found elsewhere, well away from the word in question (default span, or horizons, we consider for being neighbours is 5). The relationship between words which is measured by MI is bi-lateral. There are various different formulae for computing the strength of collocational relationships. The MI in WordSmith is computed using a formula derived from Gaussier, Lange and Meunier described in [5, p. 174]; here the probability is based on the total corpus size in tokens. An MI score of 3 or higher is proposed to be "taken as evidence that two items are collocates" [3, p. 71].

We used default settings with exception for minimum frequency which was set to 10 (default 5) to find collocates for the lemmas *вы* "you" (as well as in oblique cases *вас, вам*), *ваш* (as well as forms *ваша, ваши, вашего, вашу*) "your" as one of the most frequent words in EC. The collocates of the word *Вы* with the highest MI are *disturbs, themselves, blow up, kill, they will*. The word *Ваш* collocates with the words *territory, ideology, side, people*. Due to the lack of space, we cannot investigate the collocations of other frequent words of the corpus, however this example supports the revealed pattern of polarized thinking and contrasting, which indicates that "collocation can be a micro textual resource for a macro ideology-making process" [11, p. 337].

The revealed pattern of extremist ideology related to polarized thinking and opposition *we – you* (*they*), reference to religion is similar to that revealed by Payne [6], Prentice et al. [8], etc. It also should be noted that an elevated number of words describing *them* could be a sign of fixation-warning behaviour which Meloy et al. [4] define as "any behaviour indicating an increasingly pathological preoccupation with a person or a cause, for instance increasing perseveration on the object of fixation, increasingly strident opinion, or increasingly negative characterization of the object of fixation. The fixated person expresses a preoccupation with the group or person considered responsible for the subject's grievance by allocating large amounts of time to discussing, theorizing about, or studying the perceived enemy". The revealed pattern of constructing discourse of war for "higher cause" is close to what is called "warrior mentality" which is considered to be one of the types of warning behavior which indicates radicalization [4].

5 Conclusions

The analysis of one of the branches of the forum of the Islam extremists KavkazChat on the terror attack on the Moscow subway showed that the use of the corpus text analysis tools allows the patterns of the word use to be identified to get a more profound insight into extremist ideology. In particular, by using such tools as frequency lists, identifying word clusters, collocates and concordances by means of the software WordSmith tool 4.0, we found that in their rhetoric Caucasian extremists make use of the *we vs. you, them* contrast, build up a "war" discourse avoiding calling the event a terrorist attack. These patterns (us-versus-them dichotomy, justification of the attack as a part of the war for justice) are also typical of other Islamic extremist groups, as reported in literature.

The users commenting on the event on news sources build up a discourse of tragedy calling what happened a terrorist attack, i.e. a crime. They are widely discussing the role of authority, especially Russian president, in the 2010 Moscow Metro bombings. The users also try to find those groups who get benefit from this attack.

Our corpus-based study revealed that extremist discourse differs significantly from the "normal" discourse on the same topic with respect to most frequent words, word clusters and collocations which reflects different views on the same event by extremists and non-extremists.

6 Limitations and Future Work

This study has a number of limitations as one only segment of the extremist forum was analyzed and only a few functions of the software WordSmith were employed. Another limitation is related to the small number of media resources which were used for designing the reference corpus.

Here are some of the future directions in linguistic studies of texts of the extremist forum.

1. The analysis using more recent versions of the software WordSmith to allow the texts to be analyzed in their dynamics, which is particularly important for investigating the texts created shortly after a particular event.
2. The design of the classifiers to identify the most significant parameters that distinguish texts by extremists and those by a control group.

3. The analysis of texts of the extremist forum using the Linguistic Inquiry and Word Count (LIWC) software for unveiling hidden motives and interests of Islamic extremists.
4. The analysis of extremist texts of the forum by means of the thematic modeling methods, in particular the software TopicMiner developed by the Laboratory of Internet Studies of the National Research Institute Higher School of Economics in Saint Petersburg. TopicMiner is the first professional software for thematic modeling and visual analysis for the Russian language.
5. A comparative corpus study of the texts from the extremist corpus compiled for the current study and the other KavkazChat sections with discussion of terrorist attacks in Russia (2011 The Domodedovo International Airport bombing, etc.) aimed at revealing the dynamics of terrorist rhetorics.
6. The comparison of the rhetoric of Russian-language Islamic extremists with the discourse of Islamic extremists from other countries which is possible due to the Dark Web Project.

Acknowledgments. Funding of the project "Speech portrait of the extremist: corpus-statistical research (on the material of the extremist forum "KavkazChat")" from RF President's grants for young scientists (No. MK-5718.2018.6) for T.L. is gratefully acknowledged.

References

1. Chen, H., Wang, F.-Y., Zeng, D.: Intelligence and security informatics for homeland security: information, communication, and transportation. IEEE Trans. Intell. Transp. Syst. **5** (4), 329–341 (2004)
2. Chen, H.: Dark Web: Exploring and Data Mining the Dark Side of the Web. Springer, New York (2012). https://doi.org/10.1007/978-1-4614-1557-2
3. Hunston, S.: Corpora in Applied Linguistics. University Press Cambridge, Cambridge (2002)
4. Meloy, J.R., Hoffmann, J., Guldimann, A., James, D.: The role of warning behaviors in threat assessment: an exploration and suggested typology. Behav. Sci. Law **30**(3), 256–279 (2012)
5. Oakes, M.P.: Statistics for Corpus Linguistics. Edinburgh University Press, Edinburgh (1998)
6. Payne, K.: Winning the battle of ideas: propaganda, ideology, and terror. Stud. Confl. Terror. **32**, 109–128 (2009)
7. Pennebaker, J.W., Chung, C.K.: Computerized text analysis of Al-Qaeda transcripts. In: Krippendorff, K., Bock, M.A. (eds.) A Content Analysis Reader, pp. 453–465. Sage, Thousand Oaks (2008)
8. Prentice, Sh., Rayson, P., Taylor, P.J.: The language of Islamic extremism: towards an automated identification of beliefs, motivations and justifications. Int. J. Corpus Linguist. **17** (2), 259–286 (2012). https://doi.org/10.1075/ijcl.17.2.05pre
9. Prentice, Sh., Taylor, P.J.: Psychological and behavioral examinations of online terrorism. In: McAlaney, J., Frumkin, L. A., Benson, V. (eds.) Psychological and Behavioral Examinations in Cyber Security (Advances in Digital Crime, Forensics, and Cyber Terrorism Series), pp. 151–171. IGI Global (2018)

10. Qian, Y.: Discursive Constructions around Terrorism in the "People's Daily" (China) and "The Sun" (UK) before and after 9.11. Bern, Switzerland: Peter Lang UK (2010). https://www.peterlang.com/view/product/43720. Accessed 09 May 2018
11. Salama, A.: Ideological collocation and the recontextualization of Wahhabi-Saudi Islam post-9/11: a synergy of corpus linguistics and critical discourse analysis. Discourse Soc. **22**(3), 315–342 (2011). http://www.jstor.org/stable/42889747. 09 May 2018
12. Scott, M.: Oxford WordSmith Tools Version 4.0 (2007). http://www.lexically.net/downloads/version4/wordsmith.pdf
13. Smith, A.: Words make worlds: terrorism and language. FBI Law Enforcement Bulletin, 12–18 (2007)
14. Stepin, D.S.: Features of the implementation of terrorist agitation and propaganda using Internet resources (on the example of the "KavkazChat" forum). In: Problems of Theory and Practice of Combating Extremism and Terrorism. North-Caucasian Federal University, Stavropol (2015, in Russian)
15. Vergani, M., Bliuc, A.M.: The evolution of the ISIS' language: a quantitative analysis of the language of the first year of Dabiq magazine. Secur. Terror. Soc. **2**(2), 7–20 (2015)
16. Vergani, M., Bliuc A.M.: The language of new terrorism: differences in psychological dimensions of communication in Dabiq and inspire. J. Lang. Soc. Psychol. 1–18 (2018)

Image of International Migration in Russian Online Mass Media

Veronika Romanenko[✉] [iD]

Saint Petersburg State University, Saint Petersburg, Russia
nikar@yandex.ru

Abstract. Our objective is to assess the formation of public opinion on the topic of migration in Russian electronic media. This study is suggested as a reflection motivated, on one hand, by the common practice of the intensive Internet use in everyday life, and, on the other hand, by active migration processes in Russia. For this purpose, within the framework of the project "Social Risks of International Youth Migration in Contemporary Russia", we carried out a content analysis of articles published in popular Internet resources which contained the lexical category "migrant" and its derivatives. By comparing frequencies of mentioning of certain keywords in selected publications, we have tried to characterize the presentation in Internet media of topics related to the image of migrants and migration as a phenomenon, to the main measures of social policy, and to the activities of migrants and their problems. In addition to the analysis of the broadcasted content on migration, we also studied the opinion of Russians on that content and its presentation in media. As a result, a number of trends have been revealed in presentation of international migration processes by electronic mass media and the formation of public opinion on this issue.

Keywords: Migration · Internet · Online media · Image of a labor migrant International migrants · Content analysis

1 Introduction

Today, mass media are not only a mirror reflecting events in the world or in a country, but also are an instrument that influences public attitude towards various social phenomena. Information on migrants is widely presented in Russian mass media that helps understand possible mechanisms constructing public opinion about migration processes and characterize tolerance of the host community to immigrants. In the situation of turbulent societal development and economic crises in Russia, a negative media discourse concerning foreign labor migrants can contribute to population deconsolidation and to the increase of tension in society. Mechanisms of generalizing and transferring the properties of individuals to all members of the ethnic community, as well as broadcasting to mass media audience of unreasonable cause-and-effect relationships, were described in detail in the works of Van Dijk [1]. These techniques are actively used by the media to create the image of a migrant, due to which, on the one hand, existing stereotypes about newcomers acquire a new rationale [2–4], and, on the other hand, the attitude towards migrants in the media is dictated rather by the topic of the

© Springer Nature Switzerland AG 2018
S. S. Bodrunova (Ed.): INSCI 2018, LNCS 11193, pp. 66–77, 2018.
https://doi.org/10.1007/978-3-030-01437-7_6

day than by real qualities of the newcomers [5]. Obviously, popular Internet resources present readers with the information they are expected of, otherwise they will lose their subscribers. Thus, the "spiral of silence" is unwound [6], when some aspects of the phenomenon (for example, migration) are simply not covered, because the reader will react much more intensively, for example, to shocking news than to ordinary facts. In the Russian socio-political discourse, migration is most often recognized as an inevitable and justified phenomenon relevant to the era of globalization. However, some negative cases or qualities of migrants, interpreted by the media as sensational news, can stir up the population's dislike for the whole ethnic groups.

2 Importance and Research Premises

Immigrants are numerous in Russia. According to the Interior Ministry on short-term migration, in 2016, 4.3 million foreigners registered to work for the first time[1], while in 2017 the number of primary registrations reached 4.9 million[2]. According to the Federal State Statistics Service, in 2016, the principal departure countries rated relatively to the number of migrants in descending order were: Ukraine, Kazakhstan, Uzbekistan, Tajikistan, Armenia, Moldova, the Republic of Kyrgyzstan, Azerbaijan, Belarus, China, North Korea, and Turkmenistan[3]. Concerning the long-term migration, until recently, the number of arriving migrants generally grew up[4] (see Fig. 1). However the existing population growth due to international migration is still less than 300–400 thousand people, the estimated value needed to fully compensate the natural loss of the able-bodied population [7]. Achieving this threshold and reducing the social risks of international immigration [8] is one of the strategic goals of the state demographic policy[5].

In the mid to late twentieth century, researchers tried to evaluate the influence of public discussions about migrants and other groups different from the majority of the population on the formation of negative prejudices and increased conflict in the society (Allport, LeVine and Campbell, Harris, Miller and Slater) [9–12]. At the same time, the threats described in the media do not always have an objective basis in the form of real

---

[1] Ministry of Internal Affairs of the Russian Federation: Statistical information on the migration situation in the Russian Federation in 2016 with distribution over regions, https://мвд.рф/Deljatelnost/statistics/migracionnaya/item/9359228/, last accessed 2018/05/20.

[2] Ministry of Internal Affairs of the Russian Federation: Separate indicators of the migration situation in the Russian Federation in January–December 2017 with distributions over regions, https://мвд.рф/Deljatelnost/statistics/migracionnaya/item/12162171/, last accessed 2018/05/20.

[3] Federal State Statistics Service: Population of Russia and its migration in 2016, http://www.gks.ru/bgd/regl/b17_107/Main.htm, last accessed 2018/05/20.

[4] Federal State Statistics Service: Number and migration of the population of the Russian Federation in 2012–2013 http://www.gks.ru/bgd/regl/b14_107/Main.htm, in 2014: http://www.gks.ru/bgd/regl/b15_107/Main.htm, in 2015: http://www.gks.ru/bgd/regl/b15_107/Main.htm, in 2016: http://www.gks.ru/bgd/regl/b17_107/Main.htm, last accessed 2018/05/20.

[5] The concept of the demographic policy of the Russian Federation for the period until 2025 (approved by Presidential Decree No. 1311 of 9 October 2007). Demoscope Weekly, http://www.demoscope.ru/weekly/knigi/koncepciya/koncepciya25.html, last accessed 2018/05/20.

qualities of the ethnic group. Most often, the image of a social group is influenced by various representation manners existing in media rather than by particular real experience of communication with members of those groups (illustrated by Slater [13]).

The provocation of rather emotional than rational reaction to news about migrants is noted by some Russian researchers (for example, Iakimova, Vesnina) [14, 15]. According to estimates of studies on migration issues in print media by Mukomel, the discourse dominant in the Russian media often creates "the protrusion of the ethnicity of migrants, exaggerated importance" [16], as well as metaphorical models with negative connotations (for example, the image of a migrant as an external enemy discussed by Vesnina). In general, in the materials appearing in modern print media, accentuation on the negative consequences of migration processes is often traced [17].

Electronic resources on the issue of migration have been subjected to sociological analysis to a much lesser extent than printed ones. However, the results of such studies are partially similar to the conclusions obtained by the analysis of print media. For example, the analysis of electronic media and comments by Fedorov showed that the frequency of negative emotions experienced by the encoder is higher than of positive ones [5]. Similarly, the amount of negative information exceeds the one of positive information in the analyzed messages of electronic media. Other researchers (Bodrunova, Litvinenko, Gavra, Yakunin) studying the reflection of interethnic conflicts in Twitter emphasize the significant impact of electronic media on the communicative environment of this social network, as well as the substantial politicization of messages [18]. According to a study of posts from the Russian-language LiveJournal, it was suggested that political threats are more disturbing than predominantly social threats coming from migration. Immigrant groups differ by the level of hostility towards them (Bessudnov, Bodrunova and all) [19, 20]. For example, Central Asians are perceived as passive sources of social problems, North Caucasians are considered as active and aggressive.

Representation of the image of a migrant and migration in online Russian media is of considerable interest, since most people in Russia, firstly, use the Internet in their daily lives, and, secondly, they draw new information from there. According to the Public Opinion Foundation[6] and the Russian Center for the Study of Public Opinion[7], about 80% of Russians have access to the Internet, 60% of them use it on a daily basis. According to Yandex.Metrics[8], every fourth Internet user in Russia visits local websites at least once a month. Therefore, in order to study the risks of international youth migration in Russia, it is important to analyze how information about foreign migrants is interpreted by the electronic mass media, as well as to assess the potential of the media in the prevention of these risks.

---

[6] Internet in Russia: the dynamics of penetration. Summer 2017. Public opinion fund, http://fom.ru/SMI-i-internet/13783, last accessed 2018/05/20.

[7] Life on the Internet and without it. Russian Public Opinion Research Center, https://infographics.wciom.ru/theme-archive/society/mass-media/internet/article/zhizn-v-internete-i-bez-nego.html, last accessed 2018/05/20 (in Russian).

[8] Yandex.ru. News on the Internet: Media and Readers. https://yandex.ru/company/researches/2014/ya_news, last accessed 2018/05/20.

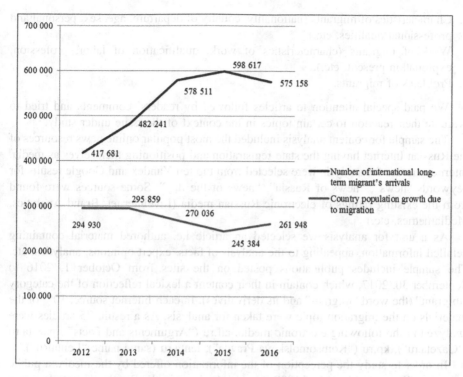

Fig. 1. International migration to Russian Federation in 2012–2017 (Federal State Statistics Service data).

3 Research Methodology

The principal research method used here is the interpretive content analysis of the media, combining qualitative and quantitative methods of analytics. It assumes, on the one hand, the interpretation of the encoder's interpretations [21] (including an assessment of the emotional coloring of the article, general impression from reading, contextual aspects in the response option choice, etc.) On the other hand, the method includes some elements of statistical data analysis. In other words, the method allows not only to fix explicit meanings according to unambiguous rules of text recognition, but also to take into account the latent content of the text (images of the problem under consideration, attitude to the problem), starting from the context perceived by the encoder [22].

The statistical map developed for analysis includes several blocks:

1. Characteristics of the article (type of text, its volume, the availability of visual materials, etc.),
2. Attitudes towards migration (associations with migration, the image of a migrant, the impact of migration on society, etc.),
3. Social control (measures of social policy, illegal actions of migrants and punishment for them, etc.),

4. Characteristics of migrants (nationality, country of departure, age, sex, personal and professional qualities, etc.)
5. Work of migrants (characteristics of work, qualification of labor, profession, exploitation present, etc.),
6. Problems of migrants.

We paid special attention to articles followed by readers' comments and tried to evaluate their reaction to certain topics in the context of the issue under study.

The sample for content analysis included the most popular online news resources of the Russian Internet having the state registration and positioning themselves as media. Internet sources for analysis were selected from top ten Yandex and Google results for keywords "news", "news of Russia", "news of the day". Some sources were found from the existing ratings of electronic Russian media (Liveinternet, Brand Analytics, Mediametrics, etc.)

As a unit for analysis we selected an article i.e. authored material containing detailed information, appealing to the analysis of facts, expert opinions, analytics, etc. The sample includes publications posted on the sites from October 1, 2016 to September 30, 2017, which contain in their content a lexical reflection of the category "migrant" (the word "migrant" and its derivatives). In each Internet source, 10% of the materials on the migration topic were taken for analysis. As a result, 75 articles were analyzed in the following electronic media: aif.ru ("Arguments and Facts"), gazeta.ru ("Gazeta.ru"), kp.ru ("Komsomolskaya Pravda"), lenta.ru (same name "LentaRu").

In order to study the perception of the information offered by the media, a public opinion poll was conducted of 1029 respondents born in the Russia. The study was a part of a large-scale national poll on migration issues in the framework of the project "Social risks of international youth migration in modern Russia". Data on 1029 participants were collected by the Center for Sociological and Internet Research of Saint-Petersburg State University in 2017. The data presented in this article are intended to provide additional understanding of the results of content analysis in terms of the information perception by the Russian audience.

4 Results

4.1 Subject and Material Presentation in Articles on Migrants

Despite that the aforementioned online media position their content as articles, an analytical component usually assumed to important for this kind of texts was present in a minority of cases. A major part (45%) of the considered articles on the topic of international migration was mostly descriptive and focused on specific situations, human history, crime, etc.). 35% of the material was of informational character (reporting on changes in legislation, migration policy in the country and etc.) Only 20% of publications contained evaluations or attempts to analyze facts. 96% of the analyzed articles were accompanied by photographs, 56% of which caused an unpleasant, repulsive impression, 28% - neutral feelings, 12% - pity, sympathy, 4% - positive emotions. Quite often (41% of cases), in addition to the author's position, expert opinions were cited.

Practically all available content concerns European countries (51%) and Russia (48%); one article analyzed was about Africa. Amongst European countries, the interest was focused at Germany, France, and the UK. The principal subjects in most cases were an offense or a crime committed by migrants (22%), migration policies in Russia or in Europe (22%), terrorist attacks (17%), offensive actions against migrants and violation of their rights (9%), increasing migration flows, and cultural expansion (9%). Other topics (about 3–4% for each) concerned were the organization of illegal migration, irregular migrants, war and military conflicts, and law enforcement actions. Even less number of articles were devoted to international cooperation, the epidemiological situation, nationalism and ethnic conflicts (1% each).

Some news resources (aif.ru, kp.ru) are accompanied by readers' comments. Out of 35 articles commented on, the largest number of comments was received on articles on crime (1346), as well as on war and military conflicts (904), on increased influx of visitors and expansion (846), illegal migration (303), terrorist attacks (277) and social policies in Russia or in another country (247). Each comments thread consisted of statements of a different nature; out of 35 commented articles, 80% of cases contained negative evaluations of migrants' actions of migrants against 30% expressing positive assessment or support. Most frequently (90% of cases), the responses contained blames towards authorities and officials or criticism on their actions. The latter also concerned migration policies in Europe, such as installation of refugee camps, etc.

4.2   Attitude to Migration Expressed in Internet Media

Each of the articles to some extent translates a certain attitude to migration, which could be inferred from the context and tone set by the author. Most often in the article, migration was positioned relatively neutrally, as a social phenomenon (43%). Nevertheless, in 33% of cases it could be defined as a social problem, and in 11% of cases as a social evil. 12% of sources broadcast the attitude to this phenomenon as a necessity, and 1% considers it as a public good.

After reading the articles, the following associations appear (in descending order of frequency): illegal (48%), crimes and violence (40%), terrorism (39%), Islam and Muslims (33%), war and refugees (25%), violation of migration legislation (23%). Other associations are recorded much less frequently: victimization, exploitation (15%), ethnic conflicts (12%), poverty (11%), unsanitary conditions (9%), earnings (7%), hard work (8%), and diseases (7%).

The impact of migration on the host community in the vast majority (64%) of articles was considered as negative, whereas it was positive in 7% of cases, and in 29% migration consequences were estimated in a neutral way or not considered. The image of the migrant in the article most often also has a negative character (55% vs. 33% neutral and 12% positive). At the same time, it is worth noting that amongst articles on migration in Europe negative connotations appear in 85% of cases, while the analogous fraction of papers about Russia equals 60% only. This inequality also applies to the image of migrant which is negative in 48% of articles on Russia and in 79% of articles about European countries. In the analyzed sources, the effect of migration on the host society frequently consists in terrorist acts (36%) and in increasing crime rate (29%). At the same time the idea that migration brings economic benefits to the society is expressed in 12% of sources.

4.3   Crime and Social Control of Migration in Internet Media

In 70% of articles (54 out of 75) criminal actions of migrants are described including (in descending order) terrorism (46%), rape (24%), murder (22%), grievous bodily harm (21%), fights and brawls (15%), forgery and forged documents (13%). More rarely (frequency of mentioning less than 10%) the considered criminal actions were robbery, racket, drug trade, exploitation and trafficking in persons, road accidents, minor offenses. 42 articles out of 75 describe not only crimes, but also punishment such as imprisonment (52%) or deportation (31%). The inaction of law enforcement bodies and authorities (17%) and the entry denial into the country for migrants (17%) were also mentioned.

The issue of limiting the afflux of migrants, in one way or another, was concerned in more than half of the analyzed articles. In 15% of cases it was suggested that the number of migrants to Russia or another country it should not be limited, in 41% of articles that it should be limited, while in the remaining 44% the issue was not considered. Among the possible reasons for limiting migration flows, the most frequently mentioned ones were: ensuring the safety of the population, reducing the crime rate (56%), reducing the threat of terrorist attacks (53%), restricting the flow of illegal immigrants (47%), stopping the spread of foreign culture and religion (34%), the adaptation of foreign visitors (25%), the reduction of the state budget expenditures, the burden on social and medical institutions (13%), and the lack of jobs for the indigenous population (13%).

As a whole, migration policy measures were identified in 51 articles out of 75. The most frequently mentioned were several possible measures, the main ones being: actions against illegal migrants (39%), complicating procedures for obtaining residence permits (29%), anti-terrorism measures and strengthening police supervision (22%). The simplification of legislation for visitors (12%) and adaptation programs, courses, social assistance (14%) as a measure of migration policy was covered less frequently. The least attention was paid to attracting qualified specialists, resettlement programs, quotas for jobs, etc.

Out of 75 articles analyzed, 23 articles deal with the reasons why migration is necessary for the country. Most often such reasons are humanism (help to refugees and to the poor, etc.) and the need for cheap labor. The idea that migrants can have good professional skills and therefore migration is necessary was not expressed in any article. It should be noted that some sources positively describe personal and professional qualities of individual visitors, mostly in the frameworks of their life stories). But there were few such articles.

4.4   Characteristics of Migrants and Their Work

75% of articles talk about migrants while female migrants appear more seldom, in 11% of cases. Both male and female migrants are mentioned in 14% of sources. The age of described persons is usually in the range from 19 to 30 years (68% of cases).

Nationality of migrants (often several nationalities) was indicated in 58 articles out of 75, i.e. in materials from electronic media a strong ethnic accentuation is present. Basically, it was (in descending order of frequencies) about Tajiks, Kirghiz, Uzbeks, Ukrainians, Turks, Afghans, Arabs, Syrians, foreigner from various countries of Africa. In articles covering life abroad, religious identification of immigrants and refugees - Muslims - was very often added.

As concerns parts of the world where the migrants come from which is referred to in 62 articles, it is Central Asia (45%), Middle East (34%), North and West Africa (27%), Eastern Europe (26%), Central, Eastern and Southern Africa (11%), South-East Asia (3%). Obviously, in articles where the action takes place in Russia, migrants from Central Asia and Ukraine are most often mentioned, while in Europe they are from countries of the Middle East and North Africa.

The articles very rarely spoke of the marital status of migrants, the presence of children, or education. Similarly, any characteristics of their appearance and character were sparsely given. When analyzing some selected lexical signs of professional and personal qualities of people coming from abroad, we found both positive and negative connotations describing appearance and behavior of migrants, such as "diligent", "inept", "hard-working", "lazy", "friendly", "aggressive"). In general, most articles in their context create a negative perception of the image of the migrant (for example, describing the fact of the terrorist act), but in the lexicon, adjectives associated with aggression or other negative factors are rarely used.

In 18 articles there was a talk about labor qualifications of migrants, and in 16 of them it was designated as low. The areas of activity of migrants were identified in 33 cases. Most often it was (in decreasing order of frequencies): illegal activities, vehicles (driver), construction and repair, housing and communal services, agriculture, trade, domestic work, entertainment.

The following characteristics of the work of migrants were used most often (in 18 articles, in descending order of the number of mentions): simple/unskilled, usual/ common, illegal, hard/exhausting, underpaid, exploiting/discriminating, significant/ relevant, dangerous/risky, and unnecessary/irrelevant.

In 36 articles out of 75, problems of migrants were identified. The first place in terms of the frequency of references among them is illegal status (53%), the second one is the lack of money (36%), followed by poor housing conditions and problems with housing rental (32%), involvement into a criminal activity (29%), problems with documents (19%), ignorance of the language of the receiving country (19%), bureaucracy (17%), ethnic conflicts (17%), and other problems (problems with the police, health problems, etc.)

4.5   Opinion of Russian Citizens on Migration Expressed in the Media

1029 respondents born in the territory of the Russian Federation answered the question "Are you interested in issues related to migration?" With a small number of ignorant and undecided relatively to migration issues (10%), the majority of respondents tended to deny their interest in this issue (54%), but more than one third (36%) expressed their interest (see Fig. 2).

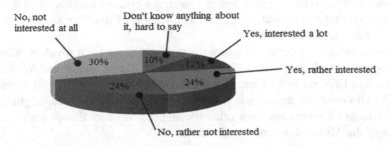

Fig. 2. Answers to question "Are you interested in issues related to migration?"

One of the indicators of interest in migration issues can be the fact that the respondent read/saw some information on this issue, and remembers this fact (i.e. the information was reflected and captured in his mind). Answering the question "When did you read, watched, listened to anything on the topic of migration last time?" 27% said that they do not remember or they did not read and did not look at anything on this topic. Nevertheless, 45% of respondents recalled that they faced the problem of migration in the media and the Internet today, yesterday or last week (see Fig. 3).

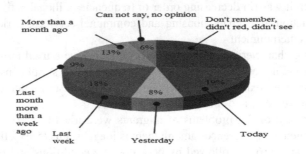

Fig. 3. Answers to the question "When did you read, watched, listened to anything on the topic of migration last time?"

Responding to the question "How do you think the information about the situation of migration and migrants in your region is available to you today in the media and the Internet?", the majority of people answered that they are not familiar with such information or could not answer this question (42%), 16% felt that the information on migration in the media is displayed truthfully, the equal amount (16%) think that the information is displayed incorrectly, 26% believe that both options are possible in different situations.

Since half of the respondents remembered that they were facing news about migration in the media during the last week, it is most probable that this news was presented in such a way that people paid noticed and remembered it. However, the general low interest in the topic of migration is unlikely to contribute to the development of critical thinking and the desire to analyze and assess information on migrants and migration received from the mass media. This is also indirectly confirmed by the inability of most respondents to assess the reliability of information on the topic of migration provided by media.

5 Conclusions

Most of the articles presented in electronic media are rather descriptive than not critical. Although expert opinions are present in many materials, real analytical information is presented in a few of. In this case, the publication of an expert opinion can be more likely referred to a journalistic method designed to enhance the impression of news, rather than provide the audience with exhaustive information for analysis. According to our public opinion poll, residents of Russia mostly do not show interest in the problems of migration, despite they confirm to see news on this topic on the Internet and other media quite regularly. This means that most of electronic media readers do not have inclination to deeply analyze the information received. Also, most of the respondents could not assess whether the issue of migration is truly covered in the media; the number of people believing they receive correct information equals the number of people who have the opposite opinion.

The main topics discussed in the electronic media in the context of migration, are crime committed by migrants and terrorism. Impressive or shocking news ensures the audience response; the greatest number of reader's comments is received by news about migrant's crimes, military conflicts, cultural expansion. Practically all materials on migration in the EU countries express the idea of cultural expansion and the growth of crime among expatriates. Thus, on the one hand, Russian electronic mass media broadcast the idea of the inadequacy of the migration policy of foreign countries, but on the other hand, they push the readers to project the situation on the Russian reality. As a result, many readers in the comments tend to condemn the authorities' excessive tolerance to migrants (humanitarian actions, refugee camps, granting citizenship on preferential terms, etc.). The image of an alien or even an enemy, created for most articles talking about refugees in Europe, can extend to readers' perception of migrants in Russia. The positive effects of migration are described to a small extent.

In summary, the following aspects are worth noting:

- The overwhelming majority of articles in Russian electronic media describes negative effects associated with migration and transmit negative image of migrants.
- While maintaining neutral vocabulary (pronounced negative connotations are absent), news items for covering the issues of migration are mostly negative.

- The media try to cover topics that cause an active reader's reaction and present them in a way that induces rather emotional than rational perception (for example, most visual materials in articles contain repulsive content).
- Profound information on migrants is practically absent; very rarely is it mentioned about their marital status, education, professional skills, etc. The basic information communicated is reduced to the designation of their sex (male, in most articles) and to the description of their actions, most often - misdemeanors, crimes.
- Articles often feature nationality, religion and the countries of migrants' departure, i.e. in the materials cultural and ethnic accents are quite actively made.
- Most readers are not prone to a critical evaluation of the reading, but judging by the number of comments, they tend to actively "digest" negative news, especially those related to criminal acts committed by migrants.

Certainly, news about the negative effects of migration should not be hushed up, but in terms of preventing ethnic conflicts, special attention should be paid to the study and description of the positive effects of migration. This may concern not only Russian, but also foreign experience, as well as international cooperation, the work of specialists including ones of high qualification, clarification of the need to attract temporary workforce of various competencies to the country economy, etc. A hot agenda, shocking news, etc. remain the important survival technique for commercial media, since it is exactly such news that inspires interest and discussion among the readers. Nevertheless, the publication of materials aimed at building intercultural dialogue and increasing tolerance for other ethnic groups among the indigenous population could reduce social tension and affect positively the population consolidation.

Acknowledgements. This publication was supported by Russian Science Foundation, Project No 16-18-10092 "Social risks of the international youth migration in contemporary Russia".

References

1. Van Dijk, T.: On trends in discursive suppression, European nationalism and a humanitarian nuclear bomb. In: Sovremennyj diskurs-analiz [The Today's Discourse Analysis], vol. 9, pp. 4–10 (2013). http://discourseanalysis.org/ada9.pdf. Accessed 20 May 2018 (in Russian)
2. Titov, V.N.: On the construction of an image of the ethnic immigrant (press publications analysis). In: Sotsiologicheskie issledovaniia [Sociological Studies], vol. 11 (2003). http://www.isras.ru/files/File/Socis/2003-11/titov.pdf. Accessed 20 May 2018. (in Russian)
3. Transnational migrants and the host society: the mechanisms and practices of mutual adaptation: a monograph. In: Dyatlov, V.I. (ed.). Izd-vo Ural. un-ta, Ekaterinburg (2009). (in Russian)
4. Nam, I.V., Karageorgij, E.M., Ermolova, A.I., Nikitina, E.V.: Designing the image of a labor migrant in regional media (example of Tomsk). In: Sibirskie istoricheskie issledovanija [Siberian Historical Research], vol. 1, pp. 166–192 (2017). (in Russian). https://doi.org/10.17223/2312461x/15/11
5. Fedorov, P.M.: The role of the Internet media in shaping the social attitudes of Russians towards migrants (based on the content analysis of regional news Internet sites). Monit. Public Opin. **6**(124), 119–134 (2014). https://doi.org/10.14515/monitoring.2014.6.09. (in Russian)

6. Noelle-Neumann, E.: Public Opinion: Opening a Spiral of Silence, Moscow (1996)
7. Deminceva, E.B., Mkrtchjan, N.V., Florinskaja, Ju, F.: Migration policy: diagnostics, challenges, proposals. https://www.hse.ru/mirror/pubs/share/218427665. Accessed 20 May 2018. (in Russian)
8. Borodkina, O., Sokolov, N., Tavrovskii, A.: Social risks of international immigration into Russia. Econ. Soc. Changes Facts Trends Forecast **10**(3), 114–133 (2017). https://doi.org/10.15838/esc.2017.3.51.6. (in Russian)
9. Allport, G.W.: The Nature of Prejudice. Perseus Books, Cambridge (1954)
10. LeVine, R.A., Campbell, D.T.: Ethnocentrism: Theories of Conflict, Ethnic Attitudes, and Group Behavior. Wiley, London (1972)
11. Harris, R.: Psychology of Mass Communications. Olma Press, Moscow (2002). (in Russian)
12. Miller, D., Slater, D.: The Internet : An Ethnographic Approach. Berg Publishers, Oxford (2000)
13. Slater, M.D.: Processing social information in messages: social group familiarity, fiction versus non-fiction, and subsequent beliefs. Commun. Res. **17**, 327–343 (1990)
14. Iakimova, O.A.: Media discourse on foreign migration to Russia in the context of interethnic interaction design. J. Sociol. Soc. Anthropol. **18**(80), 123–136 (2015). (in Russian)
15. Vesnina, L.E.: Metaphorical modeling of migration in the Russian print media. In: Politicheskaja lingvistika [Political Linguistics], vol. 1, no. 131, pp. 84–89 (2010). (in Russian)
16. Mukomel, V.I.: Russian discourses on migration: "zero" years. In: Demoscope Weekly, pp. 479–480 (2011). http://demoscope.ru/weekly/2011/0479/demoscope0479.pdf. Accessed 20 May 2018. (in Russian)
17. Varganova, O.F.: The image of the labor migrant in the national and regional mass media (based on the content analysis results)]. In: Sotsiologicheskaia nauka i sotsial'naia praktika [Sociological Science and Social Practice], vol. 3, no. 11, pp. 81–93 (2015). (in Russian)
18. Bodrunova, S.S., Litvinenko, A.A., Gavra, D.P., Yakunin, A.V.: Twitter-based discourse on migrants in Russia: the case of 2013 bashings in Biryulyovo. Int. Rev. Manag. Mark. **5**(1S), 97–104 (2015)
19. Bessudnov, A.: Ethnic hierarchy and public attitudes towards immigrants in Russia. Eur. Sociol. Rev. **32**(5), 567–580 (2016). https://doi.org/10.1093/esr/jcw002
20. Bodrunova S., Koltsova O., Koltcov S., Nikolenko S.: Who's bad? attitudes toward resettlers from the post-soviet south versus other nations in the Russian blogosphere. Int. J. Commun. **11**, 3242–3264 (2017). http://ijoc.org/index.php/ijoc/article/view/6408/2109. Accessed 20 May 2018
21. Semjonova, A.V., Korsunskaja, M.V.: Media content analysis: problems and experience of application. In: Mansurov, V.A. (ed.). Institute of Sociology RAS, Moscow (2010). (in Russian)
22. Laswell, H.: The technique of symbol analysis (content analysis). Experimental Division (1941)

The Internet and Consumption of Pornography

A Case of Generation Y in the Czech and Slovak Republic

Zdenek Smutny[(✉)] [iD] and Zdenek Sulc[(✉)]

Faculty of Informatics and Statistics, University of Economics, Prague,
W. Churchill Sq. 4, 130 67 Prague, Czech Republic
{zdenek.smutny, zdenek.sulc}@vse.cz

Abstract. Sexuality influences a number of the motives of people's behavior, e.g. at work, at school, or in free time, and it affects their values and everyday needs. The paper presents exploratory pre-research focused on the sociotechnical aspects connected with pornography consumption, carried out on a sample of Generation Y members from the Czech and the Slovak Republic. The aim of the paper is to describe the behavior and attitudes of Generation Y in connection with the use of ICTs for the purpose of accessing pornographic material and the consumption of pornography outside of privacy, e.g. at school or at work. The conclusion is interesting to social informatician as a basis for further empirical research or theoretical perspectives and company policy makers in connection with Generation Y entering work environment. The respondents access pornography almost exclusively on mobile devices via the Internet (streaming) and prefer free pornographic content. Only 5.9% of men and 3.6% of women stated that they also view porn at school or at work. Although some studies from the UK and US have highlighted the growing consumption of pornography at work, so in this study, the same trend was not identified in the Generation Y from the Czech and the Slovak Republic. A recommendation for organizations is presented in the context of a possible future change of the selected social group attitudes.

Keywords: Attitude · ICT · Internet · Policy · Porn · Social informatics
Sexuality · Workplace

1 Introduction

The positive reception of new information and communication technologies (ICT) also changes human habits and behavior – e.g. at work, at school or at home [1, 2]. An important change that affects mainly the ontological development of the members of the younger generation is the online availability of pornographic material, and the related change in sexual behavior and habits in contrast with older generations [3, 4]. Sexual instinct applies to every person and it affects their values and everyday needs. Human sexuality is part of a number of conscious and unconscious motives of behavior

© Springer Nature Switzerland AG 2018
S. S. Bodrunova (Ed.): INSCI 2018, LNCS 11193, pp. 78–91, 2018.
https://doi.org/10.1007/978-3-030-01437-7_7

both at work and in free time [5, 6]. Sexuality and its manifestations are considered a private matter that is most often carried out at home. But recent research [7–9] has pointed out that sexual practices are also carried out at work or in public places, which is connected to the online availability of pornographic material [10] via modern ICTs – tablet, mobile phone, etc.

Development of ICT offers new opportunities that are accelerated especially by the Internet and related technology solutions. Services and hypermedia content are easily available thanks to the Internet. This development allows the introduction of new ICT artefacts (e.g. mobile phone or Internet-based service), which subsequently alters the behavior of users. The behavior connected with the use of ICT is different for every generation, see e.g. changes in the understanding of privacy in connection with the use of social media [11] and cf. [12, 13].

This paper is focused on Generation Y members, that have more positive attitude towards using ICT than Baby Boomers or Generation X [14]. Therefore, it is interesting to focus on studying the use of the Internet and technical devices to access porno-graphic material and to identify the attitudes of Generation Y to the pornography consumption. The term Generation Y refers to young people who are newly eco-nomically active or are soon to become so. Among the characteristics of this generation is the fact that they were the first to use ICTs since childhood [15]. Currently this generation is in the center of research because their members are newly economically active, and they have different attitudes and needs than the earlier generations [11]. It is also one of the reasons why this generation was selected for the following explorative research. Generation Y is divided into three generation sub-units [16]: Generation Why, Millennials and iGeneration. This paper focuses on the sub-unit of Millennials, who were born between the latter half of 1980s and the first half of 1990s.

Research on Generation Y's attitudes towards pornography consumption is relevant to the area of porn studies. Porn studies are focused on the wide area of pornography-related topics and are understood as a "beginning of critical academic discussion about pornography, moving away from a 'porn debate' centred on disagreements about pornography's harmfulness" [17].

On the other hand, research focused on the use of ICT for access to pornographic content at the personal, organizational and societal level is also a relevant issue for social informatics. This paper discusses, in particular, the aspects related to the use of ICT and the associated behavior of the selected social group. Thus, the presented pre-research was conducted from the perspective of social informatics, which focuses on the study of social aspects of computerization, including the use of ICTs in various social contexts on a personal, organization, or social level [18]. The theoretical and methodological basis of this paper is the approach of social informatics to the research in applications of ICTs or e-activities in the selected social area and study of sociotechnical interaction between ICT and humans [19]. Research on the means how a social group approaches to using ICT for pornography consumption is important not only for understanding this type of sociotechnical interaction, but also for under-standing how it influenced their behavior.

Articles from the UK and US [7, 9], which are introduced in more detail in the Background section, point out that one in 10 workers in the UK and 2 in 10 workers in the US access pornography at work outside of their home space (privacy). This may lead to a reconsideration of the boundaries between public and private spaces, which can subsequently affect the organizational environment and also public space (e.g. culture, policy, relations). An important accelerator of pornographic material availability is the Internet usage [3]. Thus, it would be interesting to find out whether the consumption of pornography outside the home is equally trendy for the young generation in Central Europe (Czech and Slovak Republic) with different culture background.

There are two social informatics perspectives from which the results of this research are of particular interest: (1) From an organizational perspective, because sexual instinct and its gratification or related behavior also affects social groups at work. The discovered behavioral trends of a generation of people currently entering the job market and becoming economically active should be reflected particularly by midsized and large employers on corporate level in the implementation of information technologies and policies that are part of the information system of a company. (2) From a social perspective, because the online availability of pornographic materials via modern ICTs affects the sexual habits and development of individuals, who are part of various social groups. This gradually transforms the needs and values that affect the social and sociotechnical interaction in a given social group.

The social research focused mainly on the attitudes of a selected social group to pornography was carried out also in the Czech and Slovak Republic, but the research does not deeper address the use of ICT and ways to access pornography – it means sociotechnical aspects. An example might be article [20] dealing with adolescent attitudes towards consume pornography or experience with sexting in everyday communication [21]. Another perspective brings a comparison of the availability of pornography and number of sex crimes in the Czech Republic in a review article [22]. The sociotechnical aspects of pornography and its consumption outside the home have not yet been dealt with in this region.

The aim of the paper is to describe the behavior and attitudes of Generation Y (a sample from the Czech and the Slovak Republic) in connection with the use of ICTs for the purpose of accessing pornographic material. Emphasis is placed on pornography consumption outside the privacy in the home that is connected with mobility and the Internet availability e.g. at school or work. Based on these results could be discuss possible impact on working environment in organizations, that concerns mainly information system policy and corporate culture. The paper is based on exploratory pre-research, which by definition precedes main research and focuses only on selected areas of interest using both primary and secondary sources.

Based on the defined goal of the research, the general research problem was formulated: *The rapid change of the Internet availability could influence the Generation Y attitudes to pornography and its consumption.* There were also formulated the following research questions (RQ) that are directly linked to the research problem:

- RQ 1: What is the proportion of Generation Y members who regularly view pornography?
- RQ 2: What is the attitude of Generation Y members to using ICT for pornography materials access?

- RQ 3: Is the Generation Y members' use of pornography related to their dissatisfaction with their sex life?

There is a linear continuity in RQ 1–3 in connection with the conducted research. The first question focuses on the phenomenon of pornography use in Generation Y. The second question focuses on how Generation Y accesses pornographic materials, which includes the role of ICT. The last question follows the reasons for this activity in connection with sexual satisfaction. This set of questions provides a basic insight into the behavior of the selected group in connection with the use of ICT as a means of distribution that increases the availability of pornographic material. This contribution is a crossover between socially and technologically oriented research – it offers a sociotechnical perspective on the behavior and attitudes of the selected generation in connection with the use of ICT.

2 Background

Pornography is a multibillion-dollar industry [23] and the pornography market has acquired economic relevance since the 1970s [24]. Current empirical studies in this field focus mainly on the social and psychological perspectives connected to pornography itself. Psychologically and behaviorally oriented studies [25–27] deal mainly with the negative consequences of internet pornography use or the constant availability of online content (e.g. addiction, compulsive thoughts), or they are concerned with the sexual attitudes and behavior of a given generation in relation to pornography use [28–30].

Technological articles address a certain pornography related issue by designing an artefact (design or constructive research). In recent years, research in this field has been aimed at two subfields: the methods for protecting children from exposure to pornographic material [31–33], and systems for detecting child pornography [34–36]. Fighting child pornography in particular is an issue that resonates across social and technological fields of research [37]. The regulation of Internet pornography is subject to the legislation of individual countries, but punishment is very problematic due to the spreading of pornography via the Internet. The amorphous nature of Internet unfortunately enables the growth of child pornography that is illegal in most countries [38], or of other undesirable content catering to some people's specific sexual deviation.

Another source of information about this issue are interest groups and organizations that make available their own surveys and estimates, the results of which are closely linked to the online availability of pornography. Survey result in the USA [7] show that 20% of men access pornographic materials at work, and 10% of adults admit that they are addicted to pornography. Even among Christians nearly a half (47%) is of the opinion that pornography is a major problem. The numbers have also grown among women, with 13% of women accessing pornographic materials at work and 17% of all women struggling with porn addiction, see also the UK results [9]. World statistics and estimates concerning the use of ICT for satisfying pornographic needs point out that [39, 40]:

- 1 in 5 mobile searches are for pornography;
- 24% of smartphone users admit that they have pornographic material in their phone;
- porn sites attract more visitors each month than Amazon, Netflix, and Twitter combined;
- approximately 30% of Internet content can be described as pornographic.

These statistics show that pornography in connection with its accessibility via ICTs is a major problem on a cultural (e.g. religion), social (e.g. addiction) as well as corporate (e.g. work) level. An important issue are also sexual deviations, that can be satisfied in a positive sense by the use of pornography (reducing sexual delinquency), or in a negative sense pornography can increase the desire to actualize such practices. Pornographic videos unfortunately distort the reality of the sexual act and thus not only become the measure of what a sexual act should look like but also condition sexual maturation of young pornography users [27, 29]. As an example of undesirable patterns of behavior, it is often pointed out that pornographic videos contain violence against women, which affects men's attitudes to women in real life [39]. Modern approaches in diagnostics and treatment using e.g. virtual reality [41] enable the identification of persons with minor sexual preference that is perceived as dangerous to society.

On the other hand, the statistics provided by interest groups and organizations should be treated with caution; some long term researches do not show such radical changes in the habits and behavior related to the accessibility of pornographic material via the Internet. This can be illustrated by the study [42] based on General Social Survey data in the USA collected between 1973 and 2010 from a sample of men in the range of 401–852 respondents. There is only a slight increase in positive answers to the question about whether they viewed pornography in the past year: "In 1970s GSSs, 26% of participants said they viewed pornography. The percentage rose to 30% in the 1980s, 32% in the 1990s, and 34% in the 2000s." In the case of this research it can be stated that there is only a very slight increase. But the limitation of the results of this study is the fact that the respondents are mainly the members of older generations (Silent Generation, Baby Boomers and Generation X), for whom ICT is not a fixed component of everyday professional and private life as it is for example in the case of Generation Y.

The last source of information about accessing pornographic material via ICT are the web portals that provide this content. The portal PornHub publishes extensive annual statistics [43] concerning the behavior of the users of their service. To select some of the more interesting statistics from 2016: 26% of the users of this pornographic service are women, the average age of visitors is 35, and 60% of visitors are under 35. To access pornographic content, people use the mobile phone (61%), desktop (28%) and tablet (11%). There was a year-on-year (2015–2016) increase of almost 10% traffic via mobile phone at the expense of desktop access. There is therefore a distinct trend in accessing pornographic material via mobile devices, which is also related to pornography use being independent of a physical location.

3   Materials and Methods

The data for this explorative research were acquired by means of a questionnaire survey among a sample Czech and Slovak members of Generation Y (Table 1). The survey was conducted in a period from 5 December 2016 to 27 February 2017 via online form distributed by social media and websites of student and professional organizations. The questionnaire comprised 19 questions (6 demographic and 13 closed questions), that were divided into two thematic parts: sexual behavior and the use of social media; pornography use and mediation by ICT. This contribution only deals with the latter. There were 412 respondents participating in the questionnaire survey, of whom 54 were excluded – either because the answers were incomplete or because their age did not fall into the defined Generation Y. An implicit limitation of the contribution is given by the used sample of Generation Y members in the Czech and the Slovak Republic. The results of this explorative research are also interesting in relation to the further research planned in this field.

Table 1. Composition of respondents from Generation Y.

Demographics		Count	Column valid N %
Sex	*Man*	123	34.4%
	Woman	235	65.6%
Education	*High school*	15	4.2%
	Studying college	217	60.6%
	University	126	35.2%
Sexual orientation	*Heterosexual*	337	94.1%
	Homosexual	21	5.9%
Sexual behavior	*Heterosexual*	318	88.8%
	Homosexual	13	3.6%
	Bisexual	27	7.5%
Marital status	*Single*	136	38.0%
	In a relationship	222	62.0%

The data were processed by the IBM SPSS Statistics 24 software. There were performed methods of descriptive statistics, mainly frequency distribution tables and tables containing multiple-choice questions. When examining relationships between two variables, contingency table analyses were performed, where the chi–square test statistic G and p-value were calculated. 5% significance level is used in the whole paper. In the case of dependence, the value of the Pearson contingency coefficient C was also computed.

4 Results and Discussion

In order to answer the RQ 1, it was decided to examine a structure of the people who watch pornography in detail. In the Generation Y, 71.8% of people watch a pornographic content, see Table 2. Concerning gender, it is almost 96% of men and 59% of women. This strong discrepancy is also statistically significant ($G = 53.947, p < 0.001$, $C = 0.362$). It is likely caused by the fact that men's sexuality is more visual-oriented [44]. For comparison, the study [20] focused on Czech members of Generation Z in adolescent age (11–17 years), where 61.8% of men and 56.8% of women watch a pornographic content.

Table 2. The percentage of people who watch/do not watch pornography (n = 358).

Do you watch pornography?	Men	Women	Total
Yes	95.9%	59.1%	71.8%
No	4.1%	40.9%	28.2%

Based on data in Table 3, none of the young people was willing to pay regularly for a premium porn content. 7.6% of men tried out the paid content, but they preferred the free content in the end. There can be several reasons for it. It could be the price itself, unwillingness to pay on untrustworthy websites, or the insufficient difference in content quality.

Table 3. Willingness to pay for a porn content (n = 257).

Do you visit paid porn sites?	Men	Women	Total
Yes, I prefer the quality	0.0%	0.0%	0.0%
I tried, but I am not willing to pay for it	7.6%	0.0%	3.9%
If I see an exciting ad, I like to pay to see it	0.8%	0.0%	0.4%
No, there is a lot of free porn content	95.7%	100.0%	95.7%

Statistically significant ($G = 169.550, p < 0.001, C = 0.567$) differences between men and women also occur in the frequency of watching pornography, see Table 4. Whereas 25.4% of men watch pornography every day, by women, this ratio is only 1.4%. The majority of men watch porn 2–5 times a week, whereas the majority of women a few times a month. Almost 30% of women watch a porn content only occasionally. Thus, although both men and women in this subsample claim to consume a porn content, their attitudes towards watching it differ substantially.

Table 4. Frequency of watching pornography (n = 257).

How often do you watch pornography?	Men	Women	Total
Several times a day	11.0%	0.7%	5.4%
Once a day	14.4%	0.7%	7.0%
2–5 times a week	52.5%	14.4%	31.9%
A few times a month	18.6%	54.7%	38.1%
Very rarely	3.4%	29.5%	17.5%

To answer RQ2, attitudes of the Generation Y to accessing a porn content need to be examined. Particularly, what devices do the young people use to watch porn, where do they consume a porn content, and how do they access to pornography.

Table 5 presents three most used devices for watching pornography for men and women, where the respondents were allowed to use more than one answer. Watching porn on a notebook dominates for both sexes. Men use more often PC whereas women more often a smartphone. 57% of men also use more than one device for watching pornography compared to 33% of women.

Table 5. Three most used devices for watching pornography (n = 257).

Men		Women	
Notebook	70.3%	*Notebook*	73.4%
PC	44.9%	*Smartphone*	33.8%
Smartphone	41.5%	*PC*	20.9%

Another multiple-choice question dealt with the place, where the young people watch pornography, see Table 6, there are no substantial differences between men and women. Almost all of them watch porn in privacy. Small percentages of people also watch porn at work or school.

Table 6. Three most frequent places for watching pornography (n = 257).

Men		Women	
In privacy	99.2%	*In privacy*	100.0%
At work	3.4%	*At school*	2.2%
At school	2.5%	*At work*	1.4%

People from the Generation Y almost exclusively use the Internet to get access to pornography, see Table 7. The order of preferences does not differ for men and women. Most of the young people watch porn online on porn websites. Approximately 90% of them always look for a new porn content. Others, especially men, save their favorite porn content to bookmarks in an Internet browser. 14.4% of men and 5% of women download porn to a hard drive and watch it offline. There is 24% of men who combine at least two ways of accessing pornography, whereas the 94% of women use only one source.

Table 7. Three most frequent accesses to pornography (n = 257).

	Men	Women
Online, I am always looking for something new	89.8%	90.6%
Online, the links are saved in bookmarks	22.9%	9.4%
Downloading porn to a hard drive	14.4%	5.0%

Lastly, to answer RQ3, a relationship between watching pornography by young people and their satisfaction in their sexual life was examined. It was surveyed if the people who watch pornography change their sexual partners more often and if they need sex more often to be satisfied. Emphasis was also put on reasons why single people and people in a relationship to watch pornography.

Table 8 describes low dependence between the number of sexual partners and watching porn ($G = 9.761$, $p = 0.045$, $C = 0.163$). Young people who do not watch porn tend to have less sexual partners, but the difference is rather small. For example, in the US study [45] was greater pornography consumption significantly associated with more sexual partners.

Table 8. Relationship between the number of sexual partners and watching pornography (n = 358).

Number of sexual partners	Watch porn	Do not watch porn
Without sexual experience	5.1%	4.0%
1 to 2 partners	28.4%	42.6%
3 to 5 partners	28.8%	29.7%
6 to 10 partners	19.1%	14.9%
More than 10 partners	18.7%	8.9%

According to Table 9, people from the Generation Y who watch a pornographic content need more sex than those who do not watch it. 21% of them need sex every day, i.e., twice as many as the people who do not watch porn. In other categories, the differences are not so big, so the strength of the dependence is considered as low but statistically significant ($G = 11.476$, $p = 0.009$, $C = 0.176$).

Table 9. Relationship between an ideal sexual frequency and watching pornography (n = 358).

Frequency of sex to be satisfied	Watch porn	Do not watch porn
Every day	21.0%	9.9%
2–5 times a week	61.5%	59.4%
A few times a month	15.6%	25.7%
I do not need sex	1.9%	5.0%

The young people were also asked a direct question if they are satisfied with their sexual life. From Table 10, it is apparent that there were no substantial differences between people who watch or do not watch pornography. The lack of dependence was also confirmed by a statistical test ($G = 5.190$, $p = 0.158$).

Table 10. Relationship between sexual life satisfaction and watching pornography (n = 358).

Satisfaction with sexual life	Watch porn	Do not watch porn
Very satisfied	20.6%	24.8%
Rather satisfied	45.1%	52.5%
Rather dissatisfied	23.0%	12.9%
Dissatisfied	11.3%	9.9%

There are 77% of single people who watch porn, the ratio for the people in a relationship is only a slightly lower, 69%. Thus, there arises a question if a motivation to watch porn changes with a relationship. Table 11 presents five most often reasons for watching porn for both groups, where the respondents were allowed to use multiple answers. It is evident that there are no substantial differences between single people and the people in a relationship. The most frequent reasons are satisfaction and relaxation in both the groups.

Table 11. Five most important reasons for watching pornography (n = 257).

Single		In a relationship	
Satisfaction	66.7%	Satisfaction	59.9%
Relaxation	52.4%	Relaxation	47.4%
Entertainment	31.4%	Inspiration for sex life	38.8%
Inspiration for sex life	21.0%	Entertainment	34.2%
Satisfaction secret desires	17.1%	Satisfaction secret desires	12.5%

It can be summarized, that people from the presented sample of Generation Y almost exclusively access pornography on mobile devices via the Internet (streaming), and 90% of them always search for new material. Almost a half of the men and a third of the women who view porn do so on their mobile phones. The majority of men watch porn 2–5 times a week, whereas the majority of women a few times a month. They prefer mainly free pornographic content and only a small percentage of the respondents consume pornography outside the privacy in the home. The lack of dependence was found between satisfaction with sexual life and watch pornography. The low dependence was found between the number of sexual partners and watching pornography and between the frequency of sex and watching pornography. From a social perspective, the respondents do not believe that viewing pornography affects satisfaction with sex life, and the reasons for viewing pornography are almost the same for single people as for people in a relationship.

5 Conclusion

The paper presented the sociotechnical aspects associated with the attitudes and access to pornographic material by Generation Y from the Czech and Slovak Republic. This conclusion focuses on results from an organizational perspective and compares them with overviews from the UK and US. The mentioned overviews [7–9] and statistics of the web portal PornHub [43] providing pornographic content show an increasing trend in the use of mobile devices for access to such materials. The great popularity with Generation Y of accessing pornographic materials via mobile devices is confirmed by the presented explorative research.

Although it may be supposed that this development would lead to a change in behavior in connection with the place where pornography is consumed, a vast majority of Generation Y respondents prefers the privacy of their home. The potential problem from an organization perspective, i.e. accessing pornographic material at work, only concerns a small number of people from the sample contrary to mentioned studies from the US and UK where up to 20% employees watch pornography at work. It can be concluded that there is no threat connected with Czech and Slovak Generation Y and the possibility of radical change in pornography consumption, e.g. in the workplace.

If attitudes of the Generation Y to pornography consumption at work change in future, so at the organizational level can be recommended: establish rules on the level of a company's internal regulations (company code of conduct) that define inappropriate behavior, which should include viewing and sharing pornographic material in the workplace and related other possible inappropriate sexual behavior – see e.g. [10]. The possibilities of identifying certain behavior (using the statistics of employee access to these portals) and possible penalization depend on the legislation in a given country and on the corporate culture of a particular organization.

Limitation of the paper is associated with the fundamental constraint of the research method that was chosen. There was no way to verify that the respondents responded truthfully when they fill out the survey. Therefore the next research can focus directly on data traffic and the statistics of employee or students access to the pornography portals.

Acknowledgment. The authors thank to Oldrich Kopecky from *PricewaterhouseCoopers Czech Republic* for helping with data collection and discussion about corporate issues connected with the sexual behavior of employees.

References

1. Kalwar, S.K.: Human behavior on the internet. IEEE Potentials 27(5), 31–33 (2008)
2. Smahel, D., Vondrackova, P., Blinka, L., Godoy-Etcheverry, S.: Comparing addictive behavior on the internet in the Czech Republic, Chile and Sweden. In: Cardoso, G., Cheong, A., Cole, J. (eds.) World Wide Internet: Changing Societies, Economies and Cultures, pp. 544–579. University of Macau, Macau (2009)
3. Wolak, J., Mitchell, K., Finkelhor, D.: Unwanted and wanted exposure to online pornography in a national sample of youth internet users. Pediatrics 119(2), 247–257 (2007). https://doi.org/10.1542/peds.2006-1891
4. Willoughby, B.J., Young-Petersen, B., Leonhardt, N.D.: Exploring trajectories of pornography use through adolescence and emerging adulthood. J. Sex Res. 55(3), 297–309 (2018). https://doi.org/10.1080/00224499.2017.1368977
5. Flood, M.: The harms of pornography exposure among children and young people. Child Abuse Rev. 18(6), 384–400 (2009). https://doi.org/10.1002/car.1092
6. Carroll, J.S., et al.: Generation XXX: pornography acceptance and use among emerging adults. J. Adolesc. Res. 23(1), 6–30 (2008). https://doi.org/10.1177/0743558407306348
7. Logue, J.: Pornography Statistics: Who uses Porn? https://www.sagu.edu/thoughthub/pornography-statistics-who-uses-pornography. Accessed 01 June 2018
8. Conner, C.: Who Wastes The Most Time At Work? https://www.forbes.com/sites/cherylsnappconner/2013/09/07/who-wastes-the-most-time-at-work/. Accessed 01 June 2018
9. Curtis, J.: One in ten UK employees 'watch porn at work'. https://www.telegraph.co.uk/technology/internet-security/11614886/One-in-ten-UK-employees-watch-porn-at-work.html. Accessed 18 July 2018
10. Chelliah, J.: Policing pornography in the workplace: the case of Australia Post. Hum. Resour. Manag. Int. Dig. 22(2), 39–41 (2014). https://doi.org/10.1108/HRMID-03-2014-0031
11. Smutny, Z., Janoscik, V., Cermak, R.: Generation Y and internet privacy: implication for commercialization of social networking services. In: Benson, V., Saridakis, G., Tuninga, R. (eds.) Analyzing the Strategic Role of Social Networking in Firm Growth and Productivity, pp. 95–119. IGI Global, Hershey (2017). https://doi.org/10.4018/978-1-5225-0559-4.ch006
12. Sheahan, P.: Generation Y: Thriving and Surviving with Generation Y at Work. Hardie Grant Books, Prahran (2005)
13. Combi, C.: Generation Z: Their Voices, Their Lives. Windmill Books, London (2015)
14. Valentine, D.B., Powers, T.L.: Generation Y values and lifestyle segments. J. Consum. Mark. 30(7), 597–606 (2013). https://doi.org/10.1108/JCM-07-2013-0650
15. Becan, M., Smutny, Z.: The use of enterprise social networks in organizations from the perspective of generation Y in the Czech Republic. Sci. Ann. Econ. Bus. 63(1), 83–96 (2016). https://doi.org/10.1515/saeb-2016-0106
16. Pendergast, D.: Getting to know the Generation Y. In: Benckendorff, P., Moscar, G., Pendergast, D. (eds.) Tourism and Generation Y, pp. 1–15. CABI, Wallingford (2010)
17. Attwood, F., Smith, C.: Porn studies: an introduction. Porn Stud. 1(1–2), 1–6 (2014). https://doi.org/10.1080/23268743.2014.887308
18. Fichman, P., Rosenbaum, H.: Social Informatics: Past, Present and Future, 1st edn. Cambridge Scholars Publishing, Cambridge (2014)
19. Vehovar, V.: Social informatics: an emerging discipline? In: Berleur, J., Nurminen, M., Impagliazzo, J. (eds.) Social Informatics: An Information Society for all? In Remembrance of Rob Kling, pp. 73–85. Springer, Boston (2006). https://doi.org/10.1007/978-0-387-37876-3_6

20. Sevcikova, A., Daneback, K.: Online pornography use in adolescence: age and gender differences. Eur. J. Dev. Psychol. **11**(6), 674–686 (2014). https://doi.org/10.1080/17405629. 2014.926808

21. Sevcikova, A.: Girls' and boys' experience with teen sexting in early and late adolescence. J. Adolesc. **51**, 156–162 (2016). https://doi.org/10.1016/j.adolescence.2016.06.007

22. Diamond, M., Jozifkova, E., Weiss, P.: Pornography and sex crimes in the Czech Republic. Arch. Sex. Behav. **40**(5), 1037–1043 (2011). https://doi.org/10.1007/s10508-010-9696-y

23. Keilty, P.: Desire by design: pornography as technology industry. Porn Stud. (2018). https://doi.org/10.1080/23268743.2018.1483208

24. D'Orlando, F.: The demand for pornography. J. Happiness Stud. **12**(1), 51–75 (2011). https://doi.org/10.1007/s10902-009-9175-0

25. Allen, A., Kannis-Dymand, L., Katsikitis, M.: Problematic internet pornography use: the role of craving, desire thinking, and metacognition. Addict. Behav. **70**, 65–71 (2017). https://doi.org/10.1016/j.addbeh.2017.02.001

26. Grubbs, J.B., Exline, J.J., Pargament, K.I., Volk, F., Lindberg, M.J.: Internet pornography use, perceived addiction, and religious/spiritual struggles. Arch. Sex. Behav. **46**(6), 1733–1745 (2017). https://doi.org/10.1007/s10508-016-0772-9

27. Harper, C., Hodgins, D.C.: Examining correlates of problematic internet pornography use among university students. J. Behav. Addict. **5**(2), 179–191 (2016). https://doi.org/10.1556/2006.5.2016.022

28. Brown, C.C., Conner, S., Vennum, A.: Sexual attitudes of classes of college students who use pornography. Cyberpsychol. Behav. Soc. Netw. **20**(8), 463–469 (2017). https://doi.org/10.1089/cyber.2016.0362

29. Donevan, M., Mattebo, M.: The relationship between frequent pornography consumption, behaviors, and sexual preoccupancy among male adolescents in Sweden. Sex. Reprod. Healthc. **12**, 82–87 (2017). https://doi.org/10.1016/j.srhc.2017.03.002

30. Wright, P.J., Sun, C., Steffen, N.J., Tokunaga, R.S.: Pornography, alcohol, and male sexual dominance. Commun. Monogr. **85**(2), 252–270 (2015). https://doi.org/10.1080/03637751. 2014.981558

31. Haz, L., Guarda, T., Zambrano, I., Sánchez, C.: Internet based parenting control application on teenagers. In: 12th Iberian Conference on Information Systems and Technologies. IEEE, New York (2017)

32. Yiallourou, E., Demetriou, R., Lanitis, A.: On the detection of images containing child-pornographic material. In: 24th International Conference on Telecommunications. IEEE, New York (2017)

33. Kumar, M.S., Kumar, P.N., Deepa, R.: Protection against Pornography. In: IEEE International Conference on Engineering and Technology. IEEE, New York (2016)

34. Sae-Bae, N., Sun, X., Sencar, H.T., Memon, N.D.: Towards automatic detection of child pornography. In: IEEE International Conference on Image Processing, pp. 5332–5336. IEEE, New York (2014)

35. Moreira, D., et al.: Temporal robust features for violence detection. In: IEEE Winter Conference on Applications of Computer Vision, pp. 391–399. IEEE, New York (2017)

36. Zaidan, A.A., Karim, H.A., Ahmad, N.N., Zaidan, B.B., Sali, A.: A four-phases methodology to propose anti-pornography system based on neural and Bayesian methods of artificial intelligence. Int. J. Pattern Recognit. Artif. Intell. (2014). https://doi.org/10.1142/s0218001414590010

37. Godejord, P.A.: Fighting child pornography: exploring didactics and student engagement in social informatics. J. Am. Soc. Inform. Sci. Technol. **58**(3), 446–451 (2007). https://doi.org/10.1002/asi.20522

38. Joyce, R.A.: Pornography and the internet. IEEE Internet Comput. **12**(4), 74–77 (2008). https://doi.org/10.1109/MIC.2008.83

39. Castleman, M.: Dueling Statistics: How Much of the Internet Is Porn? https://www.psychologytoday.com/blog/all-about-sex/201611/dueling-statistics-how-much-the-internet-is-porn. Accessed 01 June 2018

40. CovenantEyes: Pornography Statistics: 2015 Report. http://www.covenanteyes.com/pornstats/. Accessed 01 June 2018

41. Riha, D., Bartova, K., Binter, J.: Use of virtual reality and human–computer interface for diagnostic and treatment purposes in human sexuality research. In: Marcus, A. (ed.) Design, User Experience, and Usability: Technological Contexts, pp. 294–305. Springer, New York (2016). https://doi.org/10.1007/978-3-319-40406-6_28

42. Wright, P.J.: U.S. males and pornography, 1973–2010: consumption, predictors, correlates. J. Sex Res. **50**(1), 60–71 (2013). https://doi.org/10.1080/00224499.2011.628132

43. PornHub: Pornhub's 2016 Year in Review. https://www.pornhub.com/insights/2016-year-in-review. Accessed 01 June 2018

44. Schmidt, G.: Male–female differences in sexual arousal and behavior during and after exposure to sexually explicit stimuli. In: Rubinstein, E.A., Green, R., Brecher, E. (eds.) New Directions in Sex Research: Perspectives in Sexuality, pp. 31–43. Springer, Boston (1975). https://doi.org/10.1007/978-1-4684-2280-1_4

45. Willoughby, B.J., Carroll, J.S., Nelson, L.J., Padilla-Walker, L.M.: Associations between relational sexual behaviour, pornography use, and pornography acceptance among US college students. Culture Health Sex. **16**(9), 1052–1069 (2014). https://doi.org/10.1080/13691058.2014.927075

The Changing Meaning of Privacy in Information Technology Debates: Evidence from the Internet Governance Forum

Artem Antonyuk[(✉)]

Centre for German and European Studies, St. Petersburg State University,
St. Petersburg, Russia
artem.antonyuk@protonmail.com

Abstract. In this paper we present the analysis of the changing meaning of privacy in Internet governance discourse. In order to uncover different facets of the issue, we apply computer-aided textual analysis to analyse transcripts of discussions at the Internet Governance Forum, an annual UN-supported event that brings together representatives of major stakeholders. Analysis of longitudinal data from 2010 to 2017 shows that privacy is a contested issue, addressed by different groups of interests. During the studied period, privacy was mostly framed in the human rights and technical perspectives. We show how specific connections between words enacted these frames and illustrate them with quotations from the data. We also show that there are routine and reflective ways in which participants enact these perspectives.

Keywords: Privacy · Internet governance · Multistakeholderism
Semantic network analysis

1 Introduction

Privacy on the Internet has recently become the focus of heated debates, bringing about increased media attention, changes in Internet usage habits and, ultimately, shifting regulatory frameworks. The whole issue has developed in a matter of a few years, making it an interesting and rare case of a problem emerging, spreading beyond professional communities and national boundaries and finally resolving in large-scale policy changes. As such, it became topical for different groups of people, some of which did not have prior engagement with the issue of privacy or Internet governance in general. It is therefore necessary to analyse how different groups of actors understand privacy in the context of coexisting plurality of interests and rapid rate of change of Internet infrastructure and services. How do they define privacy? What other issues do they consider relevant? Do they try to persuade other groups? While some of these questions were addressed by researchers [1, 2], it is necessary to update their findings in light of the most recent developments. In what follows we describe the object of our study, explain the methodological framework and present our findings.

© Springer Nature Switzerland AG 2018
S. S. Bodrunova (Ed.): INSCI 2018, LNCS 11193, pp. 92–100, 2018.
https://doi.org/10.1007/978-3-030-01437-7_8

2 Influencing Policy Through Debate at the Internet Governance Forum

According to a shared understanding, the Internet is not governed by a single organization or any other formal body. Its global outreach spans various jurisdictions, political regimes and cultures, making centralized regulation difficult. Coordination between different actors becomes needed for stable functioning of the global communication infrastructure and its services. While this setting is already complicated, it is even more difficult to ensure that it enables democratic participation. In response for the call for democratic engagement, a multistakeholder approach to Internet governance was proposed to take into account the interests of all parties potentially affected by regulatory policies [3]. Its stated advantage over multilateral government-level approach is its openness for all participants regardless of their official status, nationality or technical expertise. Multistakeholder approach to governance seeks to be inclusive, open to alternative viewpoints and respectful of the plurality of existing interests. The approach was employed most notably in the Internet Governance Forum (further referred to as the Forum or IGF).

IGF is an annual international event aimed at promoting information technology policy discussions among different stakeholders, including governments, civil society, private companies, academic and technical communities, and intergovernmental organizations. The Forum does not have any decision-making capabilities, thus—at least in theory—promoting open expression of opinions and exchange of information. While some have regarded this feature as a drawback inhibiting change in the official policies, others have stressed that such an approach may still influence policy in an indirect way [3].

The Forum's strategic withdrawal from decision-making indicates that it can serve as a neutral platform for bringing together different, sometimes opposite interests. It thus has a mediating function, and its influence comes from establishing and maintaining connections to multiple otherwise separated entities. The venue is likely to stimulate a complex dynamic of conflict, influence and cooperation between representatives of different stakeholder groups. This process, in turn, may stimulate consolidation of interests and emergence of new ideas, which will then extend their influence beyond the boundaries of the Forum by providing values and definitions of core terms or by legitimating certain perspectives.

In terms of organizational structure, discussions at Internet Governance Forum occur at different levels, including the Multistakeholder Advisory Group (its organizing committee), main sessions, several thematic subgroups called 'dynamic coalitions' and numerous workshops and open fora. Discussions at all levels seek to embody the principles of multistakeholder policy dialogue, bringing together representatives of all stakeholder groups. In our study we focus on dynamic coalitions as representing stable points of convergence of various interests.

Previous research on Internet governance has revealed the main features of the discursive dynamics in question [1, 2]. With regard to the issue of privacy, it was found that the issue plays an important part in discussions of Internet policy, stimulating expression of opposing perspectives. During the period of 2006–2011, there were several dominant ways of talking about privacy, and the most stable of them utilized the security frame. The view of privacy as a threat to security was stated mainly by government actors, while civil society actors argued for privacy protection as a cornerstone of security [1]. Competition of this kind illustrates the core problem of the multistakeholder model. Stakeholders are likely to influence discussion by providing definitions of core concepts and establishing connections with certain ideas, while omitting connections with other ideas. In this way they aim not only to secure their own positions, but also to influence the way other stakeholders perceive their own interests. In the example above, the government representatives influence the existing perceptions of privacy by raising security concerns. In turn, civil society actors accept the connection between two ideas but attempt to redefine its nature and tip the balance in favour of privacy. Discursive struggle rather than dialogue seems to occur at the Forum, with certain stakeholders trying to monopolize discourse and impose their own limited perspective on others. The meanings of key terms of Internet governance are at stake. This problem leads us to formulate the following research question: How does the meaning of privacy change in multistakeholder Internet governance discussions?

3   Data and Method

The longitudinal dataset includes the corpus of transcripts of discussions at a number of dynamic coalitions at the Internet Governance Forum, spanning the period from 2010 to 2017.[1] We include discussions at six dynamic coalitions with the largest amount of mentions of 'privacy'. These are the coalitions on Internet Rights and Principles, Core Internet Values, Platform Responsibility, Internet of Things, Network Neutrality and Publicness. Three of these coalitions were active for almost every year of the studied period, while others were active from two to four consecutive years (See Fig. 1). The total size of the corpus is 360,377 words.

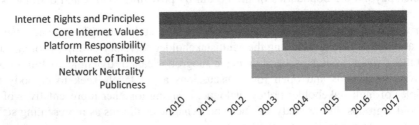

Fig. 1. Dynamic coalitions at the IGF included in the study, per year.

---

[1] The transcripts are publicly available at Internet Governance Forum website: https://www.intgovforum.org/.

In order to describe the changing meaning of privacy in the discussions, we employ semantic network analysis to study the corpus of texts. Semantic network analysis is a computer-aided textual analytic method well-suited for studying large amounts of data [4]. It allows the researcher to uncover the semantic network of words—meaningful connections between words based on their co-occurrences in a given text. The theoretical assumption behind the method is that the meaning of a word is inherently relational, being formed by connections with other words. Semantic network analysis aims to address this feature as it deals with mapping and studying the connections between words as they are articulated in specific contexts. It allows to explain why the same word has multiple meanings in different contexts or how the word's meaning changes when it is connected to words from another, previously unrelated context. The main advantage of the method over conventional content analysis methods lies in taking into account the relations between linguistic elements [5]. Also, it does not presuppose the coding phase, thus reducing researcher's bias which is a common issue in content analysis and probabilistic methods of textual analysis [6].

Semantic networks were mapped based on the corpus using semi-automatic procedure in Automap software [7]. Prior to mapping semantic networks, the texts in the corpus were pre-processed according to a conventional procedure: lowercasing, stemming, removal of stop words (such as articles, prepositions, trivial words and junk words or phrases). Then, semantic networks for each text were mapped based on co-occurrences of words within a maximum distance of one word.[2] The resulting networks consist of word stems and links of word associations between them. In other words, semantic networks represent aggregated meaning structures for each dynamic coalition session. Semantic networks also capture the frequencies of word associations by recording them as link values in the networks. Next, we reduced the complexity of semantic networks by removing links with values of 1 to remove word associations that occurred only once during a session and that could be regarded as less important (see Fig. 2). We also removed isolated nodes that did not have any persistent associations with other words. In the final network dataset, the smallest network consisted of 91 words and 67 word association links, and the largest one consisted of 289 words and 325 word association links. We analysed the networks by visually examining them, describing their structural properties and focussing on the meaning structures associated with privacy-related keywords. Then we interpreted the findings looking at the examples of how these keywords were used in the original discussions.

---

[2] E.g., for the expression 'internet governance forum', three links with values of 1 would have been produced: internet–governance, internet–forum, and governance–forum.

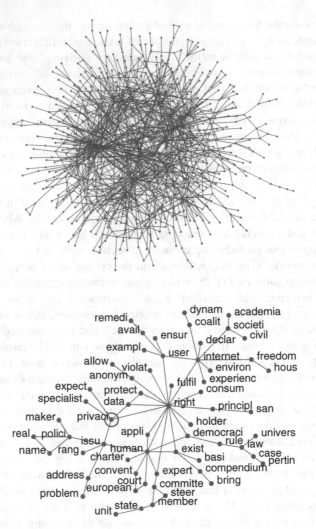

Fig. 2. Top: The main component of the full semantic network of the discussions at the dynamic coalition on Internet Rights and Principles, 2012. Links are based on *one and more* co-occurrences of words in the text. Labels are hidden. Bottom: The main component of the simplified version of the same semantic network. Links are based on *two and more* co-occurrences of words in the text. Link width does not reflect link value. Stemmed form of the keyword 'privacy' is circled.

4   Findings

Analysis of semantic networks indicates that in most cases privacy is not a persistent or central element of discussions. Only two dynamic coalitions, on Internet of Things and on Platform Responsibility, mention privacy consistently over the course of their functioning, although particular associations of privacy with other words are not stable even in the same dynamic coalition. This suggests that attention to the issue was shifting, dependent on stakeholder activity and possibly being triggered by external events. In cases when the word is found in the semantic networks, it is often located on the periphery of the network and has few links to other words. Instead, the semantic networks are focused on such words as 'internet', 'right', 'people', 'access', 'freedom', and others. It is these words that structure the discourse of Internet governance. Thus, despite being recognized as an important topic, privacy largely stands on its own, having few connections to other topics.

The observed word associations can be roughly grouped into technological and human rights perspectives that tend to be expressed together.

4.1 Privacy as a Human Right

The view of privacy as a human right is consistently promoted by the coalition on Internet Rights and Principles. Here privacy is seen as a right similar to other human rights, with all the usual normative implications: "I'm part of a group of people who think that our rights to privacy are violated by the data retention practice that exists in Switzerland."[3] Here the speaker refers to the 'right to privacy' rather than, say, 'the value of privacy'. The invoked frame determines that practice in question is regarded as a violation and not as a necessary measure, as would be the case if the government's point of view was expressed. In another case a speaker invokes the human rights frame to explicitly stress the connection between different rights. She argues that "... the issue of freedom of association and privacy at the workplace is absolutely linked."[4] This expression exemplifies how actors explicitly draw connections between an established notion of human rights and a contested concept in order to define their viewpoint and persuade their opponents.

The human rights frame is also used to contrast privacy with other rights, as in the case of discussion of regulatory decisions facing online platforms: "Of course, this [obligation to protect a core set of values on the Internet] raises a number of questions, who's core values, which core values, what is a core value, is it freedom of expression or right to privacy, who is to make that decision, so how is the platform supposed to be responsible for everyone's core values?"[5] This expression attests that human rights framing of privacy does not always convey a universally shared meaning: there is no clear dividing line between privacy protection and freedom of expression. It also indicates that the human rights frame can be challenged by different parties. In the expression above it even may have been displaced. Note that the speaker equates human rights with values. While values that drove the development of the Internet can be aligned with human rights, the crucial difference lies in the nature of regulatory model. In the context of discussion of policies aimed at platforms, protection of values entails informal regulatory approaches, e.g. self-governance by private companies. Protection of human rights entails a more complex framework that includes

---

[3] Participant at the dynamic coalition on Internet Rights and Principles, 2012.

[4] Participant at the dynamic coalition on Internet Rights and Principles, 2010.

[5] Participant at the dynamic coalition on Platform Responsibility, 2016.

government agencies and intergovernmental organizations as equal or superior actors. Thus, the choice of words in the example above indicates an ongoing tension between different regulatory models which may be not evident at the first sight.

4.2 Technological Perspective on Privacy

The technical approach to privacy is expressed in the dynamic coalition on Internet of Things. It seems to exemplify technological determinism in Internet governance, an approach that argues that most Internet-related problems, including social and cultural, can be solved with the right hardware or software. For example, the search for technical solutions for privacy protection focuses on the stage of product development: "good practice in IoT [Internet of Things] products, ecosystems and services requires meaningful transparency to users and user control of data produced by and associated with an application, ensuring security and respect for privacy."[6] Another feature of this approach evident in this expression is focus on data rather than information as an object of regulation and protection.

In another coalition a speaker makes an effort to explicitly connect the technical solutions of privacy issues with the their legal aspects: "So that's why for me the discussion about terms of services has to be done in conjunction with the discussion about privacy by design, privacy by default, and how the applications are developed to be able to protect regularly the privacy."[7] In a different context, a speakers talks about a potentially privacy-violating technology in a positive vein: "the traffic management techniques may be perfectly reasonable and legal as long as they do not jeopardize the right to privacy and the protection of users."[8]

4.3 Stable Perspectives and Creative Redefinition

There are only two coalitions that tend to regard privacy within one dominant approach. Technical standpoint on privacy is mostly expressed in the Internet of Things coalition, while the human rights approach is a major feature of the Internet Rights and Principles coalition. Other groups tend to mix both approaches to privacy or discuss it in terms of well-established frameworks, such as security versus privacy opposition. In this plural context the meaning of core concept may also be questioned: "We [dynamic coalition organizers] thought that the spreading of Right to be Forgotten is fuelled by lack of discourse or lack of discussion on the publicness as opposed to privacy."[9]

Apart from using the main approaches to privacy, the meaning of the concept can be shaped by the ways participants make their arguments. Close reading of transcripts reveals that most often an actor uses the key concept of privacy in an unreflective way, reproducing such stable associations of words as 'the right to privacy'. Another way is less common, as it requires explicitly drawing connections between an established

---

[6] Participant at the dynamic coalition on Internet of Things, 2015.

[7] Participant at the dynamic coalition on Platform Responsibility, 2015.

[8] Participant at the dynamic coalition on Network Neutrality, 2015.

[9] Participant at the dynamic coalition on Publicness, 2016.

notion such as 'human rights' and a contested concept such as 'network neutrality'. As the new notion becomes accepted, it forms a stable meaning structure that in turn may provide meaning and legitimacy to novel or contested concepts and ideas.

5 Conclusions

Our analysis of transcripts of discussions at the IGF allowed us to understand how the meaning of privacy is shaped. First, it does not play a prominent role in shaping Internet governance discourse. It forms relatively few connections with other topics, unlike other words like 'freedom' or 'people'. Next, the meaning of privacy is shaped by two main frames: human rights and technology. We found that human rights frame is often central in the semantic networks and thus plays an important role in structuring Internet governance discourse. Human rights are invoked to legitimize a contested concept, but also to distinguish between different rights. We have also found that the human rights frame can be challenged. The technological frame is mostly about how infrastructure, technologies and software influence privacy in negative and positive ways. These elements of the Internet, in addition to user data, become the main objects and even means of regulation and protection. Finally, qualitative analysis of data suggests that participants tend to reproduce stable meanings, but in some cases they explicitly draw connections between different ideas.

Future research on the topic can be done on the question of embeddedness of the meaning of privacy on the Internet in broader institutional contexts. In particular, one can ask how different stakeholder groups articulate their own positions and how coordination occurs inside and between different stakeholder groups. Overall, the approach adopted here can be extended to addresses the changing meanings of core policy concepts in other spheres, and thus to shift the research focus from dominant predictors of policy change such as legal frameworks, economic conditions, or political influence to the broader domain of culture. This will allow researchers to understand how this often overlooked yet powerful dimension influences issue perceptions, everyday habits and policy change.

Acknowledgements. The author of this paper has benefited from the support of The Russian Foundation for Humanities grant 15-03-00722 "Coevolution of knowledge and communication networks: structural dynamics of creative collectives in European cultural capitals", 2015–2017, Russian Foundation for Basic Research grant 18-011-00796 "Dynamic of Socio-cultural Network Structures", 2018–2020, and the Centre for German and European Studies—Bielefeld University and St. Petersburg State University supported by the DAAD with funds from the German Foreign Office.

References

1. Epstein, D., Roth, M.C., Baumer, E.P.: It's the definition, stupid! Framing of online privacy in the internet governance forum debates. J. Info. Pol'y. **4**, 144–172 (2014). https://doi.org/10.5325/jinfopoli.4.2014.0144
2. Pavan, E.: Frames and Connections in the Governance of Global Communications: A Network Study of the Internet Governance Forum. Lexington Books, Lanham (2012)
3. Malcolm, J.: Multi-stakeholder Governance and the Internet Governance Forum. Terminus Press, Perth (2008)
4. van Atteveldt, W.: Semantic Network Analysis. Techniques for Extracting, Representing, and Querying Media Content. BookSurge, Charleston (2008)
5. Doerfel, M.L.: What constitutes semantic network analysis? A comparison of research and methodologies. Connections **21**(2), 16–26 (1998)
6. Lee, M., Martin, J.L.: Coding, counting and cultural cartography. Am. J. Cult. Sociol. **3**(1), 1–33 (2015). https://doi.org/10.1057/ajcs.2014.13
7. Diesner, J., Carley, K.M.: AutoMap 1.2: Extract, Analyze, Represent, and Compare Mental Models from Texts. Carnegie Mellon University, School of Computer Science, Institute for Software Research International, Pittsburgh (2004)
8. Phillips, N., Lawrence, T.B., Hardy, C.: Discourse and institutions. Acad. Manag. Rev. **29**(4), 635–652 (2004). https://doi.org/10.5465/AMR.2004.14497617

Freedom of Expression and Regulation of Extremism in Russia in the Context of the Council of Europe Standards

Elena Sherstoboeva and Valentina Pavlenko[✉]

National Research University Higher School of Economics, 20 Myasnitskaya
Ulitsa, Moscow, Russia
esherstoboeva@hse.ru, v-tina13@yandex.ru

Abstract. This study examines the development of Russian anti-extremist legislation with the purpose to identify the extent to which it correlates with the legal standards of the Council of Europe (CoE) on the right to freedom of expression. Apart from Russian national legislation, the article also considers judicial visions of extremism – for the first time in the field. The analysis goes beyond the issue of compliance and non-compliance and shows the fundamental differences of Russian and CoE legal visions of the issue. It is suggested that the differences have considerably increased over the last few years which is mainly explained by the shift of priorities of the Russian political establishment, rather than by pressing social needs. It is concluded that the Russian concept of extremism has the worrying potential for further expansion both in Russia and beyond it, including in what we call "alternative" international law.

Keywords: Russia · Extremism · Hate speech · Council of Europe
Freedom of expression

1 Introduction

Against the background of increased immigration in Europe, risks of terrorist attacks and other threats to public security, governments often introduce or expand the laws forbidding speech that is deemed extremist or in support of terrorism. At the same time, these laws, as Banisar [1] argues, often become a pretext for curtailing freedom of expression. This fundamental human right is guaranteed in the main United Nations (UN) human rights documents, such as the 1948 Universal Declaration of Human Rights (UDHR)[1] as well as the 1966 International Covenant on Civil and Political Rights (ICCPR),[2] and in the 1950 European Convention on Human Rights (ECHR)[3] of the Council of Europe (CoE), the leading human rights organization in Europe.

---

[1] Universal Declaration of Human Rights 1948, GA Res 217A (III), A/810 at 71 (1948).
[2] International Covenant on Civil and Political Rights 1966, 999 UNTS 171.
[3] Convention for the Protection of Fundamental Rights and Freedoms 1950, ETS 5.

© Springer Nature Switzerland AG 2018
S. S. Bodrunova (Ed.): INSCI 2018, LNCS 11193, pp. 101–115, 2018.
https://doi.org/10.1007/978-3-030-01437-7_9

The Russian anti-extremist law have been criticized for being too broad and vague by the UN and CoE[4] as well as scholars (Grigorieva [3]; Richter [5]; Verhovskij, Ledovskih, and Sultanov [8]). However, the Russian government is of a position that the anti-extremist legal concept is in line with the international human rights law[5] and with the Russian Constitution that guarantees freedom of speech and a total ban on censorship in Article 29. The Russia's annexation of Crimea caused the aggravation of the relationships between Russia and CoE, and Russian officials have often challenges the CoE criticism of the national human rights situation as merely politically biased.[6]

Since its emergence in 2002 to combat terrorism, the Russian anti-extremist law has been expanded. At present, the legal notion of extremism encompasses many violations varying in their meanings and danger including terrorism, separatism, hate speech, libel of public officials, insult of religious feelings, proselytism, desecration of military monuments as well as public calls for executing any of this violation.[7] Several neighbouring countries have already incorporated similar legal visions. Russian legal documents[8] view anti-extremist laws as one of the main tool to neutralize increasing threats to the country's "information safety" undermining Russia's national sovereignty, political and social stability, and the Constitutional order. Therefore, most of extremist acts are criminalized in Russia, and the number of extremist crimes has more than doubled from 2010 to 2017.[9]

---

[4] European Commission for Democracy through Law, Opinion on Federal Law of the Russian Federation, "On Combating Extremist Activity," adopted by the Venice Commission at its 91 Plenary Session, Venice, 15–16 June, No. 660/ 2011, CDL-AD(2012)016, Strasbourg, 20 June 2012; the UN Human Rights Committee's Concluding Observations on the Seventh Periodic Report of the Russian Federation (CCPR/C/RUS/7), adopted on 28 April 2015.

[5] The Strategy of counteraction to extremism in the Russian Federation until 2025 (Approved by the President of the Russian Federation no. Pr-2753 as of 28 November 2014). http://www.consultant.ru/ document/cons_doc_LAW_194160/7327668c04c0470317b26d354e36cb828a4af319, last accessed 2018/05/11.

[6] The Ministry of Foreign Affairs of the Russian Federation (2017, June 30) Zayavlenie MID Rossii v svyazi s priostanovkoj uplaty vznosa Rossii v Sovet Evropy za 2017 god [Statement of the Ministry of Foreign Affairs of the Russian Federation Concerning the Suspension of Payment of Russia's Contribution to the Council of Europe for 2017]. http://www.mid.ru/web/guest/foreign_policy/rso/ coe/-/asset_publisher/uUbe64ZnDJso/content/id/2805051, last accessed 2018/05/11.

[7] Article 1 of Federal Statute of the Russian Federation of 25 July 2002, No. 114-FZ "On Counteracting Extremist Activity." http://www.consultant.ru/document/cons_doc_LAW_37867/, last accessed 2018/05/10.

[8] The Strategy of counteraction to extremism in the Russian Federation until 2025 (Approved by the President of the Russian Federation no. Pr-2753 as of 28 November 2014). http://www.consultant.ru/ document/cons_doc_LAW_194160/7327668c04c0470317b26d354e36cb828a4af319, last accessed 2018/05/11; Rossiiskaia gazeta (2009, May 19) Ukaz Prezidenta Rossiiskoi Federatsii ot 12 maia 2009 g. N 537 "O Strategii natsional'noi bezopasnosti Rossiiskoi Federatsii do 2020 goda" [Decree of the President of the Russian Federation of 12 May 2009, N 537 "On the National Security Strategy of the Russian Federation until 2020"]. https://rg.ru/2009/05/19/strategia-dok.html, last accessed 2018/05/12.

[9] See the official Web Portal on Legal Statistics of the Office of the General Prosecutor of the Russian Federation. http://crimestat.ru/offenses_chart, last accessed 2018/06/08.

Anti-extremist law has a considerable impact on online speech and media freedom in Russia. As technology advances and the Internet audience grows, this impact becomes increasingly serious. Extremism is one of the most popular grounds for restricting freedom of expression on the Internet and, in particular, for blocking websites. From 2005, the Russian Ministry of Justice has maintained a blacklist of the so called "extremist materials" that are defined very broadly.[10] As of 13 June 2018, the blacklist included 4,461 online and offline publications [4]. Since the excessive restriction of freedom of expression under the guise of combating extremism may lead to limitation of citizen empowerment on the Internet, it is particularly important to consider anti-extremist legislation in the context of Internet freedoms.

Despite more than twenty years of Russia's membership in the CoE, there have been no scholarly studies that would comprehensively consider the Russian anti-extremist law in the light of the CoE standards, and this study aims to fill this gap. This paper suggests that the Russian legal notion of extremism is mostly inconsistent with the CoE standards on free speech and represents Russian government's own interpretation (or, in fact, misinterpretation) of several CoE legal concepts.

2 Research Design and Method

The research method of the study is a qualitative comparative analysis of the Russian and CoE legal standards. It implies applying the so-called three-tier test provided in Article 10 part 2 of the ECHR. The test means that any limitation to this right must (i) be provided by law; (ii) pursue a legitimate aim; (iii) be necessary in a democratic society. The ECHR test is used by the European Court of Human Rights (ECtHR), the CoE's judicial institution, to judge on the admissibility of the governmental interference with freedom of expressions. The ECtHR's mechanism on human rights protection is often viewed as the most effective in the world, and its judgment on one member state is legally binding on all other member states. Similar test is established in Article 19 part 3 of the ICCPR[11] as well as in Article 55 part 3 of the Russian Constitution.

The ECtHR distinguishes between expressions that may shock, disturb or offend but deserving protection under Article 10 of the ECHR, and expressions that cannot be

---

[10] "Extremist materials" mean documents or information "calling for the perpetration of extremist acts or explaining or justifying the need to commit such activities; [such information] includes works by the leaders of the Nazi Party of Germany, the fascist party of Italy as well as publications explaining or justifying national or racial superiority, or justifying the practice of committing military or other crimes aimed at the full or partial elimination of any ethnic, social, racial, national or religious group."

[11] ICCPR in Article 19 of Part 3 states: "The exercise of the rights provided for in paragraph 2 of this article carries with it special duties and responsibilities. It may therefore be subject to certain restrictions, but these shall only be such as are provided by law and are necessary: (a) For respect of the rights or reputations of others; (b) For the protection of national security or of public order (ordre public), or of public health or morals."

tolerated in a democratic society.[12] Because Article 17 of the ECHR[13] excludes speech abusing rights guaranteed in the ECHR from its protection, the ECtHR declares applications seeking to protect such speech as being inadmissible.

Under the CoE standards, this paper understands not only legally binding standards of the ECHR and ECtHR but also the CoE non-binding legal standards because they help to grasp the legally binding vision. Particularly important for this paper are non-binding standards elaborated by main governing CoE institutions, such as the Parliamentary Assembly (PACE) and the Committee of Ministers (CM). Additionally, the paper often quotes the non-binding opinion of the European Commission for Democracy through Law (or the Venice Commission)[14] that specifically addressed the main Russian statute regulating extremism in 2012. The CoE standards are of secondary concern for the study as it focuses on the Russian legal concept of extremism.

This concept has been explored through the comprehensive study of Russian national legislation and judicial interpretations including the documents of the Russian highest courts, the Supreme Court and the Constitutional Court, as well as 150 decisions of Russian general jurisdiction courts selected randomly over the period from March 2012 to March 2018 from the RosPravosudiye Database.[15] The paper also examines the statistical data on the application of Russian extremist laws in 2012–2017 collected by the SOVA Center for Information and Analysis,[16] an independent Russian NGO monitoring extremist crimes in the country, as well as of Roskomnadzor,[17] the state media and mass communication regulator in Russia.

3 Hate Speech and Extremism

Both Russia and the CoE exclude hate speech from protection under free speech provisions. Article 20 of the ICCPR requiring that member-states ban racial, national or religious hatred.[18] According to the CoE, hate speech undermines the foundation of

---

[12] See, for instance, the ECtHR judgments, *Jersild v Denmark* of 23 September 1994; *Lehideux and Isorni v France* of 23 September 1998.

[13] Article 17 of the ECHR stipulates that: "Nothing in this Convention may be interpreted as implying for any State, group or person any right to engage in any activity or perform any act aimed at the destruction of any of the rights and freedoms set forth herein or at their limitation to a greater extent than is provided for in the Convention."

[14] The European Commission for Democracy through Law (or the Venice Commission) is an advisory body of the CoE designed to improve operation of democratic institutions and the protection of human rights in the member-states.

[15] "RosPravosudiye" is an open-access Russian-language database of all judicial decisions of the Russian courts.

[16] See SOVA Center's database. http://www.sova-center.ru/en/database/sentences/, last accessed 2018/05/10.

[17] See Roskomnadzor's Public Reports. http://rkn.gov.ru/press/annual_reports/, last accessed 2018/05/25.

[18] Article 20 of the ICCPR states: "1. Any propaganda for war shall be prohibited by law.
2. Any advocacy of national, racial or religious hatred that constitutes incitement to discrimination, hostility or violence shall be prohibited by law."

democracy based on the ideas of tolerance of differences, promotion of social peace and non-discrimination. According to the definition in the CoE's CM Recommendation 97 (20) "On Hate Speech,"[19] it may cover various forms of expression based on intolerance. The ECtHR tends to refuse protection for racist,[20] xenophobic or anti-Semitic speech;[21] expressions denying, challenging or diminishing the Holocaust;[22] or Nazi and neo-Nazi speech.[23] The ECtHR qualifies hate speech as such if only it incites violence.

Russian concept of hate speech is much broader. Apart from banning racial, national or religious hatred, constitutional Article 29 part 2 also prohibits "*social* hatred and strife," "racial, national or religious *strife*" as well as "propaganda of social, racial, national, religious or linguistic *superiority*". Article 282 of the Russian Criminal Code criminalising these actions forms the main part of anti-extremist legal mechanism in Russia, although Article 280 of the Criminal Code overlaps Article 282 by criminalising "public calls for extremism." Thus, Russian government has created a unique legal concept—incitement to extremism—that goes by far beyond incitement to violence.

Neither the UN nor the CoE standards use the notions of "social hatred," "strife" and "superiority" nor Russian statutes as well as Russian highest courts define them. Their aim is unclear and their meaning is too vague. The ban on "social hatred" in Russia has already led to punishing for criticism towards public officials or bodies that had been misinterpreted as social groups [8]. In contrast, the ECtHR tend to protect even harsh criticism of public officials to facilitate the public's control over their activities.[24] Article 9 part 1 of the ECHR specifically acknowledges one's right to religious expression or belief in "worship, teaching, practice and observance." The ECtHR protects expressions claiming religious "superiority" as expressions of opinions if they do not incite violence.[25] Therefore, the Venice Commission called for Russia to abolish their ban but Russia have only expanded it over the last few years.

The ECtHR does not explicitly ban Nazi propaganda as such, but tends to exclude it from protection as incompatible with the values protected by the ECHR.[26] However, the Russian legislation bans not only Nazi symbols, but also any symbols of extremist

---

[19] Recommendation 97(20) of the CoE's Committee of Ministers on Hate Speech, adopted on 30 October 1997, at the 607th meeting of the Ministers' Deputies.

[20] See, for instance, the ECtHR judgments, *Jersild v Denmark* of 23 September 1994; *Seurot v France* of 18 May 2004; *Norwood v United Kingdom* of 16 November 2004.

[21] See, for example, the ECtHR judgment, *Pavel Ivanov v Russia* of 20 February 2007.

[22] See, for example, the ECtHR judgment on the case of *Garaudy v France* of 24 June 2003.

[23] See the ECtHR judgment on the case of *H., W., P. and K. v. Austria* of 12 October 1989.

[24] See, for instance, the ECtHR judgments, *Castells v Spain* of 23 April 1992; *Janowski v Poland* of 21 January 1999; *Sürek v Turkey* of 8 July 1999; *Nilsen v Norway* of 25 November 1999; *Jerusalem v Austria* of 27 February 2001; *Karman v Russia* of 14 December 2006; *Lepojić v Serbia* of 6 November 2007; *Renaud v France* of 25 February 2010; *Axel Springer AG v. Germany* (No. 2) of 10 July 2014; and *Stankiewicz and others v Poland* of 14 October 2014.

[25] See, for example, *Kokkinakis v Greece* of 25 May 1993.

[26] See, for instance, the ECtHR judgments, *Kühnen v Federal Republic of Germany* of 12 May 1988 and *B. H., M. W., H. P. and G. K. v Austria* of 12 October 1989.

organisations that are defined very broadly. Such organisations are blacklisted by the Russian Ministry of Justice.[27] As of 15 June 2018, its register consisted of 64 organisations including five Ukrainian one added after the annexation of Crimea.

Another miscorrelation emerges from the fact that Article 20.3 of the Russian Code of Administrative Offences bans not only propaganda of the symbols or attributes of Nazi or extremist organisations or confusingly similar symbols or attributes, but also their public display. An example may be the 2015 case of a journalist Polina Danilevich who was penalised under Article 20.3. On her social media account on the Internet, she placed a picture showing what the common area next to her house had looked like back in 1941–1943 when fascists had occupied it. In 2012, a Russian politician Vitold Fillippov was fined for "liking" a photo from the film, *American History X*, depicting the actor Edward Norton with tattoos of the Nazi swastika on his body. The film, however, had not been banned in Russia. The 2017 proposal would allow public display of Nazi symbols in creative works, for educational and information purposes, but it was not adopted.

Since 2014, Russian Criminal Code has separately prohibited "the rehabilitation of Nazism." Article 354.1 criminalises not only the denial or acceptance of crimes established in decisions of the International Military Tribunal but also public dissemination of "knowingly false information of the USSR activities in the period of World War II" that goes far beyond the CoE's legal concepts. Although the ECtHR tends to exclude from protection the expressions if they deny "clearly established historical facts," it shields the debates on historical events under Article 10 of the ECHR.[28] Unlike crimes established in decisions of the International Military Tribunal, activities by the USSR during World War II may hardly constitute established facts.

Article 354.1 also provides another ambiguous ban on disseminating materials that express "explicit disrespect for [Russian] society," such as defamation of the "days of military glory as well as memorable dates in Russian history connected to the protection of the Fatherland," and public desecration of symbols of Russian military glory. No register of the days of military glory or memorable dates of Russia exists, and, therefore, this ban may also hardly comply with the ECHR as it lacks clarity.

The liability for insult of religious feelings was increased after the landmark case of a punk-rock band Pussy Riot. In 2012, Russian courts ruled on blocking the video of their punk prayer, which could be considered as contributing to political discussion because of the content of the song [2]. Therefore, most likely, it would be protected by the ECtHR. However, the Constitutional Court justified the ban of the video by stating that the religious issues are sensitive and any "form of expression concerning religion

---

[27] The register of NGOs banned on the grounds of the Federal Statute of the Russian Federation, "On Counteraction of Extremism Activity," accessed from the official website of the Ministry of Justice of the Russian Federation. http://minjust.ru/ru/nko/perechen_zapret, last accessed 2018/06/15; The register of NGOs whose activities have been suspended for committing extremist acts, accessed from the official web site of the Ministry of Justice of the Russian Federation. http://minjust.ru/nko/perechen_priostanovleni, last accessed 2018/06/15.

[28] See, for example, the ECtHR judgments on the cases of *Ochensberger v Austria* of 2 September 1994; *Honsik v Austria* of 18 October 1995; *D. I. v Germany* of 26 June 1998; *Lehideux and Isorni v France* of 23 September 1998; *Garaudy v France* of 24 June 2003.

that may insult public morals" is inadmissible.[29] Although anti-extremist law had already allowed punishing Pussy Riot, its case triggered specific criminalisation of public acts expressing "explicit disrespect to society and perpetrated with the aim to insult religious feeling" in 2013 (Article 148 of the Russian Criminal Code). The CoE standards provide a wide margin of appreciation to member-states with regards to insults of religious feelings[30] but it is under the supervision of the ECtHR. From its standpoint, such expressions may be limited if only they "are gratuitously offensive to others" and "do not contribute to any form of public debate."[31] However, Russian law overlooks this perspective and provides no criteria for defining or assessing such crimes.

While the ECtHR suggests that the ban on hate speech covers homophobic speech,[32] in Russia such speech is allowed. In 2013, the Russian government prohibited "propaganda of untraditional sexual relationships among minors,"[33] which is an unclear notion preventing from any discussions on homosexuality. In 2014, the Russian Constitutional Court found the limitation being constitutional.[34] No reference was made to the opposing ECtHR position on homophobic speech. We suggest that the ban on "social hatred" might correlate with the CoE standards and even be useful to fight hate speech in case of interpretation as protecting socially vulnerable groups from such speech, including homophobic speech.

4 Terrorism and Extremism

Savchenko [6] notes that extremism emerged in a Russian legal discourse after the adoption of the Shanghai Convention "On Combating Terrorism, Separatism and Extremism"[35] by Russia, China, Kazakhstan, Kyrgyzstan, Tajikistan and Uzbekistan. The Russian government argued that terrorist acts are instigated by political extremism inciting violence [5]. This vision was incorporated to the Convention. It has given rise to legitimizing the extremist concept in Russian national law under the claims that— from now on—extremism is banned in international law.

---

[29] Resolution of the Constitutional Court of the Russian Federation on the admissibility of the complaint by citizen N. A. Tolokonnikova, complaining about the violation of her constitutional rights by part 2 Article 213 of the Criminal Code of the Russian Federation, Saint-Petersburg, 25 September 2014, No. 1873-O.

[30] See, for example, the ECtHR judgment, *Otto-Preminger-Institut v Austria* of 20 September 1994.

[31] See, the ECtHR judgments, *Gündüz v Turkey* Application of 4 December 2003; *Erbakan v Turkey* of 6 July 2006.

[32] See the ECtHR judgment, *Vejdeland and Others v Sweden* of 9 February 2012.

[33] Article 6.21 of the Russian Code of Administrative Offences.

[34] Resolution of the Constitutional Court of the Russian Federation on the case of the constitutionality test of Article 6.21 Part 1 of the Russian Code of Administrative Offences in response to complaints of citizens, N. A. Alexeev, Y. N. Yevtushenko and D. A. Isakov, Saint-Petersburg, 23 September 2014.

[35] Shanghai Convention "On Combating Terrorism, Separatism and Extremism," adopted on 15 June 2001 and entered into force on 29 March 2003. http://www.mid.ru/sanhajskaa-organizaciaso trudnicestva-sos-/-/asset_publisher/0vP3hQoCPRg5/content/id/579606, last accessed 2018/05/18.

The initial vision of extremism in Russian law was close to the Convention that refers only to violent acts of extremism[36] or terrorism and does not directly connect them to speech. However, since the adoption of 2006 anti-terrorist statute,[37] Russia has banned not only terrorist practices but also the "ideology of violence,"[38] a concept that remains undefined in Russian legislation. The 2012 amendments to the anti-extremist statute allowed qualification of speech as extremist regardless of whether it incites violence. The connection between the Russian legal notions of extremism and terrorism has become very unclear. Russia ratified the 2005 CoE Convention on the Prevention of Terrorism[39] on 20 April 2006. Although the Convention prohibited "public provocation" and incitement to terrorism, it introduced several criteria to distinguish expressions protected under Article 10 of the ECHR and terror speech that the Russian law overlooks. The decree on terrorism of the Russian Supreme Court[40] has made this notion more in line with the CoE standards but this step is insufficient for full compliance.

The CoE standards has never required that member-states criminalise justification of terrorism, while Russia bans not only "public calls to commit terrorist activities" but also "propaganda of terrorism" and "public justification of terrorism." The latter is defined in Article 205.2 of the Russian Criminal Code as a "public claim recognising that the ideology and practice of terrorism are correct and need support as well as emulation." Additionally, the anti-terrorist statute bans "propaganda of terrorist ideas; dissemination of materials or information calling for the commitment of terrorist activities; or explaining or justifying the need to commit such activities." Thus, Russian ban on terror speech could cover any material trying to explain why terror acts could have happened. This approach contrasts with the CoE standards suggesting not to adopt "measures equating media reporting on terrorism with support for terrorism."[41]

---

[36] Shanghai Convention defines extremism as an act aimed at seizing or keeping power through the use of violence or changing violently the constitutional regime of a State, as well as a violent encroachment upon public security, including the organisation, for the above purposes, of illegal armed formations and participation in them, criminally prosecuted in conformity with the national laws of the Parties.

[37] Federal Statute of 6 March 2006, No. 35-FZ "On Counteracting Terrorism."

[38] Article 3 of this statute defined terrorism as an "ideology of violence" or "practice of influence" on the decisions of state bodies or international organisations combined with intimidation of the population or other unlawful violent activities.

[39] CoE Convention on the Prevention of Terrorism, No. 196, Adopted on May 16, 2005 in Warsaw. https://rm.coe.int/CoERMPublicCommonSearchServices/DisplayDCTMContent?documentId=090000168008371c, last accessed 2018/05/21.

[40] Decree of the Plenum of the Supreme Court of 9 February 2012, No. 1 "On Certain Issues of Judicial Practice on Terrorist Crimes."

[41] Declaration of the Committee of Ministers of the CoE "On Freedom of Expression and Information in the Media in the Context of the Fight against Terrorism," adopted on 2 March 2005 at the 917th meeting of the Ministers' Deputies. https://wcd.coe.int/ViewDoc.jsp?id=830679&Site=CM, last accessed 2018/05/12.

5   Calls for the Violation of Territorial Integrity and Extremism

Article 280.1, criminalising public calls for violating territorial integrity was added to the Russian Criminal Code in 2013, although more general Article 280, banning public calls for extremism, had already served that aim. Now, both articles may be used for that—at the discretion of courts or governmental bodies. The sanctions in Article 280.1 were tightened in July 2014, possibly in connection with the annexation of Crimea by Russia whose legitimacy was debated by some journalists and online users.

Russian law does not define what "calls for violation of territorial integrity" means and does not specify criteria for the consideration of such cases, thus allowing the perpetrators of such calls to be criminally convicted, even in cases when they have neither incited nor advocated violence. This represents a significant difference between the Russian and the CoE's approaches distinguishing speech inciting violence or armed resistance and sharp criticism of state policies, authorities, or institutions. While the former cannot be protected, from the CoE perspective, the latter may be shielded by ECHR as it serves free debates on the issues of public interest.[42]

6   Protection of Public Officials and Extremism

Article 128.1 of the Russian Criminal Code criminalises libel, which contradicts the CoE's perspective calling for decriminalisation of defamation.[43] The notion of libel is not sufficiently clear in Russian law that may have a "chilling effect" on free speech. The anti-extremist statute specifically bans "libel of public officials that alleges that they have committed extremist acts during the execution of their official duties." Therefore, courts are free to give more severe convictions for "extremist" libel including website blocking or media outlets shutdowns.

7   Sanctions for Extremist Speech in the Media and on the Internet

Article 20.29 of the Russian Code of Administrative Offences—the one most often applicable to media—bans the mass production and dissemination of extremist materials or the storage of such materials with the intention to distribute them. It is usually very complex to prove that media organisations store extremist materials without intending their dissemination. The Code in Article 13.15 also bans producing or disseminating media content that incites or justifies extremism. Additionally, it provides sanctions against media outlets for mentioning extremist organisations without saying that they have been banned in Russia.

---

[42] The ECtHR judgments, *Erdoğdu and İnce v. Turkey* and *Sürek and Özdemir v. Turkey.*

[43] Resolution 1577 (2007), "Towards Decriminalization of Defamation," adopted by the Assembly on 4 October 2007 (34th Sitting). Retrieved from http://assembly.coe.int/nw/xml/XRef/Xref-XML2HTML-en.asp?fileid=17588&lang=en, last accessed 2018/05/12.

Violations of anti-extremist law may lead to the closure of media outlet. The procedure is initiated by the Russian media regulating body Roskomnadzor or the Russian General Prosecutor. If an outlet gets two warnings within a year's time or fails to remedy the violation, it can be shut down. Such sanctions, as temporary or permanent closures of media outlets, are too severe and incompatible with the CoE standards.[44]

Since 2013, websites containing extremism can be blocked without a court's consideration, upon requests from the General Prosecutor or his deputies.[45] According to the latest available Roskomnadzor's Public Annual Report,[46] in 2016, 3,500 websites and/or webpages with extremist materials were blocked upon prosecutors' requests. The blocking procedure allows blocking access to entire websites, in contradiction to the ECtHR case law[47] suggesting removing illegal content only. Russian law lacks clear procedure for restoring access after removals of illegal information.

Russian law also allows blocking websites if they call for mass disorder or participation in mass actions "conducted in contravention of established procedures." No statute explains what it means, and by bringing this action under one umbrella with extremism, the statute virtually equates opposition activists with extremists. However, invitations for peaceful protest are protected under the ECHR and Russian Constitution.

In 2017, Russian law banned anonymizers and virtual private networks (VPNs) and legitimized blocking websites containing materials of "undesirable" foreign or international organisations as well as "information allowing access" to such content.[48] According to the SOVA Centre, links to the websites of "undesirable" organizations as well as any websites containing materials of such organisations or information calling for participation in mass actions are subject to the new regulations.

8 The Russian Higher Courts' Position on Anti-extremist Legislation

In 2013, the Russian Constitutional Court rejected consideration of the complaint[49] on the ambiguity of the notions of extremism and extremist materials. The Court justified their constitutionality by quoting the confusing provision of the Shanghai Convention

---

[44] The ECtHR judgment, *Ürper and Others v Turkey* of 20 October 2009.

[45] Federal Statute of the Russian Federation of 27 July 2006, No. 149-FZ "On Information, Information Technologies and Protection of Information."

[46] Retrieved from the official website of the Federal Service for Supervision of Communications, Information Technology, and Mass Media (Roskmnadzor). https://rkn.gov.ru/docs/doc_1646.pdf, last accessed 2018/05/25.

[47] The ECtHR judgment, *Ahmet Yildirim v Turkey* of 18 December 2012.

[48] Federal Statute of the Russian Federation "On Amending Articles 10.4 and 15.3 of the Federal Statute of the Russian Federation 'On Information, Information Technologies, and Protection of Information' and Article 6 of the Statute of the Russian Federation 'On Mass Media'," No. 327-FZ of 25 November 2017.

[49] Resolution of the Constitutional Court of the Russian Federation on the admissibility of the complaint by citizen V. S. Kochemarov, complaining about the violation of his constitutional rights by Article 1 paragraphs 1 and 3 and Article 13 paragraph 3 of the Federal Statute of the Russian Federation "On Counteraction of Extremism Activity," 2 July 2013.

that provides no justification for terrorism, separatism or extremism under any circumstances. Thus, the Court implied that no balancing test is required in extremist cases, which is inconsistent with the ECtHR standards. The only relatively positive development for Russian anti-extremist law were the Russian Supreme Court's efforts to prevent its excessive or arbitrary application by clarifying the legal concept of extremism and bringing it closer to the CoE's perspective. In the decree on extremism,[50] the Supreme Court specifically called for courts to ensure a balance between protecting of public interests, such as the constitutional order, territorial integrity and national security, and protecting of human rights and freedoms, such as freedoms of religion, speech and assembly. The Court also clarified that criticism of political or religious organisations, visions, national or religious customs cannot constitute incitement to hatred or strife. The Supreme Court attempted to incorporate a more nuanced approach used by the ECtHR to consider cases concerning on media. Its 2010 decree on the statute "On Mass Media"[51] instructed courts considering media cases to examine the language of a publication or a broadcast, its context, aim, genre, style and several other criteria. It also suggested that courts would check whether the media publications or broadcasts concern political debates, issues of public interest, whether they are based on interviews and what is a journalistic opinion to extreme speech in question. The decree on extremism also tried to diminish the protection of public officials by the anti-extremist legislation—it directly referred to the CoE standards stressing that public officials must accept wider criticism, particularly in the media, because it is "necessary for ensuring transparency and the responsible exercise of their functions."

Nonetheless, both highest Russian courts failed to limit the anti-extremist legal mechanism to the incitement of violence only.

9   The Court Practice on Extremism

In 2012–2017, 1,286 sentences for public extremist speech were given in Russia, according to the SOVA Center. It suggests that about 90% of them were imposed "lawfully," while others were deemed as "might be unlawful," "most likely, unlawful" or simply "unlawful." The increase in sentences on extremist speech—especially in 2013 and 2015 (see Fig. 1)—might be explained with the tightening of control over online speech in Russia as a consequence of the 2011–2012 mass protest movement as well as with the crackdown on critical speech after the Crimean conflict. The upward trend also results from the growth of the number of Internet users in the country.

Article 282 of the Criminal Code on public excitation of hatred or strife was by far the most applicable article among all others concerning extremist speech (see Fig. 2) in 2012–2017 (79% of all sentences on extremist speech). A possible explanation for this is the growth of racism and xenophobia in Russia, which was observed by the UN

---

[50] Decree of the Plenum of the Supreme Court of 28 June 2011, No. 11 "On Judicial Practice on Extremist Crimes."

[51] Decree of the Plenum of the Supreme Court of 15 June 2010, No. 16 "On the Practice of Application of the Statute of the Russian Federation 'On Mass Media' by Courts."

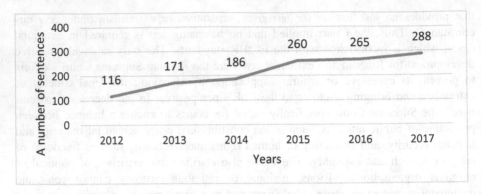

Fig. 1. An increase in sentences on extremist speech in Russia, 2012–2017.

Human Rights Committee in the 2015 Seventh Periodic Report on Russia. Interestingly, the share of lawful judgments under this article is high (91.24%), as follows from the SOVA Centre Database. The second largest group of sentences on extremist speech was for public calls to extremism (Article 280 of the Criminal Code). It represents around 16% of the total number of decisions on public extremist speech.

Sentences under "anti-terrorist" Article 205.2 amount to 3.58% of all judgments on extremist speech in 2012–2017. Decisions on the grounds of Articles 280.1 (public calls for violating territorial integrity) and 354.1 (rehabilitation of Nazism) together made up 1.56% (20 sentences) of the total number of sentences, most likely because these articles are relatively recent.

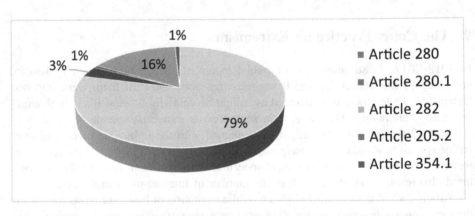

Fig. 2. Number of sentences on extremist speech in Russia, 2012–2017.

As SOVA Center [7] notes, in 2017, the focus was shifted from crackdown on the criticism of Russia's alleged role in the Ukraine conflict to strengthening of control over the opposition, local activists, and unconventional religious organizations but criminal convictions over incitement of hatred or enmity kept growing.

10   CoE Standards in Russian Court Practice

Cases for the analysis have been mostly selected proportionately to the frequency of the application of certain criminal articles by Russian courts. The largest group (77) is represented by decisions held on incitement of hatred or enmity (Article 282); 33 sentences have been examined on public calls for extremism (Article 280), 16 decisions on public calls for terrorism or its justification (Article 205.2), 3 decisions on public calls for violating territorial integrity (Article 280.1) and 2 decisions on rehabilitation of Nazism (Article 354.1). Additionally, we have included another 19 court rulings on administrative article (20.29) banning mass dissemination of extremist materials.

As the analysis showed, only a few sentences mention or quote the ECHR or other CoE standards. The Russian courts have mostly ignored the developments of the Supreme Court on extremism and refrained from explaining how they established a balance between the protection of free speech and of other legal rights and interests. Among all selected rulings, there were no not-guilty verdicts. Most of the sentences mentioned incitement to violence as the main cause for criminally convicting the accused persons. However, the decisions did not explain why or how the courts drew the conclusion that the publications' aim was to incite violence.

The overwhelming majority of sentences (97%) were given for the dissemination of extremist materials on the Internet, especially on the VK (77%), the most popular Russian-language social media platform in the world.[52] Rulings are largely based on conclusions of lower courts or experts. As Verhovskij, Ledovskih, and Sultanov [8] argue, the experts, tasked with making legal conclusions on extremism, often have no relevant qualifications. About 90% of sentences reviewed for the research provided no analysis of impugned publications—Russian courts mostly fail to thoroughly examine aims of publications, their genre, style, background, context and other criteria, as suggested by the Russian Supreme Court and ECtHR.

Russian general jurisdiction courts have mostly ignored the CoE concepts of public interest and broader limits of criticism towards public officials. For instance, sanctions under Article 280 were imposed on the citizen Karandaev[53] for posting on his VK account the comment, "We don't believe. We are for honest elections!!! Ufa." The court ruled that his publication was intended to interfere with the legitimate activity of government authorities during elections and, therefore, was extremist.

When considering media cases, courts said nothing on the important media's role in democracies, as prescribed by the CoE standards. In 2013, Klinkov, a journalist for the local newspaper, was criminally convicted for hate speech.[54] His publication represented harsh criticism of religious ideologies and institutions and stated the following: "Buddhism—to Asia. Judaism—to Palestine. Islam—to Mecca. Christianity—to

---

[52] Data about platforms for dissemination of information were removed from some rulings.

[53] Decision on the case of E. Karandaev, No. 1-8/14 of 14 January 2014, Magistrate Judge L. Fazlyeva of the Judicial District No. 5 in Kirovskiy District of the City of Ufa of the Republic of Bashkortostan.

[54] Decision on the case of A. Klinkov, No. 1-83/2013 of 4 April 2013, Central District Court of the City of Tyumen.

Byzantium and 'Tsarigrad'." Klinkov was a journalist whose article could deserve special protection, according to the CoE standards. While his article might be capable of inciting violence, it could also contribute to public debates on the increasing authority of religious institutions in secular Russia. This does not necessarily mean that the ECtHR would have protected Klinkov's speech, but it would have paid attention to these factors, while the Russian court ignored them.

In general, Russian courts tend to label speech as extremist even if it has no intention to incite violence—and this fundamentally contradicts the CoE approach. In 2017, Volkov, a supporter of the Russian oppositional leader Alexei Navalny, was charged under Article 354.1 for posting on his VK account a collage that shows "The Motherland Calls" Monument in the city of Volgograd painted in green.[55] This picture was posted after Alexei Navalny had been attacked with "brilliant green" dye, and it was aimed at drawing attention to this incident. Law enforcement authorities viewed this as public desecration of symbols of Russian military glory.

11 Conclusion

Russian legal concept on extremism mostly considerably contradicts the CoE standards on freedom of expression, and the contradiction has only increased over the last few years. Given the development of information and communication technologies and Russia's political alienation from the CoE, this national strategy does not seem to be unexpected. At the same time, the Russian case is an interesting example of how national (and "alternative" international) law can evolve to address ideological challenges. The Russian concept of extremism has the potential for further expansion including in other countries, where civil society allows to do so.

Russian government—or, better say, political establishment—consistently "improves" the legal concept on extremism by excessively limiting the opportunity to discuss the issues that may be sensitive from a political perspective. As a result, Russian legal concept on extremism lacks balance between protection of freedom of expression and public interests, that are, in fact, the interests of political establishment.

While the Russian anti-extremist law has emerged as a measure against terrorism and largely relies on the international legal ban on hate speech, its scope goes far beyond this aim. Russian law applies legal notions that may look similar to the one used by the CoE standards, such as "falsification of history," "insult of religious feelings," "justification of terrorism" but these notions are broadly misinterpreted in national legislation and arbitrarily applied in practice. In other words, the Russian law tries to imitate human rights concepts, rather than bringing them into line with the CoE vision in practice. Some of the unique Russian legal notions, such as "social hatred" or "the ban on supremacy," remain undefined. Many Russian free speech restrictions are untied under the notion of extremism nearly artificially. The redundancy and uncertainty of anti-extremist limitations and sanctions leaves a room for their selective

---

[55] Decision on the case of A. Volkov, No. 2-26/2017 of 23 October 2017, the Volgograd Regional Court.

implementation, promotes self-censorship and creates an effective mechanism for punishing political dissent in Russia.

Russian highest courts has differently contributed to the compliance of Russian law on extremism with the CoE perspective. The Russian Supreme Court has incorporated several CoE standards to the Russian policies. However, its contribution has been insufficient. The Constitutional Court's interpretations on extremism mostly deter proper implementation of the CoE standards. Russian courts of general jurisdiction mainly negate them in cases on extremism.

The increasing number of cases on extremism and extremist speech in Russia is worrying. While the share of unlawful decisions on these cases is not negligible, it is not very high. This may mean that the strategy of tightening regulation and introducing more severe sanctions does not lead to a decrease in the number of violations of anti-extremist legislation. To tackle these complex social phenomena, Russia should pay more attention to the CoE approach, which focuses on promoting tolerance, particularly in the media, rather than on banning and concealing information. The balance between countering extremism and respecting the right to freedom of expression should be found so that Internet freedom could be fully implemented by citizens.

References

1. Banisar, D.: Speaking of Terror. Council of Europe, Strasbourg (2008)
2. BBC: Pussy Riot: the story so far, 23 December 2013. http://www.bbc.com/news/world-europe-25490161. Accessed 21 May 2018
3. Grigorieva, L.V.: O nauchnom podhode k ugolovno-pravovoj ocenke dejstvij jekstremistskoj napravlennosti [On the scholarly approach to criminal and legal assessment of extremist actions]. Sovrem. Pravo 7, 99–105 (2015)
4. Ministry of Justice of the Russian Federation: The Federal Register of Extremist Materials (2018). http://minjust.ru/ru/extremist-materials. Accessed 15 June 2018
5. Richter, A.: One step beyond hate speech: Post-Soviet regulation of "extremist" and "terrorist" speech in the media. In: Herz, M., Molnar, P. (eds.) The Content and Context of Hate Speech: Rethinking Regulation and Responses, pp. 290–305. Cambridge University Press, New York (2012)
6. Savchenko, E.Y.: Jekstremizm i voprosy grazhdansko-pravovoj otvetstvennosti [Extremism and issues of civic and legal responsibility]. Pravoporjadok: istorija, teorija, praktika 1, 32–36 (2014)
7. SOVA Center: The illegal application of anti-extremist legislation in Russia in 2017 (2018). https://www.sova-center.ru/misuse/publications/2018/03/d38945. Accessed 30 May 2018
8. Verhovskij, A., Ledovskih, M., Sultanov, A.: Ostorozhno, extremism! Analiz zakono-datel'stva o protivodejstvii extremistskoj dejatel'nosti i praktiki ego primenenija [Be cautious, extremism! Analysis of the legislation on counteracting extremist activity and the practice of its application]. Elist, Voronezh (2013)

Methodologies for Studies of Online Audiences

A Self-organized Method for Computing the Epidemic Threshold in Computer Networks

Franco Bagnoli[1,2(✉)] ⓘ, Emanuele Bellini[3] ⓘ, and Emanuele Massaro[4] ⓘ

[1] Department of Physics and Astronomy and CSDC, University of Florence,
via G. Sansone 1, 50019 Sesto Fiorentino, Italy
franco.bagnoli@unifi.it
[2] INFN, Sez. di Firenze, Sesto Fiorentino, Italy
[3] Department of Information Engineering and CSDC, University of Florence,
via S. Marta 3, 50139 Florence, Italy
emanuele.bellini@unifi.it
[4] HERUS Lab, École Polytechnique Fédérale de Lausanne (EFPL),
GR C1 455 (Bâtiment GR) - Station 2, 1015 Lausanne, Switzerland
emanuele.massaro@epfl.ch

Abstract. In many cases, tainted information in a computer network can spread in a way similar to an epidemics in the human world. On the other had, information processing paths are often redundant, so a single infection occurrence can be easily "reabsorbed". Randomly checking the information with a central server is equivalent to lowering the infection probability but with a certain cost (for instance processing time), so it is important to quickly evaluate the epidemic threshold for each node. We present a method for getting such information without resorting to repeated simulations. As for human epidemics, the local information about the infection level (risk perception) can be an important factor, and we show that our method can be applied to this case, too. Finally, when the process to be monitored is more complex and includes "disruptive interference", one has to use actual simulations, which however can be carried out "in parallel" for many possible infection probabilities.

Keywords: Multiplex networks · Risk perception
Epidemic spreading

1 Introduction

We deal here with the problem of the spreading of tainted information in an unsupervised computer network, such as algorithmic (high frequency) trading [7],

The main competitive advantage (given the same information) is the processing time [13], which prevents the possibility of checking the information against a central database. However, in this way a tainted information may quickly spread and "contaminate" the whole network, in a way similar to what happens for epidemic in the human world. We have to consider, however, that in many cases

© Springer Nature Switzerland AG 2018
S. S. Bodrunova (Ed.): INSCI 2018, LNCS 11193, pp. 119–130, 2018.
https://doi.org/10.1007/978-3-030-01437-7_10

the information is processed in a redundant way, so that the tainted information can actually diffuse only if it is able to survive and spread in the network, much like an infection which has to fight against the defences of hosts.

Well-known results from the theoretical epidemiology field show that there is a strict relationship between the infection probability τ, the average number of contacts $\langle k \rangle$ and its variance, i.e., $\langle k^2 \rangle$: the critical value τ_c for the onset of an epidemic is $\tau_c = \frac{\langle k \rangle}{\langle k^2 \rangle} \simeq \langle k \rangle^{-1}$ for sharp-distributed networks [12]. In many cases however the contact network can be approximated by a scale-free distribution with diverging variance, for which there is no hope of controlling epidemics only by reducing the infection probability [14,16].

The influence of risk perception in epidemic spreading has been studied for human epidemics [3], where the knowledge about the diffusion of disease among neighbours (without knowing who is actually infected) lowers the effective probability of transmission. For regular, random, Watts-Strogatz small-world and non-assortative scale-free networks with exponent $\gamma > 3$ there is always a finite level of precaution parameter for which the epidemic goes extinct [12]. For scale-free networks with $\gamma < 3$ the precaution level depends on the cut-off of the power-law, which at least depends on the finite number of the nodes of the network.

In humans, information about the disease may not come from physical contacts, but rather from the "virtual" social contact networks [8,10,15]. Clearly, one expects that if these two networks are completely different, the perception of the risk is of less value than when the two networks coincide. Again, this is a common situation also for automatic trading and computer networks.

In a computer network, a node can indeed choose not to accept the processing of an incoming information, but this refusal also has a certain cost. In other words, it is sometimes preferable to suspend the information processing than risking the elaboration of false data, according with the cost of such operation. We can model this situation by assuming that the tainted information can propagate with a certain probability, that may depend on the knowledge one has about the infection levels in the network or at least in its neighbourhood. This infection probability is however also a measure of the cost of processing. In order to lower the infection probability one may have for instance to contact a central server, lowering also the transaction frequency. On the other hand, information processing paths are often redundant, so a single infection occurrence can be easily "cured" by other nodes, assuming that all nodes cooperate, sharing the cost.

It is therefore vital to quickly assess the epidemic threshold for a given network (that may change in time), with real-time estimates of the infection probability threshold, that may change from node to node. The optimal probability is that just below the epidemic threshold, in which the cost of checking is minimal but the tainted information cannot diffuse and is eliminated in the long time limit by the redundancy of information-processing paths.

We present here a method (first introduced in Ref. [4] and extended in Ref. [12]) that can be applied in such situations. The proposed method allows

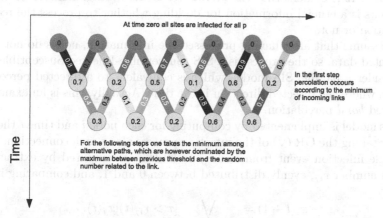

Fig. 1. Evolution of the local minimum value of the percolation parameter p_i for a 1D regular network with $k = 2$.

to obtain the epidemic threshold in just one run, without having to repeat the simulation with many tentative infection probabilities, looking for the outbreak threshold. This method can be considered an example of self-organized criticality [6], in which a system automatically discovers the critical value of a parameter. In particular, it is very reminiscent of the Bak-Sneppen evolutionary model [5]. The proposed method can be directly implemented in computer networks, allowing nodes to exchange also their estimated epidemic threshold.

Epidemic models are characterized by a monotone increasing of the probability of being contaminated with the number of infected neighbours, and this characteristic allows to explicitly obtain the epidemic threshold by the self-organized critical method. We can consider also other processes, for instance with an "interference" among infective agents, and in general processed based on generic local rules like cellular automata [9]. However, in this cases the monotonicity is lost and one has to consider more complex data structures [4].

2   The Infection Model

We consider a set of N nodes x_i, with two states: 0 for "healthy" and 1 for "tainted" (or contaminated). Node i process information coming from other nodes j, defined by an adjacency matrix $a_{ij} = 1(0)$ for connected (disconnected) nodes. We define the input connectivity of node i as $k_i = \sum_j a_{ij}$. We assume that if a node i is tainted, it can "infect" other nodes with a probability τ, that for the moment is fixed.

Let us start with a simple percolation model: a node i can be infected by each of its k neighbors separately with a probability τ, so that if s of them are infected, the total infection probability $q(s, k_i)$ is

$$q(s, k_i) = 1 - (1 - \tau)^s \simeq s\tau$$

for small τ. It is evident that the knowledge of the average number of infected neighbours is a crucial information for deciding whether to process the received information or not.

We assume that after having processed the information, nodes do not retain any tainted data, so the process is a SIS (Susceptible-Infected-Susceptible) one. We consider a parallel SIS model, which is equivalent to a directed percolation problem where the directed direction is the time. Actually, this is an example of a directed *bond* percolation.

This model is implemented by computing for each node i and time t the state $x_i(t)$ by taking the OR ($\vee$) of the infection process along each connection, where the single infection event from node j to node i is computed by extracting a random number r_{ij}, evenly distributed between 0 and 1, and comparing it with τ, i.e.,

$$x_i(t+1) = \bigvee_{j=j_1^{(i)},\ldots,j_{k_i}^{(i)}} [\tau > r_{ij}(t)] x_j(t), \tag{1}$$

where $\vee$ represents the OR operator and the multiplication represents the AND. The square bracket represents the truth function, $[\cdot] = 1$ if "$\cdot$" is true, and zero otherwise. The quantity $r_{ij}(t)$ is a random number between 0 and 1, drawn independently for each triplet i, j, t.

Alternatively one can study the *site* percolation process, where the node x_i first processes all incoming information and then, probabilistically (π), checks the result. In this case the dynamics is

$$x_i(t+1) = [\pi > r_i(t)] \bigvee_{j=j_1^{(i)},\ldots,j_{k_i}^{(i)}} x_j(t). \tag{2}$$

In the case of risk perception, we assume that τ is replaced by a probability $u(s, k_i)$ that a site i with connectivity k_i is infected by any one of its s infected neighbours as

$$u(s, k_i) = \tau f(s; J), \tag{3}$$

where τ is the "bare" infection probability and $f(s; J)$ is a monotonic decreasing function of the number of infected neighbours s, depending on some parameter J. For instance, in Ref. [3], the probability $u(s, k_i)$ was assumed to be

$$u(s, k_i) = \tau \exp\left(-J \frac{s}{k_i}\right), \tag{4}$$

The idea is that the perception of the risk, given by the percentage of infected neighbours and modulated by the factor J, effectively lowers the infection probability because the node checks the received information against the central server, paying the delay.

3   The Self-organized Percolation Method

The basic idea is that each node i estimates its own minimum value τ_i of the infection probability, or the maximum value of the precaution J_c for barely being

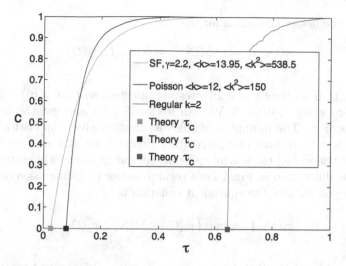

Fig. 2. Asymptotic number of infected individuals c versus the bare infection probability τ for the SIS dynamics for different networks. From left to right, for $c = 0$: Scale Free (SF), Random (Poisson), Regular. Here $N = 10000$.

infected. Iterating this procedure for long time, we find the critical value of the parameters for having the smallest surviving epidemics, for the given choice of the random numbers $r_i(t)$.

Once chosen, these random numbers behave like a quenched field. In principle the epidemic threshold is given by the average over the statistical ensemble, i.e., over many repetitions of the processes. However, in many cases the process is self-averaging [1], i.e., a large enough system gives the same results as the whole statistical ensemble, possibly inducing some small error in the determination of the critical threshold, since in this case the correlation length diverges.

Let us pretend that we are performing several simulations of the bond percolation process in parallel, with different values of τ but using the same set of random numbers. Due to the "monotonic" character of the infection, if, for a given site i and time t, the percolation stops for some value of τ, it stops also for all lower values. We can therefore replace $x_i(t)$ by $[\tau > \tau_i(t)]$ (or $[\pi > \pi_i(t)]$ for the site problem).

For the bond percolation problem, Eq. (1) becomes:

$$[\tau > \tau_i(t+1)] = \bigvee_{j=j_1^{(i)},\dots,j_{k_i}^{(i)}} [\tau > r_{ij}(t)][\tau > \tau_j(t)]. \qquad (5)$$

Since $[\tau > a][\tau > b]$ is equal to $[\tau > \max(a,b)]$ and $[\tau > a] \vee [\tau > b]$ is equal to $[\tau > \min(a,b)]$, Eq. (5) becomes:

$$[\tau > \tau_i(t+1)] = \left[\tau > \left(\min_{j=j_1^{(i)},\dots,j_{k_i}^{(i)}} \max\big(r_{ij}(t),\tau_j(t)\big)\right)\right], \qquad (6)$$

and we get the desired equation for the τ_i's

$$\tau_i(t+1) = \underset{j=j_1^{(i)},\ldots,j_{k_i}^{(i)}}{\text{MIN}} \max\big(r_{ij}(t), \tau_j(t)\big). \tag{7}$$

Let assume that at time $t = 0$ all sites are infected, so that $x_i(0) = 1 \ \forall \tau$. We can therefore write $\tau_i(0) = 0$. We can iterate Eq. (7) and get the asymptotic distribution of τ_i. The minimum of this distribution gives the critical value τ_c for which there is at least one percolating cluster with at least one "infected" site at large times, i.e., there is an epidemic spreading in the whole system. This procedure is illustrated in Fig. 1 for a regular lattice in 1 dimension and $k = 2$.

For site percolation, the equivalent equation is

$$\pi_i(t+1) = \max\Big(r_i(t), \underset{j=j_1^{(i)},\ldots,j_{k_i}^{(i)}}{\text{MIN}} \pi_j(t)\Big). \tag{8}$$

We investigated the SIS dynamics over regular, Poisson and scale-free networks as shown in Fig. 2. In particular we evaluated the critical epidemic threshold values τ_c for which there is at least one percolating clusters with at least one infected nodes (points marked "Theory τ_c" in Fig. 2).

Considering a regular lattice with connectivity degree $k = 2$, we found $\tau_c \simeq 0.6447$ which is compatible with the results of the bond percolation transition in the Domany-Kinzel model [9]. In the case of random networks with Poisson degree distributions the critical epidemic threshold is $\tau_c = \langle k \rangle / \langle k^2 \rangle \simeq \langle k \rangle^{-1}$ if the distribution is sharp [14]. Indeed, for a Poisson network with $\langle k \rangle = 12$ the self-organized percolation method gives $\tau_c \simeq 0.08 \simeq 1/12$. For a scale-free network with $\langle k \rangle = 13.95$ and $\langle k^2 \rangle = 538.5$ we get from simulations $\tau_c \simeq 0.026$, in agreement with the expected value.

Now, let us apply the method to a more difficult problem, for which the percolation probability depends on the fraction of infected sites in the neighbourhood (risk perception), es expressed by Eq. 3. In this case we want to find the extremal value of the parameter J for which there is no spreading of the infection at large times.

Again, we can replace $x_i(t)$ by $[u > u_i(t)]$ and invert the relation $u_i(t) = \tau f(s; J)$ so that at the end one gets an equation for the $x_i(t)$ like $[J \lessgtr J_i(t)]$ which can be iterated.

Let us consider for illustration the case of Eq. (4). The quantity $[u > r] = [\tau \exp(-Js/k) > r]$ is equivalent to $[J < -(k/s)\ln(r/\tau)]$. Therefore Eq. (5) is replaced by

$$[J < J_i(t+1)] = \bigvee_{j=j_1^{(i)},\ldots,j_{k_i}^{(i)}} \Big[J < -\frac{k_i}{s_i}\ln\Big(\frac{r_{ij}(t)}{\tau}\Big)\Big] [J < J_j(t)] \tag{9}$$

where

$$s_i \equiv s_i(J) = \sum_{j=j_1^{(i)},\ldots,j_{k_i}^{(i)}} x_j = \sum_{j=j_1^{(i)},\ldots,j_{k_i}^{(i)}} [J_j(t) \geq J]. \tag{10}$$

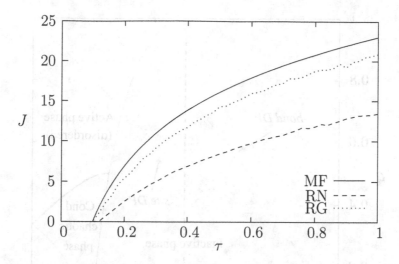

Fig. 3. Critical level J_c for which the infection is stopped, for networks with fixed or peaked connectivity $k = 10$ and $N = 1000$ in the mean-field (MF), regular (RN) and random (RG) case.

So

$$[J < J_i(t+1)] = \bigvee_{j=j_1^{(i)},\dots,j_{k_i}^{(i)}} \left[J < -\frac{k_i}{s_i(J_j(t))} \ln \left(\frac{r_{ij}(t)}{\tau} \right) \right] [J < J_j(t)] \quad (11)$$

and therefore

$$J_i(t+1) = \underset{j=j_1^{(i)},\dots,j_{k_i}^{(i)}}{\text{MAX}} \min \left(-\frac{k_i}{s_i(J_j(t))} \ln \left(\frac{r_{ij}(t)}{\tau} \right), J_j(t) \right). \quad (12)$$

Analogously to the previous case, the critical value of J_c is obtained by taking the maximum value of the $J_i(t)$ for some large (but finite) value of t.

The results are quite interesting compared with the simple SIS dynamics, for which there is always an epidemic threshold (Fig. 2). By inserting the risk perception it is possible to stop the epidemic for every value of the bare infection probability τ up to $\tau = 1$, for networks with finite variance. Let us consider for instance the case of random networks with $\langle k \rangle = 10$; for which for the simple infection process we found a critical value $\tau_c = 0.165$. As shown in Fig. 3, beyond this value of τ_c the epidemics can still be stopped if all agents adopt a sufficiently high precaution level J. The same consideration can be done also for the other scenarios.

However, as reported in Ref. [3], for some scale-free networks even the perception of the risk is not able to stop the epidemics, and one has to resort to more specialized techniques, like using special precautions for hubs, which is what is usually done also in the computer world.

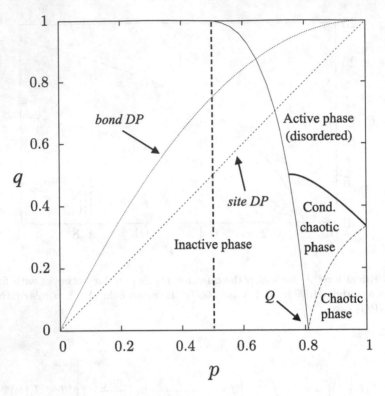

Fig. 4. The phase diagram of the Domany-Kinzel cellular automaton model. In the quiescent phase only the state with 0 infected sites is stable. In the active phase the state 0 is unstable and the average number of infected sites is larger than 0. In this phase the long-time evolution only depends on the initial condition, so it may be defined disordered. In the conditionally chaotic and chaotic phase the evolution depends on the initial condition and therefore varies when the configuration is varied (therefore "chaotic"). In the chaotic phase this dependence occurs for all implementations, in the conditionally chaotic one only for some particular computational scheme.

4   Non Monotonic Infection Probability

The self-organized method for finding the epidemic threshold relies on the monotonicity of the infection probability f with respect to the considered parameter, Eq. (3).

However, not all processes fulfils this requirement. In particular, if there is a "disruptive interference" among possible spreaders that diminishes the infection probability, it may happen that a larger number of infected neighbours actually slows down the epidemics.

In order to illustrate this problem, let us consider the Domany-Kinzel model [9]. It is probably the simplest model on a regular one-dimensional lattice with nearest-neighbours interactions still presenting an interesting phase diagram 4. The DK model is a totalistic cellular automaton with $k = 2$ inputs, so

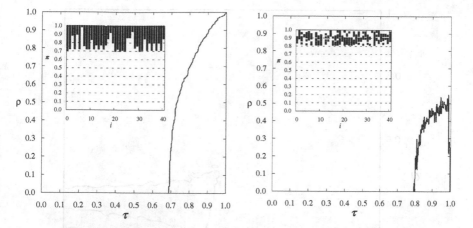

Fig. 5. Left: the average density (ρ) as a function of the bare infection probability τ and in the inset the distribution of the values of π_i for which the infection reaches site i (black bar) for the site percolation problem in a regular network with $k = 2$ (DK model, $p = q$). Right: the average density (ρ) as a function of the bare infection probability τ and in the inset the distribution of the values of π_i for which the infection reaches site i (black bar) for the a "nonlinear" (XOR) percolation problem in a regular network with $k = 2$ (DK model $q = 0$).

it is defined by 3 transition probabilities $\tau(1|n)$ which is the probability that a site will be infected in the following time step if n of its neighbours are infected, $n = 0, 1, 2$. Since the appearance of new infected individuals in a healthy population is a rare event, we set $\tau(1|0) = 0$. The other two parameters are $p = \tau(1|1)$ and $q = \tau(1|2)$.

This model generalizes the bond and site percolation problems, as shown in Fig. 4. Above the line marked "bond DP" there is a synergistic infectious effect: the probability of being infected by two contaminated neighbours is higher that the "superposition" of the two separate events. Below the line marked "site DP" there is an interference effect, and the probability of being infected by two simultaneous contaminated neighbours is less than the probability of being infected by just one of them.

The self-organized method works above the site DP line, as illustrated in Fig. 5 for $q = p$ and $q = 0$. In the insets, the asymptotic distribution of the infection for sites and for all values of the parameter p is shown. One can see that the corresponding segments are compact for the site percolation problem $q = p$, white they are fragmented for $q = 0$. This means that in the first case one can simply iterate the computation for the lower end of the segment, which is the essence of the self-organized method (Fig. 1 and Eq. (7)).

For the rest of the phase diagram, one can resort to a parallel computation for many values of the parameters, simply by coding the possible statuses using multi-bit technique, as described in Ref. [4]. In Fig. 6 the result of such computation keeping fixed q and sampling p using 64 bits (indicated by p_j, $j = 1, \ldots, 64$)

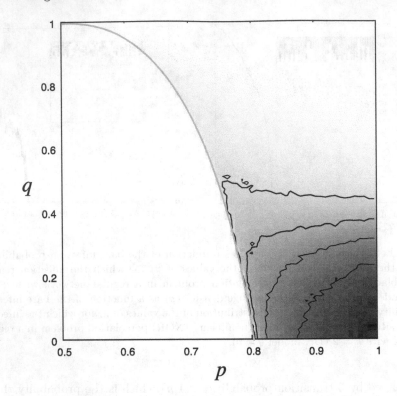

Fig. 6. Regions in the DK model where the infection probability shows negative variation (non-monotonicity). The implementation scheme coincides with that giving the conditionally chaotic phase in Fig. 4. The contour curves are for the density of negative variation equal to 0.10, 0.15, 0.20, 0.25. Computation for 10,000 time steps, $N = 10,000$, q fixed in steps of 0.01 and p sampled in 64 equally-spaced points from 0.5 to 1.

is reported. The quantity shown is the number of "holes" in the segments, i.e., the number of times for which is a given site one has infection for a certain value p_j while the site is not infected for p_{j+1}. One can see that the region for which the infection probability shows such negative changes is concentrated around the corner $p = 1, q = 0$, i.e., where the interference effect is larger. By comparison with Fig. 4, is seems that this region coincides with the chaotic one, i.e., the region in which the evolution of the system depends also on the initial conditions, and not only on the choice of the random numbers [2,11].

5   Conclusions

We investigated the problem of epidemic spreading of tainted data on computer networks, exploiting a self-organized method, that automatically gives the percolation threshold in just one simulation.

We showed that this method can be extended by considering the knowledge of the local infection level, and that this element may allow to halt an infection even for large "bare" infection probabilities. The method can be extended also to the case in which the knowledge about the infection comes from sourced partially different from the ones that actually communicate the "disease", provided that this difference is not too large.

Finally, we considered the case of more complex processes, including "disruptive interference" among spreaders. In this case the probability of being infected for a given site at an asymptotic time is not monotonous with the control parameters, and our self-organized method cannot be used. In these cases one can however exploit the self-averaging character of the problem, and carry out parallel simulations using multi-bit coding and just one or two random numbers per site. For the Domany-Kinzel cellular automaton, the region for which the self-organized method is not applicable seems to coincide with the "chaotic" one, for which the evolution is not only given by the choice of random numbers, but is still dependent on the initial state.

In the future, we shall work to develop a security protocol based on such scheme and test it on more realistic computer networks and processes.

References

1. Aharony, A., Harris, A.B.: Absence of self-averaging and universal fluctuations in random systems near critical points. Phys. Rev. Lett. **77**, 3700–3703 (1996). https://doi.org/10.1103/PhysRevLett.77.3700
2. Bagnoli, F.: On damage-spreading transitions. J. Stat. Phys. **85**, 151 (1996). https://doi.org/10.1007/BF02175559
3. Bagnoli, F., Liò, P., Sguanci, L.: Risk perception in epidemic modeling. Phys. Rev. E **76**, 061904 (2007). https://doi.org/10.1103/PhysRevE.76.061904
4. Bagnoli, F., Palmerini, P., Rechtman, R.: Algorithmic mapping from criticality to self-organized criticality. Phys. Rev. E **55**, 3970–3976 (1997). https://doi.org/10.1103/PhysRevE.55.3970
5. Bak, P., Sneppen, K.: Punctuated equilibrium and criticality in a simple model of evolution. Phys. Rev. Lett. **71**, 4083–4086 (1993). https://doi.org/10.1103/PhysRevLett.71.4083
6. Bak, P., Tang, C., Wiesenfeld, K.: Self-organized criticality: an explanation of the 1/f noise. Phys. Rev. Lett. **59**, 381–384 (1987). https://doi.org/10.1103/PhysRevLett.59.381
7. Carrion, A.: Very fast money: high-frequency trading on the NASDAQ. J. Financ. Mark. **16**(4), 680–711 (2013). https://doi.org/10.1016/j.finmar.2013.06.005. High-Frequency Trading
8. Chew, C., Eysenbach, G.: Pandemics in the age of Twitter: content analysis of tweets during the 2009 H1N1 outbreak. PLoS One **5**(11), e14118 (2010). https://doi.org/10.1371/journal.pone.0014118
9. Domany, E., Kinzel, W.: Equivalence of cellular automata to Ising models and directed percolation. Phys. Rev. Lett. **53**, 311–314 (1984). https://doi.org/10.1103/PhysRevLett.53.311

10. Ginsberg, J., Mohebbi, M., Patel, R., Brammer, L., Smolinski, M., Brilliant, L.: Detecting influenza epidemics using search engine query data. Nature **457**, 1012–1014 (2009). https://doi.org/10.1038/nature07634

11. Hinrichsen, H., Weitz, J.S., Domany, E.: An algorithm-independent definition of damage spreading–application to directed percolation. J. Stat. Phys. **88**(3), 617–636 (1997). https://doi.org/10.1023/B:JOSS.0000015165.83255.b7

12. Massaro, E., Bagnoli, F.: Epidemic spreading and risk perception in multiplex networks: a self-organized percolation method. Phys. Rev. E **90**, 052817 (2014). https://doi.org/10.1103/PhysRevE.90.052817

13. Menkveld, A.J.: High frequency trading and the new market makers. J. Financ. Mark. **16**(4), 712–740 (2013). https://doi.org/10.1016/j.finmar.2013.06.006

14. Pastor-Satorras, R., Vespignani, A.: Epidemic spreading in scale-free networks. Phys. Rev. Lett. **86**, 3200–3203 (2001). https://doi.org/10.1103/PhysRevLett.86.3200

15. Scanfeld, D., Scanfeld, V., Larson, E.L.: Dissemination of health information through social networks: Twitter and antibiotics. Am. J. Infect. Control. **38**(3), 182–188 (2010). https://doi.org/10.1016/j.ajic.2009.11.004

16. Yang, L.X., Yang, X., Liu, J., Zhu, Q., Gan, C.: Epidemics of computer viruses: a complex-network approach. Appl. Math. Comput. **219**(16), 8705–8717 (2013). https://doi.org/10.1016/j.amc.2013.02.031

Exploring Influence of Topic Segmentation on Information Retrieval Quality

Gennady Shtekh[1], Polina Kazakova[1(✉)], Nikita Nikitinsky[2],
and Nikolay Skachkov[3]

[1] National University of Science and Technology MISIS,
Leninsky Avenue 4, 119049 Moscow, Russia
kazakova1537@gmail.com
[2] Integrated Systems, Vorontsovskaya Street 35B Building 3, Room 413,
109147 Moscow, Russia
[3] Lomonosov Moscow State University, Leninskie Gory 1, 119991 Moscow, Russia

Abstract. In the present paper we address the issue of how an information retrieval system might be improved via text segmentation and to what extent. We assume that topic text segmentation allows one to better model text structure and therefore language itself, which influences the quality of text representation. We propose a search pipeline based on text segmentation by means of *BigARTM* tool and *TopicTiling* algorithm. We test the initial hypothesis by conducting experiments with several baseline models on two textual collections. The results are rather contradictory: while one collection showed that segmentation does improve the quality of retrieval, the other one demonstrated that segmentation does not influence the quality significantly.

Keywords: Information retrieval · Text segmentation
Topic modeling · Querying by example

1 Introduction

Nowadays, search interfaces such as Google or Yandex has become a de-facto standard for accessing the Internet. Most users choose a search engine according to the quality of retrieved documents ranking. Accordingly, one may name the quality of search the most crucial parameter of any search engine.

In the present paper we address the issue of how an information retrieval (IR) system might be improved via text segmentation and to what extent. Some researchers (see [6,7,16]) discussed applying text segmentation in IR tasks but the results appear to be rather disputable and the present state of the field thereby remains unclear.

P. Kazakova, N. Nikitinsky and N. Skachkov—Equal contribution.

© Springer Nature Switzerland AG 2018
S. S. Bodrunova (Ed.): INSCI 2018, LNCS 11193, pp. 131–140, 2018.
https://doi.org/10.1007/978-3-030-01437-7_11

In the domain of text segmentation there are various approaches to splitting text into semantically homogeneous blocks. Among them, segmentation methods by means of lexical chains and topic modeling are predominant. The former technique is based on the hypothesis that the vocabulary within a segment is coherent while a change in the vocabulary indicates a topic shift and therefore a segment boundary [2,5]. The main disadvantage of the segmentation based on lexical chains is that it requires thesauri such as WordNet.

Segmentation by means of topic modeling does not have this disadvantage while it requires a reasonably large document collection for building a topic model. This segmentation approach usually implies incorporating additional assumptions about text structure into standard topic models, mainly LDA. For instance, [4] proposes a complex LDA-based topic segmentation model that allows one to detect segment boundaries in documents while training a model. Another approach is *TopicTiling* [17]: it allows one to use any pretrained topic model for segment boundaries estimation.

The rest of the paper is structured as follows. In the next section we introduce the main hypothesis that topic segmentation could be useful in IR tasks and provide motivation behind it. Section 3 briefly describes the method for topic text segmentation used in our experiments. Section 4 proposes the general pipeline of a search process and Sect. 5 provides details about the experiments where we test the proposed pipeline based on segmentation against the same pipeline without segmentation. Section 6 presents the results of the experiments and in Sect. 7 we formulate the main contribution of the paper and suggest the ideas for future research.

2   Motivation

Intuitive motivation for the fact that text segmentation would improve the quality of search could be expressed in two abstract ideas. The former one is a rather fundamental notion that the better we model a language and its features, the better should work any model or algorithm applied to language data. We suppose that a natural language text is not a chaotic set of topics but a topically structured entity: in real speech we first introduce a topic, then move to another one, and in such a way topics follow each other, and it might be useful in computational tasks to model this segment structure. Topic segmentation would allow one to separate semantically distinctive parts of texts revealing more coherent and homogeneous segments that are easier to operate.

The latter argument comes from practical considerations. In the standard ad hoc retrieval task a user usually does not need whole documents in the output of an IR system, but only short paragraphs best matching to a given query. Thus, the objective of the ad hoc retrieval is not only to find relevant documents, but also to select the most relevant parts of them (this idea was previously discussed in [16]). In the present paper we describe a slightly different IR case where users query not by short keyword phrases but by document examples. In this situation splitting long documents into shorter parts might be useful for users too as it helps them to understand the connection between a query document and a retrieved document by demonstrating which segments of a query document match to which segments of a retrieved document. These matching segments also function as quasi-snippets.

Technical motivation for operating on relatively short paragraphs instead of long documents in information retrieval (as well as in other NLP) tasks is rather straightforward: a great number machine learning algorithms, including topic modeling and embedding techniques, may demonstrate significant quality loss while processing long texts.

Consider the case of *tf-idf* or BM-25 ranking formula. Suppose we have a query of a certain length and a document that is consisted of several paragraphs so that one of these paragraphs contains a sufficient rate of keywords from the given query (i.e. one paragraph is extremely relevant and others are not). If an IR retrieval system works on paragraphs instead of documents, the score between the query and the relevant paragraph would be higher (and the scores between the query and the other paragraphs would be lower) than the score between the query and the document in standard situation as the document-length penalty would be lower. Operating on document constituents thereby allows one to distinguish the most relevant parts of texts.

Considering more complex techniques, for example, various algorithms of paragraph embeddings (`doc2vec` or even simple averaging of `word2vec` vectors), one might notice that embeddings of large documents are usually inconcrete. The reason is again that as the document length increases, the number of various meanings contained in it usually increases too, and more diverse contexts appear. Any averaging (simple or more complex) of these contexts would therefore give rather inaccurate results.

3 Topic Segmentation

In our work, for text segmentation we propose to use a technique introduced in [18]. It is based on topic modeling, namely Additive Regularization of Topic Models [20].

As in [18], topic segmentation is done in two steps:

1. First, a topic model is constructed under the so-called sparsity assumption which states that words in a segment should have the same small set of topics. This assumption allows one to impose additional regularizer at the E-step of the expectation-maximization algorithm that is used to build the model. Segment borders are then estimated gradually: at the first iteration sentence boundaries are used as an initial segmental structure, at each further E-step adjacent segments are merged if they have the same topics since we suppose that topics stay permanent within segments while two adjacent segments should not have a lot of topics in common; for more detail see [18]. This step is done via *BigARTM* tool [19].

2. Second, *TopicTiling* algorithm [17] is applied to the output of the model build during the previous step. For each sentence boundary, the algorithm considers

left and right windows of a certain length and computes a cosine distance between them. Then the calculated distances are smoothed (the resulting scores are called *depth scores*) and the candidates with the final score more than a chosen threshold are proposed to be segment borders.

We compute the threshold using the following formula:

$$threshold = \mathbb{E}[ds] - \alpha\sqrt{\mathbb{E}[ds^2] - (\mathbb{E}[ds])^2},$$

where $\mathbb{E}[ds]$ is the mean of depth scores, $\sqrt{\mathbb{E}[ds^2] - (\mathbb{E}[ds])^2}$ is the standard deviation of depth scores, and α is a coefficient that one might vary to change the granularity of segmentation. The default α value is 0.5.

Figure 1 demonstrates an example of segments boundaries determination for a document. Each sentence ending with a depth score higher than a chosen threshold (a horizontal dotted line) are considered to be a segment border.

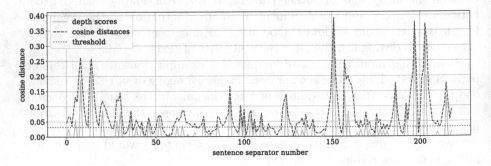

Fig. 1. Depth scores and cosine distances for an example document.

4   Methodology

We propose to use the following search pipeline.

First, common text preprocessing steps have to take place.

The next step is to divide whole documents into quasi-paragraphs - relatively small semantically coherent parts. At this step we use the method described in Sect. 3.

Next, an inverted index (paragraphs-to-documents) is constructed to enable further paragraph-to-document matching.

The resulting paragraphs have to be vectorized. In the next section we describe several baseline models that are used at this step in our experiments.

Thus, the retrieval process is done as follows:

1. The query document is segmented into paragraphs.
2. Paragraphs of the query document are vectorized.

3. For each paragraph vector relevant paragraphs from the corpus are retrieved by means of *Faiss* library [9]. These retrieved paragraphs could also be used as snippets to the corresponding documents.
4. Documents corresponding to the resulting relevant paragraphs are retrieved using inverted index, relevance scores are aggregated.
5. Documents are ranked and outputted.

Figure 2 illustrates the process described above. Note that such a methodology is based on the assumption that documents might be relevant if they have relevant paragraphs.

The question of scores aggregation poses another challenge. The result of the steps 1–4 for each pair of query and corpus documents is the $n \times m$ matrix where n is the number of paragraphs in a query document, m is the number of paragraphs in a corpus document, and elements are similarities between corresponding paragraphs. What is the best way to compute the distance between two documents given this matrix and the fact that one would prefer more discriminative and semantically informative paragraphs to contribute more to the final score? Furthermore, segmentation granularity influences the dimensionality of this matrix.

5   Experimental Setup

5.1   Data

As training data we use two publicly available collections: a collection of electronic preprints from the arXiv repository and a collection of Wikipedia articles. These datasets are used to train the segment model (see Sect. 3). We trained two segment models separately.

To test the quality of retrieval we use the automatically generated triplet datasets following the methodology described in [3]: the arXiv test set consists of triplets containing a query paper, a paper relevant to the query one (has the same subject), and a paper that is not relevant (two papers do not have any common subjects); the Wikipedia test set is constructed following the same principle: two articles are considered to be relevant to each other if they share at least one category. Approximately 140 000 preprints in total was collected. For the arXiv collection the train dataset consists of 95 000 preprints, and the test set consists of 45 000 unique preprints that form 15 715 triplets. For the Wikipedia collection the train dataset consists of 100 000 articles, and the test set consists of 58 000 articles that constitute 19 244 triplets.

We use *spaCy*[1] toolkit [8] to perform the preprocessing steps including tokenization and lemmatization. Note that we preserve sentence separators to allow further topic segmentation (since they are used as the initial approximation of segment boundaries, see Sect. 3). Additionally, as the arXiv data comes from processed pdf files, we use a set of rules to clean the text of preprints (removing short strings and mathematical symbols and formulae).

---

[1] https://spacy.io/.

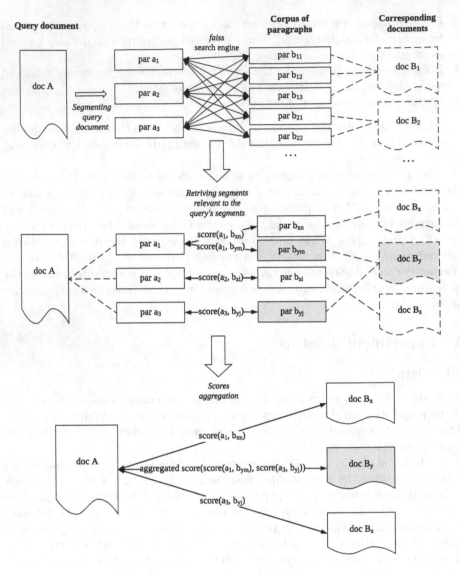

Fig. 2. General schema of the proposed retrieval process.

5.2   Baselines

We test several vectorization models:

- *ARTM:* the same model that was used for text segmentation. Unlike all the other baselines, the model is trained on the arXiv or Wikipedia training data.
- `word2vec`: a well known tool [13] for producing vectors corresponding to a given word. We obtain an embedding corresponding to a given segment by averaging its component word embeddings. We use a publicly available

word2vec model trained on Wikipedia[2]. We test two various approaches: simple averaging ($avW2V$) and averaging of normalized word vectors ($avnormW2V$).

- *GloVe:* an alternative approach for producing word vector representations [15]. We use a publicly available model trained on Wikipedia and Gigaword dataset with 300 dimensions[3]. Again, we test two various approaches: simple averaging ($avGloVe$) and averaging of normalized word vectors ($avnorm-GloVe$).

- *fastText:* an approach to learning word representations based on the skipgram model, where each word is represented as a bag of character n-grams [1] which allows one to exploit morphological patterns of words. We use a publicly available model trained on English Wikipedia, UMBC webbase corpus and statmt.org news dataset with 300 dimensions[4] [12]. We test two approaches: simple averaging of word embeddings ($avfastText$) and using sentence embeddings available from the original *fastText* implementation ($fastText$).

- doc2vec: a simple extension [11] to word2vec that allows one to average word embeddings for obtaining word sequences embeddings. We use a publicly available doc2vec model trained on English Wikipedia[5] [10].

- sent2vec: sent2vec algorithm [14] allows one to jointly train both word and paragraph embeddings. We expect sent2vec to demonstrate better results than paragraph2vec. We use a publicly available sent2vec model trained on English Wikipedia (only on unigrams) with 600 dimension[6].

5.3 Aggregation and Segmentation Granularity

We try several basic aggregation strategies:

- *mean* strategy: relevance score for each document is computed as the mean of scores of paragraphs which are constituents of a given document.
- *best N* strategy: relevance score for each document is computed as the mean of scores of paragraphs with best N scores corresponding to a given document, where N could be 1, 3 or 5.

We also try to compare different granularities of segmentations (by chosing different thresholds). For the arXiv collections we created two segmentations: finer ($\alpha = 0.5$) and coarser ($\alpha = 0.3$). Then, for the Wikipedia collection we tried three different segmentations, with $\alpha = 0.5, 0.3, -2$.

5.4 Evaluation

We evaluate the quality of retrieval and compare several baseline models by measuring *accuracy*. Accuracy here is defined as $1 - \frac{Number\ of\ inversions}{Total\ number\ of\ triplets}$, where

---

[2] https://github.com/jhlau/doc2vec#pre-trained-word2vec-models.
[3] https://nlp.stanford.edu/projects/glove/.
[4] https://fasttext.cc/docs/en/english-vectors.html.
[5] https://github.com/jhlau/doc2vec#pre-trained-doc2vec-models.
[6] https://github.com/epfml/sent2vec#downloading-pre-trained-models.

Number of inversions is the absolute number of cases where the ranking of the intruder document is better than the ranking of the corresponding relevant reference document.

6   Results

The results of the experiments are presented in Tables 1 and 2. Bold numbers denote the best configuration for each line (i.e. for each baseline model). The results demonstrate that while for the arXiv papers segmentation does improve the majority of the models, it is not so salient for the Wikipedia articles. Possible explanation for this result could be that text structure is more prominent in scientific papers than in simple texts generated by Wikipedia users, which are topically rather homogeneous. Moreover, Wikipedia articles are usually shorter. Therefore, the Wikipedia texts are vectorized rather well without any segmentation, while in case of the arXiv, segmentation improves the quality of vectorization and retrieval.

Different aggregation strategies influence accuracy scores rather significantly. For the Wikipedia dataset one can observe the tendency that scores gradually increase from *mean* to *best-1* aggregation strategy. For the arXiv dataset the most successful strategy is primarily *best-3*. Apparently, different paragraphs should make different contribution to the final similarity score so that only a small number of paragraphs are accounted for with big weights. It also appears that coarser segmentation is slightly better in both test collections. However, these are preliminary remarks and the effect of various aggregation strategies and segmentation approaches should be explored further.

Table 1. Experimental results on the arXiv dataset.

Model	No segm.	Segmentation, $\alpha = 0.5$				Segmentation, $\alpha = 0.3$			
		best 1	best 3	best 5	mean	best 1	best 3	best 5	mean
ARTM	**0.817**	0.761	0.771	0.773	0.780	0.765	0.772	0.774	0.783
sent2vec	0.770	0.807	0.808	0.807	0.783	0.808	**0.809**	0.807	0.775
fastText	0.751	0.784	**0.785**	0.782	0.684	0.784	**0.785**	0.782	0.680
doc2vec	**0.814**	0.783	0.785	0.782	0.628	0.780	0.781	0.778	0.636
avW2V	0.817	0.820	**0.824**	0.822	0.774	0.821	0.823	0.822	0.768
avnormW2V	0.580	0.584	0.583	0.587	**0.620**	0.584	0.582	0.586	0.616
avGloVe	**0.779**	**0.779**	**0.779**	0.778	0.712	0.777	0.778	0.777	0.709
avnormGloVe	0.573	0.601	0.609	0.609	0.588	0.602	0.609	**0.610**	0.589
avfastText	0.662	0.746	**0.751**	0.746	0.638	0.746	0.750	0.745	0.632

Table 2. Experimental results on the Wikipedia dataset.

Model	No segm.	Segmentation, $\alpha = 0.5$				Segmentation, $\alpha = 0.3$				Segmentation, $\alpha = -2$			
		best 1	best 3	best 5	mean	best 1	best 3	best 5	mean	best 1	best 3	best 5	mean
ARTM	**0.696**	0.672	0.675	0.674	0.678	0.674	0.678	0.677	0.680	0.665	0.662	0.665	0.678
sent2vec	**0.745**	0.740	0.708	0.696	0.705	0.739	0.706	0.696	0.704	0.742	0.720	0.709	0.710
fastText	**0.717**	0.717	0.680	0.660	0.652	0.715	0.678	0.660	0.652	0.714	0.694	0.671	0.648
doc2vec	0.672	**0.684**	0.627	0.606	0.594	**0.684**	0.625	0.604	0.591	0.670	0.629	0.609	0.570
avW2V	**0.744**	0.741	0.717	0.703	0.702	0.741	0.715	0.700	0.699	0.743	0.724	0.714	0.705
avnormW2V	0.590	0.613	0.609	0.604	0.602	0.610	0.608	0.602	0.601	**0.616**	0.611	0.604	0.603
avGloVe	0.726	**0.727**	0.695	0.682	0.677	0.726	0.693	0.681	0.679	**0.727**	0.705	0.693	0.681
avnormGloVe	0.602	0.610	0.610	0.610	0.608	0.610	0.611	0.610	0.608	0.607	0.605	0.605	**0.612**
avfastText	0.653	**0.671**	0.631	0.612	0.595	0.668	0.627	0.611	0.595	0.670	0.643	0.622	0.600

7 Conclusion

The aim of the present research was to test the hypothesis that topic segmentation could improve the quality of information retrieval.

We conducted experiments with several baseline models on two text collections. The experiments demonstrated that the quality is slightly improved when using segmentation but the text structure should be taken into account: it might be argued that the approach presented in this paper is more appropriate for segmentally structured texts such as scientific papers.

Further work could be comparing various text segmentation approaches as well as different granularity levels and investigating what segmentation techniques give better results in the IR tasks. Furthermore, the influence of various aggregation strategies also should be explored.

Acknowledgements. We would like to acknowledge the commitment from Anton Lozhkov throughout this study. We are also thankful to Viktor Bulatov for help in editing the present paper.

This research was supported by the Ministry of Education and Science of the Russian Federation under the unique research id RFMEFI57917X0143.

References

1. Bojanowski, P., Grave, E., Joulin, A., Mikolov, T.: Enriching word vectors with subword information. arXiv preprint arXiv:1607.04606 (2016)
2. Chan, S.K., Xie, L., Meng, H.: Modeling the statistical behavior of lexical chains to capture word cohesiveness for automatic story segmentation. In: Eighth Annual Conference of the International Speech Communication Association (2007)
3. Dai, A.M., Olah, C., Le, Q.V.: Document embedding with paragraph vectors. arXiv preprint arXiv:1507.07998 (2015)
4. Du, L., Buntine, W., Johnson, M.: Topic segmentation with a structured topic model. In: Proceedings of the 2013 Conference of the North American Chapter of the Association for Computational Linguistics: Human Language Technologies, pp. 190–200 (2013)

5. Galley, M., McKeown, K.R., Fosler-Lussier, E., Jing, H.: Discourse segmentation of multi-party conversation. In: Proceedings of the 41st Annual Meeting of the Association for Computational Linguistics (2003)
6. Galuščáková, P.: Application of topic segmentation in audiovisual information retrieval
7. Ganguly, D., Leveling, J., Jones, G.J.: Utilizing sub-topical structure of documents for information retrieval. In: Proceedings of the 4th Workshop on Workshop for Ph. D. Students in Information & Knowledge Management, pp. 75–78. ACM (2011)
8. Honnibal, M., Montani, I.: spaCy 2: natural language understanding with bloom embeddings, convolutional neural networks and incremental parsing (2017, to appear)
9. Johnson, J., Douze, M., Jégou, H.: Billion-scale similarity search with GPUs. arXiv preprint arXiv:1702.08734 (2017)
10. Lau, J.H., Baldwin, T.: An empirical evaluation of doc2vec with practical insights into document embedding generation. arXiv preprint arXiv:1607.05368 (2016)
11. Le, Q., Mikolov, T.: Distributed representations of sentences and documents. In: International Conference on Machine Learning, pp. 1188–1196 (2014)
12. Mikolov, T., Grave, E., Bojanowski, P., Puhrsch, C., Joulin, A.: Advances in pre-training distributed word representations. In: Proceedings of the International Conference on Language Resources and Evaluation (LREC 2018) (2018)
13. Mikolov, T., Sutskever, I., Chen, K., Corrado, G.S., Dean, J.: Distributed representations of words and phrases and their compositionality. In: Advances in Neural Information Processing Systems, pp. 3111–3119 (2013)
14. Pagliardini, M., Gupta, P., Jaggi, M.: Unsupervised learning of sentence embeddings using compositional n-gram features. arXiv preprint arXiv:1703.02507 (2017)
15. Pennington, J., Socher, R., Manning, C.: GloVe: global vectors for word representation. In: Proceedings of the 2014 Conference on Empirical Methods in Natural Language Processing (EMNLP), pp. 1532–1543 (2014)
16. Prince, V., Labadié, A.: Text segmentation based on document understanding for information retrieval. In: Kedad, Z., Lammari, N., Métais, E., Meziane, F., Rezgui, Y. (eds.) NLDB 2007. LNCS, vol. 4592, pp. 295–304. Springer, Heidelberg (2007). https://doi.org/10.1007/978-3-540-73351-5_26
17. Riedl, M., Biemann, C.: Text segmentation with topic models. J. Lang. Technol. Comput. Linguist. 27(1), 47–69 (2012)
18. Skachkov, N., Vorontsov, K.: Improving topic models with segmental structure of texts. In: Computational Linguistics and Intellectual Technologies: Papers from the Annual International Conference Dialogue, pp. 652–661 (2018)
19. Vorontsov, K., Frei, O., Apishev, M., Romov, P., Dudarenko, M.: BigARTM: open source library for regularized multimodal topic modeling of large collections. In: Khachay, M., Konstantinova, N., Panchenko, A., Ignatov, D., Labunets, V. (eds.) AIST 2015. CCIS, vol. 542, pp. 370–381. Springer, Cham (2015). https://doi.org/10.1007/978-3-319-26123-2_36
20. Vorontsov, K., Potapenko, A.: Additive regularization of topic models. Mach. Learn. 101(1–3), 303–323 (2015)

Combining Behaviors and Demographics to Segment Online Audiences: Experiments with a YouTube Channel

Bernard J. Jansen[1], Soon-gyo Jung[1], Joni Salminen[1,2(✉)], Jisun An[1], and Haewoon Kwak[1]

[1] Qatar Computing Research Institute, Hamad Bin Khalifa University, Doha, Qatar
{bjansen,sjung,jsalminen,jan,hkwak}@hbku.edu.qa
[2] University of Turku, Turku, Finland

Abstract. Social media channels with audiences in the millions are increasingly common. Efforts at segmenting audiences for populations of these sizes can result in hundreds of audience segments, as the compositions of the overall audiences tend to be complex. Although understanding audience segments is important for strategic planning, tactical decision making, and content creation, it is unrealistic for human decision makers to effectively utilize hundreds of audience segments in these tasks. In this research, we present efforts at simplifying the segmentation of audience populations to increase their practical utility. Using millions of interactions with hundreds of thousands of viewers with an organization's online content collection, we first isolate the maximum number of audience segments, based on behavioral profiling, and then demonstrate a computational approach of using non-negative matrix factorization to reduce this number to 42 segments that are both impactful and representative segments of the overall population. Initial results are promising, and we present avenues for future research leveraging our approach.

Keywords: Audience segmentation · Audience analytics · User profiling

1 Introduction

Understanding the audience is a critical task in many domains, including marketing, advertising, system development, online content creation, and website design. In the wake of social media proliferation, companies and other organizations now have access to much more user data than ever before [1] However, dealing with "big data" has been found to be cumbersome [2], so that the cognitive limitations assign much greater constraints for utilizing user data than the availability of the data itself [3, 4]. One of the means to counter the overload of data is through efficient audience segmentation.

Although there has been considerable work in many domains focused on segmenting audiences by information consumption patterns [5], as this is often critical to successful online content creation, identifying audience segments in many situations is difficult due to lack of data, too much data, or privacy concerns [6]. It is also problematic to determine what a meaningful audience segment is, especially for large,

© Springer Nature Switzerland AG 2018
S. S. Bodrunova (Ed.): INSCI 2018, LNCS 11193, pp. 141–153, 2018.
https://doi.org/10.1007/978-3-030-01437-7_12

diverse, and complex audiences, such as international social media followership. This difficulty motivates our work, as the question of determining the right number of audience segments for efficient decision making [7] is constrained by finding meaningful segments. By meaningful, we mean an audience segment that is *behaviorally and demographically different* than one or more other segments from the same overall audience.

Given the increased interest in micro-targeting [8], i.e., focusing on extremely small audience segments, we do not aim at maximizing the size of the segment in our approach of combining behavioral and demographic information. In contrast, we utilize online videos from the content collection of a major news organization, along with associated behavioral and demographic attributes to identify *the maximum possible number* of distinct audience segments within the overall total audience. We then develop an approach for reducing this set of audience segments to the smallest number of meaningful audience segments. This reduction permits a narrower focus by organizations on the most impactful (i.e., distinct and actionable) audience segments for decision making in content creation, marketing, or other uses.

In this manuscript, we lead off with a short background section, introduce our data, and present our methods and results. We conclude with discussion, implications, and directions for the next stages of the on-going research effort.

2 Related Literature

Audience segmentation [9] is the process of separating a group of people into homogenous sub-segments, typically based on behaviors, demographics, or both, with the grouping most commonly grounded around some goal, product, system, or content [10]. Each audience segment can be defined as a group of people from the overall audience who are similar in specific ways but different from the other segments of the population. The identification of audience segments has long been central to marketing [11], and it is increasingly important in online content publishing. The purpose of segmentation is typically to increase understanding of users or customers, often using some key performance indicators capturing a strategic goal, such as increasing content views [12].

However, prior research has identified several challenges related to segmentation. Firstly, deriving actionable results from segmentation is not easy. For example, Tkaczynski, Rundle-Thiele, and Prebensen [13] analyze more than two thousand customers using a clustering, arriving at two segments, neither of which were actionable according to the researchers. In examine online news consumption, An and Kwak [14] attempt to segment audiences across 129 countries and by topic, and find it challenging to summarize the complex audience. Secondly, demographic differences are typically used for segmentation, but there is a need for more meaningful segmentation criteria, such as behavioral differences [15]. Prior work has shown that social media analytics can inform aspect of information behavior, such as information sharing [16]. Social media data can thus offer insights into understanding audience information preferences driving the online behavior [17]. This is extremely important, as social media actors, such as YouTube channels, often have complex audiences [18].

As an example of behavioral segmentation, online data has been used to segment audiences into various purchasing groups [12]. Behavioral segmentation using Hidden Markov Models shows that there are consistent behaviors within searching stages [19]. Garcia et al. [20] report on a variety of behavioral attributes of a YouTube audience. Zhou and Zhang [21] use data from Weibo, one of the most popular social media platforms in China, to detect patterns of dietary preferences. In the broadcast domain, with the increased use of social media sites for news distribution, there is a concern of audience fragmentation. Fletcher and Nielsen [22] use audience segmentation to show that online audiences are no more fragmented than off-line audiences, although they found that cross-platform audiences vary by country. Lo, Chiong, and Cornforth [23] leverage large-scale social media data to identify the top-k audience members. Araújo et al. [24] explore YouTube audiences by country and age in online adolescence channels, finding large and diverse segments of audiences.

Overall, segmentation has been researched in a variety of contexts, including system design [25], health care [26], crisis response [27], journalism [28], and marketing [29]. However, prior work typically focuses on either demographic or behavioral segmentation, but they are rarely applied simultaneously. In particular, there is a lack of research into complex populations [33] that may contain multiple behavioral audience segments *within a certain demographic group*, such as with popular social media channels that provide content ranging over a variety of topics. In these cases, the content preferences of individuals belonging to the same demographic group might drastically differ, requiring behavioral segmentation. However, even in these cases decision makers are interested in retaining some demographic information in the segments, as having this information facilitates audience insights and immersion [30]. Therefore, dealing with large and demographically and behaviorally diverse audience populations can be quite challenging. One approach is to simplify these complex populations by identifying the most impactful audience segments, which is the approach we investigate here.

3   Research Objectives

Our goal is to develop a methodology for reducing audience segments from large and diverse audience populations to the most meaningful segments that retain both demographic and behavioral information. In other words, we trim the audience segments to achieve a practical number of segments by focusing on reducing the audience segments to a minimal but still informative number. In practice, this number is somewhat arbitrary and requires further empirical work with decision makers of audience segments. Here, we simply measure how much we can *reduce* the number of segments in order to simplify the audience without losing its essential characteristics.

With this goal in mind, we define B as a behavioral audience segment, which is a segment based on interactions (behavior) with a set of content (C). D is a demographic audience segment, which is segment based on demographic characteristics. U is an integrated audience segment composed of both behavioral and demographic attributes.

In this research, we will:

1. Identify the number of behavioral segments (B) within a total audience.
2. Associate each of these behavioral segments with a set ($D_{1 \text{ to } X}$) of weighted demographic segments (D_i), resulting in a set of integrated segments U, defined as ($B \times D_{1 \text{ to } X}$), where X is the maximum number of segments.
3. Develop an approach for reducing the set ($D_{1 \text{ to } X}$) while retaining the most descriptive demographic segments ($D_{1 \text{ to } i}$) resulting in a reduced set of U.

We present our data and methodology in the following sections.

4 Methodology

4.1 Data Collection

For our research, we collect actual audience data from a major online media and mobile channel based with millions of audience members with varying interests in the online content and geographically distributed worldwide. Our data source is the *online news channel AJ+*[1], which was designed from its founding to serve news in the medium of the viewer, with no redirect to a website or other platform. AJ+ is based on social platforms, meaning the digital content developed is specifically designed to be viewed by audiences on the Facebook, YouTube, Twitter, or Instagram, depending on the audience members who are most active on each platform.

For the data collection platform for the research reported in this manuscript, we use the AJ+ YouTube Channel, reserving analysis of the Twitter, Facebook, and other platforms for future work. However, the technique presented here is generalizable to any social media channel providing aggregated audience statistics [31]. As with many other social media platforms, the YouTube channel's analytics platform provides detailed statistics for every video. As an example of an AJ+ YouTube video, see Fig. 1.

Fig. 1. Example of YouTube video from the AJ+ YouTube channel, with number of views.

---

[1] Part of the Al Jazeera Media Network.

For this research, we collect data on 4320 videos produced from June 13, 2014 to July 27, 2016. Collectively, these videos have had more than 30 million views from people in 190 countries at the time of the data collection. The YouTube analytics platform provides, for each piece of the content collection, user attributes (e.g., gender, age, country location) at an aggregate level. One can access the data via the YouTube application programming interface (API), through which data can be collected automatically if permission is granted by the channel owner. We obtained the permission and collected the data. The attributes used for this research are listed in Table 1.

Table 1. Demographic and behavioral variables in the dataset.

Type	Description
Demographic attributes	**Agegroup:** YouTube viewers are classified into multiple age categories (13–17, 18–24, 25–34, 35–44, 45–54, 55–64, and 65 years and older); 7 possible age categories for a customer **Gender:** YouTube viewers are classified as either male or female, so there are 2 possible categories **Country:** YouTube uses the two-letter ISO-3166-1 country code index to classify where viewers are from, with 249 current officially assigned country codes at the time of this study
Behavioral attribute	**Viewcount:** YouTube provides the number of views per video for a given [country] by [gender, ageGroup]

We operationalize a demographic segment as a unique combination of (country, gender, age group). With 2 genders, 7 age groups, and 249 counties, this yields an upper limit of 3,486 audience segments. However, our data has 2,214 demographic segments, as not all countries and not all age groups for each country are represented. Even so, the dataset can be said to describe a large and diverse social media audience.

4.2 Segmentation Procedure

To isolate audience behavior patterns, the embedded structures in the aggregated data should be discovered. We employ a matrix decomposition technique, specifically non-negative matrix factorization (NMF), for this purpose. As this process is outlined in [32], we only conceptually present it here (see Table 2).

Using this matrix approach as the basis, we can decompose (i.e., separate into simpler components) the overall matrix V into two matrices: W and H. In other words, one complex matrix V can be approximated as the product of smaller matrices W and H. The matrix H contains the audience behaviors and matrix W contains the user demographics. The matrix H encodes an association between the behavioral segments and the individual pieces of content. The resolution in finding user behavioral segments can be adjusted by the number of rows in H. The outcome of this step is the determination of B. Although one can present as many behavioral segments as the data contains, cognitive limits of the end users of the system pose a practical upper bound. It is not purposeful to show end users hundreds of customers segments.

Once we have the matrix H, we discover, via NMF, the underlying latent patterns, which describe the user segment interactions with the sets of individual content. These

Table 2. Matrix decomposition process using non-negative matrix factorization (NMF). The original matrix V is decomposed into two matrices, H and W.

Step	Description
Step 1	We first develop a matrix representing users' interaction with online content
Step 2	The columns of the matrix are the online content pieces, e.g. videos (e.g., c contents $(C_1, C_2, ..., C_c)$)
Step 3	The rows of the matrix are the user groups or customer demographic segments (e.g., g user groups $(G_1, G_2, ..., G_g)$)
Step 4	Therefore, the matrix describing the association between user groups and contents is denoted by V the $g \times c$ matrix of g user groups or customer demographic segments and c contents
Step 5	The element of the matrix V, V_{ij}, is any statistic that represents the one interaction or set of interactions of the user group G_i for content C_j

latent patterns become the basis of the user demographic segments, $D_{1\ to\ x}$, in the next step. The matrix **W** encodes an association between user demographic groups and behavioral user segments (i.e., latent content interaction patterns) with the set of corresponding user demographic segments each with an associated weight indicating how strongly each demographic segment is associated with the given behavioral segment. Each row in **W** represents how each demographic segment can be characterized by different behavioral patterns. The columns in **W** show how each latent behavioral pattern is associated with different demographic segments.

The resolution in finding demographic segments can be adjusted by the number of columns in **W**. We identify the most impactful demographic segments associated with the previously defined behavioral segments. A single behavioral segment can have multiple associated demographic segments, as shown in Table 3. This reflects the fact that users within the same demographic attributes can interact with different content.

Table 3. Demographic segments (D_1 to D_{10}) associated with behavioral Segment 1 (B_1). Shaded areas are below the elbow and with negative z-scores.

Seg.	Country	Age	Gender	Weight	z-score
	User Behavioral Segment #1 (B1)				
D_1	US	25	male	415.73	2.330935
D_2	US	35	male	313.00	1.215947
D_3	US	45	male	221.56	0.223497
D_4	CA	25	male	216.42	0.167709
D_5	CA	35	male	176.54	-0.26513
D_6	US	55	male	165.83	-0.38137
D_7	GB	25	male	147.47	-0.58064
D_8	CA	45	male	124.21	-0.8331
D_9	US	65	male	114.93	-0.93382
D_{10}	GB	35	male	113.99	-0.94402

Given our dataset, we define a behavioral audience segment as a pattern of video viewing. With 4,320 videos, we have an extremely high number of combinations of videos viewed by different segments. However, prior research has shown that individuals struggle to work with large volumes of information [34]. For this research, we use 15 behavioral segments, each associated with 10 demographic segments. Therefore, we have a total of 150 potential segments, which is the number we aim to reduce.

5 Results of Simplification

We have four variables to utilize for simplifying our segmentation, which are: (a) weight, (b) country, (c) gender, and (d) age. Leveraging first weight, we want to determine a cut-off beyond which the demographic segments are less meaningful.

For this, we employ the *elbow approach*, in which one chooses the number of segments so that adding another segment does not add much information. For many phenomena, the marginal gain will drop, giving an angle, or elbow, in a graph. The number of segments is chosen at this point. The elbow can be verified using the z-score, which is a measure of how many standard deviations above or below a population's mean a raw score is. The z-score is calculated with $z = (X - \mu)/\sigma$ where z is the z-score, X is the value of the element, μ is the population mean, and σ is the standard deviation.

We utilize both the graphical elbow graph and the z-score for all 15 behavioral segments (with three sample graphs shown in Fig. 2, eliminating the demographic segments below the elbow (i.e., where the z-score becomes negative). Figure 2 displays the graphical display of the demographic weights of behavioral Segment 1 with the critical z-score shown as a vertical line. Using elbow and z-score approaches, we reduce our entire data set of 150 audience segments to 63 segments (a 58% reduction).

Table 3 shows the z-score calculations for the set of demographic segments (D_1 to D_{10}) for behavioral Segment 1 (B_1). For each behavioral segment, we group demographic segments based on country, specifically using the ISO 3166-1 country codes utilized by most of the major online platforms. Keeping the demographic segments distinct by country makes sense, as privacy, marketing, and other legal restrictions often vary by country. If two or more demographic segments are from the same country, then those audience segments are candidates for consolidation (see Table 4).

We group demographic segments based on gender, specifically in this research using a binary of male and female. If demographic segments are of the same gender from the same country, those segments are candidates for consolidation (see Table 5).

We group demographic segments based on age category. As this is initial research, we take a heuristic approach: (a) if the age bracket is bounded by corresponding age brackets from the same country and gender, then the age brackets are aggregated, or (b) if the age bracket is adjacent to a corresponding age bracket from the same country and gender, then the two age brackets are aggregated (see Table 6).

We then apply the country, then gender, and then age consolidations to each of the 15 behavioral segments. Table 7 presents an example of the overall simplification approach for behavioral segment 1, with the original 10 demographic segments reduced to 2. The *Weight* attribute reduced the set to 6. The *Country* and *Gender* attributes can reduce the segments to 2, which was the result when the *Age* heuristic was applied.

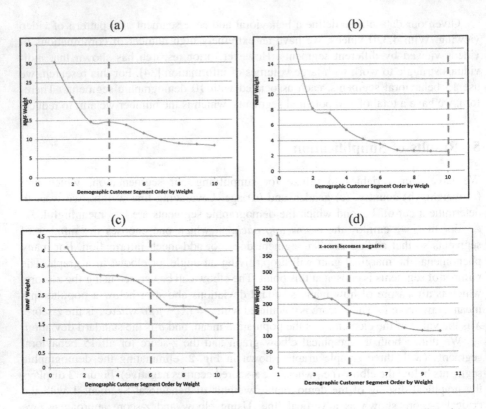

Fig. 2. Segment 2 with elbow at demographic segment 4 (a); segment 10 with no elbow in top ten demographic groups (note: elbow at segment 10) (b); segment 15 with elbow at demographic segment 6 (c); segment 1 with elbow at demographic segment 5.

Table 4. Segment 10 grouped into 6 possible demographic segments from the original 10 based on country variable.

Country	Age	Gender	Weight
GB	25	male	15.97
GB	35	male	8.16
GB	18	male	7.53
DE	25	male	5.38
CA	25	male	4.15
GB	45	male	3.52
IT	25	male	2.7
AE	25	male	2.64
CA	18	male	2.54
CA	35	male	2.49

Table 5. Segment 4 grouped into two possible demographic segments of four based on gender variable.

Country	Age	Gender	Weight
PH	25	male	3.4
PH	18	male	1.59
PH	35	male	1.21
PH	25	female	1.18

Table 6. Segment 11 grouped into one demographic segment based on age variable.

Country	Age	Gender	Weight
MY	55	male	9.26
MY	25	male	7.13
MY	65	male	6.71
MY	45	male	6.42
MY	35	male	5.76

Table 7. Segmentation simplification process, reducing 10 demographic segments (D_1 to D_{10}) into 2 (D_{US} and D_{CA}) for behavioral segment 1.

Country	Age	Gender	Weight	z-score
US	25	male	415.73	2.330935
US	35	male	313.00	1.215947
US	45	male	221.56	0.223497
CA	25	male	216.42	0.167709
CA	35	male	176.54	-0.26513
US	55	male	165.83	-0.38137
GB	25	male	147.47	-0.58064
CA	45	male	124.21	-0.8331
US	65	male	114.93	-0.93382
GB	35	male	113.99	-0.94402

Table 8 shows the results for all 15 behavioral segments after applying the reductions discussed above. Our original 150 integrated audience segments were reduced to 42 segments, a 72% simplification, with each segment distinct in terms of behaviors. The average simplification was 2.8 segments, with a maximum of 9 and a minimum of 1.

Table 8. Set of 150 segments simplified to 42 by applying first weight and then country-gender-age reduction.

Behavioral segment (B)	No. of demographic segments (D)	Applying weight (D)	Applying country-gender-age (D)
1	10	4	2
2	10	4	4
3	10	3	3
4	10	4	2
5	10	3	1
6	10	3	2
7	10	5	5
8	10	3	2
9	10	3	3
10	10	10	9
11	10	5	1
12	10	3	1
13	10	4	2
14	10	4	1
15	10	5	4
	150	63	42

6   Discussion and Conclusion

The abundance of social media data has been transformative for online content creation. However, at the same time it has resulted in an overwhelming number of potential audience segments, especially for channels with large international audience.

In this research, we show that meaningful audience segmentation that retains both demographic and behavioral information is achievable. Our research results show that audience segmentation can be accomplished rapidly and dynamically using a large-scale user data from major online social media platform, reflecting the content consumption behavior of real people forming the channel's online audience.

Furthermore, we show that one can employ consistent techniques to reduce the number of audience segments in complex user populations. With our approach on the example dataset, we achieved a 72% simplification of the audience segments, while considering both demographic and behavioral variation in the output personas.

Concerning limitations, a known shortcoming of the applied elbow method is that the elbow cannot always be unambiguously identified, even when using the z-score. In future research, we are investigating ways to solve this issue.

Moreover, while we limited our focus here to understanding the meaningful audience segments with social media data, it would be interesting to apply the approach to the long tail of audience segments to investigate possible micro-audience segments, cultural differences [35], and content topics [36].

From a practical point of view, although this manuscript is specifically focusing on digital content on YouTube, our approach can be applied in a wide range of contexts, given that the data structure remains similar. Increasingly, audience segmentation processes are leveraging aggregated audience data [37], having the advantage of retaining the privacy of individual users. Our approach, utilizing aggregated data from the YouTube API, has this benefit as the privacy of users is kept safe.

Overall, the strength of the research is that we use real content and user data from a major social media platform to investigate novel ways for audience segmentation, with promising areas for future research. We are actively investigating the use of other social media and data sources to provide richer audience segments for online content creators.

References

1. Nguyen, T., Zhou, L., Spiegler, V., Ieromonachou, P., Lin, Y.: Big data analytics in supply chain management: a state-of-the-art literature review. Comput. Oper. Res., 254–264 (2017)
2. Agarwal, R., Dhar, V.: Editorial—big data, data science, and analytics: the opportunity and challenge for IS research. Inf. Syst. Res. **25**, 443–448 (2014)
3. Gandomi, A., Haider, M.: Beyond the hype: big data concepts, methods, and analytics. Int. J. Inf. Manag. **35**, 137–144 (2015)
4. Edwards, J.S., Taborda, E.R.: Using knowledge management to give context to analytics and big data and reduce strategic risk. Proc. Comput. Sci. **99**, 36–49 (2016)
5. Hendahewa, C., Shah, C.: Evaluating user search trails in exploratory search tasks. Inf. Process. Manag. **53**, 905–922 (2017)
6. Salminen, J., et al.: From 2,772 segments to five personas: summarizing a diverse online audience by generating culturally adapted personas. First Monday **23** (2018). Article no. 8415
7. Sweller, J.: Cognitive load during problem solving: effects on learning. Cogn. Sci. **12**, 257–285 (1988)
8. Cho, M., Auger, G.A.: Extrovert and engaged? Exploring the connection between personality and involvement of stakeholders and the perceived relationship investment of nonprofit organizations. Publ. Relat. Rev. **43**, 729–737 (2017)
9. Shafto, A.: Mastering audience segmentation: how to apply segmentation techniques to improve internal communication. Melcrum (2006)
10. Stern, B.B.: A revised communication model for advertising: multiple dimensions of the source, the message, and the recipient. J. Advert. **23**, 5–15 (1994)
11. Smith, W.R.: Product differentiation and market segmentation as alternative marketing strategies. J. Mark. **21**, 3–8 (1956)
12. Ortiz-Cordova, A., Jansen, B.J.: Classifying web search queries to identify high revenue generating customers. J. Am. Soc. Inf. Sci. Technol. **63**, 1426–1441 (2012)

13. Tkaczynski, A., Rundle-Thiele, S.R., Prebensen, N.K.: To segment or not? That is the question. J. Vacat. Mark. **24**, 16–28 (2018)
14. An, J., Kwak, H.: Multidimensional analysis of the news consumption of different demographic groups on a nationwide scale. In: Ciampaglia, G.L., Mashhadi, A., Yasseri, T. (eds.) SocInfo 2017. LNCS, vol. 10539, pp. 124–142. Springer, Cham (2017). https://doi.org/10.1007/978-3-319-67217-5_9
15. Jansen, B.J., Booth, D.: Classifying web queries by topic and user intent. In: CHI 2010 Extended Abstracts on Human Factors in Computing Systems, pp. 4285–4290. ACM, New York (2010)
16. Liu, Z., Jansen, B.J.: Questioner or question: predicting the response rate in social question and answering on Sina Weibo. Inf. Process. Manag. **54**, 159–174 (2018)
17. Gonzalez Camacho, L.A., Alves-Souza, S.N.: Social network data to alleviate cold-start in recommender system: a systematic review. Inf. Process. Manag. **54**, 529–544 (2018)
18. Nguyen, H.T., Le Nguyen, M.: Multilingual opinion mining on YouTube—a convolutional N-gram BiLSTM word embedding. Inf. Process. Manag. **54**, 451–462 (2018)
19. Han, S., He, D., Chi, Y.: Understanding and modeling behavior patterns in cross-device web search. Proc. Assoc. Inf. Sci. Technol. **54**, 150–158 (2017)
20. Garcia, D., Abisheva, A., Schweitzer, F.: Evaluative patterns and incentives in YouTube. In: Ciampaglia, G.L., Mashhadi, A., Yasseri, T. (eds.) SocInfo 2017. LNCS, vol. 10540, pp. 301–315. Springer, Cham (2017). https://doi.org/10.1007/978-3-319-67256-4_24
21. Zhou, Q., Zhang, C.: Detecting dietary preference of social media users in China via sentiment analysis. Proc. Assoc. Inf. Sci. Technol. **54**, 523–527 (2017)
22. Fletcher, R., Nielsen, R.K.: Are news audiences increasingly fragmented? A cross-national comparative analysis of cross-platform news audience fragmentation and duplication. J. Commun. **67**, 476–498 (2017)
23. Lo, S.L., Chiong, R., Cornforth, D.: Ranking of high-value social audiences on Twitter. Decis. Support Syst. **85**, 34–48 (2016)
24. Araújo, C.S., Magno, G., Meira Jr., W., Almeida, V., Hartung, P., Doneda, D.: Characterizing videos, audience and advertising in Youtube channels for kids (2017). arXiv:1707.00971 [cs]
25. Salminen, J., Jung, S.-G., An, J., Kwak, H., Jansen, B.J.: Findings of a user study of automatically generated personas. In: Extended Abstracts of the 2018 CHI Conference on Human Factors in Computing Systems, pp. LBW097:1–LBW097:6. ACM, New York (2018)
26. Burkell, J., Fortier, A.: Could we do better? Behavioural tracking on recommended consumer health websites. Health Inf. Libr. J. **32**, 182–194 (2015)
27. Kim, Y., Miller, A., Chon, M.-G.: Communicating with key publics in crisis communication: the synthetic approach to the public segmentation in CAPS (communicative action in problem solving). J. Conting. Crisis Manag. **24**, 82–94 (2016)
28. Nelson, J.L.: And deliver us to segmentation. J. Pract. **12**, 204–219 (2018)
29. Ashley, C., Tuten, T.: Creative strategies in social media marketing: an exploratory study of branded social content and consumer engagement. Psychol. Mark. **32**, 15–27 (2015)
30. Nielsen, L., Storgaard Hansen, K.: Personas is applicable: a study on the use of personas in Denmark. In: Proceedings of the SIGCHI Conference on Human Factors in Computing Systems, pp. 1665–1674. ACM (2014)
31. An, J., Kwak, H., Jansen, B.J.: Personas for content creators via decomposed aggregate audience statistics. In: Proceedings of Advances in Social Network Analysis and Mining (ASONAM 2017), Sydney, Australia (2017)

32. Jung, S.-G., An, J., Kwak, H., Ahmad, M., Nielsen, L., Jansen, B.J.: Persona generation from aggregated social media data. In: Proceedings of the 2017 CHI Conference Extended Abstracts on Human Factors in Computing Systems, pp. 1748–1755. ACM, New York (2017)

33. Jansen, B.J., An, J., Kwak, H., Salminen, J., Jung, S.-G.: Viewed by too many or viewed too little: using information dissemination for audience segmentation. Presented at the Association for Information Science and Technology Annual Meeting 2017 (ASIST2017), Washington DC, USA, 27 November 2017

34. Miller, G.A.: The magical number seven plus or minus two: some limits on our capacity for processing information. Psychol. Rev. **63**, 81–97 (1956)

35. Salminen, J., et al.: Generating cultural personas from social data: a perspective of middle eastern users. In: Proceedings of the Fourth International Symposium on Social Networks Analysis, Management and Security (SNAMS-2017), Prague, Czech Republic (2017)

36. AL-Smadi, M., Jaradat, Z., AL-Ayyoub, M., Jararweh, Y.: Paraphrase identification and semantic text similarity analysis in Arabic news tweets using lexical, syntactic, and semantic features. Inf. Process. Manag. **53**, 640–652 (2017)

37. Jansen, B.J., Sobel, K., Cook, G.: Classifying ecommerce information sharing behaviour by youths on social networking sites. J. Inf. Sci. **37**, 120–136 (2011)

The Platform Effect: Analysing User Activity on Tumblr

Nora Alrajebah[1](✉), Leslie Carr[2], and Thanassis Tiropanis[2]

[1] King Saud University, Riyadh, Saudi Arabia
nrajebah@ksu.edu.sa
[2] University of Southampton, Southampton, UK
{lac,t.tiropanis}@soton.ac.uk

Abstract. One of the fundamental aspects of online social network platforms is that they provide a number of core affordances. The actual mechanisms of these affordances vary in different platforms but their main purposes are similar: allowing users to create content and connect with each other. In this paper, we study user activity on Tumblr, we analyse user activity around the most popular posts in one year, reflecting on the effects of Tumblr's affordances, communication style, and content discovery mechanisms on its users' behaviour. Our findings show that the majority of user activity on Tumblr is non-verbal, users reblog and like posts but they rarely engage in conversations with others.

Keywords: Social network analysis · User activity · Tumblr

1 Introduction

Since their emergence, online social networks (OSNs) are considered as one of the most vital Web applications. As they were evolving, these platforms were viewed from various angles. In their early days, OSNs were identified as services that allow users to create profiles, create a designated list of connections and be able to traverse the list of connections of others [1,9]. However, this description has developed to include other aspects such as the ability to publish content and form virtual communities based on common interests [32]. The core purpose of these platforms is to allow users to publish content and get exposed to others' content. Nonetheless, each platform has its own flavour in terms of the affordances it offers and the culture that evolves around it [9].

Platforms' affordances are facilitated by a mixture of functionalities that schematise and organise what users can do on each platform. The differences in functionalities is what differentiates one platform from the other. There has been a ongoing debate concerning the accurate interpretation of the term 'affordance' in Human-Computer Interaction literature [17]. It is useful to briefly explain the difference between 'affordance' and 'functionality' in the context of OSNs. An affordance refers to the ability to perform a particular action, but a functionality is the mechanism by which the action is performed. For instance, the ability to

© Springer Nature Switzerland AG 2018
S. S. Bodrunova (Ed.): INSCI 2018, LNCS 11193, pp. 154–168, 2018.
https://doi.org/10.1007/978-3-030-01437-7_13

connect with each other is an affordance that is facilitated by two distinctive functionalities 'follow' on Twitter and Tumblr and 'friend' on Facebook.

As mentioned earlier, on OSNs affordances have been added gradually throughout a decade including the ability to spread content, add comments, mention other users, and express admiration. On one hand, these affordances have shaped the way users perceive and behave on social networks. On the other hand, the trails users leave as they interact with each other via these affordances have provided an enormous source of data about user activity. A number of studies have investigated user activity on OSNs for four purposes; first, to understand how platforms' functionalities are used in practice because users adopt different conventions while using them [8,29]. Second, to examine user behaviour during a particular event e.g. presidential debates [25] or scientific conferences [34]. Third, to study a particular aspect of social networking such as conversations [20] or to determine user intentions and identify user categories [21].

Motivated by the above purposes, this paper aims at establishing an understanding of user activity on Tumblr, a platform that has not been studied in depth in previous studies. It is a hybrid platform, a fusion of blogosphere with social networking features. This fusion creates an environment that encourages faster communication [27] because it needs the least amount of both effort and time. In addition, Tumblr employs a number of content promotion mechanisms such as: staff picks, trends, tracked tags, etc. which increase the chances of content exposure which will attract more users to the published content. This paper investigates Tumblr as a platform for content sharing and analyses Tumblr users' activity and the effects of Tumblr's affordances on its users.

Recently, many OSNs publish a special review at the end of each year to showcase the most popular posts that have been shared during that past year. Such reviews are very useful as a proxy to catalogue popular content, enabling researchers to analyse them in a retrospective manner. Few days before the New Year, Tumblr publishes its "Year in Review" blog, a showcase of the most popular content on Tumblr during the past year. This blog allow us to analyse user activity within a subset of the community, those interested in the popular content. Our aim is to analyse Tumblr's user activity around the most popular content. We chose Tumblr because it is a medium that has a different objective and style compared to Facebook and Twitter. We analyses Tumblr users' activity around three functionalities: reblogging, liking and commenting. We compare Tumblr with other platforms while reflecting on the effects Tumblr's affordances, content exposure and discovery mechanisms, communication style on its users' activity.

The contributions of this paper are:

- An in depth analysis of Tumblr, its affordances and users' activities.
- An insight into the activities around the most popular posts, hence, providing an insight into users' activity in viral content.
- An understanding of the value of Tumblr to the users and how it fits the social network application ecosystem.

Our analysis revealed a number of interesting findings about user activity on Tumblr. First, although the most popular posts attract large number of users; most of the user interaction on Tumblr is non-verbal. Users reblog and like but they rarely engage in conversations either via comments or direct replies. In other words, users are interested in the content but they do not attempt to start conversations with other users. Second, reblogging is more popular than liking which indicates that Tumblr users are more engaged with the content because reblogging means that posts will be added to the reblogger's blog. Third, using the total number of reblogs as an estimate of the size of a community on Tumblr; we found that 'animals', 'plants', 'lgbtq', 'feminism', 'education' and 'parenting' categories are the largest communities on Tumblr. Fourth, Tumblr employs different mechanisms to attract users' attention and expose them to content they might be interested in, which explains the high reblogging and liking rates within the most popular content in comparison with other platforms.

This paper is organised as follows. Section 1 explores the most relevant work to the work presented in this paper. Section 2 provides a description of Tumblr affordances and the dataset used in this paper. In Sect. 3 we present the finding of the analyses we carried out and Sect. 4 discusses these finding reflecting on the effects of Tumblr's affordances on its users' behaviour. And the conclusions are discussed in Sect. 5.

2   Related Work

The work presented in this paper is related to analysing user activity on OSNs. This topic has attracted researchers' attention since the early days of OSNs. There are two approaches to analysing user behaviour or activity: qualitative and quantitative. In the qualitative approach researchers conduct surveys asking users about their perception and usage of OSNs, whilst the quantitative approach relies on analysing user activity utilising the traces users leave as they interact with each other on such platforms. We will briefly review both approaches highlighting the main purposes of each approach and the methodology used in the analysis.

In the quantitative camp, there are a number of related work that studied user activity for various purposes. Based on the data type available for researchers, we can divide quantitative approaches into two main sub-approaches: analysing clickstream data and analysing functionality data. The former allows analysing all of the users activity, including visible and invisible ones or silent activity such as browsing. Silent activity accounts for the majority of user activity on social networks (92%). Hence, user activity captured via web crawling or API requests comprises a small fraction of what users do on such platforms [5]. However, collecting clickstream data is more challenging than collecting data directly from the platform either by crawling or via APIs. Clickstream data can be collected using different methods such as: social network aggregator [5], anonymized HTTP header traces from ISPs [32], or using an extension added to the web browser [28]. The former two methods requires anonymisation while the latter requires recruiting users who are willing to share their data. However, [22] argue that clickstream data can be incomplete as it is limited by the collection duration and the location.

Beside clickstream data analysis, Java et al. [21] utilised community detection algorithms to determine user intentions and categories on Twitter. They used network analysis to detect communities then they analysed the content shared within these communities to categorise users and interpret their intentions. However, their approach focuses on the users not the platform, i.e., they utilised the Twitter's functionalities and users' activity record to unveil users' behaviours. Another early work on Twitter looked at the nature of conversations that emerge on the platform; the researchers used content analysis methods to assess the use of @, responses to tweets with @ and the coherence of the exchange of messages [20]. Boyd et al. [8] analysed the practice of retweeting as a conversation mechanism on Twitter; in particular, they analysed the non-conventional retweet practices on Twitter i.e., using "RT @username". Kendall et al. [23] analysed users interaction about health-related topics on Twitter identified using a set of keywords. Retweeting, sharing and reblogging activities on Twitter, Facebook and Tumblr respectively received the majority of researchers' attention [4,10–12,16,24,35–37].

On the qualitative side, Meier et al. [29] studied the motivation of favouriting on Twitter, after conducting a survey they introduced a taxonomy of 25 different motivation to use the favourite button which can be categorised into two types: as a response or for other purposes such as: reuse or non-verbal communication. On Facebook, Meixner et al. [30] conducted a survey asking users about their impression after a content they liked or commented on it is altered. Also, Scissors [33] examined user perception when liking or receiving a like on Facebook. [18, 19] investigated Tumblr's fandoms and the nature of interaction within such communities.

While few studies considered Tumblr [10,35], their focus was on the reblogging functionality only, other functionalities (such as liking and commenting) receive little to no attention. Thus, the work presented in this paper aims at establishing an understanding of user activity on Tumblr and it makes use of a rich dataset of user interaction around the most popular content. Our work utilises quantitative methods and reflects on the finding in related work on Tumblr and other platforms.

3   Experimental Settings

Tumblr is a hybrid OSN platform that exhibits several characteristics of blogging and social networking [10]. Tumblr allows its users to write long posts in any multimedia form, also, it allows a number of functionalities such as following, reblogging and liking [35]. There are two mechanisms to communicate verbally on Tumblr, either by adding comments to reblogs or by replying directly to a post. In addition, for more personal attribution Tumblr introduced @mention in early 2014, which can be used in either a comment or a reply. Reblogs, likes, comments, and replies appear in the list of notes attached to each post in the following format: *username* **reblogged this from** *username*, *username* **liked this**, *username* **reblogged this from** *username* **and added** "a comment", and *username* **said:** "a reply".

Dataset Description: The dataset we use in this paper was collected from Tumblr's 2014 "Year in Review" blog curated by Tumblr's staff; it consists of the most reblogged posts and popular topics in one year. Using this blog means that we can leverage Tumblr's staff privileged access that catalogue the most popular posts. Consequently, our dataset is biased towards popular content, however, we believe that analysing user activity within popular content is as important as analysing it in ordinary posts. Because both types of content exist on any platform. We collected the URLs of the most reblogged posts according to their category. For each post we obtained the following: URL, author (blog-name), publishing timestamp, type and category. We then used a web scraper to extract the list of notes that include all activities (reblogging, liking, commenting and replying) in a chronological order. A web crawler was used because Tumblr's API does not provide the list of notes or any information related to user activity. The dataset contains all activities in the top posts in 57 different categories. There are 1292 posts, and the number of distinct activities in the dataset are as follows: reblogs: 73,048,903, likes: 48,822,318, reblogs with comments: 1,133,096, and replies: 315.

4   User Activity Analysis

Tumblr users can perform a number of activities including reblogging, liking, commenting and replying. These activities are facilitated by a number of functionalities namely: reblog, like, reblog with comment and reply. Each one of these functionalities indicates a different level of users' engagement with the published content. In this section, we will look into these functionalities and compare them across categories. We also considered two affordances of Tumblr i.e., the ability to reblog more than once and reblog deletion.

4.1   Reblogging

We found that on average a post is reblogged 56539 times, and the maximum number of reblogs a post has is 581895 while the minimum is 3. In fact, about 78% of the posts were reblogged 10000 times or more but only 18% were reblogged more than 100000 times. As we can see there is a huge margin in the total number of reblogs per post. One reason is that these posts are selected as the top ones in 57 categories curated by Tumblr's staff. Hence, they appeal to different communities based on users' interests. Figure 1a shows the distribution of the number of reblogs. Heavy-tailed distributions have been widely observed in previous studies; posts on Tumblr have similar characteristics.

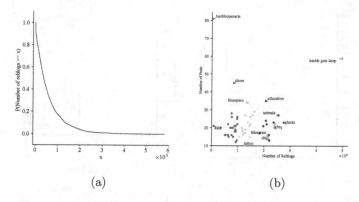

(a)   (b)

Fig. 1. (a) The distribution of the number of reblogs per post, (b) categories clustered according to the size of the category (number of posts) and the total number of reblogs in each category (Color figure online)

Figure 1b illustrates the relation between the number of posts in each category and the corresponding total number of reblogs in that category. We used K-means clustering to divide categories into four groups. Figure 1b, shows that the number of posts for the majority of categories ranges between 10 and 30, while few categories stand out both in terms of the number of posts and the total number of reblogs.

The first group contains one category 'tumblr gets deep' which acquires the majority of reblogging across all categories and also it stands out in terms of the size of the category i.e., the total number of posts in the category. The second group includes: education, plants, animals, nostalgia, video, lyrics, feminism, parenting and chill. The categories in this group have large number of reblogs but they vary in terms of the size of category. The third and fourth groups (in yellow and blue respectively) contains the majority of categories. The third group contains categories with total number of reblogs below 2M and above 1M, while the fourth contains categories with total number of reblogs below 1M. 'tumblropenarts' and shoes stand out in terms of the size of the categories. 'tumblropenarts' has the highest number of posts, but it has the smallest total number of reblogs across all categories. The category shoes, on the other hand, has many posts but its total reblogs is relatively smaller than the categories in both group four and three. One noticeable category is kale, which has an average number of posts but its total number of reblogs is remarkably smaller than the majority of categories.

4.2 Reblogging Rate

Unlike most of the other platforms, Tumblr allows its users to reblog the same post more than once. This particular ability is said to be used as Tumblr's users' means of communication [10]. We want to explore the rate at which this happens i.e., if Tumblr users are allowed to reblog more than once, how often does this

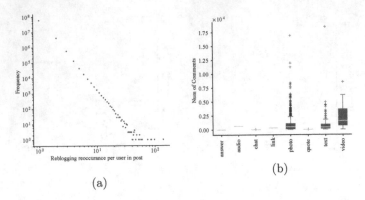

(a)   (b)

Fig. 2. (a) Reblogging reoccurrences per user in a post, (b) the number of comments by post type

occur? This is particularly important for two reasons: first, to examine whether this ability is being used at all. Second, to examine the rate at which users' communicate with each other given the remark that reblogging is being used as a way of communication. Figure 2a illustrates the distribution of reblogging reoccurrences made by one user in one post. As we can see most users reblog a post only once. This means that even though Tumblr allows reblogging more than once, most users reblog a post on one occasion only. Nonetheless, only 7.33% of the reblogs in the dataset are reoccurrences, while the majority (92.66%) are one reblog per user in each post.

4.3   Commenting

We looked at reblogging rates and we have seen that users rarely reblog more than once. Thus, if we assume that reblogging is Tumblr's users' means of communication, the low reblogging rate means that Tumblr users rarely engage in conversations with each other. Despite the low reblogging rate, comments were suggested as an explanation for the reoccurring reblogging behaviour [10]. Our analysis shows that the number of reblogs with comments is exceptionally low in comparison to the total number of reblogs. Overall only 1.55% of reblogs are with comments. The average number of comments in each post equals 877 and on average, there are 0.16 comments per 10 reblogs (median: 0.13). To examine if personal attribution (using @) is being used widely on Tumblr, we analyse comments' text finding that only a tiny percentage of comments include @ in the text (0.32%). Replies, on the other hand, are also rare, there were 315 replies only across all categories.

Additionally, video posts have higher comment rates per post, which is consistent with the fact that posts that belong to the video category have high numbers of comments per post. Photo posts, the dominant post type in the dataset, have lower commenting rate in comparison with videos. Also, text posts, which comprise only 10.90% of all posts, show very low degrees of commenting although one would expect that these posts will be intriguing for others to comment (Fig. 2b).

4.4 Reblog Deletion

In an ideal situation, the first reblog must be from the same user (post's author). However, that was not the case in 486 posts in the dataset (37.61%). In these posts the authors were not the source for the first reblogs. After investigating the causes we noticed that some times users might delete posts or reblogs. Reblog deletion is detected if there is a reblog but the source (rebloggee) doesn't appear as a target (reblogger) in all of the earlier reblogging cases. This occurs if the author or a reblogger deletes their post/reblog after which other users have reblogged from them. Hence, there will be some missing data and it is difficult to estimate the amount of the deleted reblogs before the data collection, it might be one reblog only or many consecutive reblogs. Our analysis shows that, on average, there are 1150 deleted reblogs (median: 747) in each post. In other words, there are 27 deleted reblogs for each 1000 reblogs. Moreover, around 60% of the posts have 1000 deleted reblogs or less, while the rest have higher deletion rates.

4.5 Liking

On Tumblr, Liking is the second main functionality available for users. It allows users to express their admiration towards a post without adding it to their blogs. However, we found that the total number of reblogs per category is higher than the total number of likes. This means that reblogging is more popular among Tumblr users in comparison to liking. However, they are correlated and relationship between the two is linear, so as the post becomes more popular by being reblogged, more people attempt to like the post. On average, there are 7.99 likes per 10 reblogs. Having the option to like and reblog the same post, on average 22.37% of users reblogged and liked the same post.

5 Discussion

The functionalities provided by any social network platform shape its users' behaviour. These functionalities schematise, and sometimes control and limit what users are able to do within the platform. These functionalities provide a form of non-textual and non-verbal communication on social networks, a task that is central to any Computer-Mediated Communication [29]. This section discusses Tumblr's affordances and how they affect user activity. it highlights some remarks, discusses the findings obtained from user activity analysis and compares Tumblr with other platforms.

Table 1. Category clusters ordered by the total number of reblogs per category

Groups	Categories
Group 1:	Tumblr gets deep
Group 2:	Plants, animals, lgbtq, chill, feminism, lyrics, nostalgia, education, video, parenting
Group 3:	Internet, school, beauty, business, cosplay, funny, home and decor, bluespace, health and fitness, tech, ice+bucket+challenge, hair, gaming, webcomics, healthcare, tattoo, puns, bathtub, music video, sculpture
Group 4:	Marriage-equality, menswear, mobile-movement, history, science, skeleton war, pizza, pixel art, gif art, sports, shoes, architecture, maps, crowdfunding, food, autos, street art, 3d gif, diy, 3d printing, sponsored posts entertainment, archaeology, sponsored posts brands, net art, kale, tumblropenarts

5.1 Categories as Community Identifiers

The most popular posts belong to different categories; thus, they attract a different group of users based on their interests. Therefore, the total number of reblogs per category can be used as an estimate of the size of a particular community on Tumblr. However, not all categories can be easily associated with a particular community. Table 1 lists the four groups as identified in Fig. 1b ordered by the total number of reblogs per category. Our analysis showed that 'tumblr gets deep' category acquires a number of the most reblogged posts in the dataset. Typically, posts in 'tumblr gets deep' category start off as a text or a photo that becomes popular when users reblog and comment on it, then the nested comments spread as a one piece of content. However, it is hard to associate 'tumblr gets deep' category with a particular community. In contrast, the second group has a number of communities that can be identified such as: animals, plants, lgbtq, feminism, education and parenting. The rest (lyrics, nostalgia, video and chill) appear to be appealing to a large number of Tumblr users, but it is not possible to associate those categories with a specific community. Group three contains another set of categories that can be used as indicators of communities such as: school, beauty, business, home and decor, health and fitness, tech, gaming, and healthcare.

Posts in 'tumblropenarts' category have remarkably small number of reblogs. This category contains posts from the 'tumblropenarts' blog, which is known as Tumblr official hub of art where users submit their art-work to be published. The low reblogging rate might indicate that this blog might not be well-known, especially that there are a number of other art-related categories that have larger number of reblogs such as: net art, street art, pixel art and sculpture. Another category that has a remarkably small number of reblogs is kale, possibly because it attracts an audience with a very specific interest in vegetarian and vegan food based on the tags that are added to its posts.

5.2   Reblogs vs. Comments

Our analysis showed that the number of comments on Tumblr is remarkably low; there are only 0.16 comments per 10 reblogs. Among the small minority of reblogs with comments, only 0.32% contain the @ sign. On Twitter, Liu et al. [26] report that about 35% of tweets are actually replies. In our dataset there are 315 replies only, while the total number of reblogs and likes are 73,048,903 and 48,822,318 respectively. Which means that most communication between users is non-verbal: users like and reblog but rarely express their opinions in textual form. In contrast, Java et al. [21] identify conversation as one of the intentions to use Twitter. They found that 21% of users used Twitter for conversations, composing about 12.5% of the whole tweets identified by the @ sign.

Looking at the effect of posts' type on the number of comments it has, we found that posts that contain videos are the ones that exhibit higher number of comments per post (Fig. 2b). One explanation for the low commenting rate is the nature of personas that Tumblr users choose and the types of connections they seek. Hillman et al. [18] reported that Tumblr users often choose informal user-names. They also mentioned that, in contrast to Twitter and Facebook, most of their connections are not personal but based on common interests. Hence, users are gathered around the content they find interesting. However, Tumblr recently added a number of communication functionalities such as replies (@mentions) and private messages. Replies were found rare in the dataset, both replies and messages are fairly new features; replies was introduced in early 2014[1] while messages was introduced in November 2015[2]. Before that, the only way for users to communicate was via 'Ask'. Hillman et al. [18] mentioned that Tumblr users hesitate to communicate with each other using this 'Ask' feature because the question (message) and the response will be publicly visible.

Comparing reblogging reoccurrences and commenting rates across categories, we can notice that the number of comments is lower than reblogging reoccurrences, meaning that most reblogging reoccurrences are comment-less (Fig. 2b). This particular behaviour raises the following question: why do the users reblog the same content more than once if they are not using them for communication? A possible answer might be that these users might be bots, or it might be that these users are deliberately reblogging the same post at a different time of the day to get attention from a different audience.

5.3   Reblogs vs. Likes

The reblogging functionality shows higher degree of users' engagement with the content than liking. When users reblog, their interest is publicly shown because reblogged posts are added to the users' blogs. Liking, on the other hand, has been associated with a number of motivation such as bookmarking or giving a non-verbal feedback. On Tumblr, likes will only be shown on the same post or

---

[1] https://unwrapping.tumblr.com/post/74972171775/user-mentions-tumblr-apps.
[2] https://support.tumblr.com/post/132943845192/youve-asked-us-for-real-instant-messaging-and.

for some users who chose to show their likes in a designated tab. This aligns with what is stated on Tumblr help pages: "Replies are Tumblr's way of responding to a post that's more specific than a like, less of a commitment than a reblog, and more public than a message."[3]

One of the most important findings is the fact that reblogging is slightly more popular than liking: for each 10 reblogs there are 7.9 likes. The higher reblogging rates mean that users on Tumblr are highly engaged with the shared content. This finding is also aligned with Tumblr's CEO's remark about the platform's high reblogging rates: "Ninety percent of content on Tumblr is actually reblogged". Agarwal et al., in their analysis of extremism on Tumblr, found that reblogging is a better indicator of relation between two users than liking [2]. On Twitter, 43% of tweets get at least one favourite and 36% of them get at least one retweet [14]. Hence, it seems that favouring is more popular on Twitter than retweeting, while it is the opposite on Tumblr, especially for the most popular content.

On the other hand, 22.37% liked and reblogged the same post. This behaviour shows the degree of 'interestingness' in the post's content [29]. This raises an important question: what is the user's perception of the functionalities available on OSNs? Users will always use such functionalities in innovative ways [6]. Thus, while the intended purpose of these functionalities is defined by the platform, users might exploit them for other purposes. Boyd et al. [8] surveyed Twitter users on their perception of the retweet functionality while Meier et al. [29] surveyed favourite functionality. Both reported that users' motivations to use the functionality were diverse, both in terms of its meaning and purpose. It will be interesting to investigate Tumblr's functionalities perception and motivations of usage given the rates that we have seen in the analysis.

5.4   The Value of Deleted Reblogs

We have seen that it is common for users to revisit their reblogging decisions and they might either delete reblogs or deactivate their accounts. Deletion is an important aspect of social network behaviour. The rate of deletion indicates that the state on OSNs is dynamic; the state of Tumblr can rapidly change. Thus, this must be taken in consideration during the data collection and analysis. In addition to accounting for this behaviour for practicality during data collection and analysis; deletion is important for other purposes including calculating the probability of rumour deletion [15] and identifying regrettable tweets [38].

5.5   Content Exposure

For a post to be seen, reblogged or liked, users must first be exposed to it. Tumblr incorporates a number of mechanisms that help exposing users to content and enable the discovery of new content. By following other users, a user will be exposed to friends' newly published content. On Tumblr and many OSNs,

---

[3] https://tumblr.zendesk.com/hc/en-us/articles/231855648-Replies.

following others is the main mechanism for content exposure. However, Tumblr has other mechanisms in place to promote content and increase its exposure. For instance, the majority of Tumblr users are young [10] and most of the time they get involved in fandoms. Fandoms are communities of users with similar interests, mainly of TV shows, films, celebrities, musical groups, etc. [31]. Through these fandoms users express and share their devotion, passion and feelings [13]. Fandoms are not explicit entities but rather they are implicit communities that are identified with a number of tags [7].

Members of fandoms discover content through a set of designated tags; from the list of tags attached to posts they can also discover other tags [13]. Tags are important of Tumblr, they help making posts more visible. Since Tumblr's search mechanism searches tags only, posts with no tags can hardly be discovered unless the user follows the blog [35]. Tags reside in a separate component apart from the content, allowing users to include as many tags as they wish. On Twitter, hashtags are part of the tweet's text. Therefore, Tumblr's mechanism increases posts' exposure. The top posts analysed in this paper have on average about 8.33 tags, while the maximum number of tags for one post was 31. Tumblr also allows users to track tags, hence, each time a post that contain a tracked tag is posted it will appear in the user's feed. In fact Agarwal et al. suggested that tracked tags allow users to create virtual communities without following each other [2].

Additionally, Tumblr has a number of content promotion tools. E.g., each day Tumblr shows what is trending and it has a staff picks page that includes a list of curated posts selected by Tumblr staff. Also, 'fandometrics' is an official Tumblr page that provides a weekly review of the most popular fandoms. It rates fandoms according to the number of posts posted in a tag and the number of searches, reblogs and likes on posts with that tag. In addition, at the end of each year, Tumblr publish its 'Year in Review' blog. In fact, we have seen that 'tumblr open art' category has the lowest reblogging rates, nonetheless, its posts were considered as the most popular in a year. This indicates that promoting posts on the 'Year in Review' blog is a way to get more users' attention to the posts published in 'tumblr open art' blog. The mechanisms mentioned above increase the likelihood that a piece of content get reblogged and liked. This explains why Tumblr posts are reblogged and liked more in comparison with popular content on other platforms [3].

6   Conclusions

In this paper we analysed the way Tumblr's functionalities are being utilised within the most popular posts in one year. This curated list of posts allows us to unravel users activity around popular content on Tumblr, a platform that has its own culture and distinctive features. One of most interesting finding is that reblogging is more popular among Tumblr's users than liking, while the rate of comments is significantly low. This means that most of the time, users communicate using non-verbal mechanisms; they are interested in the content, they reblog it or like it but they rarely talk to each other about it. The high reblogging rates indicates that Tumblr users are highly engaged with the content in comparison to popular content on other platforms. This is facilitated by the many content exposure and discovery mechanisms that Tumblr use to increase its users' exposure to new and interesting content which will eventually cause a surge in popularity represented by likes and reblogs.

References

1. Adamic, L., Adar, E.: How to search a social network. Soc. Netw. **27**(3), 187–203 (2005). https://doi.org/10.1016/j.socnet.2005.01.007
2. Agarwal, S., Sureka, A.: A topical crawler for uncovering hidden communities of extremist micro-bloggers on Tumblr. In: CEUR Workshop Proceedings, vol. 1395, pp. 26–27 (2015)
3. Alrajebah, N., Carr, L., Luczak-Roesch, M., Tiropanis, T.: Deconstructing diffusion on Tumblr: structural and temporal aspects. In: Proceedings of the 2017 ACM on Web Science Conference, WebSci 2017, pp. 319–328. ACM (2017). https://doi.org/10.1145/3091478.3091491
4. Bakshy, E., Rosenn, I., Marlow, C., Adamic, L.: The role of social networks in information diffusion. In: Proceedings of the 21st International Conference on World Wide Web, WWW 2012, pp. 519–528. ACM, New York (2012). https://doi.org/10.1145/2187836.2187907
5. Benevenuto, F., Rodrigues, T., Cha, M., Almeida, V.: Characterizing user behavior in online social networks. In: Proceedings of the 9th ACM SIGCOMM Conference on Internet Measurement Conference, pp. 49–62 (2009). https://doi.org/10.1145/1644893.1644900
6. Berners-Lee, T., Hall, W., Hendler, J.A., O'Hara, K., Shadbolt, N., Weitzner, D.J.: A framework for web science. Found. Trends Web Sci. **1**(1), 1–130 (2006). https://doi.org/10.1561/1800000001
7. Bourlai, E., Herring, S.C.: Multimodal communication on Tumblr: "I have so many feels!". In: Proceedings of the 2014 ACM Conference on Web Science, WebSci 2014, pp. 171–175. ACM (2014). https://doi.org/10.1145/2615569.2615697
8. Boyd, D.M., Golder, S., Lotan, G.: Tweet, tweet, retweet: conversational aspects of retweeting on Twitter. In: 2010 43rd Hawaii International Conference on System Sciences (HICSS), pp. 1–10. IEEE Computer Society, January 2010. https://doi.org/10.1109/HICSS.2010.412
9. Boyd, D.M., Ellison, N.B.: Social network sites: definition, history, and scholarship. J. Comput.-Mediat. Commun. **13**(1), 210–230 (2007). https://doi.org/10.1109/EMR.2010.5559139
10. Chang, Y., Tang, L., Inagaki, Y., Liu, Y.: What is Tumblr: a statistical overview and comparison. ACM SIGKDD Explor. Newsl. **16**(1), 21–29 (2014). https://doi.org/10.1145/2674026.2674030
11. Cheng, J., Adamic, L., Dow, P.A., Kleinberg, J.M., Leskovec, J.: Can cascades be predicted? In: Proceedings of the 23rd International Conference on World Wide Web, WWW 2014, pp. 925–936. ACM (2014). https://doi.org/10.1145/2566486.2567997
12. Cheng, J., Adamic, L.A., Kleinberg, J.M., Leskovec, J.: Do cascades recur? In: Proceedings of the 25th International Conference on World Wide Web, WWW 2016, pp. 671–681. International World Wide Web Conferences Steering Committee (2016). https://doi.org/10.1145/2872427.2882993

13. DeSouza, M.E.: A case of the red pants Mondays: the connection between fandom, Tumblr, and consumption. Major Papers by Master of Science Students (2013)
14. Enge, E.: Twitter engagement unmasked: a study of more than 4M tweets (2014). https://www.stonetemple.com/twitter-engagement-umasked/
15. Friggeri, A., Adamic, L., Eckles, D., Cheng, J.: Rumor cascades. In: International AAAI Conference on Web and Social Media Eighth International AAAI Conference on Weblogs and Social Media (ICWSM), pp. 101–110. AAAI (2014)
16. Goel, S., Anderson, A., Hofman, J., Watts, D.: The structural virality of online diffusion. **22**, 26 (2013, preprint)
17. Hartson, R.: Cognitive, physical, sensory, and functional affordances in interaction design. Behav. Inf. Technol. **22**(5), 315–338 (2003)
18. Hillman, S., Procyk, J., Neustaedter, C.: alksjdf;lksfd: Tumblr and the fandom user experience. In: ACM Conference on Designing Interactive Systems, pp. 1–10 (2014). https://doi.org/10.1145/2598510.2600887
19. Hillman, S., Procyk, J., Neustaedter, C.: Tumblr fandoms, community & #38; culture. In: Proceedings of the Companion Publication of the 17th ACM Conference on Computer Supported Cooperative Work & #38; Social Computing, CSCW Companion 2014, pp. 285–288. ACM (2014). https://doi.org/10.1145/2556420.2557634
20. Honeycutt, C., Herring, S.C.: Beyond microblogging: conversation and collaboration via Twitter. In: 42nd Hawaii International Conference on System Sciences, HICSS 2009, pp. 1–10. IEEE (2009). https://doi.org/10.1109/HICSS.2009.89
21. Java, A., Song, X., Finin, T., Tseng, B.: Why we Twitter: understanding microblogging usage and communities. In: Proceedings of the 9th WebKDD and 1st SNA-KDD 2007 Workshop on Web Mining and Social Network Analysis, pp. 56–65. ACM (2007). https://doi.org/10.1145/1348549.1348556
22. Jin, L., Chen, Y., Wang, T., Hui, P., Vasilakos, A.V.: Understanding user behavior in online social networks: a survey. Commun. Mag. IEEE **51**(9), 144–150 (2013). https://doi.org/10.1109/MCOM.2013.6588663
23. Kendall, L., Hartzler, A., Klasnja, P., Pratt, W.: Descriptive analysis of physical activity conversations on Twitter. In: CHI 2011 Extended Abstracts on Human Factors in Computing Systems, CHI EA 2011, pp. 1555–1560. ACM (2011). https://doi.org/10.1145/1979742.1979807
24. Kwak, H., Lee, C., Park, H., Moon, S.: What is Twitter, a social network or a news media? In: Proceedings of the 19th International Conference on World Wide Web, WWW 2010, pp. 591–600. ACM (2010). https://doi.org/10.1145/1772690.1772751
25. Lin, Y.R., Margolin, D., Keegan, B., Baronchelli, A., Lazer, D.: # bigbirds never die: Understanding social dynamics of emergent hashtag. arXiv preprint arXiv:1303.7144 (2013)
26. Liu, Y., Kliman-Silver, C., Mislove, A.: The tweets They are a-Changin: evolution of Twitter users and behavior. In: Proceedings of the Eighth International AAAI Conference on Weblogs and Social Media, pp. 305–314. AAAI (2014)
27. Marquart, E.: Microblog sensation: the growing popularity of Tumblr. 3PM J. Digit. Res. Publ. Sess. **2**, 70–75 (2010)
28. Meier, F., Aigner, J., Elsweiler, D.: Using sessions from clickstream data analysis to uncover different types of Twitter behaviour. In: Proceedings of the 15th International Symposium of Information Science (ISI 2017), pp. 237–250 (2017)
29. Meier, F., Elsweiler, D., Wilson, M.L.: More than liking and bookmarking? Towards understanding Twitter favouriting behaviour. In: Proceeding of the 8th International AAAI Conference on Weblogs and Social Media, pp. 346–355. AAAI (2014)

30. Meixner, B., Marlow, J.: Like it or not: how do users understand the relationship between likes and edited social media content? In: Proceedings of the 2017 CHI Conference Extended Abstracts on Human Factors in Computing Systems - CHI EA 2017, pp. 1893–1900 (2017)
31. Renwick, L.: Audience research project: Tumblr study group research How do Fandoms' on Tumblr react to new media content? Enq.-ACES J. Undergrad. Res. 4, 1–24 (2014). https://doi.org/10.1145/3027063.3053119
32. Schneider, F., Feldmann, A., Krishnamurthy, B., Willinger, W.: Understanding online social network usage from a network perspective. In: Proceedings of the 9th ACM SIGCOMM Conference on Internet Measurement, IMC 2009, pp. 35–48. ACM (2009). https://doi.org/10.1145/1644893.1644899
33. Scissors, L., Burke, M., Wengrovitz, S.: What's in a like?: attitudes and behaviors around receiving likes on Facebook. In: Proceedings of the 19th ACM Conference on Computer-Supported Cooperative Work & Social Computing, CSCW 2016, pp. 1501–1510. ACM (2016). https://doi.org/10.1145/2818048.2820066
34. Wen, X., Lin, Y.R., Trattner, C., Parra, D.: Twitter in academic conferences: usage, networking and participation over time. In: Proceedings of the 25th ACM Conference on Hypertext and Social Media, pp. 285–290. ACM (2014). https://doi.org/10.1145/2631775.2631826
35. Xu, J., Compton, R., Lu, T.C., Allen, D.: Rolling through Tumblr: characterizing behavioral patterns of the microblogging platform. In: Proceedings of the 2014 ACM Conference on Web Science, WebSci 2014, pp. 13–22. ACM (2014). https://doi.org/10.1145/2615569.2615694
36. Yang, J., Counts, S.: Predicting the speed, scale, and range of information diffusion in Twitter. In: Fourth International AAAI Conference on Weblogs and Social Media ICWSM, pp. 355–358 (2010)
37. Yang, Z., et al.: Understanding retweeting behaviors in social networks. In: Proceedings of the 19th ACM International Conference on Information and Knowledge Management, CIKM 2010, pp. 1633–1636. ACM (2010). https://doi.org/10.1145/1871437.1871691
38. Zhou, L., Wang, W., Chen, K.: Tweet properly: analyzing deleted tweets to understand and identify regrettable ones. In: Proceedings of the 25th International Conference on World Wide Web (WWW 2016), pp. 603–612. ACM (2016). https://doi.org/10.1145/2872427.2883052

Rationality or Aesthetics? Navigation vs. Web Page Ergonomics in Cross-cultural Use of University Websites

Alexander V. Yakunin[iD], Svetlana S. Bodrunova[✉][iD], and Maria Gourieva[iD]

School of Journalism and Mass Communications, St. Petersburg State University, Saint Petersburg, Russia
s.bodrunova@spbu.ru

Abstract. The article looks at one of the factors that may cast impact upon interest to educational programs of today's universities in various regions of the world, namely at effective web presence of a university in the global information space. To successfully advance the university in the World Wide Web, efficient interaction with the global networked audience is necessary.

The quality of this interaction depends primarily on web design of the university portals, which are the main communication tool of any educational organization with potential studentship and professorship. However, for efficient communication with the audience in different regions of the world, it is necessary to take into account the peculiarities of visual culture peculiar to those regions. The paper suggests that the perception patterns of the Western audiences and people in South-East Asia can differ, which can affect communication efficiency for web portals with unified structures, adapted only in terms of language. In order to test this assumption, we carry out an experiment in which we compare the results of interaction experience of two representative groups of the global audience – students from Russia and from China – with 23 university portals around the world selected based on webometrics rankings. The results of the experiment show that, in the perception patterns of Western and Eastern users, there are differences in perception of information architecture and page layouts. In particular, perception of the representatives of South-East Asia is more sensitive to the composition and visual aesthetics of single web pages than to the rationality of the structure of the website as a whole. This result allowed the authors to propose recommendations for developing a strategy for promoting university brands on the Internet.

Keywords: Web usability · Web presence · University websites Russia · China

1 Introduction

In a globalized communication sphere of today, any modern university needs an efficient system of information dissemination and of communicating with potential and existing target audiences, be it the student community, professorship, or global

© Springer Nature Switzerland AG 2018
S. S. Bodrunova (Ed.): INSCI 2018, LNCS 11193, pp. 169–180, 2018.
https://doi.org/10.1007/978-3-030-01437-7_14

audience at large. For the vast majority of the universities around the globe, the central element of such communication system is a university portal. Online activities have started to affect the university ratings [1].

Among the factors important for the university rankings, those measured the most often may be formulated as 'efficiency of web presence' and 'impact of web presence upon...' (various parameters). These indicators are perceived not only as directly influencing the university performance; high positions by these parameters are also a sign of overall high quality of education and competitiveness of a given university on the world stage.

University web portals are also assessed within global webometric systems that include web portals of various origins and goals. High positions in such ratings, too, may affect the perception of overall success of a university. One of such global ratings is the Webometrics rating (since 2004) by Cybermetric Laboratory of the Spanish National Research Council (CSIC). This metric is considered independent and may be used for selecting universities on the basis of their efficient web presence.

But both university rankings and webometric ratings do not assess the parameter which may be called 'cultural adaptation'. Despite the significant amount of research done on cross-cultural use and affordances of institutional web spaces (for a review, see below) [2], the university rankings still oversee this parameter of web presence assessment. Also, if English-language and Eastern users are often the case for cross-cultural analysis, mainly due to the fact that such research is conducted either in Anglo-American world or in China and Japan, other languages and cultures important on the Internet, are almost completely overlooked. This is especially true for Russian, which is second only to English in terms of the number of web domains established, and has long been ranked #4 in the volume of blogs and overall space occupied.

Another gap lies in the fact that, when assessed even cross-culturally, usability is often understood in very pragmatic terms and does not include the difference in aesthetic appeal; thus, many of the results may be misleading or misinterpreted.

Our research addresses both these gaps. First, we use Russian students as assessors along with the Chinese students; also, we assess both navigational and layout elements, as based on our previous research [4–6]. The paper is organized as follows: in Sect. 2, we review the literature and reconstruct the theoretical framework for the research design. In Sect. 3, we explain our method and the research design. In Sect. 4, we show the conduct of the experiment; in Sect. 5, we describe and explain its results. Section 6 provides the discussion upon the results at the background of previous studies.

2 Theoretical Framework

In usability studies, there is a range of works on the relationship between the usability of a university site and its efficiency of web presence [13, 21, 24, 27, 31]. Thus, one study [27] shows that, with the growth in the position of a university in the Webometrics ranking, the quality of design of its website also increases. The author believes that design influences web presence, which Webometrics evaluates, and the improvement of design promotes the university to be ranked higher.

Typically, most studies that examine the factors of web presence of Internet media pay special attention to the role of an efficient organization of the information architecture and navigation system [15, 20, 29, 33]. Web navigation retains leadership in the number of mentions in studies on usability and user-interface interaction [11, 25, 26].

The main problems that are actively investigated at the present stage are the determination of the elements of a navigation system that affect the users' behavior, as well as assessment of menu quality. However, obvious prioritizing of navigation makes the scholars overlook compositional and aesthetic aspects of web design and their role in efficient user interaction with the university websites (see, e.g., [19, 24]). Also, the result of interaction largely depends on mental models of the audience, which change due to the visual culture dominant in a certain region. Even in navigation systems, different preferences are possible due to the cognitive styles inherent to different cultures [9, 23].

To date, there are a fairly large number of comparative studies on impact of cultural features upon website design. In all these studies, the selection of cultural markers in design is based on application of criteria of a particular model – for example, the Hofstede's model [6, 7, 14, 17, 28]. However, as some studies show [9, 16, 18], there is a problem of relativity in understanding Hofstede's criteria by representatives of different cultures. Evaluation of design with the use of the Hofstede's criteria also ignores the aesthetic traditions of the regions under scrutiny.

When the scholars discuss the relativity of universal criteria in the evaluation of design, attention is also paid to studies devoted to the method of heuristic evaluation [1, 25, 26]. In these studies, traditional methods of evaluating the structure and the website layout are criticized. Nielsen's criteria of usability, long considered universal, in fact reflect the Western understanding of efficacy of visual perception and ignore the cultural characteristics of audience in other regions. At the same time, in several rare works, direct dependence of web design upon the aesthetic traditions of certain cultural regions is discussed. Thus, one paper [22] investigates the relationship between the design parameters of the websites in Australia, China, and Saudi Arabia. As the design parameters the authors take the layout, navigation, links, multimedia, visual representation, color, and text. Significant differences were found in each of the listed design attributes, suggesting that different interfaces may be needed for successful communication with different cultural groups. However, in such studies, it is not clear which features and to what extent are responsible for the variations in perception of the website interfaces. While research upon the usability of university websites is plentiful, comparative studies of the relative role of navigation and page layout in efficacy of user experience is virtually non-existent.

3 Methodology

For the current study, we assume that the relative importance of information architecture and page composition may differ in different cultures.

In particular, we expect that the visual culture of South-East Asia will make the assessors to be more sensitive to composition and visual aesthetics than to the rationality of the website structure.

To (dis)prove this assumption, we test navigation and layouting of university web portals within two groups of assessors representing the 'western' type of perception (Russian students) and the 'eastern' type of perception (People's Republic of China).

In the design of the study, we were guided by two research questions:

RQ1. Are there differences between the groups in the efficiency of task performance on the websites with different parameters of layouting and navigation?

RQ2. Which factors – navigational or those of the layout – are more important for each group? In other words, if the page has poor usability and poor navigation, what needs to be improved for a certain segment of the audience – the overall design of the page, or would navigation be enough to optimize?

In accordance with the questions raised, we have developed a research design with the following stages:

- sampling of websites and single web pages for which the differences in navigation and layouting would be definable and measurable;
- choice and justification of the factors of webpage layout and navigation that, to our mind, would most affect the user experience;
- assessment of web pages based on U-index and N-index (see below), grouping of web pages for our experiment;
- establishment of parameters and metrics for assessment of efficacy of the users' experience;
- testing of the sampled websites during an experiment by measuring user experience in both groups;
- comparing user experience regarding navigation and layouting parameters in order to reveal regularities characteristic for each of the groups.

3.1 Justification of the Factors of Webpage Design and Navigation

In developing the assessment system for the layouts, we relied on studies examining pragmatic and aesthetic aspects of user experience in the context of the visual architecture of a web page [6, 10, 12]. Earlier, we had elaborated the concept of two-level organization of a layout [6], which is useful also for the current study, as, according our previous research results, the quality of ergonomics of a web page can be estimated by an integrated usability index (U-index). This index summarizes the impact of individual elements of a layout, such as font, spacing, columns, color balance, creolization of textual blocks etc., upon user experience. In effect, the index is a list of assessment criteria with options providing for higher or lower marks for each of the criteria. We had shown that this index can provide a quantitative metric for the quality of a web page in terms of usability without the necessity to test the page on eye trackers or any other apparatus [4, 6].

In developing the navigation assessment system, we relied upon a range of academic papers on models of menu organization and optimization. Out of them, we have derived N-index – a generalizing index for the assessment of navigation quality, similarly to the aforementioned U-index. This index demands in-depth description, as we have tested it for the first time. It also consists of a list of criteria that provide for higher or lower marks; all the marks together form the index value for a particular website.

The first of these criteria is the type of navigation system in terms of the number of its components and their location on the page (that is, the navigation pattern). Based on studies examining different types of menus [3, 5, 30], we have developed a scale for assessing the navigation system of a website as follows (see Table 1). The works on comparison of menus, including our own, suggests that the fewer menus on the page the better for both user performance and satisfaction.

Table 1. Options of positioning of the components of a navigation system

Navigation pattern	Components	Score
One-component top (T)	Only the upper menu (expandable/non-expandable)	3
Two-component on the left (TL)	'Top + left menu'	2
Two-component top (2T)	The top two in different categories	2
Two-component on the right	'Top + right menu'	1
Three-component	'Left + top menu + content navigation in center'	1

The second important factor was the color zoning of the menu, the importance of which was also noted by a number of researchers [22, 32].

For this criterion, three possible options and their corresponding estimates were adopted:

- high-contrast zoning – 2 points;
- low-contrast – 1 point;
- no contrast – 0 point.

These two criteria have formed the N-index with the estimates from 1 to 5.

3.2 Assessment and Sampling of University Web Pages for the Experiment

Using the considered factors of page layout design and navigation as criteria, we estimated all pages of the sample on two coding sheets.

The next step was the selection of four types of pages in the design of which the difference in the usability of navigation indicators and that of layouts reached the maximum. Thus, for the experiment, the following four pages were selected:

1. pages with a maximum layout usability index and a maximum menu usability index (Umax+Nmax);
2. pages with a maximum layout usability index and a minimum menu usability index (Umax+Nmin);
3. pages with a minimum layout usability index and a maximum menu usability index (Umin+Nmax);
4. pages with a minimum layout usability index and a minimum menu usability index (Umin+Nmin).

Thus, for the page Umax+Nmax the expected result implies the maximum search speed and low perceived complexity; for the page Umin+Nmin, minimum search speed and high perceived complexity is expected. For the pages with mixed U-index and N-index, that is, (2) and (3), the expected search speed and perceived complexity will be culturally dependent.

Our initial sample included the websites of 23 universities – leaders of the Webometrics ranking. We have chosen three pages on each website that were key in the website topologies: these pages were leaders by betweenness centrality (that is, they were linked to the maximum number of other pages within the university web spaces). Thus, the sample for coding consisted of 69 web pages.

Then, we have coded all the web pages for U-index and N-index values and ranged the pages accordingly. The coding data are available on request. Then, for pre-testing, we have selected the typical representative pages – one per each combination of index values, from Umax+Nmax to Umin+Nmin. The detailed descriptions of the selected pages, including the index values calculated, are presented in Table 2.

Table 2. Sampled web pages and their U- and N-indices' values

Page URL	Quality indication	Indices	
		U-index (out of 22)	N-index (out of 5)
http://www.ucf.edu/locations	Umax+Nmax	15	4
http://www.uu.se/en/students	Umax+Nmin	15	2
http://www.iastate.edu/students	Umin+Nmax	7	4
http://www.berkeley.edu/atoz/	Umin+Nmin	9	2

3.3   The Research Hypotheses

In accordance with the research design, we have formulated five hypotheses, for them to be tested using an experiment with the four key pages:

H1 (testing N-index and double-testing U-index). Both groups will perform best on the Umax+Nmax page, and both groups will show the worst results for Umin+Nmin pages.

H2a. For a group with the 'western' perception type, navigation design casts more impact upon task performance than the layout design. Thus, their performance on the page Umin+Nmax will be better than on the page Umax+Nmin.

H2b. For a group with the 'western' perception type, navigation design is subjectively more important than the layout design. Thus, their evaluation of the page Umin+Nmax will be higher than that of the page Umax+Nmin.

H3a. For a group with the 'eastern' type of perception, layout usability casts more impact upon task performance than navigation design. Thus, their performance on the page Umax+Nmin will be better than on the page Umin+Nmax.

H3b. For a group with the 'eastern' type of perception, layout usability is subjectively more important than navigation design. Thus, their evaluation of the page Umax+Nmin will be higher than that of the page Umin+Nmax.

4   The Conduct of the Pre-test

After selecting the web pages for the pre-test, we asked the assessors to perform tasks on each of the four pages. The tasks aimed at finding information fragments.

The experiment involved 20 people aged 20 to 22; among them, 10 Russian students in the 'western' group and 10 Chinese students in the 'eastern' group. The level of technological literacy and the experience of working on the Internet for all the assessors were equally high. Also, both groups performed the tasks in English, which was a non-native language for both groups; the assessors had more or less comparable command of English, and, thus, the groups were in equal conditions in terms of linguistic workload.

As performance and subjective satisfaction metrics, the speed of performing the search task and the perceived level of complexity of the page design were chosen, respectively. After testing, each assessor was asked to evaluate the perceived complexity of the design by answering a simple request: 'Please rate how easy it was for you to find the information on this page'. The assessors rated the pages using the 5-point Likert scale with the following answers:

1. extremely inconvenient and difficult, the process caused irritation;
2. slight discomfort in finding the information;
3. normal, average degree of complexity, typical for most websites;
4. pretty easy;
5. too easy, intuitive and effortless.

The testing took place in a quiet room, each assessor had equal conditions for performing the tasks, and no student was familiar with the pages selected for pre-tests before the experiment.

5   Results

The aggregate results of the pre-test are shown in Table 3 (for the 'western' group) and Table 4 (for the 'eastern' group).

Table 3. Aggregate pre-test results for the 'western' group of assessors

Page type	Execution time, ms	Perceived difficulty, average points
Umax+Nmax	8.5	4.0
Umax+Nmin	41	1.4
Umin+Nmax	10	3.6
Umin_Nmin	39	1.0

Table 4. Aggregate pre-test results for the 'eastern' group of assessors

Page type	Execution time, ms	Perceived difficulty, average points
Umax+Nmax	19	2.7
Umax+Nmin	22	2.6
Umin+Nmax	51	2.9
Umin_Nmin	52	3.9

As can be seen from the results in Tables 3 and 4, the visual perception of layout of the web pages and the efficiency of the task performance differ for different groups.

H1. The results prove that the indices work, indeed; as expected, the page Umax +Nmax provoked the best performance, and the page Umin+Nmin has induced the lowest performance. H1 is proven for objective measurement, and we can use the indices for the pre-test.

But we also see that, in terms of subjective evaluation, the 'western' group has shown the expected difference (1.0 vs. 4.0), while the 'eastern' group has shown a reverse patent (3.9 vs. 2.7); we also see that the three pages with some maximum values have all invoked worse evaluation, As we discuss below, this may be linked to the differing perception of what constitutes subjective satisfaction and ease of use, as for the eastern cultures subjective satisfaction of the use is not strictly linked to timing of task performance.

H2 – a and b. As expected, the performance of the 'western' group showed that, for them, navigation, indeed, plays a bigger role in faster task fulfilment, as well as in subjective satisfaction. Moreover, the figures for the pages with better navigation (Umin+Nmax) end up in performance similar to the page with maximum navigation *and* layout (Umax+Nmax) – 8.5 ms and 4.0 points vs. 10 ms and 3.6 points, respectively. At the same time, the page Umax+Nmin has shown the results similar to the page Umin+Nmin: 41 ms and 1.4 points vs. 39 ms and 1.0 points. Thus, for the 'western' type of perception, both hypotheses are supported.

With all the limitations of the study taken into account, we may still say that we see the following implications of the result discovered. First, web designers and prototype constructors should put their primary attention into the menu functionality, and also try to minimize the number of menus on the page. Second, improvement of web design or redesign should take into account the menu; it may be so that complete redesign is unnecessary, while eliminating the mess in navigation may raise significantly the users' satisfaction and search efficiency of the website. This is especially important for large web spaces like university portals, where hierarchization of information is oftentimes one of the main issues.

H3a. As it follows from Table 4, for the group of Chinese students representing the 'eastern' type of perception, the speed pattern was as expected. Thus, the page Umax +Nmin showed better performance than the page Umin+Nmax. Moreover, the results for the page with better layout and minimal navigation index provoked the aggregate result comparable with the best page (22 ms vs. 19 ms, respectively), while the page Umin+Nmax provoked the aggregate result comparable to the worst page (51 ms vs. 52 ms, respectively). Thus, H3a is supported by our data, and we see that pre-testing shows high relative importance of overall layout for task fulfilment for the 'eastern' group. This has to be taken into account by web designers and prototypists; also, improving the menu structure may not solve all the design problems when you deal with the Eastern audiences.

We also need to note that the 'eastern' group performed 2.2 times worse than the 'western' group for the best page and 1.3 times worse on the worst page. This difference in the aggregate speed cannot be explained by the fact that they performed the task in non-native language (English); it may need additional testing and further investigation if proven again. The difference may be caused by the fact that Chinese portals have vertical layouts due to their hieroglyphic content, while Russian websites are much more similar to English-language ones; the latter may result in faster search on the pages laid out horizontally for the Russian speakers. This also needs to be taken into account by the prototypists who lay out the web portals for universities where Chinese students are one of the primary target groups.

H3b. As already stated above, this hypothesis is not supported by our results, and this clearly contradicts with the performance results. This, in effect, means that the measurement system for subjective evaluation (the Likert scale) was perceived differently by the two groups, and they link their assessment of 'hard' and 'easy' to different factors. One explanation offered above is that, for the Chinese students, the efficiency and ease of use was not linked to timing of their search but may have been linked to other factors; this needs further investigation, and this also needs to be taken into consideration by design practitioners.

These results allow for drawing a conclusion relevant for developing a strategy of promotion of universities in the global networked space. To increase the efficiency of a university website in terms of interaction with global audience, it is crucial to take into account the peculiarities of visual culture of different regions of the world. For example, when developing several language versions of a website, it is recommended to modify the design in accordance with the perception patterns of a certain region of the world. In particular, the versions of websites in the languages of South-East Asia need layouts that differ from those in European languages. In 'Eastern' layouts, more attention is to be paid to the aesthetics and overall layout, such as frame proportions, fonts, and spacing. And if information search on a university website in the Eastern languages turns out to be ineffective, it is necessary to improve not only the navigation system of the website but also the composition of the page as a whole.

6 Discussion and Conclusion

Modern research pays much attention to the search for the factors that affect cross-cultural user interaction with university websites. But the common problem of such studies is that they do not take into consideration that navigational (rational) and layout (aesthetic) aspects of web design and prototyping may vary in significance for different culturally-based target audiences.

In our study, we have shown that, for various visual traditions ('western' and 'eastern', personified by Russian and Chinese students, respectively) the roles of navigation and web page design play different roles in task performance. We have shown that, for the Russian students, navigational aspects were way too more important, and minimization of the number of menus, as well as correct page zoning, helped a lot in raising the speed of task performance for this group. At the same time, for the Chinese students, the changes in navigation did not save the situation, while perfection of the page layout has helped raise the performance. As stated above, this needs to be taken into account in the process of website prototyping, web design, and redesign. Our main recommendation to the developers of the university websites is that, for global audiences, they need to develop the versions adapted to regional cultural features, not only linguistically, but also visually.

Another, perhaps even more intriguing result was received when we have measured the subjective user satisfaction with the process of information search. Thus, we have seen that the best result for the 'eastern' group was perceived for the page that we had ranked as the worst by both indices, and other results were all close to the middle of the Likert scale. This allows us to put a question mark on the accuracy of traditional methods of cross-cultural web design research. That is, to what extent can the Likert scale be considered universal? The meanings that the westerners consider inherent for this scale may not at all be perceived as such by other cultures.

Of course our study is a pre-test pilot one, and it has a lot of limitations. Thus, the use of non-native language for both groups needs to be further explored; here, it has been used to put both groups into equal ground, but the results suggest that real-world sampling might have been substituted by an elaborated prototype that would have contained the tasks on the assessors' native languages. Also, we have pre-tested only four pages, and the statistical data are too little to make reliable conclusions; this is why we do not provide the information on standard deviations of the aggregate results and other statistical data. But the topic definitely deserved further development and enlargement of the sample and the groups of assessors. Another limitation lies in the fact that N-index so far does not allow for wide differentiation of websites; we will further work on its refinement.

But, with all the aforementioned limitations, the results that we have received still make us rethink both website design strategies and the method of measuring user satisfaction, if today's universities wish to successfully compete for the global audiences online.

References

1. Aguillo, I.F., Ortega, J.L., Fernández, M.: Webometric ranking of world universities: introduction, methodology, and future developments. High. educ. Eur. **33**(2–3), 233–244 (2008)
2. Alexander, R., Murray, D., Thompson, N.: Cross-cultural web usability model. In: Bouguettaya, A., et al. (eds.) WISE 2017. LNCS, vol. 10570, pp. 75–89. Springer, Cham (2017). https://doi.org/10.1007/978-3-319-68786-5_6
3. Blustein, J., Ahmed I., Instone K.: An evaluation of menu breadcrumbs for the WWW. In: Proceedings at the Sixteenth ACM Conference on Hypertext and Hypermedia (HT 2005), pp. 202–204. ACM Press, New York (2005)

4. Bodrunova, S.S., Yakunin, A.V.: Impact of menu complexity upon user behavior and satisfaction in information search. In: Yamamoto, S., Mori, H. (eds.) HIMI 2018. LNCS, vol. 10905, pp. 55–66. Springer, Cham (2018). https://doi.org/10.1007/978-3-319-92046-7_5
5. Bodrunova, S.S., Yakunin, A.V., Smolin, A.A.: Comparing efficacy of web design of university websites: mixed methodology and first results for Russia and the USA. In: ACM International Conference Proceeding Series, 22–23 November 2016, pp. 237–241 (2016)
6. Bodrunova, S.S., Yakunin, A.V.: U-index: an eye-tracking-tested checklist on webpage aesthetics for university web spaces in Russia and the USA. In: Marcus, A., Wang, W. (eds.) DUXU 2017. LNCS, vol. 10288, pp. 219–233. Springer, Cham (2017). https://doi.org/10.1007/978-3-319-58634-2_17
7. Chiu, W.H., Chu, L.S., Lin, P.K., Chi, H.R., Chiu, H.N.: Comparing cultural differences in trading website management between mainland China and Taiwan. In: Proceedings of the 9th International Conference on Service Systems and Service Management (ICSSSM'2012), pp. 431–434. IEEE (2012)
8. Chun, W., Singh, N., Sobh, R., Benmamoun, M.: A comparative analysis of Arab and US cultural values on the web. J. Glob. Mark. 28(2), 98–112 (2015)
9. Cui, T., Wang, X., Teo, H.: Building a culturally-competent website: a cross-cultural analysis of web site structure. J. Glob. Inf. Manag. 23(4), 1–25 (2015)
10. Deng, L., Poole, M.S.: Affect in web interfaces: a study of the impacts of web page visual complexity and order. MIS Q. 34(4), 711–730 (2010)
11. Garret, R., Chui, J., Zhang, L., Young, S.D.: A literature review: website design and user engagement. Online J. Commun. Media Technol. 6(3), 1–4 (2016)
12. Geissler, G., Zinkhan, G., Watson, R.T.: The influence of home page complexity on consumer attention, attitudes, and purchase intent. J. Advert. 35(2), 69–80 (2006)
13. Hasan, L.: Using university ranking systems to predict usability of university websites. JISTEM J. Inf. Syst. Technol. Manag. 10(2), 235–250 (2013)
14. Juric, R., Kim, I., Kuljis, J.: Cross cultural web design: an experiences of developing UK and Korean cultural markers. In: Proceedings of the 25th International Conference on Information Technology Interfaces (ITI'2003), pp. 309–313. IEEE (2003)
15. Kaur, S., Kaur, K., Kaur, P.: Analysis of website usability evaluation methods. In: 3rd International Conference on Computing for Sustainable Global Development (INDIACom), pp. 1043–1046. IEEE (2016)
16. Khanum, M.A., Fatima, S., Chaurasia, M.A.: Arabic interface analysis based on cultural markers. Int. J. Comput. Sci. Issues 9, 1 (2012)
17. Khashman, N., Large, A.: Measuring cultural markers in Arabic government websites using Hofstede's cultural dimensions. In: Marcus, A. (ed.) Design, User Experience, and Usability. Theory, Methods, Tools and Practice, vol. 6770, pp. 431–439. Springer, Berlin (2011). https://doi.org/10.1007/978-3-642-21708-1_49
18. Ko, D., Seo, Y., Jung, S.U.: Examining the effect of cultural congruence, processing fluency, and uncertainty avoidance in online purchase decisions in the US and Korea. Mark. Lett. 28(3), 377–390 (2015)
19. Lautenbach, M.A.E., Schegget, I.S., Schoute, A.M., Witteman, C.L.M.: Evaluating the usability of web pages: a case study (2006). www.phil.uu.nl/preprints/ckipreprints/PREPRINTS/preprint011.pdf
20. Liu, Y.: Developing a scale to measure the interactivity of websites. J. Advert. Res. 43(2), 207–216 (2003)
21. Mentes, S.A., Turan, A.H.: Assessing the usability of university websites: an empirical study on Namik Kemal University. Turk. Online J. Educ. Technol. 11(3), 61–69 (2012)

22. Michailidou, E., Haper, S., Bechhofer, S.: Visual complexity and aesthetic perception of web pages. In: Proceedings of the 26th Annual ACM International Conference on Design of Communication, pp. 215–224 (2008)
23. Mimouni, H.E., MacDonald, C.M.: Culture and information architecture: a study of American and Arab academic websites. Proc. Assoc. Inf. Sci. Technol. **52**(1), 1–4 (2015)
24. Murano, P., Sander, M.: User interface, menu design performance and user preferences: a review and ways forward. IJACSA Int. J. Adv. Comput. Sci. Appl. **7**(4), 355–361 (2016)
25. Paz, F., Pow-Sang, J.A., Collazos, C.: Validation of a usability evaluation protocol based on the heuristic inspection method: an experimental case study in the web domain. Adv. Sci. Technol. Lett. **142**, 63–68 (2016)
26. Paz, F., Pow-Sang, J.A., Collazos, C.: Formal protocol to conduct usability heuristic evaluations in the context of the software development process. Int. J. Eng. Technol. **7**(2.28), 10–19 (2018)
27. Peker, S.: Exploring the relationship between web presence and web usability for universities: a case study from Turkey. Program **50**(2), 157–174 (2016)
28. Singh, N., Fassot, G., Chao, M.C.H., Hoffmann, J.A.: Understanding international web site usage: a cross-cultural study of German, Brazilian and Taiwanese online consumers. Int. Mark. Rev. **23**(1), 83–97 (2006)
29. Sohn, D.: Anatomy of interaction experience: distinguishing sensory, semantic, and behavioral dimensions of interactivity. New Media Soc. **13**(8), 1320–1335 (2011). https://doi.org/10.1177/1461444811405806
30. Teng H.: Location breadcrumbs for navigation: an exploratory study. Unpublished Master's thesis, Faculty of Computer Science, Dalhousie University, NS, Canada (2003)
31. Tuzun, H., Akinci, A., Kurtoglu, M., Atal, D., Pala, F.K.: A study on the usability of a university registrar's office website through the methods of authentic tasks and eye-tracking. TOJET Turk. Online J. Educ. Technol. **12**(2), 26–38 (2013)
32. Van Oostendorp, H., Ignacio Madrid, R., Carmen Puerta Melguizo, M.: The effect of menu type and task complexity on information retrieval performance. Ergon. Open J. **2**(1), 64–71 (2009)
33. Zheng, G.: Web navigation systems for information seeking. In: Encyclopedia of Information Science and Technology, 3rd edn, pp. 7693–7701. IGI Global, Hershey (2015)

Similarity Measures and Models for Movie Series Recommender System

Bliznuk Danil, Yagunova Elena, and Pronoza Ekaterina(✉)

St.-Petersburg State University, Saint-Petersburg, Russian Federation
blizda@outlook.com, iagounova.elena@gmail.com,
katpronoza@gmail.com

Abstract. In this paper we propose a method of movie series recommender system development. Our recommender system is content-based, and movie series are represented by their scripts. We experiment with several semantic similarity measures, lexico-morphological metrics, keywords and vector space models to extract similar movie series. Evaluation is conducted in the experiment with informants. The best results are achieved by distributional semantic approach (i.e., using word2vec technology).

Keywords: Recommender system · Semantic similarity measure
Vector space model · Clustering algorithm · Movie series scripts

1 Introduction

Nowadays many companies are engaged in the development of recommender systems. Such IT giants as Google or Yandex use them to target advertising to users. Many online stores, such as Ozon, Amazon and Ebay, use recommender systems to sell their products to users. There are online content stores (iTunes, Netflix, Amedi-ateka and others [1, 2]) which try to guess users preferences as accurately as possible in order to sell their content to them.

There are four types of recommendation systems [3]:

- Collaboration
- Knowledge based
- Content based
- Hybrid

Collaborative recommender systems usually work as follows [4]: similar user profiles are found, and recommendations are provided based on the data from similar profiles.

Knowledge-based recommender systems [3] recommend similar items based on knowledge (the data are usually collected manually). Kinopoisk (url https://www.kinopoisk.ru) where users add similar movies to the movies list themselves is an example of such recommender system.

Content-based recommender systems [3] often use tags extracted from text using metrics like TF-iDF and recommend similar content based on these tags. The most

© Springer Nature Switzerland AG 2018
S. S. Bodrunova (Ed.): INSCI 2018, LNCS 11193, pp. 181–193, 2018.
https://doi.org/10.1007/978-3-030-01437-7_15

advanced systems use vector space model for document representation (term-document matrix is built), and further apply standard vector similarity measures like cosine distance to assess documents closeness. Such a recommendation system, for example, is used by Lops [4]. As an object for analysis, it uses the description of songs prepared by users. The recommender system described in this paper is also content-based.

Hybrid recommender systems may combine several approaches to obtain the best result.

The recommender system developed in our project is a content-based on (it is based on the corpus of movie series scripts). Although the idea of such a system is not new, however, we are not aware of any cases of the use of scripts of movie series as source data, or the use of distributional semantic tools like word2vec [30]. Moreover, according to recent studies (see Fig. 1), movie series are becoming increasingly popular nowadays [22, 23], and therefore there is a demand for helping users find movie series according to their tastes.

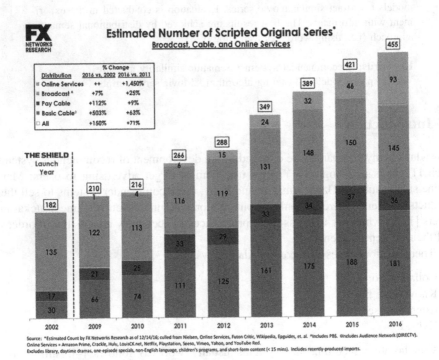

Fig. 1. The growing popularity of movie series since 2002 according to FX Network Research

The aim of our research is to find out the most appropriate method for extracting similar movies and to develop a recommender system using such method. Our hypothesis is that semantic similarity of movie series scripts correlates with the similarity of movies themselves, i.e., that movie series can be compared using their scripts. In other words, we reduce the problem of finding similar movie series to the problem of finding movie series with similar scripts.

We acknowledge that there is no strict definition of similarity between movies (the same problem takes place for books, songs, etc.), and users of recommender systems often find it hard to decide whether two movies are similar or not. Another problem is that movie series do not always belong to one genre; in fact, the situation is usually quite the opposite (see "Appendix A"). The data (scripts of movie series) suggest the abundance of spoken language, which makes it hard to analyze for any natural language processing (NLP) tool. The described problems demand another research, and a thorough one, and are beyond the scope of this paper.

In our research we experiment with various methods of extracting similar movie series: keywords, low-level statistical measures, vector space models. We evaluate the effectiveness of these methods using statistics and experiments with informants.

It should be mentioned that the constructed recommender system can recommend similar movie series for each particular movie series (like Kinopoisk or Imhonet) but such a system can easily be adapted to movies, books or even songs.

2 Related Work

There are a lot of articles on the recommender systems published in the Internet [12–15]. Of course, we cannot but mention Recommender Systems Handbook [3, 4] as the main source of information about recommender systems. However, in the overwhelming number of publications on recommender systems, common methods of analyzing the similarity of texts [9, 16], genre detection [7, 8] and authorship detection [6] are not used.

TF-iDF is often used to construct a dictionary from text [8, 16] and statistical metrics (Pearson's criterion [6], Jacquard measure [10], etc.) are used for the determination of semantic similarity of dictionaries. In some papers a different approach is suggested: the use of probabilistic metrics like surprisal [17] to determine the general "surprisingness" of the text, as well as the use of purely statistical metrics (entropy and readability index [9]).

There are also papers proposing the use of some characteristics for calculating semantic and lexical parameters (analyticity, verbality, and others [7]) to classify texts into genres and sub-genres [7], but they can also be used to create a unique "portrait" of the script in order to further search for the most semantically and stylistically close scripts.

Distributional semantic models have recently become popular in most NLP areas, however, they are rarely used in recommender systems communities. In this paper we experiment with vector space models as well as traditional statistical measures.

3 Data

We manually constructed a corpus of 100 movie series scripts of different genres and topics. They were selected based on their Kinopoisk rating scores [24, 25]. In Fig. 2, genre distribution of the selected movie series is shown.

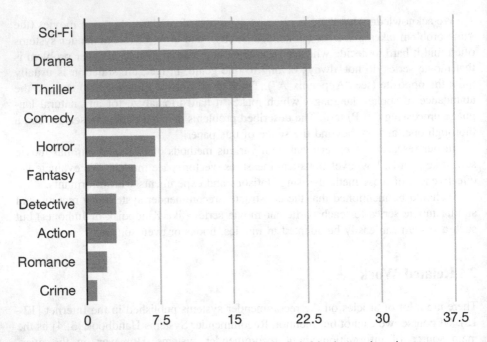

Fig. 2. Genre distribution of the movie series included in the movie series corpus

4 Method

First of all, movie series scripts are preprocessed: tags common for subtitle files are cut off. Then the text is split into sentences, lowercased and lemmatized using pymorphy2 (all the following operations are done on the lemma level).

For each movie series script we calculate several metrics.

Entropy is calculated as follows:

$$H = -\sum_{i=1}^{n} p_i log p_i \tag{1}$$

Surprisal, another metric which predicts the probability of a word occurring in a particular context, is calculated as shown in (2):

$$I = \sum_{i=1}^{n} log_2 \frac{1}{P_i(x|context)} \tag{2}$$

Readability metric measures how hard it is for a human to perceive a particular written text. In this paper we use a modified version (modified for NLP tasks) of this metric:

$$RL = R, R > 0 - 1R, R < 0, \tag{3}$$

$$R = 0.39N + V - 15.59 \tag{4}$$

where N denotes the number of words divided by the number of sentences in the text, and V denotes the number of vowels divided by the number of words in the text.

We also calculate a series of lexico-morphological metrics used to classify texts according to their genres. We use ten such metrics:

- Analyticity - the ratio of the number of service words to the total number of words in the text
- Verbs ratio - the ratio of the number of verbs to the total number of words
- Substantivity - the ratio of the number of nouns to the total number of words
- Adjectivity - the ratio of the number of adjectives to the total number of words
- Pronominality - the ratio of the number of pronominal words to the total number of words
- Autosemanticity - the ratio of the number of meaningful words (all except for service words and pronouns) to the total number of words
- Lexical diversity - the ratio of the number of different tokens to the total number of words
- The portion of high-frequency words - the ratio of the number of words in the text that are in the first hundred most frequent in Russian (they are taken from the dictionary collected by S. Sharov), to the total number of words
- Unfamiliarity - the ratio of the number of non-spoken words to the total number of words
- The portion of nominal lexicon - the ratio of the sum of the numbers of nouns and adjectives to the total number of words.

Metric values calculated for each movie series, constitute a feature space, and the problem of extracting similar movie series is reduced to the clustering problem (a standard machine learning problem) with movies represented by their feature vectors.

Other movie features are calculated using distributional semantic models. First, for each movie series script a dictionary (of keywords) is built using TF-iDF. All the words (on the lemma level) are ranged according to their TF-iDF values. The resulting dictionary consists of the words from the middle of the list as we found them to be more robust in our preliminary experiments (in other words, such terms represent movie series better than terms with top TF-iDF values). We train word2vec[1] model on another corpus of movie series scripts (other than our corpus described in Sect. 3), and thus, for each word from the constructed dictionary, there exists a 300-dimensional vector (if the word occurs in the corpus on which the model was trained). Finally, for each movie series script, a word2vec-based feature vector is obtained as the weighted sum (with TF-iDF weights) of vectors corresponding to the words from the script's dictionary.

---

[1] We also experimented with other tools for training word embeddings like FastText and tried larged word embedding models provided by RusVectores and Russian Distributional Thesaurus, but in both cases the results appeared to be worse than those achieved with word2vec trained on the movie series scripts. These results are not reported in this paper due to space limits.

Thus, we construct several feature vectors for each movie series script, and further solve the problem of extracting similar movie series by clustering these vectors in the feature space.

We also try another approach: movie series scripts are compared using Jaccard coefficient which is calculated for all pairs of scripts on the lemma level.

5   Results

To cluster movie series scripts, we experiment with such clustering algorithms as Ward hierarchical clustering [31], DBSCAN [32] and Affinity propagation [35] (as implemented in scikit-learn). The latter ones do not demand the number of clusters (which is unknown in our case). The three selected algorithms represent different approaches to the problem of clustering: creating clusters that have a predetermined ordering (hierarchy) from top to bottom, using the concept of "message passing" between data points and grouping together points that are closely packed together, i.e., are lying in high-density areas.

Parameters of the clustering models are optimized using silhouette coefficient. Parameters of word2vec model were also optimized, and the following parameters were selected: window size = 10, minimal word frequency = 5.

To evaluate the quality of clustering, we conducted experiment with informants. There were 15 informants, all of them under 27 years. They were shown (a) a list of 16 movie series, and (b) another list of 61 movie series names. For each of the movie series from list (a) the informants were asked to find one to three similar movie series from the list (b). Two movie series were considered similar if thought so by two or more informants. Results of the informants' decisions on the similarity of the movie series are shown in Table 1.

Table 1. Clusters of similar movie series selected by the informants.

Cluster 1	Cluster 2	Cluster 3	Cluster 4	Cluster 5
Секретные материалы/The X Files	Шерлок/Sherlock	Звёздный путь следующие поколение/Star Trek The Next Generation	Как я встретил вашу маму/How I Met Your Mother	Однокурсники/Community
Твин Пикс/Twin Peaks	Обмани меня/Lie to me	Звёздный путь Энтерпрайз /Star Trek Enterprise	Друзья/Friends	Друзья/Friends
Доктор Кто/Doctor Who	Лучше звоните Соулу/Better Call Saul	Звёздный Путь оригинальный сериал/Star Trek The Original Series	Теория большого взрыва/The Big Bang Theory	Как я встретил вашу маму/How I Met Your Mother
Чёрное зеркало/Black Mirror	Касл/Castle	Орвил/Orville	Офис/The Office	Американская семейка/Modern Family

(continued)

Table 1. (*continued*)

Cluster 1	Cluster 2	Cluster 3	Cluster 4	Cluster 5
Белые воротнички/ White Collar	Доктор Кто/Doctor Who		Секс в большом городе/Sex and the City	
Касл/Castle	Доктор Хаус/House M.D.		Парки и зоны отдыха/Parks and Recreation	
Доктор Хаус/House M.D.	Секретные материалы/ The X Files		Американская семейка/Modern Family	
Сверхъестественное/ Supernatural	Настоящий детектив/ True Detective			
Грань/Fringe				

Result of the number of matches between the clusters identified by the informants and the clustering algorithms are shown in Table 2 for Ward hierarchical clustering, DBSCAN and Affinity propagation.

Table 2. Results of different clustering algorithms

Algorithm	Number of matches with informants' decisions
Ward hierarchical clustering	16
DBSCAN	–
Affinity propagation	21

DBSCAN algorithm could not identify any clusters among the given movie series ad annotated all of them as noise. Thus, among the three considered clustering algorithms, Affinity propagation appeared to be the best one.

We also split movie series into clusters using Jaccard coefficients. Such clustering method achieved only 14 matches with the decisions made by the informants. Hence, vector space model approach was used in our recommender system.

Apart from calculating the number of matches between automatic clustering methods and clustering by the informants, we also analyzed the amount of similar movie series different clustering methods (and informants) were able to identify. In Fig. 3, for each of the target 5 movie series, the number of movie series identified as similar to that particular movie series by a certain clustering method (or informants), is shown.

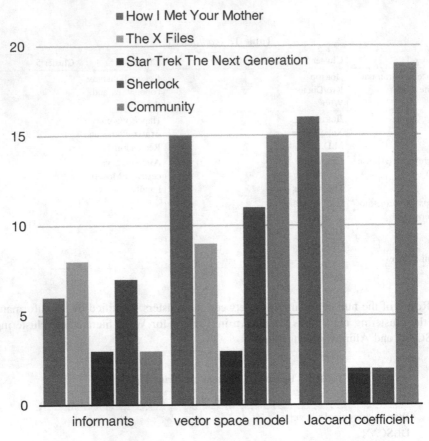

Fig. 3. Number of similar movie series identified using different methods

The percentage of correctly identified movie series in each of the five target clusters (with informants' decisions as the gold standard) is shown in Fig. 4.

It can be seen from Figs. 3 and 4 that both clustering methods (Jaccard coefficient and vector space model) show fairly good results, but vector space model achieves the best results. Moreover, if we take into account the genres the considered movie series belong to, the similarities found between comedies become evident: a large number of movie series belong to a purely comedy genre. As for other genres, they are usually combined and it is hard to tell one from another in most movie series.

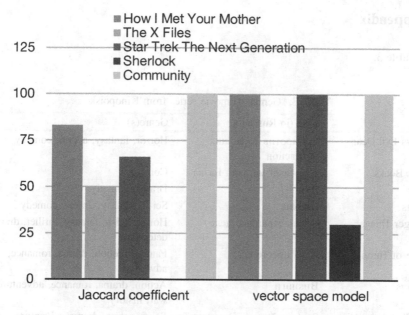

Fig. 4. Number of correctly identified movie series in the 5 target clusters

6 Conclusion

The problem of constructing a successful content-based movie series recommender system is quite important nowadays, and in this paper we describe our method of constructing such a system.

We propose a method of comparing movie series by their scripts, and according to the obtained results, such method can be used to construct a recommender system.

We experiment with different statistical metrics and also distributional semantic models and clustering algorithms and select optimal models and algorithms. The models performance is evaluated by calculating the number of matches between the clusters of movie series identified by the model and by the informants.

The system constructed as a result of the research can be used not only to recommender movie series – it can be adapted to other domains like books and songs. These domains share some problems with our current domain (movie series): the notion of similarity between two movies or songs is quite vague even for humans, and scripts of movies and lyrics of the songs are complicated objects of analysis in NLP. Nevertheless, the obtained results prove that the problem of clustering movie series can be solved, and the corresponding recommender system can be successfully constructed.

A Appendix

See Table 3.

Table 3. Genres of movie series from Kinopoisk

Title	Title (in Russian)	Genre(s)
Ash vs Evil Dead	Эш против Зловещих мертвецов	Horror, fantasy, action, comedy
Black Books	Книжный магазин Блэка	Comedy
Louie	Луи	Drama, comedy
Misfits	Плохие	Sci-fi, fantasy, drama, comedy
Stranger Things	Очень странные дела	Horror, sci-fi, fantasy, thriller, drama, detective
Game of Thrones	Игра престолов	Fantasy, action, drama, romance, adventure
Vikings	Викинги	Action, drama, romance, adventure, war, history
Star Trek Enterprise	Звездный путь: Энтерпрайз	Sci-fi, action, drama, adventure, detective
Star Trek The Next Generation	Звездный путь: Следующее поколение	Sci-fi, action, detective, adventure
Star Trek The Original Series	Звездный путь	Sci-fi, action, adventure
The Orville	Орвил	Sci-fi, drama, comedy, adventure
Downton Abbey	Аббатство Даунтон	Drama, romance
Hannibal	Ганибал	Detective, thriller, crime, drama
The Knick	Больница Никербокер	Drama
Homeland	Родина	Thriller, drama, crime, detective
House of Cards	Карточный домик	Drama
Lie to Me	Обмани меня	Thriller, drama, crime, detective
Mr Robot	Мистер Робот	Thriller, drama, crime
Narcos	Нарко	Crime, drama
Prison Break	Побег	Action, thriller, drama, crime, detective
Suits	Форс-мажоры	Drama, comedy
The Bridge	Мост	Thriller, crime, detective
The Newsroom	Служба новостей	Drama
Better Call Saul	Лучше звоните Солу	Drama, crime
Black Mirror	Чёрное зеркало	Sci-fi, thriller, drama
Breaking Bad	Во все тяжкие	Thriller, drama, crime
Fargo	Фарго	Thriller, drama, crime
Lost	Лост	Sci-fi, fantasy, Thriller, drama, detective, adventure

(*continued*)

Table 3. (*continued*)

Title	Title (in Russian)	Genre(s)
Peaky Blinders	Острые козырьки	Drama, crime
Sherlock	Шерлок	Thriller, drama, crime, detective
Southland	Саутленд	Thriller, drama, crime
The Killing	Убийство	Thriller, drama, crime, detective
True Detective	Настоящий детектив	Detective, crime, thriller, drama
Twin Peaks	Твин Пикс	Thriller, drama, crime, detective, sci-fi
Castle	Касл	Drama, romance, comedy, crime, detective
Doctor Who	Доктор Кто	Sci-fi, drama, comedy, adventure, family
Fringe	Грань	Sci-fi, thriller, drama, detective
House M.D.	Доктор Хаус	Drama, detective
The Good Wife	Хорошая жена	Drama, crime, detective
The Mentalist	Менталист	Thriller, drama, crime, detective
The X Files	Секретные материала	Sci-fi, thriller, drama, detective
White Collar	Белый воротничок	Detective, crime, drama, comedy
Altered Carbon	Видоизменёный углерод	Sci-fi, thriller, drama
Firefly	Светлячок	Sci-fi, action, drama, adventure
Westworld	Мир дикого запада	Sci-fi, drama, detective, western
Boardwalk Empire	Подпольная империя	Drama, crime
Community	Однокурсники	Comedy
Desperate Housewives	Отчаянные домохозяйки	Drama, romance, comedy, detective
Friends	Друзья	Comedy, romance
How I Met Your Mother	Как я встретил вашу маму	Comedy, romance, drama
Modern Family	Американская семейка	Romance, comedy
Parks and Recreation	Парки и зоны отдыха	Comedy
Queer as Folk	Близкие друзья	Drama, romance
Sex and the City	Секс в большом городе	Romance, comedy
Shameless	Бесстыдники	Drama, comedy
Silicon Valley	Силиконовая долина	Comedy
Supernatural	Сверхъестественное	Horror, fantasy, thriller, drama, detective
The Big Bang Theory	Теория большого взрыва	Romance, comedy
The Office	Офис	Comedy
The Wire	Прослушка	Thriller, drama, криминал
Jeeves and Wooster	Дживс и Вустер	Comedy

References

1. Gurbanov, T.: Non-personalized recommendations: method of associations. https://habrahabr.ru/post/257903/. Accessed 1 May 2018
2. Roizner, M.: How recommender systems work. https://habrahabr.ru/company/dca/blog/280700/. Accessed 1 May 2018
3. Ricci, F., Rokach, L., Shapira, B.: Introduction ton to Recommender Systems Handbook. In: Ricci, F., Rokach, L., Shapira, B., Kantor, P.B., (eds.) Recommender Systems Handbook, pp. 1–29 (2011). ISBN 978-0-387-85819-7, https://doi.org/10.1007/978-0-387-85820-3
4. Lops, P., de Gemmis, M., Semeraro, G.: Content-based recommender systems: state of the art and trends. In: Ricci, F., Rokach, L., Shapira, B., Kantor, P.B. (eds.) Recommender Systems Handbook. ISBN 978-0-387-85819-7, pp. 73–100 (2010). https://doi.org/10.1007/978-0-387-85820-3_3
5. Mikolov, T., Sutskever, I., Chen, K., Corrado, G., Dean, J.: Distributed representations of words and phrases and their compositionality. In: NIPS'13 Proceedings of the 26th International Conference on Neural Information Processing Systems, vol. 2, pp. 3111–3119 (2013)
6. Tambovcev, Y., Tambovceva, A., Tambovceva, L.: Typology of linguistic units distribution in text as a factor in author profiling task. Vestnik Omskogo universiteta **2**, 88–96 (2008)
7. Pospelova, A., Yagunova, E.: The use of stylistic and genre characteristics to describe text collection style. Novie informacionnie tehnologii v avtomatizirovannih systemah, pp. 347–357 (2014)
8. Yagunova, E., Pivovarova, L.: Experimental and computational study of N.V.Gogol' narrative stories. Struct. Funct. Stud. Russ. Linguist. **1**(3), 83–104 (2014)
9. Wojciechowski, A., Goeznynski, K.: A method for measuring similarity of books: a step towards an objective recommender system for readers. In: Human Language Technology. Challenges for Computer Science and Linguistics, pp. 161–174 (2016). https://doi.org/10.1007/978-3-319-43808-5_13
10. Pronoza, E., Yagunova, E.: Low-level features for paraphrase identification. Adv. Artif. Intell. Soft Comput. 59–71 (2015). https://doi.org/10.1007/978-3-319-27060-9
11. Movie2Vec: Clustering movies by plot. https://movie2vec.wordpress.com/2016/03/22/clustering-movies-by-plot/. Accessed 1 May 2018
12. Paramonov, S.: How to write a simple recommender system. https://habrahabr.ru/post/230155/. Accessed 1 May 2018
13. Recommender systems: introduction to the cold start problem. https://habrahabr.ru/company/surfingbird/blog/168733/. Accessed 1 May 2018
14. Bordashshenko, A., Potemkin, A., Sazanova, E., Shekshuev, S.: Algorithm for the search of similar media reports. Int. J. "Naukovedenie" **7** (2015). ISSN 2223-5167
15. Myslín, M., Levy, R.: Codeswitching and predictability of meaning in discourse. Language **91**(4), 871–905 (2015). https://doi.org/10.1353/lan.2015.0068
16. Song, Y., Roth, D.: Unsupervised sparse vector densification for short text similarity. In: NAACL HLT 2015—2015 Conference of the North American Chapter of the Association for Computational Linguistics: Human Language Technologies, Proceedings of the Conference, pp. 1275–1280 (2015)
17. MacKay, D.: Information Theory, Inference, and Learning Algorithms. Cambridge University Press, Cambridge (2003)
18. Manning, C., Raghavan, P., Schütze, H.: Introduction to Information Retrieval. Williams (2014). ISBN 978-5-8459-1623-5

19. Scripted Originals Hit Record 455 in 2016. FX Study Finds. https://www.hollywoodreporter. com/live-feed/scripted-originals-hit-record-455-2016-fx-study-finds-958337. Accessed 1 May 2018
20. Era of Peak TV Continues With 487 Scripted Shows in 2017. https://www.wsj.com/articles/ era-of-peak-tv-continues-with-487-scripted-shows-in-2017-1515182593. Accessed 1 May 2018
21. Best movie series. https://www.kinopoisk.ru/top/lists/45/. Accessed 1 May 2018
22. The most popular movie series in Kinopoisk. https://www.kinopoisk.ru/top/lists/257/. Accessed 1 May 2018
23. Gensim. https://radimrehurek.com/gensim/. Accessed 1 May 2018
24. RusVectōrēs: Russian semantic models. http://rusvectores.org/ru/. Accessed 1 May 2018
25. Russian Distributional Thesaurus. https://nlpub.ru/Russian_Distributional_Thesaurus. Accessed 1 May 2018
26. Mikolov, T., Chen, K., Corrado, G., Dean, J.: Efficient Estimation of Word Representations in Vector Space
27. word2vec. https://code.google.com/archive/p/word2vec/. Accessed 1 May 2018
28. Hierarchical clustering. https://docs.scipy.org/doc/scipy/reference/cluster.hierarchy.html. Accessed 1 May 2018
29. Ester, M., Kriegel, H.-P., Sander, J., Xu, X.: A Density-based algorithm for discovering clusters in large spatial databases with noise. In: Proceedings of the Second International Conference on Knowledge Discovery and Data Mining, pp. 226–231 (1996)
30. Frey, B.J., Dueck, D.: Clustering by passing messages between data points. Science **315** (2007). https://doi.org/10.1126/science.1136800
31. Ward Jr., J.H.: Hierarchical grouping to optimize an objective function. J. Am. Stat. Assoc. **58**, 236–244 (1963). https://doi.org/10.2307/2282967
32. AffinityPropagation. http://scikit-learn.org/stable/modules/generated/sklearn.cluster.Affinity Propagation.html. Accessed 1 May 2018

What Makes Users Trust a Chatbot for Customer Service? An Exploratory Interview Study

Asbjørn Følstad[1(✉)], Cecilie Bertinussen Nordheim[2],
and Cato Alexander Bjørkli[2]

[1] SINTEF, Oslo, Norway
asf@sintef.no
[2] University of Oslo, Oslo, Norway

Abstract. Chatbots are increasingly offered as an alternative source of customer service. For users to take up chatbots for this purpose, it is important that users trust chatbots to provide the required support. However, there is currently a lack in knowledge regarding the factors that affect users' trust in chatbots. We present an interview study addressing this knowledge gap. Thirteen users of chatbots for customer service were interviewed regarding their experience with the chatbots and factors affecting their trust in these. Users' trust in chatbots for customer service was found to be affected (a) by factors concerning the specific chatbot, specifically the quality of its interpretation of requests and advise, its human-likeness, its self-presentation, and its professional appearance, but also (b) by factors concerning the service context, specifically the brand of the chatbot host, the perceived security and privacy in the chatbot, as well as general risk perceptions concerning the topic of the request. Implications for the design and development of chatbots and directions for future work are suggested.

Keywords: Chatbots · Customer service · Trust · Interview study

1 Introduction

Chatbots are software agents that interact with users through natural language conversation [8]. As such, chatbots are seen as a promising technology for customer service. For service providers, the quality of customer service is critical for customer satisfaction and loyalty [5]. At the same time, customer service is highly resource demanding as it typically requires highly personalized customer interaction, involving skilled customer service personnel. Intelligent automation of customer service may allow for accessible and efficient support while keeping costs at an acceptable level [22].

Chatbots represent a potential means for automating customer service. In particular because customer service is increasingly provided through online chat. Chatbots are not a novel technology. However, recent advances in artificial intelligence (AI) and machine learning, as well as a general adoption of messaging platforms, has recently motivated companies to explore chatbots as a complement to customer service.

© Springer Nature Switzerland AG 2018
S. S. Bodrunova (Ed.): INSCI 2018, LNCS 11193, pp. 194–208, 2018.
https://doi.org/10.1007/978-3-030-01437-7_16

Examples of companies leading the way in such use of chatbots include food companies like Dominos Pizza and Wingstop, where customers can place orders through chatbots in Facebook Messenger, and retail platforms like Alibaba and Aliexpress, where chatbots serve as the companies' first line of support.

Customer service currently is only an emerging chatbot application area, and general uptake among the intended customer groups is not yet realized. From other technology areas, we know that user trust is critical for a broad uptake of novel interactive solutions [3]. However, our knowledge regarding users' trust in chatbots, and the factors affecting such trust, is severely limited. This is a critical if the aim is to strengthen customer service through chatbots.

In this paper, we contribute a study intended as a first step towards the needed knowledge of users' trust in chatbots. Specifically, we present the results of an in-depth interview study which involved 13 users of customer service chatbots. The study contributes insight into users' perceptions of chatbots for customer service, and shed light on factors that may affect users' trust in chatbots.

The remainder of the paper is structured as follows. First, we present an overview of background on customer service, chatbots, and the concept of trust. We then explicate our research question and detail the research method before presenting our results. In particular, we highlight our findings on users' perceptions of chatbots for customer service and factors affecting users' trust in such chatbots. Finally, we discuss our findings, present an initial set of factors of relevance to trust in chatbots, and suggest implications for practice and for future research.

2 Background

2.1 Automation in Customer Service

Customer service has always been key to service companies. With the uptake of the internet, customer service has gradually transformed from being personal and dialog-based towards being automated and self-service oriented. However, automation and online self-service solutions do not fully meet users' needs for help and assistance and service providers' costs associated with manual customer service are still increasing [9].

In an effort to provide more efficient customer service, while meeting customers in their preferred channels, service providers offer customer service through a range of online channels, such as company webpages, social media, email, and chat. Customer service through chat is increasingly prioritized. Chat represents a relatively resource effective channel for the service provider, compared to support by e-mail and telephone, as customer service personnel may handle multiple requests in parallel [19]. The chat also provide the user with a written summary of the interaction which may be helpful in terms of instruction details or links to useful online resources.

Given the increasing uptake of chat as a prioritized channel for customer service, chatbots are seen as ever more relevant as a complement to customer service.

2.2   Chatbots

Chatbots are machine agents that provide access to data and services through natural language interaction [2]. Though the term *chatbot* is relatively recent, computer systems interacting with users in natural language has been developed and researched since the 1960'ies [21]. The current surge of interest in chatbots is in part due to recent advances in AI and machine learning [20].

Promising chatbot application areas include information services [4], education [10], therapy [7], and, in particular, customer service [22]. A number of tech companies provide platforms that may support chatbots for customer service, including IBM Watson, Microsoft Bot Framework, and Google owned DialogFlow.

Users hold a range of motivations for using chatbots. Brandtzaeg and Følstad [2] found that the most frequently reported motivations for chatbot use were efficiency and convenience, and that user experience, social aspects, and a sense of novelty can also be relevant motivators. A recent study of chatbots for customer service found that customer service interactions are characterized by both emotional and factual statements from customers [22]. Interestingly, AI-powered chatbots may identify and respond to emotional customer statements nearly as well as human operators, due to machine learning capabilities for sentiment detection [13].

While the current body of knowledge include research on users' perceptions of chatbots in terms of, for example, usefulness and user experience [e.g. 14], there is a lack of knowledge on users' trust in chatbots. This is a critical knowledge gap, as trust has been shown to be a key factor in users uptake of interactive systems [3, 12].

2.3   The Concept of Trust

Trust is defined by Rousseau et al. as "a psychological state comprising the intention to accept vulnerability based upon positive expectations of the intentions or behavior of another" [17]. Trust is seen as particularly relevant in situations characterized by risk, where the trustor depends on the actions of the trustee [15]. Trust is seen as dependent on a cognitive assessment in the trustor [15], but also as depending on affective [18] and social [1] aspects.

Trust is historically investigated in the context of interpersonal relations, organizations and society [17], and is often described as inducing a sense of belonging [18] and facilitating frictionless interaction and collaboration between humans [1]. Mayer et al. [15], presenting one of the leading models of organizational trust, identified three key determinants of trust, that is, the trustee's perceptions of expertise, benevolence, and integrity in the trustor.

While the notion of trust in technology may be seen as controversial [11], there is a rapidly increasing body of research addressing this. For example, in a review article on trust in robots, Hancock et al. [12] identified a range of factors determining such trust grouped in human-related, robot-related, and environmental factors. A much cited framework of trust in interactive systems was presented by Corritore et al. [3], targeting users' trust in websites. In this framework, key determinants of trust were seen as perceptions of credibility, ease-of-use, and risk.

The current literature provides some clues to what may be important factors in determining users' trust in chatbots. However, given that chatbots hold a set of highly particular characteristics, there is a need to explore trust specifically for this interactive technology.

3   Research Question

To address the identified gap in current knowledge, the aim of this study was to explore and identify an initial set of factors assumed to affect users' trust in chatbots for customer service. While existing background suggests some factors that may be of relevance, the lack in research on this in the field of chatbots made us choose an exploratory approach. The research question for our explorations was as follows:

Which factors are relevant to users' trust in chatbots for customer service?

Our explorations of this question, will enable us to establish a tentative overview of factors that may affect trust in chatbots for customer service. This may, in turn, guide future research and support design and development of chatbots for customer service.

4   Method

In response to the research question, we chose an exploratory research design. Specifically, to gather rich in-depth insight we conducted a semi-structured interview study.

4.1   Participants and Study Context

The study participants were all users of chatbots for customer service. To ensure that all participants had recent experiences with such chatbots, they were invited to the study as part of their chat dialogue with one of a small number of customer service chatbots. Invitations were provided as the customer service dialogue was completed.

When accepting the invitation, the participants first responded to a questionnaire on their experiences and perceptions of the chatbot. The findings from this questionnaire will be presented in a later publication. Upon completing the questionnaire, the participants could volunteer for a follow-up interview. All participants indicating such interest (28) were invited to join the study; 14 answered positively to the follow-up communication from the research team. Of these, 13 were included in the final analysis; one was excluded as she was part of a chatbot development project.

The chatbots through which the participants were recruited, were the customer service chatbots of four Norwegian consumer service providers. These providers were chosen because they were advanced in implementing chatbots for customer service.

The Norwegian context arguably is useful for the purposes of this study. The population is relatively advanced in terms of mobile internet and smartphone penetration, and Norwegian service providers are relatively advanced in implementing chatbots for customer service.

All participants were provided information about the study and terms for participation as part of the invitation. All data collection was anonymous, and the participants were at the beginning of the interviews reminded not to disclose personal information. All participants were offered a gift card of 250 Norwegian kroner (approximately 25 Euro), as incentive to participate.

4.2   Study Material and Data Analysis

All interviews were conducted on the basis of a predefine interview guide. The guide included open-ended questions on the following topics:

- Customer service chatbot experience
- Perceived benefits of chatbots for customer service
- Perceived challenges or problems with chatbots for customer service
- Factors affecting trust in chatbots for customer service
- Factors affecting future use of chatbots
- Suggestions for improvements in chatbots for customer service.

The main topic was factors affecting trust in chatbots for customer service. Here, the participants were first encouraged to reflect freely on trust in chatbots for customer service and factors affecting such trust. Following this, the participants were prompted on a small set of possible factors drawn from the literature on trust in technology including risk, expertise, ease of use, reputation, and human likeness.

The interview guide also included a brief introduction, summarizing the study purpose and terms of participation, and a debrief for the participant to ask questions and make additional reflections. All interviews were conducted in Norwegian. Example quotes presented in the result section were translated to English by the first author.

The interviews were recorded, upon the participants' explicit consent, and transcribed. Analyses were done on the transcripts, following Ezzy's [6] guidelines for thematic analysis. Coding themes were identified, consolidated and applied for coding the data. The data associated with each particular code were then made subject of a final qualitative interpretation. On the basis of this analysis, an set of factors of relevance to trust in chatbots for customer service was established.

5   Results

The study participants all had experience with chatbots for customer service. The participants typically had experience with such chatbots a few times (5) or several times (6). However, two of the participants only had the one experience with chatbots for customer service when they were recruited to the study. Half the participants (6) described themselves as more than average technology interested or as advanced technology users.

In the results section, we first provide an overview of the participants' responses to the topics of perceived benefits and challenges with chatbots for customer service. We then go into the topic reflecting the research question – factors affecting trust in chatbots for customer service – before providing an overview of factors affecting future use of chatbots and suggestions for improvements.

5.1   Benefits with Chatbots for Customer Service

The main benefit of chatbots for customer service, reported by all study participants, is the opportunity for fast and accessible help and information. The rapid response of chatbots were accentuated by all study participants. For example, as in the following:

> *[…] it is really great that you get an immediate response, and not have to wait for a human to answer.* (P1)

Likewise, most participants mentioned the 24/7 access to customer service chatbots.

> *Yes, it is really simple. No waiting time. If you are to talk to the employees or the managers, there is often waiting time. But the chatbot always has time.* (P4)

A substantial proportion of the participants also noted as beneficial that the chatbot works well for simple, general questions (6) and provides answers that have gone through substantial quality control (5). For example, as detailed in the following responses:

> *For me, this seems to be a good way to get answers to questions that are simple and straight forward […]* (P8)

> *[The chatbot] is in a way more trustworthy as it does not just give a yes or no answer. Rather, you can see how it interprets the question. And then it will answer on this basis, so accuracy is better.* (P5)

Interestingly, about half the participants reported on the chatbot holding also other benefits in contrast to customer service with human personnel. First, several noted that chatbots may lower the threshold for asking questions (6). Specifically, it was reported that when asking questions to a chatbot one does not feel being judged – even when asking questions that one may consider stupid or silly.

> *You can ask really stupid questions, if you are an anonymous customer. When you call customer service you are in a way cautious not to ask too simple or banal questions. But with a bot you are in a way encouraged to ask stupid questions, so that you can be a bit more open.* (P5)

Also, some of the participants noted that since the chatbot is not human they do not feel any time pressure. Hence, they can take the time they feel necessary to formulate questions and read answers.

> *I can do this in my own speed. That is, I can use as long time as I want on the questions.* (P9)

5.2   Challenges with Chatbots for Customer Service

The main challenge with chatbots for customer service mentioned by the participants (9) was interpretational problems. That is, the chatbot does not always understand what the customer is intends to ask. For example, as in the following participant report.

It is not always the chatbot understand what I say. And when I, after formulating my question in three or four different ways and the chatbot still does not understand, then I get annoyed. Then it is not very useful and I rather want to talk to a human. (P1)

Furthermore, several of the participants also noted as a problematic issue that the chatbots as they currently are implemented, does not allow for answering complex questions or questions pertaining to the details of ones personal relationship with the service provider. This issue is in part linked to the limitations in the user intents that the chatbots can identify, but also in the limitations of customer service chatbots that does not access personal data about the customer. As reflected in the following participant quote.

My experience so far has been positive. But, of course, a chatbot is a chatbot. Which means that it will be somewhat limited what you can get out of it. (P12)

Some participants also reflected on challenges pertaining, not to the interaction with the chatbot, but to other contextual issues. Such as concern for security and privacy, and also fear for chatbots for customer service being a step towards reduced access to customer service personnel. Concerns for security and privacy focused on the need for service providers to make sure that the chatbot is just as secure as other online services. Concern for reduced access to customer service personnel in the future, was typically voiced as a need to keep access to customer service personnel as an available option also in a future with more efficient chatbots, as there in the foreseeable future likely will be need also for help and support from humans as a complement to customer service chatbots. Not having such access to customer service personnel could be detrimental, as reported in the following quote.

[Companies with chatbots for customer service] reduce efforts on regular customer service. In total. As the chatbot is not good enough, the level of customer service in total, is reduced. (P7)

5.3   Factors Affecting Trust in Chatbots for Customer Service

The key topic of the interviews was the participants' views on factors that may affect their trust in chatbots for customer service. The identified factors may broadly be structured in two high-level groups: Factors that concern the chatbot itself and factors that concern the service context or environment of the chatbot.

Before going into these two high-level groups of identified factors, we take a brief detour into the participants' willingness and ability to reflect on trust in chatbots. This because the notion of users' trust in technology has been contested in the literature [11]. Interestingly, the participants did not report it to be challenging to reflect on trust in chatbots. On the contrary, most effortlessly reported on factors they found particularly important in affecting their trust in a chatbot. The exceptions to this was one of the participants, who started his answer to the question on factors affecting trust in the chatbot with reflecting on the strangeness that he was perceiving the dialogue with the chatbot in a similar fashion with what he would expect from a dialogue with a human customer service representative. In addition, another participant argued that he likely would never fully trust a chatbot for customer service. Hence, reporting on trust in chatbots for customer service, was found to be easy for the participants.

Factors Concerning the Chatbot. The most frequently mentioned factors affecting trust in the customer service chatbots concerned the chatbot itself. Specifically, the chatbot's quality of interpretation and advice, and also the chatbot's human-likeness, self-presentation, and level of professional appearance. We detail these in the following.

Interpretation and Advice. Unsurprisingly, the chatbots' ability to correctly interpret the users' questions and requests, as well as its ability to provide helpful and informative responses were seen as a key factor affecting trust in customer service chatbots. This was reported by most participants (9), and was also for many of these the first factor mentioned. The participant reports coded as concerning this factor addressed aspects such as the chatbot's ability to efficiently provide help, its ability to match a question with an relevant response, as well as the answers' having been through thorough quality assurance. For example as in the following report.

> *It is the response you get back. That it answers correctly. And gives you relevant information. [...] Being robust and quality assures is the most important.* (P4)

Human-likeness. About half the participants also associated the chatbots character as having some kind of personal or relational flair to its style of communication to potentially enhance trust. Some of these participants argued that the chatbot communicating in a personal style with some humor when appropriate, would be beneficial to building trust. Others argued that a human-like style of communication just feels better, and that this therefore will be beneficial to trust. Yet others accentuated the benefit of the chatbot communicating in a polite and humanlike manner. The human-likeness was reported to be dependent on the communication style, but also other aspects such as the chatbots name and avatar image.

> *I know it is a robot, but I would like it to have, so to say, personal. To have a twinkle in its eye, not just pushing fact-based information, but to have a sort of human language or tone of voice.* (P1)

Three of the participants, however, argued against the potential benefit of human-likeness for trust in chatbots. Two of these argued that while human-likeness could improve the user experience of the chatbot, it would hardly affect their trust in the service. The third suggested that in some contexts, a too humanlike chatbot could even reduce levels of trust, with reference to the uncanny valley phenomenon where a too human-like robot may induce a feeling of creepiness in the user.

Self-presentation and Professional Appearance. Some of the participants suggested that the chatbots self-presentation would be important to them trusting it. Specifically, that the chatbot clearly communicates what it can do, and how it can help. Such a presentation was argued to be particularly helpful in the introduction of the dialogue. And, just as importantly, it was reported to be important the chatbot is open and honest regarding its limitations. The importance of the chatbot's self-presentation was, for example, argued in the following quote.

> *[The chatbot] seemed honest in a way. [...] This I can help you with, but not this. That is, it clearly communicated what it could do.* (P9)

Some of the participants also argued that their trust in the chatbot would depend on the degree to which it appeared as having been thoughtfully developed. This could concern the overall visual design of the chatbot, but also the degree to which is was see as using adequate and correct language. As noted in the following quote.

[The chatbot] should seem to be well made, and not be plagued by typos, for example, or poor grammar. (P8)

Factors Concerning the Service Context. The participants also reported on a number of factors seen as affecting trust that did not concern the chatbot as such but rather the overall service context. Factors concerning the service context were somewhat less frequently reported than factors concerning the chatbot, but nevertheless this was a substantial part of the user feedback. These factors included the brand hosting the chatbot, perceived security and privacy, and also perceived risk.

Brand. Nearly half the respondents reported the brand hosting the chatbot as being important to trust. A chatbot for customer service is typically developed to support customers of a particular brand, and users perceptions of this brand was argued to be a key determinant of trust. Brand was seen as potentially affecting trust through branding of the chatbot, but also by the chatbot being accessed from the brand webpage. As noted by one of the participants:

Trust for me primarily is in the brand [...] which I already trust as a service provider. (P13)

Security and Privacy. A substantial number of the respondents also reported the stated or perceived security and privacy measures in the chatbot to be important for trust. It was noted that the user needs to be certain that the security level of the chatbot is sufficient, in particular if the chatbot is to support transactions and not just provide answers to frequently answered questions. When supporting transactions, it was also argued as necessary that the responsibility in the case the chatbot failed should be on the service provider, not the user. The importance of security in the chatbot was, for example, voiced in the following quote.

The chatbot needs to be safe to use. When you start using the chatbot you need to be convinced that the security level is sufficient. (P4)

The respondents also argued that it would be important for their trust levels how their personal data from the interaction with the chatbot is used and stored. In particular, it was reported that the chatbot should make clear what is stored, and preferably store as little personal data as possible.

Risk. Finally, a few participants noted that the perceived risk associated with using the chatbot would be important to whether or not they would trust it. As noted by one of the participants:

If [the objective of the interaction] was very important to me, I would check also with another source. [...] I should not trust it, at least not 100%, if it was important. (P2)

Summarizing Factors Affecting Trust. All factors identified by the participants, both those concerning the chatbot and those concerning the service context, are summarized in Table 1. Reported frequencies in the table correspond to the number of participants addressing a particular factor as potentially affecting trust.

Table 1. Factors perceived to affect trust in chatbots for customer service

High-level group	Factor name and description	Frequency
Factors concerning the chatbot	*Interpretation and advice.* Quality in interpretation of the user request and advise in response to request	9
	Human-likeness. The chatbot's appearance as human-like, personal, or polite	6
	Self-presentation. The chatbot's communication of what it can do and its limitations	3
	Professional appearance. The chatbot's appearance as being thoughtfully developed, with correct spelling and grammar	2
Factors concerning the service environment	*Brand.* The effect of the brand of the service provider hosting the chatbot	5
	Security and privacy. The importance of security and privacy aspects of the service	5
	Risk. The perceived risk associated with using the chatbot	2

5.4 Factors Affecting Future Use and Suggestions for Improvement

Towards the end of the interview, the participants were asked about factors which in their view could affect their future use of chatbots for customer service. Specifically, factors that could make them regular users of chatbots for this purpose.

The most important factor for future use, mentioned by ten of the participants, was seen as the chatbots ability to understand and provide adequate help and information This resembles the participants' answers for what is seen as affecting their trust levels. For chatbots to be frequently used, and also to be trusted, they need to correctly interpret the users' questions, understand the users' needs, and provide the needed assistance. This view is reflected in the following user quote.

> If the chatbot solves my problem I will come back. Because then it is much more efficient that waiting in a phone or chat que to speak with an employee in the company. (P4)

The participants specifically noted that the efficiency in interaction would be decisive for their future use of customer service chatbots. Specifically, it was argued that the chatbot needs to be seen as a more efficient channel of support than other available options, as suggested in the following quote.

> I would need to experience more often that the chatbot is a more efficient channel than the alternatives. (P1)

It was also suggested that more frequent future use would depend on the accessibility of the chatbot. That is, whether or not the chatbot was promoted as an alternative to regular customer service.

If the chatbot was made available as a clearly visible option on the home page of the service provider, for example the webpage of the tax authority, it may well be that I would use it instead of trying to find an answer through search. (P6)

However, five of the participants also noted that them becoming regular users of chatbots for customer service in part depended on their own interest in technology and new services. That is, their future use of chatbot may not only depend on the chatbot as such but also on themselves as users.

I have very strong belief in this. I am a user because I want to show my support to the technology as I am quite interested in information technology. (P5)

6 Discussion

We have presented the key findings from an interview study concerning user trust in customer service chatbots. This knowledge is an important basis for future chatbot development, as trust is a determinant of user uptake of technologies and services [3].

In the following, we will discuss our findings and their theoretical and practical implications. Echoing the structure of the results presentation, we will first discuss the perceived benefits and challenges with current chatbots for customer service before discussing the findings that may shed light on which factors that affect trust. We will also address the findings pertaining to future chatbot use. Finally, we will address the study limitations and make suggestions for future research.

6.1 Chatbots Represent Benefits and Challenges

The participants reported a number of benefits of chatbots for customer service. These benefits were in part corresponding with previous research on users' motivations for chatbot use [2], suggesting that the main motivation to use chatbots is productivity. That is, the promise of efficient assistance with simple requests. Specifically, the benefits of not having to wait in queue for assistance by customer service personnel and 24/7 accessibility were accentuated as major benefits.

At the same time, chatbots' inability to address more specific or complex requests was regarded a major limitation. While this finding may be seen as an artefact of chatbots being an emerging technology for customer service, it also serves as a reminder of the importance to clearly inform the user on what the chatbot can and cannot do. Failure to do so, may lead the user to believe that the chatbot is capable of more than it actually is, which in turn may lead to frustration and reduced willingness to continue using chatbots for this purpose [14].

Interestingly, productivity was not seen as the only form of benefit in chatbots for customer service. The participants also noted other, perhaps more surprising, benefits. Among these, we find it particularly noteworthy that some users regard the machine nature of chatbots as a benefit. Customer service provided by a machine may be seen as relaxed, as the user can take the time needed to process feedback and formulate questions. The user may also see it as less embarrassing to ask questions about presumably simple issues, as the chatbot is seen as non-judgmental. These potential benefits correspond to findings in previous research, where users of therapeutic chatbots may find it easier to open up and talk about difficult topics with these than with a human therapist [7].

The reported benefits and challenges, however, clearly indicates that chatbots currently are an emerging technology for customer service purposes. The main reported challenge concerned the chatbot's ability to correctly interpret the user's request. This resembles the early days of website design, when a main challenge of ecommerce websites was the prevalence of usability problems [16]. Hence, while the reported benefits in part may be seen as expected benefits of near future chatbots, the challenges may be seen as actual challenges in current chatbots for customer service.

6.2   Trust Affected by Factors in the Chatbot and in the Service Context

While there exists a substantial body of knowledge on users' trust in technology, we currently lack insight into the factors affecting trust in chatbots. The main contribution of this study is to provide a basis for establishing such insight.

While the notion of trust in technology has been seen as controversial [11], it may be noted that the participants of the study seemed to consider the notion of trust in chatbots a relevant and timely topic.

The identified factors seen as affecting trust in chatbot for customer service to some extent corresponded to factors in the existing literature. For example, the participants' accentuation of the importance of quality in interpretation and advice is partially overlapping Corritore et al.'s [3] concept of credibility. At the same time, the identified factors also clearly represent something highly specific for chatbots. For example the identified link between the chatbot's human-likeness and trust is a factor that has received less attention in the literature. Possibly, the fact that the interaction with the chatbot is conducted in a manner similar to the interaction with a human being, makes the factor of human-likeness particularly important.

The identified factors also suggest that trust in the chatbot not only is the result of perceived chatbot characteristics. Rather, the service context in which the chatbot is situated is seen as important. In particular, it is noteworthy that the brand hosting the chatbot is critical to trust in the chatbot. If the chatbot is hosted by a trusted provider, the user is more likely to trust also the chatbot. That is, the trust in the provider spills over on the chatbot. Also contextual factors such as perceived security and privacy, and also perceived risk, was seen as decisive for users' trust in the chatbot. Hence, to fully understand trust in chatbots it may be important not only to consider the chatbot in isolation, but also to consider the chatbot as pat of a broader service context.

6.3   Implications for Future Design of Customer Service Chatbots

While this study is only a first step towards understanding users' trust in chatbots for customer service, a number of tentative implications for future design of such chatbots may be drawn. Such implications may be drawn in part on the participants responses to the questions on factors affecting future use and suggestions for improvement, and in part on the findings based on other parts of the interviews.

In the following, we list what we see as five key implications for future design of customer service chatbots, relevant for designers and developers of such chatbots.

1. **Prioritize efficient service provision.** The key determinant of users' trust in chatbots for customer service, as well as their likelihood of becoming regular users of such chatbots, is efficient service provision. Users should consistently experience the chatbot channel as superior on efficiency when choosing this option.
2. **Be transparent on the chatbots features and limitations.** Chatbots are not able to handle all customers' needs and wants, but they may be an efficient alternative for some. Hence, it is critical that the chatbot clearly communicates both what it can do, and what it cannot do, to the user. This will help the user in choosing the chatbot channel when this actually is the most efficient option.
3. **Strengthen the user experience through human-like conversation.** A courteous, personal and human-like appearance may enhance user experience and trust in the chatbot. Such human-likeness should not negatively impact efficiency, but may provide an additional experiential layer – similar to that of a pleasant and polite customer service representative.
4. **Leverage users' trust in the brand.** Users' trust in the brand likely spills over to the chatbot. Hence, strategic use of branding and hosting of the chatbot may positively affect trust. At the same time, a poorly executed chatbot design may, likewise, reflect negatively on the brand.
5. **Demonstrate that security and privacy are prioritized.** Security and privacy are important to users. The design and dialogue of the chatbot should make it clear that security and privacy are top priorities also for the chatbot channel.

6.4   Limitations and Future Research

The aim of this study is to provide an initial basis for understanding trust in chatbots for customer service. This aim has been pursued through an exploratory interview study, a consequence of which are some important limitations. In this section, we will in particular address three such limitations.

First, the study is relatively small scale, involving 13 users of chatbots for customer service. This limitation allowed us to explore a range of factors that may affect trust in such chatbots. At the same time, the generality of the identified factors may be challenged. Future research is needed to validated and expand on the findings of this study, through involvement of a larger number of users.

Second, the study is conducted in the context of a specific context; four Norwegian customer service chatbots. This limitation allowed us to make an in-depth analysis of user experience and trust for these chatbots. Furthermore, the choice of context allowed us to conduct the investigation in a market with high levels of digital technology uptake, which is beneficial for the relevance of the findings. At the same time, the study should be extended with similar data collections in other markets.

Third, the exploratory aim of the study implied that the data collection and analysis was not guided by specific theoretical constructs of trust in chatbots. This limitation is due to the study being an initial step towards increased knowledge on this topic. Future studies will benefit from being guided by a theoretical framework. Hopefully, the finding from this study may serve as a basis for establishing such a framework.

7 Conclusion

We have presented an exploratory interview study, shedding light on the factors affecting users' trust in chatbots. The identified factors concern not only the chatbots, but also the service context in which the chatbots reside. The study findings are offered as a first step towards a theoretical framework of trust in chatbots for customer service. The findings also suggest a number of implications for designers and developers of such chatbots. To fully realize the potential in chatbots for customer service, chatbots need to be trusted by users. We hope that this study motivates future research within this important field of interest.

Acknowledgement. This work was supported by the Research Council of Norway grant no. 270940.

References

1. Botsman, R.: Who Can You Trust?: How Technology Brought Us Together–And Why It Could Drive Us Apart. Penguin, London (2017)
2. Brandtzaeg, P.B., Følstad, A.: Why people use chatbots. In: Kompatsiaris, I., et al. (eds.) INSCI 2017. LNCS, vol. 10673, pp. 377–392. Springer, Cham (2017). https://doi.org/10.1007/978-3-319-70284-1_30
3. Corritore, C.L., Kracher, B., Wiedenbeck, S.: On-line trust: concepts, evolving themes, a model. Int. J. Hum. Comput. Stud. **58**(6), 737–758 (2003). https://doi.org/10.1016/S1071-5819(03)00041-7
4. Crutzen, R., Peters, G.J.Y., Portugal, S.D., Fisser, E.M., Grolleman, J.J.: An artificially intelligent chat agent that answers adolescents' questions related to sex, drugs, and alcohol: an exploratory study. J. Adolesc. Health **48**(5), 514–519 (2011). https://doi.org/10.1016/j.jadohealth.2010.09.002
5. Dixon, M., Freeman, K., Toman, N.: Stop trying to delight your customers. Harvard Bus. Rev. **88**(7/8), 116–122 (2010)
6. Ezzy, D.: Qualitative Analysis: Practice and Innovation. Routledge, London (2002)
7. Fitzpatrick, K.K., Darcy, A., Vierhile, M.: Delivering cognitive behavior therapy to young adults with symptoms of depression and anxiety using a fully automated conversational agent (Woebot): a randomized controlled trial. JMIR Ment. Health (2017). https://doi.org/10.2196/mental.7785
8. Følstad, A., Brandtzæg, P.B.: Chatbots and the new world of HCI. Interactions **24**(4), 38–42 (2017). https://doi.org/10.1145/3085558
9. Følstad, A., Kvale, K., Haugstveit, I.M.: Customer support as a source of usability insight: why users call support after visiting self-service websites. In: Proceedings of NordiCHI 2014, pp. 167–170. ACM, New York (2014). https://doi.org/10.1145/2639189.2639232

10. Friedman, B., Khan Jr., P.H., Howe, D.C.: Trust online. Commun. ACM **43**(12), 34–40 (2000). https://doi.org/10.1145/355112.355120
11. Fryer, L.K., Carpenter, R.: Bots as language learning tools. Lang. Learn. Technol. **10**(3) (2006). http://dx.doi.org/10125/44068
12. Hancock, P.A., Billings, D.R., Schaefer, K.E., Chen, J.Y., de Visser, E.J., Parasuraman, R.: A meta-analysis of factors affecting trust in human-robot interaction. Hum. Factors **53**(5), 517–527 (2011). https://doi.org/10.1177/0018720811417254
13. Liu, X., Xu, A., Sinha, V., Akkiraju, R.: Voice of customer: a tone-based analysis system for online user engagement. In: Extended Abstracts of CHI 2018. ACM, New York (2018). https://doi.org/10.1145/3170427.3188454
14. Luger, E., Sellen, A.: Like having a really bad PA: the gulf between user expectation and experience of conversational agents. In: Proceedings of CHI 2016, pp. 5286–5297. ACM (2016). https://doi.org/10.1145/2858036.2858288
15. Mayer, R.C., Davis, J.H., Schoorman, F.D.: An integrative model of organizational trust. Acad. Manag. Rev. **20**(3), 709–734 (1995). https://doi.org/10.5465/amr.1995.9508080335
16. Nielsen, J.: Designing Web Usability: The Practice of Simplicity. New Riders Publishing, Indianapolis (1999)
17. Rousseau, D.M., Sitkin, S.B., Burt, R.S., Camerer, C.: Not so different after all: a cross-discipline view of trust. Acad. Manag. Rev. **23**(3), 393–404 (1998). https://doi.org/10.5465/amr.1998.926617
18. Schoorman, F.D., Mayer, R.C., Davis, J.H.: An integrative model of organizational trust: past, present, and future. Acad. Manag. Rev. **32**(2), 344–354 (2007). https://doi.org/10.5465/amr.2007.24348410
19. Tezcan, T., Zhang, J.: Routing and staffing in customer service chat systems with impatient customers. Oper. Res. **62**(4), 943–956 (2014). https://doi.org/10.1287/opre.2014.1284
20. Vinyals, O., Le, Q.: A neural conversational model. arXiv preprint arXiv:1506.05869 (2015)
21. Weizenbaum, J.: ELIZA—a computer program for the study of natural language communication between man and machine. Commun. ACM **9**(1), 36–45 (1966). https://doi.org/10.1145/365153.365168
22. Xu, A., Liu, Z., Guo, Y., Sinha, V., Akkiraju, R.: A new chatbot for customer service on social media. In: Proceedings of CHI 2017, pp. 3506–3510. ACM, New York (2017). https://doi.org/10.1145/3025453.3025496

Online Media and Public Issues

Measuring Agenda Setting and Public Concern in Russian Social Media

Darja Judina(✉) and Konstantin Platonov

Center for Sociological and Internet Research, Saint Petersburg State University,
Saint Petersburg, Russia
dartisimus@gmail.com, konplatonov@gmail.com

Abstract. Intensified contradictions between Russian state and private media have the serious consequences related to the fragmentation of the agenda. Each media pursues its own purposes in agenda setting which determine their strategies regarding the audience concern. Our hypotheses were that the private media would follow the interests of their audience in agenda-setting, and the state ones, on the contrary, would ignore them. To test out hypotheses we decided to measure the media and public agenda in social media because on these platforms there was the opportunity to study both of them. This paper presents the investigation of agenda-setting on the SNS Vkontakte of four popular news groups which represent following media: Russia Today, TASS, RBC and Meduza. We compared the topic coverage of mentioned media and the engagement rate for the news. We discovered that only RT's agenda correspond to the audience concern. In other news groups correlations were about zero. These results did not confirm our main hypotheses, but the analysis of the communication activity suggested that there was artificial activity which could affect the engagement rate. In addition, we revealed that the state media tend to cover the unobtrusive issues while the private ones – the obtrusive issues. The main methodological result of this paper is the demonstration how to replace the surveys by social media metrics in research of agenda-setting.

Keywords: Agenda-setting · News · Social media · Vkontakte
Engagement rate

1 Introduction

Contemporary comparative studies show that the Russian media as a whole have a more powerful urge to set their own agenda and to influence public opinion than the American and European ones [12]. This tendency poses a threat to the independence of mass media. In the recent years, a number of private Russian media have faced one or more of the following sanctions: from restriction of rights and designation as "foreign agents" to compulsory blocking by Roskomnadzor (Grani.ru, Kasparov.ru). Also during this time, pro-government stakeholders have increased their share in the large mass media and the social networks sites [37]. Although the mechanisms of state influence on mass media are not always expressed in tough actions, they somehow lead to the formation of self-censorship, which is an important risk for development of civil society.

© Springer Nature Switzerland AG 2018
S. S. Bodrunova (Ed.): INSCI 2018, LNCS 11193, pp. 211–225, 2018.
https://doi.org/10.1007/978-3-030-01437-7_17

In the recent years, the state and the private media of the Russian Federation are often opposed to each other. The former are periodically accused of broadcasting false facts [8] and imposing the agenda [26] that is inadequate to the real problems [43] and concerns of the society. The latter are subjected to pressure by legislative machine, being accused of receiving and illegal use of foreign financing [37].

Competing for loyal audience, the state and the private media in Russia focus on different topics and often tell different stories about the same events, but how does the specificity of the agenda relate to engagement?

The opportunities of employing classical methods, such as surveys, to analyze the inconsistencies between broadcasting of information and a request for it, are rather limited because of the relatively low reachability of respondents, choosing specific media. Meanwhile, thanks to development of social media and participation of the traditional state and private media in disseminating their news on these platforms, it is possible to measure the relationship between the agenda and the real concern of their audiences. In this study, we analyze the correspondence of the agenda and the extent of engagement in its discussion, using as an example, news groups of popular Russian state and private media, represented on social network VKontakte.

2   Theoretical Background

Issues, related to research of composition and content of news, are traditionally studied in the framework of the theory of setting the agenda. This concept became logical continuation of the theory of public opinion, developed in parallel with the basic paradigms of sociology of mass communications. Back in the 1970s, Shaw and McCombs showed in their classic study the discrepancies in representation of socially significant topics in different mass media [19]. Setting the agenda is the process in which media influence the representations of importance of problems and events among their audience [6]. Thus, media decide what is significant and what is not, in addition, they can form their own strategies for drafting the agenda [30]. Later versions of this conception also take into account the existence of a second level of agenda-setting, in which the affective and cognitive attributes of perception of news are intertwined [21], which leads to formation of a special way of thinking for audience.

Specificity of contemporary digital media imposes certain adjustments to actual understanding of this theory. On the one hand, this implies rethinking the audience as a more heterogeneous and active entity, on the other, there emerges reduction in the "time lag" that accompanies perception of information by audience [2]. Studies examining the phenomenon of creating agendas in social networks, often refer to data from Twitter [36, 46]. A number of European studies empirically have proved that for the present this network affects the agenda significantly more than, for example, newspapers [13]. Variety of broadcast channels in modern social media allows us to compare the official channels with the informal ones, the formal opinion leaders with the informal ones [31], which opens up new opportunities for a deeper understanding of the agenda formation.

Historically, the early research of the agenda formation focused on electoral processes and in this context on reflection of specific social problems in the news [20].

Later, the methodology and the scope of these investigations were expanded and the attention shifted to such phenomena as the effects of the agenda formation, its impact on behavior and public opinion [44]. In the 90th, studies, related to specific issues, were actively developing. Among them, for example, there was analysis of the agenda setting around environmental problems [1]. These processes have been studied in the context of various communication channels: newspapers, blogging newspapers [25], radio [7], TV [4], Twitter [31] and other platforms.

Traditional research of the agenda-setting implements classical quantitative sociological methods: surveys and analysis of secondary data regarding audiences, later - analysis of time series. Occasionally, qualitative methods can also be used, for example, focus groups and interviews [15]. In current studies, there were described methods and empirical research of the agenda setting by means of network analysis and big data methodology [10, 11].

The latest research focuses not only on the setting processes, but also on the mechanisms of agenda perception. A number of experiments show that the presence of thematic content and attention to the problems, outlined in the news and posts of Twitter, increases the perceived significance of this information [38]. The mechanisms of blurring the agenda in the context of constructing non-problems are also considered [29].

Strengthening the influence of social media on the agenda formation drew the attention of researchers to the process of mutual influence between these new and traditional media, for example, between traditional publication media and Twitter, blogs, forums [23], and also Youtube [34]. In these cases, in order to prove the influence of a particular information source, the analysis of time series was used with the assumption: if a source published the topic first, and then others spread the topic, then this source is considered as an influencer. However, as the authors of the papers themselves admit, this relationship is not an unambiguous proof of direct influence.

3 Agenda Setting and Public Concern

In the context of studying intermedia influence, we would like to note that social media are not only playing the role of a new type of media, but they also are a platform for shaping and setting the public agenda. As part of this representation, users of social networks sites themselves can "vote" with their attention and activity for topics that interest or concern them. Along with this, mass media, presented in social media are actually given a choice: they are able to not pay attention to the concern of their audience, can "play along" to the public, more frequently publishing materials on popular topics, or they can try to impose their agenda contrary to the needs of users.

Variety of Russian media can be conditionally divided into the state and the private ones. State media are organizations whose work in the largest proportion is financed from the state budget. Private media form their budget from the money of private companies, private donations, or through advertising. Some media can be called conditionally private or conditionally public, if they are financed by the money of the companies owned by the state.

The key research question of this work is:

RQ1. How is the agenda of state and private media in social media correlated with the concern of their audiences?

Based on the presumption that the state media, whose funding does not depend (at least directly) on the real interest of its audience, but depends on the demands of ideology that is broadcast through these media, we assume that state media try to either impose an agenda on their audience, or simply ignore its concerns.

H1a. The share of topics, broadcast in the news of state media in social media, has negative or zero correlation with the audience concern of these media.

Following the same logic with regard to the private media, we assume that they strive to match the interests of their users in social networks, since they depend financially on them (for example, through advertising or donations) in a greater degree than state-owned media.

H1b. The share of topics, broadcast in the news of the private media in social media, has a positive correlation with the audience concern of these media.

As a result of the differences in the assumed strategies for shaping the agenda among private and state media, we expect that in the news of the state media the unobtrusive issues (foreign policy, information about other countries) are more frequent, and in the private, respectively, the obtrusive issues (economy, domestic policy) are.

H1c. Obtrusive issues take greater share in the private media agenda than in the state ones. Meanwhile the state media contain more unobtrusive issues that the private ones.

4 Data

The sample of news groups includes public pages of popular media, presented in social network "Vkontakte". This social network was chosen as the most visited in the Russian Federation with more than 491 million registered accounts[1] (at the time of writing, vk.com is the most popular website based on traffic volume calculations in Russia[2]). The groups was selected from three sources. Firstly, they are groups that are offered as media by website "VKontakte", and secondly, they are groups of media listed in the top catalogs of search engine "Yandex"[3] and expert organization "Medialogy"[4]; thirdly, the groups were received from references of the already found public pages. In total, 62 groups were included in the sample. All publicly available information in these groups was downloaded using the VK API methods[5] for the period from 2018/01/17 to 2018/03/09. The total number of posts was 112167, the total number of comments was 3501259. Only 60 groups kept the option to leave comments.

---

[1] Vkontakte. Catalog, https://vk.com/catalog.php.

[2] Alexa. Traffic Statistics, https://www.alexa.com/siteinfo/vk.com.

[3] Yandex, https://yandex.ru/yaca/cat/Media/.

[4] Medialogy, http://www.mlg.ru/ratings/

[5] Vkontakte. API methods, https://vk.com/dev/methods

Only these groups with posts more than five were considered in the further analysis. The total number of such groups was 59.

To test the hypotheses, we decided to select four newsgroups, two of which were owned by the state media, that is, openly funded from the RF budget, and two were owned by the media, whose funding comes from other means (private companies, advertising sales, etc.). Additional selection criteria were:

- High average number of views on a post;
- Media content had to be filled primarily with news, but, for example, not dedicated to private stories;
- In the posts, various topics were present (the media should not be domain-specific);
- Media had to be on type, namely the publishing, (groups, associated with television or radio, were not considered);
- The content of posts in groups should be predominantly textual; posted pictures or video should not contain significant part of information. This criterion is related to the technical limitations of our data downloading method from "Vkontakte". Because of this, we had to exclude the RIA group from the final sample, although it fit the rest of the criteria.

As a result, the selected groups are following: among the state-owned media: Russia Today in Russian[6] and TASS[7], among private ones: Meduza[8] and RBC[9] (Table 1).

Table 1. Parameters of the selected news groups.

Type	Name	Posts	Views on a post	Comments
State	Russia_Today	7632	37395	893456
	TASS	3555	13437	61977
Private	Meduza	1900	47625	115878
	RBC	1823	34600	144497
Total		14910	133057	1215808

4.1 Sampling and Coding

In each of the four media, 100 posts were collected by random sampling. In accordance with the rules for coding posts, a post was removed from this sample, if there was no text in the post, if it was unclear from the post text what the news was about or the post contained not news but an analytical or entertaining note. In this case, the procedure for sampling posts was repeated until there were 100 posts with interpreted news for each group.

---

[6] Vkontakte. RT news in Russian, https://vk.com/rt_russian.
[7] Vkontakte. TASS, https://vk.com/tassagency.
[8] Vkontakte. Meduza, https://vk.com/meduzaproject.
[9] Vkontakte. RBC, https://vk.com/rbc.

The coding scheme for posts was developed from a preliminary analysis of the most frequent nouns and adjectives (the first 4000) contained in the full corpus of posts. Since coding the news content requires significant knowledge on economics, politics, mass culture, etc., which have been impossible to provide in the coding scheme, so the posts coding was performed by two coders employing the negotiated coding methodology [9]. To facilitate the work of coders, as well as to ensure greater coding accuracy, the number of topics for each post was limited to three.

4.2 Engagement Rate

To measure the users' attention to the news, we decided to implement the popular metrics used in social networks, – engagement rate. This metric is associated with one of the key sociological concepts, namely social inclusion. Social engagement is an effect that ascertains the degree of passive or active people's participation in any socially significant collective action or initiative. The term is often used in the context of the SROI methodology for stakeholders [22], as well as in applied social work alongside the concepts of "social inclusion" and "social support" [3]. Engagement as a phenomenon in the literature is presented in three formats: as a concept, as a qualitative and as a quantitative variable [14]. To assess the degree of audience participation and subsequent analytics, the last option is used: the metric indicator is the engagement rate. Although there is no single method for calculating such an index, in the most general form it means the difference between the number of event perceptions (coverage) and the number of inspired interactions [33].

Engagement rate in one form or another is used in studies of the efficiency of modern teaching methods and pedagogical strategies [18], sports [27], m-commerce [42], health communication [39], assessment of the academic journals audience concern in certain types of content [41] and many other areas.

In online research, engagement rate remains one of the most valuable metrics in the audience research. Engagement is represented as a measure of the user experience quality [17]. Most often, as a key metric, it is used in social media marketing, where it is important to evaluate and maximize the degree of influence (usually branded) content on the audience, ensure its loyalty [16]. In addition to using the indicator as a behavioral metrics, it can be employed to assess the engagement quality of a page or an entire social network, so it is proved that Twitter, Facebook and Google Plus have different global engagement rates [24]. On Twitter data, significant correlation between engagement coefficient and, for example, such variables as the time of day and the day of the publication week have been found [35].

In general, the metrics of online engagement is based on three main initial concepts: popularity (number of users, visits to a page, clicks, views, etc.), activity (average number of pages viewed per visit, the duration of a visit, etc.), loyalty (the number of visits to a site for a user, etc.) [17]. For social networks and with respect not to websites in general, but to users, the most relevant and technically measurable, above all, are the metrics of popularity, loyalty and their modifications. Such an indicator should take into account the entire range of key user activities, represented in the social network site, as well as be able to be weighed by temporary or other factors. This is one of the simplest formula used in research to calculate the average engagement rate per page:

((likes + comments + reposts per day)/(number of posts per day/number of unique commentators per day)) × 100 [28]. There are also formulas where the publication coverage (number of views) is placed in the denominator, and the calculation methods, where different weights are assigned to the different types of activities based on an understanding of their significance (for example, like has 1, comment has 2, etc.) [40].

For measuring engagement rate for posts in Vkontakte, a formula, similar to the formula used in Facebook [5] is implemented. It includes the following activity parameters: the number of likes and the number of comments are divided by the number of views, and this fraction is multiplied by a coefficient which is a multiple of 10 for convenience of analyzing the obtained value (formula 1). Although for posts in this social network (as well as in Facebook) there is also a parameter "the number of reposts", but it is not included in this formula, because when a post is reposting, it automatically gets a like.

$$ER = ((likes + comments)/views) * 1000 \tag{1}$$

The drawback of this formula is that it does not take into account the possible artificial activity regarding the attention to posts, or the activity caused by the news presentation, and not by its content. This, for example, may lead to the fact that for certain topics engagement rate may be higher exactly due to these factors. To examine these suggestions, as a first step, we decided to find out how all available measures of activity are correlated within the selected news groups during the observation period.

As seen in Fig. 1, in the Russia Today group, the number of comments exceeds the number of likes, which is atypical relative to the other three public pages. The number of comments on the commentator in Russia Today exceeds almost twice the next RBC. Since the difference between the groups in the number of commentators per post is less than in the number of comments, we assume that replacing comments with commentators in the engagement rate formula will improve our estimation of users' attention by partially removing the influence of artificial activity.

The distribution of likes and reposts on a post shows that Meduza takes a higher position than the other three groups (Fig. 1). Perhaps the reason for this inequality is that this media publishes educational and analytical content, more frequently than others do, or the wording of the news on Meduza is more entertaining in nature, which pushes users to leave a like or make a repost. But the differences between news groups pertinent to the number and proportion of reposts are noticeably smaller than for likes. As shown by the research of social networks and microblogging, the clicking on a like or a repost depends on many factors, such as format, nature, originality and quality of the content [32, 45].

We assume that replacing likes by reposts in the engagement rate formula will allow taking into account the interest of the group audience to the news, rather than to the style of its presentation.

4.3   Postmoderation of Comments

Large communities with the commenting option available in VKontakte are often post-moderated including media public pages. This factor hypothetically can affect the engagement rate for a particular topic, so we decided to estimate how often the group administration uses this option.

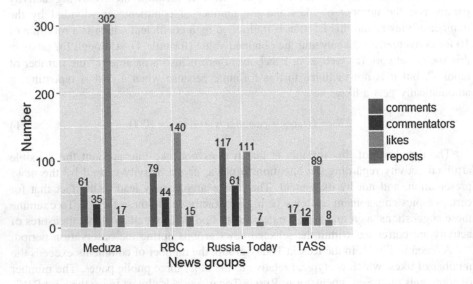

Fig. 1. Metrics of communication activity on a post in the news groups.

In some cases, restrictions on certain publications are fixed in the rules published on the public page. The Russia Today group (See footnote 6) directly indicates in the block of information the ban on the use of insults, profanity, and the spread of spam, links. RBC[10] in addition to this also declares a ban on advertising, discrimination, calls for violent change of the constitutional order of the Russian Federation, the dissemination of another's personal data, posting content related to violence, suicide propaganda, copy-paste and flood. Meduza and TASS did not register the rules for deleting comments, however this practice is also present in these public pages.

To estimate frequency of postmoderation, we took advantage of the fact that users periodically complain about deleting their own or other people's replicas directly in the comments, in some cases criticizing this practice for bias. The search for such complaints was conducted according to key words, taking into account word forms and possible misspelling. The comment was sampled, if it contained the word post or comment and one of the words: delete, remove, moderate, moderator. Then, the relevant comments were manually selected from this array.

---

[10] Vkontakte. RBC, https://vk.com/topic-25232578_32782346.

From the entire array of 1215808 comments (in 4 groups), 194 replicas have been selected which directly or indirectly contained complaints about deletion. In the selected media the relative frequency of such comments is quite low and ranges from 0.014 to 0.023%. Most likely, the real proportion of deleted comments is larger, but they hardly comprise a significant impact on the engagement rate of a post.

5 Results

As the result of posts coding, 27 topics were obtained (their distributions are presented in Table 2). It is necessary to explain particularly why the topic "Russia" was singled out separately only in the context of internal policy, although it would be possible to indicate in each topic whether this topic is relevant to Russia or not. We decided that in this case, our classification would be excessively complex, so we agreed to point out this difference only in relation to internal policy.

H1c hypothesis is partially confirmed, as in both groups of the state media, foreign issues are more common than in the private ones (p level of chi-square < 0.05). Concerning the presence of another unobtrusive issues, namely, the mentions of other countries, there is no single pattern. Only the most frequent treatment of Ukraine in the news of Russia Today shows the statistically significant difference among other media.

As for obtrusive issues, statistically significant evidence of the difference in the agenda of state and private media was in the references to the Russian internal policy due to relatively low frequency of this topic on Russia Today and high frequency on RBC. Perhaps, with a larger sample of posts, statistical differences would also be revealed in the coverage of civil society news.

Table 2. Distributions of themes

Topics	All groups, count	% of posts				
		All groups	Russia Today	TASS	RBC	Meduza
Foreign_issues	80	20.00	28	27	18	7
Internal_politics_ (Russia)	78	19.50	12	17	32	17
Crime	63	15.75	10	12	15	26
USA	63	15.75	15	19	19	10
Sports	62	15.50	22	13	16	11
Economics	49	12.25	14	13	16	6
Region_of_Russia	44	11.00	6	16	9	13
Law	37	9.25	6	5	13	13
Mass_culture	32	8.00	3	8	7	14
Europe	31	7.75	9	10	7	5
Ukraine	29	7.25	17	4	7	1
Incidents	27	6.75	6	8	3	10

(*continued*)

Table 2. (*continued*)

Topics	All groups, count	% of posts				
		All groups	Russia Today	TASS	RBC	Meduza
Education_issues	21	5.25	3	8	6	4
Internal_politics (other_countries)	19	4.75	6	6	4	3
Security_officials (siloviki)	19	4.75	4	2	7	6
Asia	16	4.00	2	7	5	2
Civil_society	16	4.00	2	1	6	7
Mass_media	16	4.00	0	2	5	9
Near_East	13	3.25	6	3	1	3
Health_issues	10	2.50	0	2	5	3
Transport	10	2.50	0	2	3	5
Latin_America	7	1.75	1	2	3	1
Religion	6	1.50	0	4	0	2
Africa	1	0.25	1	0	0	0
Canada	1	0.25	0	0	0	1
Middle_Asia	1	0.25	1	0	0	0
Housing_services	1	0.25	0	0	0	1

To test hypotheses H1a and H1b, Spearman's correlation was calculated between the frequency of the topics in each news group and the four types of engagement rate. For each topic ER was calculated by the average ER posts, in which there was a topic. In other words, the presented correlations show how the frequency of the topic appearance in media corresponds to the degree of the audience engagement?

Table 3. Correlations between engagement rate and theme frequencies

	ER1 likes + comments	ER2 likes + commentators[a]	ER3 reposts + comments	ER4 reposts + commentators
Meduza	− 0.11	− 0.1	− 0.26	− 0.20
RBC	0.09	0.14	0.07	0.01
Russia_Today	0.54*	0.44*	0.6*	0.38
TASS	0.11	0.08	0.11	− 0.07

*$p < 0.05$, $p < 0.1$

[a]Variable "commentators" was calculated as the number of unique commentators for each post.

As can be seen from Table 3, the hypothesis H1a is confirmed only with respect to TASS, since the correlations with all four types of ER are statistically close to 0. Correlations between engagement rates and the frequency of topics in the news of Russia Today are definitely positive. In our sample this is the only media whose thematic field of the news in terms of engagement rate largely corresponds to the audience concern.

H1b hypothesis is not confirmed, since all four correlations of RBC are almost equal to zero, and Meduza are negative, although they are also statistically close to zero. Our suggestions that the possible artificial activity or the news presentation may affect the measurement of the news posts popularity have been partially confirmed. In case of replacing comments with commentators, the correlation between ER and the topic proportions in the RT group fell by about 0.1 and 0.2 points, respectively. For TASS, such a change reduced the correlation only in case of the simultaneous replacement of likes and reposts. After replacement likes with reposts, the correlations of Meduza also had fell by 0.1 points on average. The same permutation reduced the correlation of the RBC by about 0.1 only together with replacing comments with commentators.

It can not be said that changes in the ER formula significantly influenced the nature of the connection between the public concern in certain news topics and their shares on the media agenda. Perhaps we did not take into account any other sources for skewness of real interest. However, the differences in the correlations between different types of ER indicate that the external factors affecting the activity around news in social media should be taken into account.

6 Discussion

The results and analysis of the data encourage to speculate what kind of correlation between the audience concern and the news agenda is "normal" or "abnormal". On the one hand, the answer is obvious - the media must adapt to the topics that concern their users. But what if it is a regular echo chamber? Perhaps, a large positive correlation indicates this. That is, the media contributes to preventing their audience from news that these people would like not to know and not to react to them. Therefore, on the other hand, "zero" correlation (or close to it) can be recognized as "normal", which indicates an independent, in a good sense, selection of news. With regard to the negative relationship between the attention of the audience and the proportions of the topics in the media agenda, it is unlikely that a significant negative correlation can be found here. We assume that users who rarely find or do not find interesting news for themselves at all will go to other media.

The problem of artificial activity around certain news or news groups in social media remains open. That suspicious activity, which we managed to cover, is hardly the only one. Perhaps, based on the parameters of the metrics used in social networks sites, there are still ways to represent issues as popular which are not. It is not ruled out that this problem causes the ethical obligations of the media and thus contributes to its resolution.

Limitations. The authors of the paper recognize some important limitations within the research. First, our sample of newsgroups is not representative of the whole multitude of newsgroups, so when analyzing a representative sample or the statistical population, the conclusions regarding the differences between the private and state media agendas may be different. Secondly, the analysis of the agenda may also be affected by coding scheme for labeling posts. Thirdly, as we have repeatedly pointed out, we can not exclude the influence of the artificial activity around news posts that we were not able to neglect, and which could lead to violation of the engagement rate validity. Fourth, distributions of the engagement rate within a media outlet depends on a site audience where a newsgroup is placed. For instance, this indicator may be higher in Facebook than in Vkontakte.

Further Work. Based on the labeled corpus of posts, we are going to create an automated algorithm for labeling news messages so that we can analyze a larger volume of the news agenda and include other media in our studies. In addition, a larger corpus will allow for more accurately assessment of the public concern about less frequent topics.

7   Conclusion

The results of the research showed that a funding source does not absolutely determine the strategy of the publishing media for shaping the news agenda in social media (in this case, newsgroups in social networks Vkontakte) regarding their audience concern. At the same time, the examined cases showed that the state media can largely meet the needs of their users (like Russia Today) and the private media can to some extent counter this interest (like Meduza).

The content of the news agenda was predicted correctly: the state media publish foreign issues more frequently, and the private – Russian internal politics. Along with this, the presented conclusions remain valid only if we have managed to escape, or significantly reduce the effect of cheating in the communication activity. We can not assert this with certainty, especially observing how the value of correlations between the different types of ER and the topics in the news group of Russia Today fell.

The main methodological result of our work is that we showed how, when using the theory of agenda-setting, it is possible to replace traditional surveys in determining the significance of news topics in the public agenda, by measuring the communicative activity in social media. Perhaps, the engagement rate formulas proposed for this purpose can somehow be complemented or made more resistant to the attempts of the artificial interest implementation.

References

1. Ader, C.R.: A longitudinal study of agenda setting for the issue of environmental pollution. Journal. Mass Commun. Q. **72**(2), 300–311 (1995). https://doi.org/10.1177/10776990 9507200204
2. Aruguete, N.: The agenda setting hypothesis in the new media environment. Comunicacion y Sociedad **28**, 35–58 (2017)
3. Bennett, K.M.: Low level social engagement as a precursor of mortality among people in later life. Age Ageing **31**(3), 165–168 (2002). https://doi.org/10.1093/ageing/31.3.165
4. Brosius, H.B., Kepplinger, H.M.: The agenda-setting function of television news: static and dynamic views. Commun. Res. **17**(2), 183–211 (1990). https://doi.org/10.1177/0093650 90017002003

5. Chan, M., Fassbender, K.: Evaluating public engagement for a consensus development conference. J. Palliat. Med. **21**, 1–20 (2018). https://doi.org/10.1089/jpm.2017.0390
6. Dearing, J., Rogers, E.M.: Agenda-setting research: where has it been, where is it going? Commun. Yearb. **11**, 555–594 (1988). https://doi.org/10.1080/23808985.1988.11678708
7. Fitzgerald, R., et al.: Generating news: agenda setting in radio broadcast news. In: Burger, M. (ed.) L'analyse Linguistique des Discours Médiatiques, Nota Bene, Québec, pp. 133–154 (2008)
8. Fletcher, R., et al.: Measuring the Reach of "Fake News" and Online Disinformation in Europe. Reuters Institute Factsheet, https://reutersinstitute.politics.ox.ac.uk/our-research/measuring-reach-fake-news-and-online-disinformation-europe
9. Garrison, D.R., Cleveland-Innes, M., Koole, M., Kappelman, J.: Revisiting methodological issues in transcript analysis: negotiated coding and reliability. Internet High. Educ. **9**(1), 1–8 (2006). https://doi.org/10.1016/j.iheduc.2005.11.001
10. Guo, L., Vargo, C.: The power of message networks: a big-data analysis of the network agenda setting model and issue ownership. Mass Commun. Soc. **18**(5), 557–576 (2015). https://doi.org/10.1080/15205436.2015.1045300
11. Guo, L.: The application of social network analysis in agenda setting research: a methodological exploration. J. Broadcast. Electron. Media **56**(4), 616–631 (2012). https://doi.org/10.1080/08838151.2012.732148
12. Hanitzsch, T., Folker, H., Corinna, L.: Setting the agenda, influencing public opinion and advocating for social change: determinants of journalistic interventionism in 21 countries. Journal. Stud. **17**(1), 1–20 (2016). https://doi.org/10.1080/1461670X.2014.959815
13. Harder, A.R., Sevenans, J., Aelst, P.: Intermedia agenda setting in the social media age: how traditional players dominate the news agenda in election times. Int. J. Press Polit. **22**(2), 1–19 (2017). https://doi.org/10.1177/1940161217704969
14. Hudson, S., Huang, L., Roth, M.S., Madden, T.J.: The influence of social media interactions on consumer-brand relationships: a three-country study of brand perceptions and marketing behaviors. Int. J. Res. Mark. **33**(1), 27–41 (2016). https://doi.org/10.1016/j.ijresmar.2015.06.004
15. Kwansah-Aidoo, K.: The appeal of qualitative methods to traditional agenda-setting research: an example from West Africa. Gazette **63**(6), 521–537 (2001). https://doi.org/10.1177/0016549201063006004
16. Lee, D., Hosanagar, K., Nair, H.: The effect of advertising content on consumer engagement: evidence from Facebook (2013). https://www.researchgate.net/publication/257409065_The_Effect_of_Advertising_Content_on_Consumer_Engagement_Evidence_from_Facebook
17. Lehmann, J., Lalmas, M., Yom-Tov, E., Dupret, G.: Models of user engagement. In: Masthoff, J., Mobasher, B., Desmarais, M.C., Nkambou, R. (eds.) UMAP 2012. LNCS, vol. 7379, pp. 164–175. Springer, Heidelberg (2012). https://doi.org/10.1007/978-3-642-31454-4_14
18. Lu, O.H.T., Huang, A.Y.Q., Huang J.C.H., Huang, C.S.J., Yang, S.J.H.: Early-stage engagement: applying big data analytics on collaborative learning environment for measuring learners' engagement rate. In: International Conference on Educational Innovation through Technology. IEEE, Tainan (2016). https://doi.org/10.1109/eitt.2016.28
19. McCombs, M., Shaw, D.L.: The agenda-setting function of mass media. Publ. Opin. Q. **36**, 176–187 (1972). https://doi.org/10.1086/267990
20. McCombs, M.: A look at agenda-setting: past, present and future. Journal. Stud. **6**(4), 543–557 (2005). https://doi.org/10.1080/14616700500250438
21. McCombs, M.: The agenda-setting role of the mass media in the shaping of public opinion. https://www.researchgate.net/publication/237394610_The_Agenda-Setting_Role_of_the_Mass_Media_in_the_Shaping_of_Public_Opinion

22. Mulgan, G.: Measuring social value. Stanf. Soc. Innov. Rev. **8**(3), 38–43 (2010)

23. Neuman, R.W., Guggenheim, L., Mo Jang, S., Bae, S.Y.: The dynamics of public attention: agenda-setting theory meets big data. J. Commun. **64**(2), 193–214 (2014). https://doi.org/10.1111/jcom.12088

24. Niciporuc, T.: Comparative analysis of the engagement rate on Facebook and Google Plus social networks. In: Proceedings of International Academic Conferences, pp. 334–339. International Institute of Social and Economic Sciences, Prague, London (2014)

25. Noguera, J.M.: The new agenda setting paradigm in the web: cybermedia towards news social filters. Int. Assoc. Media Commun. Res. (2007)

26. Paul, C., Matthews, M.: The Russian "Firehose of Falsehood" Propaganda Model. http://www.rand.org/content/dam/rand/pubs/perspetives/PE100/PE198/RAND_PE198.pdf

27. Pedro, S.D.G.: Athletes engagement, resilience, and rate of perceived exertion on Portuguese national- and international-level wrestlers. Int. J. Wrestl. Sci. **6**(1), 5–10 (2016). https://doi.org/10.1080/21615667.2016.1166299

28. Peñaflor, J.: Beyond "Likes" an assessment of user engagement in Facebook among Philippine Academic Libraries. Libr. Manag. **39**(1/2), 59–65 (2018). https://doi.org/10.1108/LM-12-2016-0100

29. Pingree, R.J., Stoycheff, E., Sui, M., Peifer, J.T.: Setting a non-agenda: effects of a perceived lack of problems in recent news or Twitter. Mass Commun. Soc. (2018). https://doi.org/10.1080/15205436.2018.1451543

30. Pinto, S., Balenzuela, P., Dorso, C.O.: Setting the agenda: different strategies of a mass media in a model of cultural dissemination. Physica A **458**, 378–390 (2016). https://doi.org/10.1016/j.physa.2016.04.024

31. Russell, F.M., Hendricks, A.M., Choi, H., Conner, S.E.: Who sets the news agenda on Twitter? Journalists' posts during the 2013 US Government shutdown. Digit. Journal. **3**(6), 925–943 (2015). https://doi.org/10.1080/21670811.2014.995918

32. Sabate, F., et al.: Factors influencing popularity of branded content in Facebook fan pages. Eur. Manag. J. **32**(6), 1001–1011 (2014). https://doi.org/10.1016/j.emj.2014.05.001

33. Salvo, M.T., et al.: Social media engagement: identifying the predictive anatomy of organic social content. https://repositories.lib.utexas.edu/handle/2152/39080

34. Sayre, B., Bode, L., Shah, D., Wilcox, D., Shah, C.: Agenda setting in a digital age: tracking attention to California proposition 8 in social media, online news and conventional news. Policy Internet **2**(2), 7–32 (2010). https://doi.org/10.2202/1944-2866.1040

35. Semiz, G., Berger, P.D.: Determining the factors that drive Twitter engagement-rates. Arch. Bus. Res. **5**(2), 38–47 (2017). https://doi.org/10.14738/abr.52.2700

36. Skogerbø, E., Bruns, A., Quodling, A., Ingebretsen, T.: Agenda-setting revisited: social media and sourcing in mainstream journalism. In: Bruns, A., Enli, G., Skogerbø, E., Larsson, A.O., Christensen, C. (eds.) The Routledge Companion to Social Media and Politics, pp. 104–120. Routledge, New York (2016)

37. Snegovaya, M.: Stifling the public sphere: media and civil society in Russia. National Endowment for Democracy. https://www.ned.org/stifling-the-public-sphere-media-and-civil-society-in-egypt-russia-and-vietnam/

38. Stoycheff, E., et al.: Agenda cueing effects of news and social media. Med. Psychol. **21**(2), 182–201 (2018). https://doi.org/10.1080/15213269.2017.1311214

39. Theiss, S.K., et al.: Getting beyond impressions: an evaluation of engagement with breast cancer-related Facebook content. MHealth (2016). https://doi.org/10.21037/mhealth.2016.10.02

40. Vadivu, V.M., Neelamalar, M.: Digital brand management—a study on the factors affecting customers' engagement in Facebook pages. In: International Conference on Smart Technologies and Management for Computing, Communication, Controls, Energy and Materials (ICSTM), pp. 71–75. IEEE, Tamil Nadu (2015) https://doi.org/10.1109/icstm.2015.7225392

41. Wadhwa, V., Latimer, E., Chatterjee, K., McCarty, J., Fitzgerald, R.T.: Maximizing the tweet engagement rate in academia: analysis of the AJNR Twitter feed. Am. J. Neuroradiol. 38(10), 1866–1868 (2017). https://doi.org/10.3174/ajnr.A5283

42. Walters, P., Hoven, K.A.: Measuring audience engagement with corporate brands, through their mobile phone. Int. J. Manag. Cases (2011). https://doi.org/10.5848/apbj.2011.00006

43. Watanabe, K.: Measuring news bias: Russia's Official News Agency ITAR-TASS' coverage of the Ukraine crisis. Eur. J. Commun. 32(3), 224–241 (2017). https://doi.org/10.1177/0267323117695735

44. Weaver, D., McCombs, M., Shaw, D.L.: Agenda-setting research: issues, attributes and influences. In: Kaid, L.L. (ed.) Handbook of political communication Research, pp. 257–282. Erlbaum, Mahwah (2004)

45. Yang, C., et al.: Research on the factors affecting users' reposts in microblog. In: International Conference on Service Systems and Service Management, pp. 1–6. IEEE, Dalian, China (2017). https://doi.org/10.1109/icsssm.2017.7996249

46. Yang, X., Chen, B.-C., Maity, M., Ferrara, E.: Social politics: agenda setting and political communication on social media. In: Spiro, E., Ahn, Y.-Y. (eds.) SocInfo 2016. LNCS, vol. 10046, pp. 330–344. Springer, Cham (2016). https://doi.org/10.1007/978-3-319-47880-7_20

Negative A/Effect: Sentiment of French-Speaking Users and Its Impact Upon Affective Hashtags on *Charlie Hebdo*

Svetlana S. Bodrunova[1](✉) ⓘ, Ivan S. Blekanov[2] ⓘ,
Mikhail Kukarkin[1] ⓘ, and Nina Zhuravleva[1] ⓘ

[1] School of Journalism and Mass Communications,
St. Petersburg State University, St. Petersburg, Russia
s.bodrunova@spbu.ru
[2] Faculty of Applied Mathematics and Control Processes,
St. Petersburg State University, St. Petersburg, Russia

Abstract. Studies of user sentiment on social networks like Twitter have formed a steadily growing research area. But there is still lack of knowledge on whether the discussion clusters tagged by emotionally opposite hashtags differ in sentiment distribution, both in terms of difference between hashtags and between user types, e.g. non-influencers and influential accounts. We look at two hashtags that marked the discussion on the *Charlie Hebdo* massacre of 2015, namely #jesuischarlie and #jenesuispascharlie. As sentiment analysis studies for the French language are rare, we elaborate our own approach to sentiment vocabulary. We apply human coding and machine learning to correct the automated sentiment assessment. Then we apply the enhanced knowledge on sentiment to both discussion segments and compare the configuration of the resulting sentiment-based nebulae in overall and francophone-only discussions. Also, we define influencers for both discussions and compare whether ordinary and institutional users differ by sentiment. We have three notable findings. First, negativity structures #jenesuispascharie more than #jesuischarlie. Second, while francophones communicate cross-sentiment inside the francophone talk, their negativity tends to cast impact upon cluster formation inside general discussions. Third, influencers in both cases tend to be more negative than positive, but institutional users bear neutral and positive sentiment more than ordinary people.

Keywords: Sentiment analysis · French · Twitter · Influencer
Charlie Hebdo

1 Introduction

Studies of user sentiment in discussions at social networking sites, including Twitter, have formed a huge and constantly expanding research area. But there are still several important gaps in our knowledge on how social conflicts are discussed online.

First, sentiment in Twitter discussions is often analyzed without taking into account the *ad hoc* nature of the online conversation [1]. But, as we know, hashtagged discussions, especially conflictual ones with high potential for user polarization, tend to be

© Springer Nature Switzerland AG 2018
S. S. Bodrunova (Ed.): INSCI 2018, LNCS 11193, pp. 226–241, 2018.
https://doi.org/10.1007/978-3-030-01437-7_18

more horizontal in terms of structure [2], less predictable in discussion dynamics [3, 4], and highly emotional due to their origin in affect [5]. This implies higher impact of personal traits of authors and of discursive features of user texts, including sentiment, upon the discussion structure. Thus, studying discussions on openly conflictual issues on social media may help detect how sentiment relates to user grouping, as well as predict the actors of potentially conflict-bearing views. Also, there is evidence that, with time, user polarization influences topic perception and news consumption [6], and that offline clusterization of sentiment towards a socially polarizing issues may have grave consequences for situational dynamics [7], while positive tone in relations between local governments and citizens increases online political participation [8]. Also, the newest works show (see, e.g. [9]) that in-platform conversational conflicts eventually reduce user discussion activity. Thus, it is important to assess whether sentiment is a ground for user polarization for conflictual topics.

But, second, in user sentiment studies, we observe striking scarcity of works that would link user sentiment to the discussion structural metrics and user positions in the discussion. Only rare works directly assess network metrics in relation to user sentiment (for the examples, see [10] and [11]). This happens despite the abundancy of works that associate sentiment with echo chamber formation in Twitter and Facebook discussions (see below). And, third, the works that would assess sentiment-based discussion structure in some comparative perspective are virtually non-existent.

Fourth, we very rarely see the cases when positive/neutral and negative hashtags could be juxtaposed. In particular, there is lack of knowledge on whether the discussion clusters tagged by emotionally opposite hashtags differ in sentiment distribution, both in terms of difference between hashtags and sentiment expressed by different types of users, e.g. 'ordinary people' and institutions. This happens partly because emotionalized discussions are difficult for sentiment analysis due to abundance of rhetoric expressions with indirect meanings (sarcasm, rhetoric questions etc.).

Fifth, sentiment analysis is mostly done for English-language texts, and other languages remain peripheral in sentiment detection on the global level [12].

We address these gaps by looking at one of the acutest online discussions of the recent years – namely, the discussion on the *Charlie Hebdo* massacre in Paris in 2015. As widely known, the hashtags #jesuischarlie and #jenesuispascharlie have set an example for further online discussions on violent ethnicity- and belief-based conflicts, and it was the first time when the societal value clash was so openly manifested. The research on this case and how it was discussed online is today quite extensive (for a review, see [13]), but it still lacks understanding of whether user sentiment formed distinct clusters and who were the bearers of this sentiment.

To fill these gaps, we use the approach that unites the discussion network analytics and sentiment analysis for the French language, and for the latter – a mixture of lexicon construction and machine learning based on data from human coders.

The remainder of the paper is organized as follows. In Sect. 2, we reconstruct the scholarly discourse that links user sentiment to the discussion structure to better identify the research gaps. We also describe the current state of research on sentiment analysis for French and research upon the *Charlie Hebdo* case. In Sect. 3, we pose the research questions and hypotheses. In Sect. 4, we explain our methodology, including data collection, formation of the sentiment lexicon, the discovered issues with it, and use of human coding for the machine-learning improvement of the sentiment detection. In Sect. 5, we show the results and (dis)prove the hypotheses. In Sect. 6, we discuss our results against earlier findings and explain them.

2   Polar Twitter Hashtags and Their Sentiment Shape

2.1   Sentiment-Based Discussion Structure: User Metrics and Echo Chambers

In the recent years, various instruments of sentiment analysis have been widely used to detect user views in relation to user groupings. Such studies mostly fall within online polarization field of studies and try to detect the so-called echo chambers based on, among other factors, user sentiment. But most of the works claim that echo chambers exist (or do not exist) based on user sentiment divergence, without assessing the relative distance of the paths between users and the users' roles in the discussions. E.g. authors of an early work on blogs [14] see individual blogs as echo chambers and, thus, by stating echo chambering based on comments, just show that individual blogs diverge in political standing. Another, more recent work [15] has taken a user's ego-network of tweets/comments as an analogue of an echo chamber and used sentiment analysis to show whether these micro-structures experience divergence of views.

Works that take large homophily-based user groups as echo chambers, e.g. the one on a long-standing issue of climate change [16], have shown that, first, sentiment does separate users in issue-based discussions and, second, is different in interactions between positively- and negatively-minded tweeters, which evidently adds to echo chamber formation. At the same time, there are works that show that 'opinion cross-roads' also exist on Twitter, be it based on sentiment [17] or on other features of user alignment like a user's position towards an issue assigned manually by researchers [18], friendship ties [19], or news sharing [20]. There are also works that link user metrics and/or discussion web graph structure to user sentiment. Thus, one work calls this approach hybrid [21] but does not go beyond just detecting the sentiment-based graph structure and showing that the seven detected communities are all heterogeneous in their sentiment. Two other works [10] and [11] show that sentiment analysis helps identify influencers, but do not describe who the influencers are and whether their status in the discussion is somehow linked to their offline social status.

The works that would try to juxtapose pre-defined pro/contra views on a given problem and detect sentiment within the expectedly clustered communities remain rare in sentiment analysis field. An attempt to discuss 'positive' ('science') and 'negative' ('conspiracy') statements in the discussion on misinformation was undertaken by the authors [22, 23]. They have supported the long-existent claim that users come out of the online discussions with their views even more polarized and radical than before; moreover, '[t]he more active a polarized user [was], the more the user tend[ed] towards negative values both on science and conspiracy posts' [22: 12]. Another work by the same group of authors [24] shows that, on Facebook, highly involved users inside echo chambers tend to express negative sentiment. Thus, we may expect that highly involved influencers may have more negative views than non-influential users in both cases. But, in contrast to this, our earlier works show that influencers in the discussions on *Charlie Hebdo* tend to have mixed sentiment [25].

Out of this research, we see that: (1) event-based emotionally-laid discussion outbursts are rarely researched upon in terms of user sentiment; (2) there are only rare attempts to juxtapose pre-defined 'positive' and 'negative' sides of issue- or event-based discussions, to detect sentiment within them, and compare the sentiment-based structure of the discussions; (3) there are no attempts to detect sentiment of particular users in connection to their offline status. We will try to address these gaps by revealing the sentiment-based structure of two hashtagged discussion segments with polar modalities, namely #jesuischarie and #jenesuispascharlie. We deliberately chose the French-language case to test our combined method of sentiment detection in a language other than English, and in the circumstances of pre-defined polarized opinion.

2.2   French-Language Sentiment Detection and Its Accuracy

Today, detecting sentiment in languages other than English is still problematic, first and foremost due to absence of well-developed and tested lexicons that would be non-case-specific. For French, there are only several works that are focused on this language only [26–29]. Authors [29] have undertaken an extensive attempt to build a lexicon in French, with yielded accuracy of 71.59%. In [27], despite the authors discuss not only lexicon but also morphology and semantics, the analysis anyway goes on the level of lexicon polarity. In [28], the authors try to enrich the French lexicon and test several machine translation techniques, but fail to significantly improve the results beyond the selected baseline.

One approach to work with French is lexicon enrichment from English or copying the lexicon development approach on the whole. A work on French and Italian elections [30], based on an approach developed for English [31], uses hand coding of sample datasets and relies on salience of n-grams. A more complicated approach that tests semi-supervised methods of lexicon enrichment and reach accuracy close to 83% by F-measure in word label propagation for French [32], but do not test the overall sentiment attribution to any short or longer texts.

But in most cases, French is used as target language to which machine translation of lexicons from English is applied. Among those, most works deal with cross-language sentiment detection and apply machine translation and (semi-)automated lexicon development from English and, sometimes, Spanish to as many other languages as possible, from two [32], three [33, 34], five [35], seven [36], eight [37] to 13 [38] to 136 [12]. For this approach (where indicated, which is not always the case), the accuracy of sentiment detection varies within 57.1% to 61.2% [33] to 67.8% [39] to 72.2% [40] to 74.9% [34] to 78.8% [37]. In one meta-evaluative work, acceptable sentiment polarity prediction ranges 66% to 83% with substantial coverage of the dataset (over 70%) [41]. One work reported accuracy to vary between 87% and 93% for seven languages [42], but with no exact scores for French. With French, this approach remains dominant, despite the fact that, for many works, 'the performance of cross-language sentiment analysis using single/multiple assisting language/languages is lower when compared to in-language sentiment analysis' [43: 8].

Sometimes French is used the other way round – as a source language, and translation is done into English to which then sentiment analysis is applied [44], but such works are rare. Language-independent (based on emoticons) approaches have also been tested for French [45], but we will leave them aside from our review, as we are interested in sentiment within two already polar discussion zones, and we expect emoticons to be used in similar ways in both clusters. We also ignore ontologies developed for analysis of visual data [46], as they do not cover the language fully.

For this work, we will focus exclusively on French and combine two-stage human coding, machine translation, and machine learning to develop the polarity-oriented lexicon for the *Charlie Hebdo* case also suitable for other sentiment analysis tasks, given that case-specific n-grams are added.

2.3   The *Charlie Hebdo* Case and Its Previous Assessment

The massacre in the editorial office of *Charlie Hebdo* and the subsequent murders in Paris suburbs have received significant attention from the scholarship around the world. Thus, authors [47] have conceptualized #jesuischarlie and #jenesuispascharlie as discourse and counter-discourse, respectively. In a later paper [48], the same authors described in detail the discourses within #jenesuispascharlie, while another paper [49] reflected upon the users' emotion-based framing; they all suggest emotional cleavages in the discussion structure. Authors [50] drew attention to the tensions between the global and the local in the conflict. Another important study [51] argued that divisions in the discussion reflected Huntington's clash of civilizations, if spatial origin of the tweets is taken into account. But our recent study [13] showed that, in language distribution, unlike in spatial one, the civilizational clash was absent, as tweets in French and English fully dominated. Also, one work [52] shows that the users' political preferences also influence the discussion structure.

Sentiment analysis has also been already applied to the case, including assessment between the influential and non-influential users. Thus, one work [53] also assessed user sentiment across a range of *Charlie Hebdo*-related hashtags for both 'super-tweeters' and 'the rest', but not via lexicon construction or human coding plus machine learning but by use of first-person pronouns and several emotionally-laid words. While this attempt is interesting in its approach, it does not explain why 'je', being just a part of a hashtag, relates to identity constructions (which authors claim to be a pre-requisite for research). Our pilot work based on small proportions of users [25] showed that the two hashtags differed in sentiment-oriented user groupings.

As we know from our previous research [13], even if the discussion was, indeed, multilingual encompassing over 30 languages, French and English vividly dominated and, moreover, formed distinct language-based clusters within the discussions. Thus, it is interesting whether we can discover a second layer of echo chambering within one language crucially important for the discussion.

3 Research Questions and Hypotheses

Based on our previous research and the literature review above, we have limited our research to French-speaking users only, as they were the main group that discussed the case in a non-English language and represented, by our estimates, over 80% of non-English speakers in the discussion. Having in mind all the aforementioned, we have developed the following research questions and hypotheses:

RQ1: *Does user sentiment have substantial impact on the discussion structure?*
H1a. In both cases, francophone users will form distinguishable discussion clusters based on positive/negative/mixed sentiment within the francophone discussion.
H1b. Sentiment of francophone users will cast impact on the overall discussion for both #jesuischarlie and #jenesuispascharlie.
H1c. The structure of the francophone discussion nebulae will differ, with positive sentiment relatively more salient and tightly grouped in #jesuischarlie and negative sentiment more salient and tightly grouped in #jenesuispascharlie.
RQ2. *What sentiment is expressed by the discussion influencers?*
H2a. In both cases, the influencers will mostly bear negative sentiment.
H2b. In both cases, institutional influencers will bear more positive/neutral sentiment, and non-institutional users will tend to express more negative sentiment.

We will also qualitatively describe the sentiment of the top influential users, in order to draw some preliminary conclusions on whether negative sentiment is linked to the users' offline status.

4 Method

4.1 Data Collection and Selection of Influencers

For data collection, we have used an API-independent web crawler capable of collecting large amounts of Twitter data with ensured quality, developed by the research group for earlier projects [54, 55]. With this, we have collected all the publicly available tweets for both hashtags for three days in the immediate aftermath of the tragedy, as we were interested in the most emotionally loaded period of the discussion.
The resulting general datasets included:

- for #jesuischarlie: tweets – 420,080; users who published them – 266,904; users who posted and interacted with the posted tweets (by likes, retweets, or comments) – 719,503, the overall number of tweets and interactions – 3,808,564;
- for #jenesuispascharlie: tweets – 7698; users who published them – 5466; users who posted and interacted with the posted tweets (by likes, retweets, or comments) – 17,872; the overall number of tweets and interactions – 68,945.

Then, we have selected the influential users (influencers). For this, we have used the strategy that we had developed for previous research on inter-ethnic conflicts [4, 56]. For this, in each of the two initial datasets, we have ranked users by 9 parameters: the number of tweets, likes, retweets, and comments, as well as by five centrality metrics, namely in-degree, out-degree, cumulative degree, betweenness, and pagerank. Then, to make the samples adequate to the sizes of the initial datasets, we established the thresholds for each parameter having in mind ∼ 100 users per parameter for #jesuis-charlie and 5–10 users per parameter for #jenesuispascharlie. After that, duplicate users were eliminated from the top lists; the final lists of influencers included: for #jesuis-charlie, 459 users, for #jenesuispascharlie, 91 users.

Out of these four datasets, we have selected the users who we considered franco-phone. We had to sample users differently for the general datasets and for influencer lists, as, for the general datasets, we were interested in how the francophone discourse was structured altogether, and for the influencers, we wanted to assess individual users, too, and thus needed those who spoke only French (or with only a tiny minority of tweets being written in other languages, which allowed us to consider these users francophones *prima facie*).

Thus, our final datasets included: for #jesuischarlie, 167,049 users, of them – 154 influencers; for #jenesuispascharlie, 2740 users, of them – 35 influencers.

4.2   Formation of Sentiment Lexicon

Our strategy of lexicon formation was two-stage and combined human- and machine-enriched French sentiment dictionaries with human correction. This method is known as the one of triangulation [36] and has shown good results in previous works. Both earlier [35] and later [41] works show that machine translation in sentiment analysis performs satisfactorily in comparison with analysis of original non-English-language texts. Thus, machine translation may help a lot in enrichment of sentiment lexicons. But, at the same time, newest works (see, e.g. [57]) tell that, for Twitter, human-coded case-specific samples work the best for non-English languages.

Within a bigger project on cross-language sentiment detection, our sentiment lex-icons were elaborated for English, French, Italian, Spanish, and Russian, and we used the same two-stage procedures. Further on, we discuss the procedure for French only.

The first stage included formation of the polarity-oriented lexicon based on WordNet (www.cs.uic.edu/∼liub/FBS/sentiment-analysis.html), the world-renowned English-language sentiment lexicon, and enriched by synonym addition (using machine translation) and human coding of frequency vocabularies of the discussions. Thus, initially, 6785 words (2005 positive and 4780 negative) formed the primary lexicon in English. Then, we have elaborated software that found synonyms to these lexemes, and the vocabulary grew to 5787 positive and 11,660 negative lexemes. The software also checked the list for duplicates and eliminated them. Then, machine translation based on Google Translate (onlinedoctranslator.com/ru/translationform) was used to build the lexicon in French; again, the procedure of elimination of possible duplicates was applied. As a result, 4928 positive and 11,299 negative lexemes remained.

Also, we have enriched the lexicon by the case-specific lexemes coded positive/negative/neutral by human coders. To form this list of lexemes, we have selected francophone users from the influencers in both cases and created a word frequency vocabulary out of their tweets. After pre-processing, the lists of 1488 lex-emes (frequency 7 or higher) for #jesuischarlie and 601 lexemes (frequency 2 or higher) for #jenesuispascharlie were hand-coded by two French-speaking coders; all the cases of disagreement were discussed by the working group. The two lists then were juxtaposed to each other and to the primary lexicon; again, duplicates were eliminated.

The resulting lexicon contained over 16,600 units and was applied to both influencers and non-influential users with 5+ tweets, in order to test-calculate the sentiment in tweets, which we conducted. But as we were interested in sentiment of users, not individual tweets, we have labeled sentiment for the users (as based on their tweets) in the following way, dissimilar to previous works:

- neutral – if a user had neutral tweets only;
- negative – if a user had negative or negative&neutral tweets only;
- positive – if a user had positive or positive&neutral tweets only;
- mixed – if a user had both negative and positive tweets.

For the three latter categories, sentiment ratios were calculated. For the users labeled positive/negative, we could see the strength of their sentiment expression; for those labeled mixed, we could see whether their sentiment was deviating towards positive or negative. And, as only a handful of users (less than 0.03% in the two cases taken together) had mixed sentiment with a ratio $|0.8| < r < |1|$ (close to positive/negative), mostly due to the fact that the overwhelming majority of users posted 7 or fewer posts in French, we did not set any threshold of turning mixed sentiment into positive or negative. Thus, mixed users with sentiment $|0.8| < r < |1|$ remained labeled mixed.

4.3 Assessing First-Stage Results and Application of Machine Learning

To assess the quality of the lexicon and to improve it, we have compared the automatized and human labeling of tweets (on the basis of which user sentiment was labeled). We have corrected sentiment for a sample dataset of 3000 tweets that had been previously labeled automatically. We found out that, for different parts of the coded sample, the accuracy of automated labeling varied from 61.3 to 68.5%, which was a bit lower than the results in the works mentioned above; thus, we needed to train the classifier with the human-coded data.

Also, we have assessed in an expert manner what caused the problems that had led to wrong automated labeling of tweets. Describing this in detail goes beyond the scope of this paper, but we need to mention that we have identified several problems on various levels that led mostly to false negative coding. Some of them are well-known, but others often elude from description. On the level of individual lexemes, there were several words like 'terrifiant' ('terrific') that had the first negative meaning but were used in its second positive one. But the major problems arose, of course, on the syntagmatic level, and they were linked to our not being able to take into account the stylistics of the speech. Thus, the first problem here was the well-described one of sarcasm, or, wider, irony in the tweets. But the second issue, the one that we consider even more important, was that negative lexemes (e.g. 'suspect') shifted the meaning of neutral headline-style tweets towards negativity, even when the tweet was emotionally neutral or even positive (e.g. 'the suspect is detained'). N-grams (bi- or trigrams) do not always resolve this issue, as both meaningful words are considered negative but the n-gram must be labeled as neutral within a headline-style tweet. Moreover, such headlines are intentionally deprived of any sentiment due to journalistic traditions of construction of objective media text. This stylistics is important for event-based discussions, as it is frequent in both original posts and massive retweets from major media outlets, but it is not captured well by lexicon-based sentiment analysis. This is why we needed to use machine learning based on corrected datasets.

The machine learning technique that we used was support vector machines method (SVM). To enhance the accuracy of classification, normalization of tweets was undertaken. This process had three steps: (1) elimination of stop-words including frequent and auxiliary lexemes, figures, dates and time, @mentions, links, and punctuation marks; (2) tokenization – in case of Twitter, the best tokens are single lexemes; (3) stemming (based on Snowball algorithms). After normalization, the lists of meaningful stems were subjected to the bag-of-words model controlled by the tf-idf measure. The tweets were represented as vectors; the hand-coded tweets were used as the training sample; then, the rest of the tweets were classified.

After training the classifier, we only conducted several manual checks with random mini-samples of machine-coded tweets. The results were higher than those at the first stage, namely from 70.5% to 79%, which was in line with most of the existing research and was enough for our goals. Now we could reconstruct and assess the graphs for the final datasets of all users and deal with influencers, too.

4.4   Reconstruction of the Web Graphs

We have reconstructed the web graphs for all users, creating four graphs: for all collected users and for francophone users only. We did that to assess whether the grouping of users is (or is not) relevant both within the overall discussion (see Fig. 1(a, b) for #jesuischarlie and #jenesuispascharlie, respectively), within the francophone one (see Fig. 2(a, b) for #jesuischarlie and #jenesuispascharlie, respectively), and for the francophone influencers.[1] We have used the YifanHu algorithm to reconstruct the overall structure of the discussions and calculated the number of edges both within and between the sentiment-based clusters in order to assess if sentiment creates echo chambers in the discussions (see Table 1).

4.5   Manual Analysis of Influencers' Profiles

To answer RQ2, we have manually assessed the user profiles of the detected influencers and used descriptive statistics to see whether user status is linked to sentiment and whether most influencers, as other researchers claimed, bore negative sentiment. To address H2b, we have assessed the number of users with the four types of sentiment for both discussions, and, to assess H2a, we combined the influencers in both discussions, as their number was too small for Spearman's rho calculations.

5   Results

As stated above, we have reconstructed the web graphs based on our labeling of user sentiment (see Figs. 1 and 2) and checked them for sentiment clusters (see Table 1).

RQ1: how sentiment affects the structure of the discussions. Visual assessment of the graphs on Fig. 2(a, b) shows that the discussions are divided into clusters based on user sentiment: thus, for #jesuischarlie, a large cluster of positive/neutral interactions is surrounded by two clusters of negative/mixed sentiment, and for #jenesuispas- charlie, two distinct negative-based clusters linked to influencers lie under a greenish positive-based nebula. But the data on interactions inside and between clusters (see Table 1) show that this is a graph construction artifact. In #jesuischarlie, users with very different sentiment all talk to each other, rather than form closed clusters; in #jenesuis-pascharlie, only neutral users tend to talk to each other substantially more than people in other clusters, but positive and negative sentiment anyway does not form any distinct group. Thus, H1a has to be rejected.

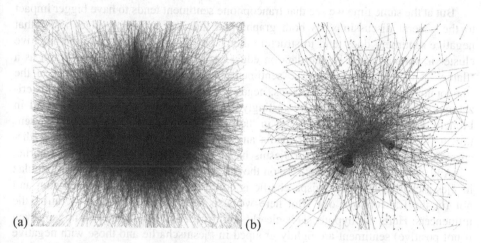

(a)   (b)

Fig. 1. Sentiment-based structure: (a) #jesuischarlie; (b) #jenesuispascharlie (graph fragments) for the overall discussion. *Green*: positive; *grey*: neutral; *red*: negative; *mixed*: brown. (Color figure online)

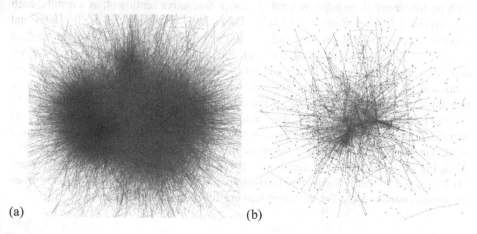

(a)   (b)

Fig. 2. Sentiment-based structure: (a) #jesuischarlie; (b) #jenesuispascharlie (graph fragments) for the francophone discussion. *Green*: positive; *grey*: neutral; *red*: negative; *mixed*: brown. (Color figure online)

Table 1. Number of edges inside and between clusters for both discussions

User sentiment	General discussion		Francophone segment		Francophone influencers	
	#jesuis	#jenesuispas	#jesuis	#jenesuispas	#jesuis	#jenesuispas
Positive	2.53%	0.25%	9.43%	3.17%	0.64%	0
Neutral	**25.03%**	16.29%	11.72%	**22.72%**	0	0
Negative	5.19%	**21.58%**	5.43%	9.04%	5.73%	**52.38%**
Mixed	3.85%	0.70%	5.87%	1.47%	**37.58%**	0
Between clusters	63.40%	61.18%	67.55%	63.59%	56.06%	47.62%

But at the same time we see that francophone sentiment tends to have bigger impact to the general discussions, as both graphs and the data on graph edges show that negative sentiment does tend to structure them. For #jesuischarlie, while the negative cluster is not supported by the data on edges, it is anyway evident in the graph as a 'flame' at its top. While positive sentiment is 'dissolved' much more than in the francophone discussion in both cases, negative sentiment casts an impact on clusterizaton for #jenesuispascharlie. Interestingly enough, negative sentiment expressed in French affects the overall discussion in the public counter-sphere, while neutral sentiment (mostly characteristic for media and institutional talk) affects the bigger discussion. Thus, H1b is rejected for #jesuischarlie but confirmed for #jenesuispascharlie.

And, as we see from above, H1c on the difference between the structure of nebulae in #jesuischarlie and #jenesuispascharlie is confirmed for the general discussion and not for the francophone one. But here we also need to take into consideration the influencers. Here, the hypothesis is clearly confirmed, as influencers with mixed (even if not positive) sentiment are tightly grouped in #jesuischarlie and those with negative sentiment are tightly grouped in #jenesuispascharlie.

RQ2: what sentiment the influencers express. As stated above, we have calculated user sentiment by assigning values as the differences between the number of tweets with positive/neutral, negative/neutral, or positive/negative sentiment; as a results, each user received a label from -1 to 0.56. User status was assigned as: 0 – personal account, 1 – individual professional account, 2 – official account/representative, as based on manual assessment of the user accounts. For #jesuischarlie, positive vs. neutral vs. negative was 50:19:85, and for #jenesuispascharlie, 2:7:26. Thus, negative sentiment (fully negative, or mixed with neutral tweets, or dominating over positive tweets) was found in 55 and 74% of the influencers, respectively. H2a is confirmed.

For H2b, we have merged the data on the influencers' sentiment and status from the two discussions and applied Spearman's rho metric to this dataset. We have found a weak but significant correlation between the users status and sentiment (0.209**). Also, Fig. 3 shows sentiment distribution for #jesuischarlie, where the cluster between -0.28 and 0.2 is clearly formed by institutions (mostly media). Thus, H2b is confirmed for #jesuischarlie, while for the other hashtag the data is too scarce to tell.

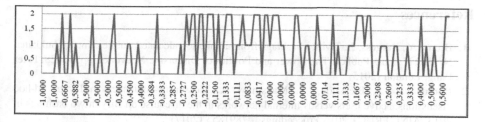

Fig. 3. Sentiment distribution in influencers' talk on #jesuischarlie

6 Discussion

In this paper, we have assessed the user sentiment in two polar hashtagged segments of the Twitter discussion on the *Charlie Hebdo* case. We have used a triangulation-based approach to detect user sentiment and have detected meaningful differences between the discussion segments.

What we have found is, first, that francophone discussions were more 'opinion crossroads' than echo chambers, but negative sentiment that the French users bore has cast impact upon the bigger general discussion of #jenesuispscharlie, making this cluster a negative-leaning counter-discourse.

Second, negative inclination was especially true for the influential users, as they formed the only negative cluster between themselves and created the centers of gravity in the general discussion. We may even say that, in terms of sentiment, non-influencers have produced more balanced pictures than the influencers. Moreover, Spearman rho has shown that the more institutionalized an influencer was, the more was the probability that the account would bear positive sentiment. We have also seen that non-institutional influencers tended to polarize, while institutional accounts bore more balanced views.

Third, we have seen that the two discussion segments did differ in how the sentiment structured the discussions, but not via formation of positive and negative echo chambers within the French-speaking community but by 'negative' users' talk to non-French speakers.

Our findings on the influencers are in line with the previous research, but what we add is a possible rethinking of the level of echo chamber formation in multi-lingual discussions. To assess how the discussion is structured in terms of sentiment, one needs to look both at one language and the overall discussion. Also, we have shown that positive and negative affective hashtags do differ in sentiment, and negative hashtags, indeed, tend to bear more negative sentiment.

Acknowledgements. This work was supported in full by Russian Science Foundation, Grant 16-18-10125.

Notes
We do not provide the web graphs for the influencers, as they are visually non-informative; but we have calculated the edges for these graphs (see Table 1).

References

1. Bruns, A., Burgess, J.: Twitter hashtags from ad hoc to calculated publics. In: Rmbukkana, N. (ed.) Hashtag Publics: The Power and Politics of Discursive Networks, pp. 13–28. Peter Lang, London (2015)
2. Bodrunova, S.S., Blekanov, I.S., Maksimov, A.: Measuring influencers in Twitter ad-hoc discussions: active users versus internal networks in the discourse on Biryuliovo bashings in 2013. AINL FRUCT 2016 Proceedings, #7891853 (2017)
3. Bruns, A., Burgess, J.: Researching news discussion on Twitter: new methodologies. J. Stud. 13(5–6), 801–814 (2012)
4. Bodrunova, S.S., Litvinenko, A.A., Blekanov, I.S.: Comparing influencers: activity vs. connectivity measures in defining key actors in twitter *Ad Hoc* discussions on Migrants in Germany and Russia. In: Ciampaglia, G.L., Mashhadi, A., Yasseri, T. (eds.) SocInfo 2017. LNCS, vol. 10539, pp. 360–376. Springer, Cham (2017). https://doi.org/10.1007/978-3-319-67217-5_22
5. Papacharissi, Z.: Affective Publics: Sentiment, Technology, and Politics. Oxford University Press, Oxford (2015)
6. Del Vicario, M., Zollo, F., Caldarelli, G., Scala, A., Quattrociocchi, W.: Mapping social dynamics on Facebook: the Brexit debate. Soc. Netw. 50, 6–16 (2017)
7. Salathé, M., Khandelwal, S.: Assessing vaccination sentiments with online social media: implications for infectious disease dynamics and control. PLoS Comput. Biol. 7(10), e1002199 (2011)
8. Zavattaro, S.M., French, P.E., Mohanty, S.D.: A sentiment analysis of US local government tweets: the connection between tone and citizen involvement. Gov. Inf. Q. 32(3), 333–341 (2015)
9. Kumar, S., Hamilton, W.L., Leskovec, J., Jurafsky, D.: Community interaction and conflict on the web. In: Proceedings of the 2018 World Wide Web Conference, pp. 933–943. International World Wide Web Conferences Steering Committee (2018)
10. Stieglitz, S., Dang-Xuan, L.: Political communication and influence through microblogging: an empirical analysis of sentiment in Twitter messages and retweet behavior. In: 45th Hawaii International Conference on System Science, pp. 3500–3509. IEEE (2012)
11. Bigonha, C., et al.: Sentiment-based influence detection on Twitter. J. Braz. Comput. Soc. 18(3), 169–183 (2012)
12. Chen, Y., Skiena, S.: Building sentiment lexicons for all major languages. In: Proceedings of the 52nd Annual Meeting of the Association for Computational Linguistics, vol. 2, pp. 383–389 (2014)
13. Bodrunova, S.S., Smoliarova, A.S., Blekanov, I.S., Zhuravleva, N.N., Danilova, Y.S.: A global public sphere of compassion? #Jesuischarlie and #Jenesuispascharlie on twitter and their language boundaries. Monitoring Obshchestvennogo Mneniya: Ekonomichekie i Sotsial'nye Peremeny 1(143), 267–295 (2018)
14. Gilbert, E., Bergstrom, T., Karahalios, K.: Blogs are echo chambers: blogs are echo chambers. In: 42nd Hawaii International Conference on System Sciences, pp. 1–10. IEEE (2009)
15. Hundt, M., Schneider, B., El-Assady, M., Keim, D.A., Diehl, A.: Visual analysis of geolocated echo chambers in social media. In: Proceedings of EuroVis (2017). http://bib.dbvis.de/uploadedFiles/2017-08-24doceurovis-2017-echochambers_FINAL.pdf
16. Williams, H.T., McMurray, J.R., Kurz, T., Lambert, F.H.: Network analysis reveals open forums and echo chambers in social media discussions of climate change. Glob. Environ. Change 32, 126–138 (2015)

17. Gruzd, A., Roy, J.: Investigating political polarization on Twitter: a Canadian perspective. Policy Internet **6**(1), 28–45 (2014)
18. Yardi, S., Boyd, D.: Dynamic debates: an analysis of group polarization over time on Twitter. Bull. Sci. Technol. Soc. **30**(5), 316–327 (2010)
19. Conover, M., Ratkiewicz, J., Francisco, M.R., Gonçalves, B., Menczer, F., Flammini, A.: Political polarization on Twitter. In: ICWSM Proceedings, vol. 133, pp. 89–96 (2011)
20. Herdağdelen, A., Zuo, W., Gard-Murray, A., Bar-Yam, Y.: An exploration of social identity: the geography and politics of news-sharing communities in Twitter. arXiv:1202.4393 (2012)
21. Alamsyah, A., Adityawarman, F.: Hybrid sentiment and network analysis of social opinion polarization. In: 5th International Conference on Information and Communication Technology (ICoICT), pp. 1–6. IEEE (2017)
22. Quattrociocchi, W., Scala, A., Sunstein, C.R.: Echo chambers on Facebook (2016). http://www.law.harvard.edu/programs/olin_center/papers/pdf/Sunstein_877.pdf
23. Zollo, F., et al.: Emotional dynamics in the age of misinformation. PLoS ONE **10**(9), e0138740 (2015). http://journals.plos.org/plosone/article?id=10.1371/journal.pone.0138740
24. Del Vicario, M., et al.: Echo chambers: emotional contagion and group polarization on Facebook. Sci. Rep. **6**, #37825 (2016). https://www.nature.com/articles/srep37825
25. Bodrunova, S.S., Blekanov, I.S., Kukarkin, M.: Multi-dimensional echo chambers: language and sentiment structure of Twitter discussions on the *Charlie Hebdo* Case. In: Stephanidis, C. (ed.) HCI 2018. LNCS, vol. 850, pp. 393–400. Springer, Cham (2017). https://doi.org/10.1007/978-3-319-92270-6_56
26. Mathieu, Y.: A computational semantic lexicon of French verbs of emotion. In: Shanahan, J., Qu, Y., Wiebe, J. (eds.) Computing Attitude and Affect in Text: Theory and Applications, pp. 109–123. Springer, Dordrecht (2006). https://doi.org/10.1007/1-4020-4102-0_10
27. Ghorbel, H., Jacot, D.: Further experiments in sentiment analysis of French movie reviews. Adv. Intell. Web Mastering **3**, 19–28 (2011)
28. Ghorbel, H.: Experiments in cross-lingual sentiment analysis in discussion forums. In: Aberer, K., Flache, A., Jager, W., Liu, L., Tang, J., Guéret, C. (eds.) SocInfo 2012. LNCS, vol. 7710, pp. 138–151. Springer, Heidelberg (2012). https://doi.org/10.1007/978-3-642-35386-4_11
29. Pak, A., Paroubek, P.: Twitter for sentiment analysis: When language resources are not available. In: 22nd International Workshop on Database and Expert Systems Applications (DEXA), pp. 111–115. IEEE (2011)
30. Ceron, A., Curini, L., Iacus, S.M., Porro, G.: Every tweet counts? How sentiment analysis of social media can improve our knowledge of citizens' political preferences with an application to Italy and France. New Media Soc. **16**(2), 340–358 (2014)
31. Hopkins, D.J., King, G.: A method of automated nonparametric content analysis for social science. Am. J. Polit. Sci. **54**(1), 229–247 (2010)
32. Rao, D., Ravichandran, D.: Semi-supervised polarity lexicon induction. In: Proceedings of the 12th Conference of the European Chapter of the Association for Computational Linguistics, pp. 675–682. Association for Computational Linguistics (2009)
33. Balahur, A., Turchi, M.: Multilingual sentiment analysis using machine translation. In: Proceedings of the 3rd workshop in computational approaches to subjectivity and sentiment analysis, pp. 52–60. Association for Computational Linguistics (2012)
34. Bader, B.W., Kegelmeyer, W.P., Chew, P.A.: Multilingual sentiment analysis using latent semantic indexing and machine learning. In: 11th International Conference on Data Mining Workshops (ICDMW), pp. 45–52. IEEE (2011)
35. Bautin, M., Vijayarenu, L., Skiena, S.: International sentiment analysis for news and blogs. In: ICWSM Proceedings, pp. 19–26 (2008)

36. Steinberger, J., et al.: Creating sentiment dictionaries via triangulation. Decis. Support Syst. **53**(4), 689–694 (2012)
37. Ruder, S., Ghaffari, P., Breslin, J.G.: A hierarchical model of reviews for aspect-based sentiment analysis. arXiv:1609.02745 (2016)
38. Steinberger, J., Lenkova, P., Kabadjov, M., Steinberger, R., Van der Goot, E.: Multilingual entity-centered sentiment analysis evaluated by parallel corpora. In: International Conference on Recent Advances in Natural Language Processing, pp. 770–775 (2011)
39. Boiy, E., Moens, M.F.: A machine learning approach to sentiment analysis in multilingual web texts. Inf. Retr. **12**(5), 526–558 (2009)
40. Kumar, A., Kohail, S., Kumar, A., Ekbal, A., Biemann, C.: IIT-TUDA at SemEval-2016 task 5: beyond sentiment lexicon: combining domain dependency and distributional semantics features for aspect based sentiment analysis. In: Proceedings of the 10th International Workshop on Semantic Evaluation (SemEval-2016), pp. 1129–1135 (2016)
41. Araujo, M., Reis, J., Pereira, A., Benevenuto, F.: An evaluation of machine translation for multilingual sentence-level sentiment analysis. In: Proceedings of the 31st Annual ACM Symposium on Applied Computing, pp. 1140–1145. ACM (2016)
42. Neri, F., Aliprandi, C., Capeci, F., Cuadros, M., By, T.: Sentiment analysis on social media. In: International Conference on Advances in Social Networks Analysis and Mining (ASONAM), pp. 919–926. IEEE (2012)
43. Balamurali, A.R., Khapra, M.M., Bhattacharyya, P.: *Lost in Translation*: viability of machine translation for cross language sentiment analysis. In: Gelbukh, A. (ed.) CICLing 2013. LNCS, vol. 7817, pp. 38–49. Springer, Heidelberg (2013). https://doi.org/10.1007/978-3-642-37256-8_4
44. Denecke, K.: Using SentiWordNet for multilingual sentiment analysis. In: 24th International Conference on Data Engineering Workshop, pp. 507–512. IEEE (2008)
45. Narr, S., Hulfenhaus, M., Albayrak, S.; Language-independent twitter sentiment analysis. In: Knowledge Discovery and Machine Learning (KDML), LWA, 12–14 (2012)
46. Jou, B., Chen, T., Pappas, N., Redi, M., Topkara, M., Chang, S.F.: Visual affect around the world: a large-scale multilingual visual sentiment ontology. In: Proceedings of the 23rd ACM International Conference on Multimedia, pp. 159–168. ACM (2015)
47. Giglietto, F., Lee, Y.: To Be or Not to Be Charlie: Twitter hashtags as a discourse and counter-discourse in the aftermath of the 2015 Charlie Hebdo shooting in France. In: AoIR Selected Papers of Internet Research. http://ceur-ws.org/Vol-1395
48. Giglietto, F., Lee, Y.: A hashtag worth a thousand words: discursive strategies around #JeNeSuisPasCharlie after the 2015 Charlie Hebdo shooting. Soc. Media+Soc. **3**(1) (2017). https://doi.org/10.1177/2056305116686992
49. Rosas, O.V.: The emotional framing of terrorism in online media: the case of Charlie Hebdo. In: Wassmann, C. (ed.) Therapy and Emotions in Film and Television, pp. 134–152. Palgrave Macmillan, London (2015)
50. Weston Vauclair, J., Vauclair, D.: De Charlie Hebdo à #Charlie: Enjeux, histoire, perspectives. Eyrolles, Paris (2015)
51. An, J., Kwak, H., Mejova, Y., De Oger, S.A.S., Fortes, B.G.: Are you Charlie or Ahmed? Cultural pluralism in Charlie Hebdo response on Twitter. In: ICWSM Proceedings, pp. 2–11 (2016)
52. Ratinaud, P., Smyrnaios, N.: The web sphere of #CharlieHebdo: a network and discourse analysis of a political controversy on Twitter. ESSACHESS J. Commun. Stud. **9**(2), 213–230 (2016)

53. Shaikh, S., Feldman, L.B., Barach, E., Marzouki, Y.: Tweet sentiment analysis with pronoun choice reveals online community dynamics in response to crisis events. In: Schatz, S., Hoffman, M. (eds.) AHFE 2016. AISC, vol. 480, pp. 345–356. Springer, Cham (2017). https://doi.org/10.1007/978-3-319-41636-6_28

54. Blekanov, I.S., Sergeev, S.L., Martynenko, I.A.: Constructing topic-oriented web crawlers with generalized core. Sci. Res. Bull. St. Petersburg State Polytech. Univ. 5(157), 9–15 (2012)

55. Bodrunova, S.S., Litvinenko, A.A., Blekanov, I.S.: Influencers on the Russian Twitter: institutions versus people in the discussion on migrants. ACM International Conference Proceeding Series, 22–23 November 2016, pp. 212–222 (2016)

56. Bodrunova, S.S., Litvinenko, A.A., Blekanov, I.S.: Please follow us: media roles in Twitter discussions in the United States, Germany, France, and Russia. J. Pract. 12(2), 177–203 (2018)

57. Mozetič, I., Grčar, M., Smailović, J.: Multilingual Twitter sentiment classification: the role of human annotators. PLoS ONE 11(5), e0155036 (2016)

Emotional Stimuli in Social Media User Behavior: Emoji Reactions on a News Media Facebook Page

Anna S. Smoliarova[(⊠)] ⓘ, Tamara M. Gromova ⓘ,
and Natalia A. Pavlushkina ⓘ

St. Petersburg State University, St. Petersburg, Russia
a.smolyarova@spbu.ru

Abstract. Emotions influence cognitive processes such as attention to a Facebook post and lead to behavioral response, such as liking, sharing and commenting. In 2016 Facebook launched a new set of icons indicating emotions in addition to the Like button, therefore the data about emotional stimuli in social media user behavior can be gathered automatically. This study examines user response to the posts published by 18 Facebook pages of Israeli news media in Russian language and investigates relationships between selective, interpretative and productive activities of a news user.

We advocate that the usage of Emoji reactions on Facebook media pages is negatively correlated with commenting and sharing. The Love icon is used in the same way as the traditional Like. Posts evoking a Sad reaction are less likely to be commented or shared than posts arousing any other reaction.

Second, we measure the congruence between different reactions expressed in a choice of one Emoji icon. The Love icon is used in the most monosemantic way. On the contrary, the post evoking a Wow reaction might be responded with any other Emoji reaction with a moderate degree of probability. Possible meanings of the homogeneity of emotions shared in a media Facebook page community are discussed.

Keywords: News users · Facebook reactions · Emotions · User engagement

1 Introduction

News were always used by individuals to communicate with others [1, 2]. Web 2.0. with its comment sections and possibilities to share news made these interactions around news items visible and measurable. Social media as decentralized platforms where everybody can disseminate content and participate in a dialogue created a next form of communication infrastructure that people use "because they like to talk to others about what is happening in the world" [3: p. 668, 4]. Among social media Facebook has shown "a further strengthening in the role played by Facebook in accessing, discussing, and sharing news" [5].

User activity with news on Facebook covers three dimensions of an active audience suggested by Picone [6]: (1) selective activity via following a particular media fan-page; (2) interpretative activity evident in choosing a Facebook reaction on a news item

© Springer Nature Switzerland AG 2018
S. S. Bodrunova (Ed.): INSCI 2018, LNCS 11193, pp. 242–256, 2018.
https://doi.org/10.1007/978-3-030-01437-7_19

(3) productive activity exposed in sharing and commenting. Introduction of a diversified spectrum of reactions by Facebook (Emoji reactions) in 2016 broadens further the research of "interpretative activity" that "implies the reader as actor of meaning making, not an actor of content production" [6: p. 127]. Thus, the paper at hand follows the intention of Picone (2016) "to grasp the full scope of how audiences are active". Studying correlations between Facebook reactions, sharing and commenting performed by followers of news media fan-pages we seek to detail the continuum of "selective, interpretative and productive dimensions of activity" [6: p. 128; 7].

Affective nature of the content has been proven to influence the user engagement with the news content [8–10], however, the data about Emoji reactions usage allows for more direct observation on user response [11]. In this article we track how the choice of a Facebook reaction (Like or one of the Emoji) relates to other types of interaction provided by Facebook – namely, comments and shares. To address this research question, this study examines Facebook pages of Israeli media in Russian language.

Previous research has shown that the internet facilitates the creation of digital diaspora [12–14] providing immigrant communities with efficient communication channels and forums for public discussion about specific immigrant experience [15, 16]. One might assume that representatives of diaspora should be more involved into online communities and interact intense with the media content [17–19]. The field of studies dedicated to diasporic news user's behavior on Facebook is growing [see for Russian speaking diaspora 20].

The role of Russian-language media remains salient for the first generation of immigrants from the former republics of the Soviet Union: not only for elder generation but also for adolescents [21]. Russian language media in Israel represent one of the most diverse media landscapes among other countries with Russian speaking diasporas. Russian language news media – two news websites and one TV channel – are ranked among 50 top visited Israeli websites [22]. Among other social media Facebook is quite popular in Israel: more than 43% of the population in Israel access Facebook, almost twice than a global usage penetration of 22.9% [23]. For Russian language media in Israel Facebook is a leading source for traffic from social networks. It takes the share of 80% or higher of traffic from social networks for two thirds of our sample, and for media outlets with smaller audience it might be the main source of traffic (see Appendix A).

The launch of a set of Emoji for expressing feelings about the items in the news feed was triggered by the attempt of Facebook management to raise the number of posts the users engage with [24]. The quality of user engagement is discussed from the perspective of "slacktivism" [25]. In this paper we look at whether the users' choice of an Emoji reactions instead of a plain Like correlates with user participation in forms of commenting and sharing. Second, the character of diasporic news users may be associated with the higher level of homogeneity among the media Facebook pages followers. In this regard, studying the usage of Emoji reactions in terms of their congruence appears to contribute in the filter bubbles research.

The remainder of this paper is organized as follows. The next section provides a literature review on user engagement with news content with an emphasis on emotional stimuli for cognitive processes and behavioral response. We then present our methodology (Sect. 3) and the findings of our study (Sect. 4). We conclude with a discussion of our results as well as limitations and potential future work.

2 Emotional Stimuli for News User Behavior

2.1 News User Behavior: From News Websites to Social Media

Even the audience of monological mass media such as TV was characterized by selective approach to media content consumption [1, 26]. Reception studies suggested that the audience consist on people able to interpret media messages [27, 28]. Online interactivity has rapidly changed the user behavior practices [29, 30] but "networked audiences on many occasions still act as broadcast audiences merely consuming broadcasted content" [32: p. 213] and still need to be stimulated by media outlets for meaningful contributions [3: p. 666].

The literature seems to suggest that implementations of users' comments created "a new phase in journalism audience participation" [33] since the media users gained more control on who might speak to the broaden audience of the media outlet [34, 35]. Commenting is associated with social-interactive motives and is driven by entertainment needs [36–38]. People want not only to interact with others but also to express a personal opinion on an issue/story [39, 40] and educate others [see a review in 38]. Indeed, the low quality of comments (abusive nature, lack of relevant debate) [41–43]; financial reasons of media business [44] or negative attitudes of journalists towards comment sections [33, 45] led to closing of comment sections on the online versions of mass media and to the movement of them to Facebook [46, 47].

Studies focusing on news sharing show similar motives [48–50]. The importance of news sharing is studied from a perspective of secondary gatekeeping: selective redissemination of journalistic content by news users results in user-generated visibility of the content [51]. People choose to disseminate items of practical utility, interest, and surprise [see review in 38]. The visibility to the others is a crucial stimulus: sharing news is "mainly a way to connect with others by means of exchanging content that might appeal to, interest or entertain one's social circle" [52: p. 929]. Kümpel et al. [9] distinguish between three possible motivations for news sharing: gaining reputation and social capital; inform others; get social approval. To some extent they are interconnected: self-presentation as an altruistic knowledge disseminator might be seen by the user as a tool for gaining status among others, self-worth as well as a request for social approval or empowerment [53, 54]. To the self-serving motives belong also entertainment via creating online content [53]. Macek interprets an act of sharing as an act of "performative self-exposure" [54: p. 295]. Overall, as Lischka and Messerli have shown in their literature review, "sharing of articles can be regarded as a social transaction actively motivated by an enhancement of the self-concept and social relations of the sender through information utility" [38: p. 3].

New forms of user engagement with news on social media [55] and on accessible and user-friendly online platforms [30] have blurred the border between production and consumption rising an active "produsage" [30]. Several researchers conceptualize "people formerly known as the audience" [31] as "active recipients of news" [11, 328, e.g. 3, 56, 57] who select sources and content pieces, express attitudes toward consumed content with likes and shares. Recent studies have shown that individuals choose less demanding forms of user engagement [46, 58]—one-button activities, such as liking or sharing news content, instead of online commenting or journalist-reader collaborations [44]. Overall, researchers estimate sharing and commenting as productive dimension of user activity [6, 48].

2.2 News in Your Pocket: News Media Facebook Pages

Social media have changed the social practices of how "news is produced, disseminated, and discussed" [59: p. 1, e.g. 46, 47]. A comparative study of news user behavior in six countries in 2016 has shown that for all cases the number of users commenting and sharing news items in social media is higher than in the websites [49]. The social practice is changing rapidly: for data from 2013 Nielsen and Schroder stated that "only a minority use them to engage in more participatory forms of news use like sharing, commenting on, or publishing their own stories" [59: p. 12]. Hence, since Facebook is a platform for personal communication and mass self-communication [29], news is only "a byproduct", as Hille and Bakker [3: p. 664] underline. This hybrid nature influences users' decisions on news engagement. As Larsson puts it, it is appropriate to form our online selves as "angry or upset over some societal malady" but Facebook users tend less to open what makes them happy or entertain them [11: p. 337].

Facebook integration with news media websites provides several possibilities for user engagement with driven from three major activities: (1) share a news item from the media website to a personal FB page; (2) comment on the media website as a registered FB user; (3) like the news media via media FB-page; (4) follow the news media via media FB-page; (5) express an attitude towards a news item published on the media FB-page with one of Facebook reactions (Like, Love, Ha-Ha, Wow, Sad, Angry); (6) comment the news item on the media FB-page; (7) comment on an other's comment; (8) express an attitude towards an other's comment; (9) share the news item from the media FB-page to the personal FB page; (10) write a post sharing news item on the personal FB page; (11) participate in a discussion about the news item on the personal FB page; (12) participate in a discussion about the news item on somebody's personal FB page.

We restrict our study to the reactions visible on the media FB-page (4–7, 9). In comparison to the personal pages engagement with news items on the media FB page assumes a certain readiness to communicate with strangers and openness to express an attitude or opinion for a broaden public. Being a follower means potentially regular consumption of the content, which again is connected to a certain level of involvement.

Media FB-pages were researched in several case studies [3, 34, 60, 61]. The page feed commonly consists on hyperlinks to the content items on the media website, thus, media tried to increase traffic to their online versions [60] or get viral dissemination of the news message.

Running FB page also diminishes risks of uncivil behavior of the commenters [62]. As a third party, Facebook "potentially offers more participation at lower costs" [3: p. 666]. As pointed above, low level of interactivity is preferable by the users, and they have been reported to comment only on the FB teaser of the news story without reading the whole [47]. Users also tend to like news posts more actively than comment or share them [11]. Sharing may require readiness for in-depth elaboration, while commenting causes a risk of other user's response and evaluation of one's comment [63].

Commenting while using a mobile app is even more complicated: "Commenting might afford nuanced responses but composing those responses on a keypad takes too much time. People needed a way to leave feedback that was quick, easy, and gesture-based", cited Stinson [24] Julie Zhuo, a product design director at Facebook. Launch of diversified range of reactions – emotional emoji icons instead of one like-button—was driven also by intense mobile consumption as well as by need to increase share of likeable posts [24]. As Facebook management has announced the main goal of the news tool, "there should be more ways to easily and quickly express how something you see in News Feed makes you feel" [64]. Five emoji were chosen based on a study of sentiments most frequently expressed by users that are evident in stickers, emoji, and one-word comments [24]. In a year after the launch the Reaction buttons were used 300 billion times, first of all, in Mexico, Chili, Suriname, Greece and Paraguay [65].

Therefore, we expect the following:

H1. Use of an Emoji reaction reduces the likelihood of the post to be commented or shared in comparison with the Like button.

2.3   Emotion-Driven Interaction

Previous research focused on emotional triggers provides rich data about the influence of emotional character of the content on the user response and behavior [see the literature review 10]. We will summarize the results to develop hypotheses about correlations between Facebook emoji reactions and sharing/commenting activities.

Cognitive and behavioral studies have indicated that emotions influence considerably cognitive processes such as attention or even lead to behavioral response, for ex., information sharing in social networks [see full literature review on emotions and information sharing in 8].

Emotions such as awe, amusement, anxiety, anger, were positively connected to user involvement [8]. Both positive and negative emotions, affective language increases feedback [66] or sharing through email [67; see also full literature review in 9]. They suppose that the emotions arouse readers, resulting in a higher engagement or in an affective action [68]. Sentiment articulated in the text on social media platforms also influences the frequency and the speed of retweets [8] proving the affective nature of user response in social media [8, 66].

Other studies provide evidence for more differentiated consequences. The data is contradictive, and many questions remain unanswered. For example, according to Joyce and Kraut, positive affect in messages encourages continued participation, while negative affect in messages might increase the feedback response rate [69]. Berger and Milkman [67] found that positive emotions are more likely to go viral than negative.

Another group of researchers have found evidences for an opposite trend. Negative stimuli often provide evidence for stronger and quicker emotional, behavioral, and cognitive responses than neutral or positive events [8]. This correlation is explained with reference to the negativity bias: more attention is paid, and stronger reactions are shown in case of negative information [70, 71]. Twitter and Facebook studies published by Steglitz and Dang-Xuan confirm this tendency for social media. Anxiety is also seen as the main trigger for disseminating rumors [8]. Finally, Lischka and

Messerli [38] found out that commenting a news item correlates with dissatisfaction of a news user.

To solve this contradiction, Heiss et al. [63] differentiate tonality (content elements – positive or negative news) from emotionality (explicit expression of emotions). They found out that negative tonality increases the number of comments and shares, while negative emotions had no effect on shares, slightly influenced the comments and have a significant effect on the number of likes. Positive tone did not affect user engagement, but positive emotions increased all three types – shares, likes and comments.

Low arousal, or deactivating, emotions (e.g. sadness) do not gain leverage by sharing [8, 67]. Humoristic elements are very likely to be shared and commented, and less but still likely to be liked [63].

Emotional nature of new range of Facebook reactions provides new opportunities for the research of user responses to the political content [72, 73], news and mass media content [11, 74] as well as for automatically conducted emotion detection [75]. According to Larsson's findings on Facebook pages of main Swedish and Norwegian newspapers, news content evoking Angry reaction also received higher amounts of shares and comments. On the contrary, such Facebook reactions as Love, Ha–Ha and Wow turned out to be significant negative predictors for sharing and commenting activities [11] "We share and comment on what makes us angry and upset but appear to act in the opposite way when the content consumed makes us happy" [11: p. 337].

Drawing on the insights summarized above, we derive the following hypotheses:

H2. Different emotional reactions correlate responsively with commenting or sharing activities

H2a. Posts evoking Angry reactions tend to be commented than shared

H2b. Posts evoking Love reactions are more likely to be commented than shared.

H2c. Posts evoking Wow reactions are more likely to be shared than commented.

H2d. The association between Sad and Ha–Ha reaction and sharing/commenting is the weakest among other reactions.

We also assume that one post may evoke diverse reactions because every user will individually perceive and interpret the message of the post. The understanding of the emoji icon's meaning is also not determined precisely and is constructed by the user. Still some patterns should be evident, for example, posts that arouse sadness, anxiety or anger might not be interpret ambivalent by most of news users. On the other hand, posts gaining support, explicitly expressed with the Love Emoji, might not be arouse Angry reaction. If our findings will support the latter the level of congruence of diametrically opposed emotional reactions such as Love and Angry could be interpret as an indicator for the audience homogeneity. The paper at hand, then, makes a small contribution into the filter bubble studies.

3 Method

Data were gathered with the Netvizz application [76] that exports data from publicly available Facebook pages and provides it anonymized to prevent individual users from being identified.

The sample includes 12322 posts published between May 1th 2017 and May 1th 2018 on the Facebook pages of 18 Russian language media in Israel. The period was selected due to features of an annual cycle in Israel and to include both annual celebration of Israel's Independence Day.

Web traffic data, including the share of traffic from social networks, in particular from Facebook, were gathered from the Similar Web database in status for May 2018. The audience size on Facebook was measured by the number of followers, i.e., the number of news media users receiving updates from the news media' Facebook page in their news feed. The data about followers is open and was collected from the Facebook pages in May 2018. We studied the general criteria of user responses to the content: how actively the posts gain reactions in general, are shared or commented; how actively in comparison to a Like button Emoji icons are used (Appendix A).

To prove our hypotheses the correlations between the number of shares, comments and Facebook reactions including Likes were measured for the whole dataset. We used descriptive statistics (Spearman's rho, because the variables are measured on a continuous scale, but Pearson's correlation cannot be run due to violations of normality). To investigate the relations between different Emoji reactions we measured the Spearmen's rho and then calculated standard deviation and range for each Emoji.

4 Findings

H1. Use of an Emoji reaction reduces the likelihood of the post to be commented or shared in comparison with the Like button.

A Spearman's correlation was run to assess the relationship between different Facebook reaction and commenting and sharing activity. We expected that the correlation between a reaction and an act of sharing/commenting is weaker for an emoji reaction than for the like reaction (Table 1).

Table 1. Spearmen's rho correlating comments and shares to Facebook reactions

	Reactions in general	LIKE	LOVE	HA-HA	WOW	SAD	ANGRY
Comments	.737**	.671**	.445**	.525**	.512**	.390**	.531**
Shares	.753**	.726**	.511**	.324**	.441**	.332**	.365**

Posts that are Liked tend to be disseminated and are positively related to the user engagement in the form of comments. There is a strong positive correlation between number of reactions to a post in general and both numbers of comments and shares of the given post. For the total amount of reactions, the Spearmen's rho is almost equal.

The same trend can be seen with Likes. A possible explanation might be that choosing an Emoji reaction is perceived by user as a full and self-sufficient expression of one's attitude towards the post. In this sense our findings correspond with concerns about "slacktivism" [25]. First, the Emoji reactions were launched to make easier the user interaction with a post that evoking one's reaction [24], that means, to some extent new variety of Facebook reactions fulfilled exactly the function they were implemented to. Moreover, due the social visibility of user interaction with a Facebook posts public expression of a sentiment may be perceived as equally challenging as taking a risk of a "performative self-exposure" or other user response and evaluation.

H2. Different emotional reactions correlate responsively with commenting or sharing activities (Fig. 1).

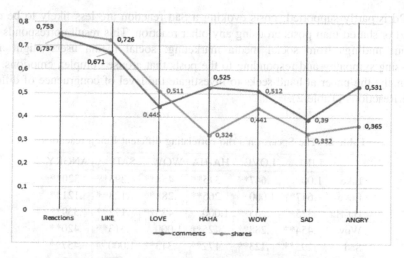

Fig. 1. Spearmens' rho correlating comments and shares to Facebook reactions

H2a. Posts evoking Angry reactions are more likely to be commented than shared.

H2a is supported: posts evoking Angry reaction are significantly more likely to be commented than shared. This result supports the previous findings on negativity bias: users tend to comment posts evoking Angry reaction rather than posts evoking other emotions represented in Emoji variety. Ha-Ha icon shows a similar trend, with the lowest correlation for shares. One might assume that both type of reactions are driven by entertainment (Ha-Ha) and social-interactive (Angry) needs that are associated with commenting and, in a contrary, are negatively related with sharing because of "performative self-exposure" as a result for the latter.

H2b. Posts evoking Love reactions are more likely to be commented than shared.

H2b is not supported: choosing a Love reaction seems to be in general the stronger version of Like reaction taking into consideration the similarity of correlation trends.

H2c. Posts evoking Wow reactions are more likely to be shared than commented.

H2c is not supported, moreover, the correlation between reaction and sharing is stronger than between reaction and commenting only for Like and Love reactions. Wow reaction has shown the third strongest correlation with shares which corresponds to the stimuli, so our data confirms the assumption that aroused readers tend to give a strong response to the content.

H2d. The association between Sad and Ha-Ha reaction and sharing/commenting is the weakest among other Reactions.

H2d is partly supported: posts evoking a Sad reaction are less likely to be commented or shared than posts arousing any other reaction. This result corresponds with previous findings from social media marketing: social media users might avoid expressing sympathy and responding to the posts that arouse complex emotions.

Finally, the paper at hand seeks to investigate the level of congruence of different Emoji Reactions (Table 2).

Table 2. The Spearmen's rho correlating different Emoji reactions

	LIKE	LOVE	HA-HA	WOW	SAD	ANGRY
Like	1.000	**.647****	.375**	.454**	.295**	.320**
Love	.647**	1.000	.265**	.288**	.123**	.121**
Ha-Ha	.375**	.265**	1.000	.425**	**.172****	.339**
Wow	.454**	.288**	.425**	1.000	.313**	.420**
Sad	.295**	**.123****	.172**	.313**	1.000	.457**
Angry	.320**	**.121****	.339**	.420**	.457**	1.000

The Love Emoji is proven to be the most monosemantic (range 0.526, standard deviation 0.214779). The use of Love Emoji correlates with the use of Like button (.647**) and the meanings of other correlations are much weaker, especially with Sad Emoji (.123**) and Angry Emoji (.121**).

Posts arousing the choice of Like button, as well as Sad and Angry Reactions have shown similar level of congruence of other Reactions (range 0.334–0.352, standard deviation 0.130462–0.141703). The more Sad reactions the post get, the less it is liked to arouse Love (.123**) or Ha-Ha (.172**) reaction. Sad reaction and Angry reaction might be expressed for the same post.

Emoji reaction with the highest level of congruence of other reactions is Wow Emoji. With range 0.166, standard deviation 0.074253 this icon might be chosen with a moderate degree of probability depending on an individual user response to the news item.

5 Conclusion

The research outlined in the paper at hand focused on emotional stimuli for social media activity of a follower of a news media Facebook page. The study addressed the correlation between different types of Facebook reactions, sharing and commenting activities. An analysis of a sample of 12322 posts gathered from 18 Facebook pages of Israeli news media in Russian language has shown that people tend to share and comment posts that they have Liked rather than posts that they have reacted with an Emoji reaction. We also made preliminary steps in observing the relationship between different types of Emoji reactions and assumed that measurement of the congruence between Emoji reactions in an online community of followers provides important insights into the filter bubble research.

This study has not examined at the micro level the correlations for each news media included in the sample. As Larsson [11] noticed, the media format as well as the content of the posts should be tested for their effect on user engagement. This should be considered as a limitation of our study. Second, we examined the correlations, therefore, the causal relationship cannot be described. The further research should take into consideration the level of activity within the community of followers. Third, the discrepancy of individual attitudes to the Emoji meanings may cause instability of results. Although for the final decision about the Emoji reactions set the universality in different cultures has been taken into consideration [24], the localization of verbal analogues may question comparative research of Facebook reaction usage across the world. For example, Russian version of reactions that is studied in the paper includes "outrageous" instead of "angry", "super" instead of "love", and "sympathize with/am sorry" instead of sad. Despite these limitations, the study provides new insights into the patterns of user engagement with news content on Facebook.

Acknowledgements. The research has been supported in full by Russian Presidential Grant for Young Ph.D. Scientists, research Grant MK-6128.2018.6.

A Appendix

See Table 3.

Table 3. Descriptive statistics for the Facebook pages

	Media type	Number of Facebook followers	Website views (M ln)	% Traffic from Facebook	% Posts without attention (no reactions, shares, comments)	Number of posts	% Posts shared	% Posts commented	% Likes of all Reactions	An average number of reactions per post	An average number of comments per post	An average number of shares per post
Channel 9	TV	113192	13.64	0.0361	4.17	912	60.75	54.71	71	96.23	37.26	52.49
Vesti	Newspaper	84281	5.85	0.2976	21.86	677	74.74	59.08	68	150.87	17.66	73.67
Mignews	Online only	38978	10.08	0.0421	5.19	770	61.69	61.04	55	21.81	6.76	3.27
ILand	Online TV	38064	0.27	0.1464	3.19	878	69.25	56.49	83	40.63	4.85	28.35
BeInIsrael	Lifestyle	15849	0.09	0.0683	0.00	289	65.74	83.04	95	48.09	4.66	8.96
Newsru	Online news	14304	15.85	0.0288	2.46	771	67.44	71.08	56	22.48	11.45	4.23
Dom	Online news	12436	0.16	0.8260	0.00	844	95.85	72.99	66	56.63	9.93	21.63
Shakshuka	Online, opinion	10758	No data	40.36	0.00	191	89.53	59.61	82	40.48	5.43	9.45
Iton-TV	Online TV, opinion	8905	0.35	0.0609	0.39	760	67.24	96.05	74	13.46	5.69	7.77
Data24	Online news	8030	0.05	0.4660	0.00	497	87.12	57.55	76	46.70	5.46	10.16
Detali	Online news	7261	2.16	No data	0.26	768	56.29	25.53	69	54.63	28.01	13.86
IsraGeo	Online magazine, opinion	5896	0.37	0.4197	13.90	842	56.29	25.53	61	7.52	1.05	2.46
Zahav	Online news and forum	4099	6.50	0.8625	31.42	662	12.39	8.91	79	1.25	0.18	0.18
Relevant	Online magazine, opinion	3908	0.11	0.4087	0.13	742	84.10	94.47	78	34.87	42.93	5.72
Newspress	Online news	3104	0.10	0.6817	0.98	1021	96.96	57.00	66	26.87	6.28	17.43
Strana	Online news	1858	0.11	0.4146	21.24	777	25.35	18.79	52	2.95	0.36	0.52
NEP	Online magazine, business	1528	0.63	0.0220	9.58	553	53.16	53.16	66	6.53	1.43	1.82
Channel 7	TV	311	1.87	0.0448	76.90	368	7.34	6.25	58	0.17	0.09	0.12
Mediana		8467.5			2.83	764	66.49	57.28	68.5	30.87	5.58	8.37

References

1. McQuail, D., Blumler, J., Brown, R.: The television audience: a revised perspective. In: McQuail, D. (ed.) Sociology of Mass Communication. Longman, London (1972)
2. Katz, E., Haas, H., Gurevitch, M.: On the use of the mass media for important things. Am. Sociol. Rev. 164–181 (1973)
3. Hille, S., Bakker, P.: I like news. searching for the 'Holy Grail'of social media: the use of Facebook by Dutch news media and their audiences. Eur. J. Commun. **28**(6), 663–680 (2013)
4. Couldry, N., Livingstone, S., Markham, T.: Media Consumption and Public Engagement: Beyond the Presumption of Attention. Palgrave Macmillan, New York (2010)
5. Fletcher, R., Radcliffe, D.: Reuters Institute Digital News Report 2015. http://reutersinstitute. politics.ox.ac.uk/sites/default/files/Supplementary%20Digital%20News%20Report% 202015.pdf. Accessed 20 May 2018
6. Picone, I.: Grasping the digital news user: conceptual and methodological advances in news use studies. Digit. J. **4**(1), 125–141 (2016)
7. Livingstone, S.: The changing nature of audiences: from the mass audience to the interactive media user. In: Valdivia, A.N. (ed.) Companion to Media Studies, pp. 337–359. Blackwell, Oxford (2003)
8. Stieglitz, S., Dang-Xuan, L.: Emotions and information diffusion in social media—sentiment of microblogs and sharing behavior. J. Manag. Inf. Syst. **29**(4), 217–248 (2013)
9. Kümpel, A.S., Karnowski, V., Keyling, T.: News sharing in social media: a review of current research on news sharing users, content, and networks. Soc. Media+Soc. **1**(2) (2015). https://doi.org/10.1177/2056305115610141
10. Hyvärinen, H., Beck, R.: Trump facts: the role of emotions in on social media: a literature review. In: Proceedings of the 51st Hawaii International Conference on System Sciences, pp. 1797–1806. HICSS, Hawaii (2018)
11. Larsson, A.O.: Diversifying likes. J. Pract. **12**(3), 326–343 (2018). https://doi.org/10.1080/ 17512786.2017.1285244
12. Castells, M.: The Internet Galaxy: Reflections on the Internet, Business, and Society. Oxford University Press, Oxford (2001)
13. Bailey, O.G., Georgiou, M., Harindranth, R.: Transnational Lives and the Media: Re-Imagining Diasporas. Palgrave Macmillan, New York (2007)
14. Khvorostianov, N., Elias, N., Nimrod, G.: 'Without it I am nothing': the internet in the lives of older immigrants. New Media Soc. **14**(4), 583–599 (2012)
15. Georgiou, M.: Diasporic communities online: a bottom-up experience of transnationalism. In: Sarikakis, K., Thussu, D. (eds.) The Ideology of the Internet: Concepts, Policies, Uses, pp. 131–146. Hampton Press, New York (2006)
16. Elias, N., Lemish, D.: Spinning the web of identity: the roles of the internet in the lives of immigrant adolescents. New Media Soc. **11**(4), 533–551 (2009)
17. Everett, A.: Digital Diaspora: A Race for Cyberspace. SUNY Press, Albany (2009)
18. Elias, N., Shoren-Zeltser, M.: Immigrants of the world unite? A virtual community of Russian-speaking immigrants on the web. J. Int. Commun. **12**(2), 70–90 (2006)
19. Morgunova, O.: National living on-line? Some aspects of the Russophone e-diaspora map. E-Diasporas atlas: exploration and cartography of diasporas on digital networks. De la Maison des Sciences de l'Homme, Paris (2012)
20. Korkonosenko, S.G., Berezhnaia, M.A.: Community media online: research approaches and practices of functioning. Case Ethnic Media HOLOS **5**, 370–381 (2017)

21. Elias, N., Lemish, D.: Between three worlds: host, homeland, and global media in the lives of Russian immigrant families in Israel and Germany. J. Fam. Issues **32**(9), 1245–1274 (2011)
22. SimilarWeb. http://similarweb.com/. Accessed 02 June 2018
23. Statista. https://www.statista.com. Accessed 02 June 2018
24. Stinson, L.: Facebook reactions, the totally redesigned like button, is here. Wired, 24 February 2016. https://www.wired.com/2016/02/facebook-reactions-totally-redesignedlike-button/. Accessed 01 May 2018
25. Morozov, E.: From slacktivism to activism. Foreign Policy, 5 September 2009. http://foreignpolicy.com/2009/09/05/from-slacktivism-to-activism/. Accessed 12 April 2018
26. Rubin, A.M.: The uses-and-gratifications perspective of media effects. In: Bryant, J., Zillmann, D. (eds). Media Effects. Advances in Theory and Research, 2nd edn, pp. 525–548. Lawrence Erlbaum Associates, Mahwah (2002)
27. Hall, S.: Encoding/decoding. In: Hall, S., Hobson, D., Lowe, A., Willis, P.: Culture, Media, Language, pp. 128–138. Hutchinson, London (1980)
28. Livingstone, S.: The challenge of changing audiences: or, what is the audience researcher to do in the age of the internet? Eur. J. Commun. **19**(1), 75–86 (2004)
29. Castells, M.: Communication, power and counter-power in the network society. Int. J. Commun. **1**, 238–266 (2007)
30. Bruns, A.: Blogs, Wikipedia, Second Life, and Beyond: from Production to Produsage. Peter Lang, New York (2008)
31. Rosen, J.: The People Formerly Known as the Audience. PressThink. http://archive.pressthink.org/2006/06/27/ppl_frmr.html. Accessed 03 Oct 2018
32. Couldry, N.: The necessary future of the audience… and how to research it. In: Nightingale, V. (ed.) The Handbook of Media Audiences, pp. 213–229. Blackwell Publishing, Malden (2011)
33. Reich, Z.: User comments. The transformation of participatory space. In: Singer, J.B. (ed.) Participatory Journalism: Guarding Open Gates at Online Newspapers, pp. 96–117. Wiley, Chichester (2011)
34. Hille, S., Bakker, P.: Engaging the social news user: comments on news sites and Facebook. J. Pract. **8**(5), 563–572 (2014)
35. Boczkowski, P.J., Mitchelstein, E.: How users take advantage of different forms of interactivity on online news sites: clicking, E-Mailing, and commenting. Hum. Commun. Res. **38**(1), 1–22 (2012)
36. Chung, D.S., Yoo, C.Y.: Audience motivations for using interactive features: distinguishing use of different types of interactivity on an online newspaper. Mass Commun. Soc. **11**, 375–397 (2008)
37. Springer, N., Engelmann, I., Pfaffinger, C.: User comments: motives and inhibitors to write and read. Inf. Commun. Soc. **18**(7), 798–815 (2015)
38. Lischka, J.A., Messerli, M.: Examining the benefits of audience integration: does sharing of or commenting on online news enhance the loyalty of online readers? Digit. J. **4**(5), 597–620 (2016)
39. Canter, L.: The misconception of online comment threads. J. Pract. **7**(5), 604–619 (2013). https://doi.org/10.1080/17512786.2012.740172
40. Nagar, N.A.: The loud public: the case of user comments in online news media. Doctoral dissertation, State University of New York at Albany (2011)
41. Hermida, A., Thurman, N.: A clash of cultures: the integration of user-generated content within professional journalistic frameworks at British newspaper websites. J. Pract. **2**(3), 343–356 (2008)

42. Diaz Noci, J., Masip P., Domingo D., Mico, J.L., Ruiz, C.: Comments in news, democracy booster or journalistic nightmare: assessing the quality and dynamics of citizen debates in catalan online newspapers. In: #ISOJ The Official Research Journal of the International Symposium on Online Journalism, vol. 2, no. 1, pp. 1–20 (2010)

43. Toepfl, F., Litvinenko, A.: Transferring control from the backend to the frontend: a comparison of the discourse architectures of comment sections on news websites across the post-Soviet world. New Media Soc. 1461444817733710 (2017)

44. Karlsson, M., Bergström, A., Clerwall, C., Fast, K.: Participatory journalism—the (r) evolution that wasn't: content and user behavior in Sweden 2007–2013. J. Comput.-Mediat. Commun. **20**(3), 295–311 (2015). https://doi.org/10.1111/jcc4.12115

45. Curran, J., et al.: Internet revolution revisited: a comparative study of online news. Media Cult. Soc. **35**(7), 880–897 (2013). https://doi.org/10.1177/0163443713499393

46. Larsson, A.O.: The news user on social media: a comparative study of interacting with media organizations on Facebook and Instagram. J. Stud. 1–18 (2017)

47. Al-Rawi, A.: News values on social media: News organizations' Facebook use. Journalism **18**(7), 871–889 (2017)

48. Bastos, M.T.: Shares, pins, and tweets. J. Stud. **16**(3), 305–325 (2014). https://doi.org/10.1080/1461670x.2014.891857

49. Kalogeropoulos, A., Negredo, S., Picone, I., Nielsen, R.K. Who shares and comments on news? A cross-national comparative analysis of online and social media participation. Soc. Media+Soc. **3**(4) (2017). https://doi.org/10.1177/2056305117735754

50. Bodrunova, S.S., Smoliarova, A.S., Blekanov, I.S., Litvinenko, A.A.: Content sharing in conflictual *Ad-Hoc* Twitter discussions: national patterns or universal trends? In: Alexandrov, D.A., Boukhanovsky, A.V., Chugunov, A.V., Kabanov, Y., Koltsova, O. (eds.) DTGS 2017. CCIS, vol. 745, pp. 3–15. Springer, Cham (2017). https://doi.org/10.1007/978-3-319-69784-0_1

51. Singer, J.B.: User-generated visibility: secondary gatekeeping in a shared media space. New Media Soc. **16**(1), 55–73 (2014)

52. Picone, I., De Wolf, R., Robijt, S.: Who shares what to whom and why? News sharing profiles amongst Flemish news users. Digit. J. **4**, 921–932 (2016)

53. Christodoulides, G., Jevons, C., Bonhomme, J.: Memo to marketers: quantitative evidence for change: how user-generated content really affects brands. J. Advert. Res. **52**(1), 53–64 (2012). https://doi.org/10.2501/JAR-52-1-053-064

54. Macek, J.: More than a desire for text: online participation and the social curation of content. Convergence **19**(3), 295–302 (2013). https://doi.org/10.1177/1354856513486530

55. Hermida, A., Fletcher, F., Korell, D., Logan, D.: Share, like, recommend. J. Stud. **13**(5–6), 815–824 (2012). https://doi.org/10.1080/1461670X.2012.664430

56. Boczkowski, P.J.: News at Work: Imitation in an Age of Information Abundance. The University of Chicago Press, Chicago (2010)

57. Singer, J.B., et al.: Participatory Journalism: Guarding Open Gates at Online Newspapers. Wiley, Chichester (2011)

58. Kalsnes, B., Larsson, A.O.: Understanding news sharing across social media: detailing distribution on Facebook and Twitter. J. Stud. 1–20 (2017)

59. Nielsen, R.K., Schrøder, K.C.: The relative importance of social media for accessing, finding, and engaging with news: an eight-country cross-media comparison. Digit. J. **2**(4), 472–489 (2014)

60. Ju, A., Jeong, S.H., Chyi, H.I.: Will social media save newspapers? J. Pract. 1–17 (2013). https://doi.org/10.1080/17512786.2013.794022

61. Valencia-Bermúdez, A., Lombao, T.F.: Public service media on social networks: the European case. In: Campos Freire, F., Rúas Araújo, X., Martínez Fernández, V.A., García, X.L. (eds.) Media and Metamedia Management. AISC, vol. 503, pp. 149–156. Springer, Cham (2017). https://doi.org/10.1007/978-3-319-46068-0_19

62. Braun, J., Gillespie, T.: Hosting the public discourse, hosting the public: when online news and social media converge. J. Pract. **5**, 383–398 (2011)

63. Heiss, R., Schmuck, D., Matthes, J.: What drives interaction in political actors' Facebook posts? Profile and content predictors of user engagement and political actors' reactions. Inf. Commun. Soc. 1–17 (2018)

64. Krug, S.: Reactions now available globally. Facebook newsroom. http://newsroom.fb.com/news/2016/02/reactions-now-available-globally/. Accessed 01 May 2018

65. Keating, L.: Facebook users shared 300 Billion reactions In: One Year. TechTimes, 24 February 2017. https://www.techtimes.com/articles/199136/20170224/facebook-users-shared-300-billion-reactions-one-year.htm. Accessed 01 May 2018

66. Huffaker, D.: Dimensions of leadership and social influence in online communities. Hum. Commun. Res. **36**(4), 593–617 (2010)

67. Berger, J., Milkman, K.: What makes online content viral? J. Mark. Res. **49**(2), 192–205 (2012)

68. Papacharissi, Z.: Affective Publics: Sentiment, Technology, and Politics. Oxford University Press, Oxford (2015)

69. Joyce, E., Kraut, R.: Predicting continued participation in newsgroups. J. Comput.-Mediat. Commun. **11**(3), 723–747 (2006)

70. Baumeister, R.F., Bratslavsky, E., Finkenauer, C., Vohs, K.D.: Bad is stronger than good. Rev. Gen. Psychol. **5**(4), 323–370 (2001)

71. Rozin, P., Royzman, E.B.: Negativity bias, negativity dominance, and contagion. Personal. Soc. Psychol. Rev. **5**(4), 296–320 (2001)

72. Mancosu, M.: Populism, selective exposure, and emotional appeals in social media: a comparative approach using Facebook reactions. In: Proceedings of the SISP Conference 2016, pp. 1–35. SISP, Milano (2016)

73. Eberl, J.M., et al.: Emotional Reactions on Austrian parties' Facebook pages during the 2017 Austrian Parliamentary Election. Computational Communication Science Lab, University of Vienna (2017)

74. Rony, M.M.U., Hassan, N., Yousuf, M.: Diving deep into Clickbaits: who use them to what extents in which topics with what effects? In: Proceedings of the 2017 IEEE/ACM International Conference on Advances in Social Networks Analysis and Mining, pp. 232–239. ACM, New York (2017)

75. Pool, C., Nissim, M.: Distant supervision for emotion detection using Facebook reactions. arXiv preprint arXiv:1611.02988 (2016)

76. Rieder, B.: Studying Facebook via data extraction: the Netvizz application. In: Proceedings of the 5th Annual ACM Web Science Conference, pp. 346–355. ACM, New York (2013)

Instant Messaging for Journalists and PR-Practitioners: A Study of Four Countries

Il'ia Bykov[1](✉) ⓘ, Aleksandr Hradziushka[2], Galiya Ibrayeva[3], and Elira Turdubaeva[4]

[1] St Petersburg State University, Saint Petersburg, Russia
i.bykov@spbu.ru
[2] Belarusian State University, Minsk, Belarus
webjourn@gmail.com
[3] Al-Farabi Kazakh National University, Almaty, Republic of Kazakhstan
galiya.ibrayeva@gmail.com
[4] American University of Central Asia, Bishkek, Kyrgyz Republic
eliraturdubayeva@gmail.com

Abstract. The paper presents the results of an exploratory research of the use of instant messaging in the professional communication of journalists and public relations specialists. The study was conducted in four countries of the Eurasian Economic Union: Belarus, Kazakhstan, Kyrgyzstan, and Russia. The main method of research was an expert poll. The authors have interviewed 256 experts in the field of journalism and PR. The data were collected in December of 2017. The participating experts had to meet two requirements: to have considerably solid job experience and to use messenger applications such as WhatsApp, Telegram, Facebook Messenger, Skype, Viber, etc. for professional purposes. The study shows that instant messaging has become an important communication tool for journalists and PR-specialists who choosing to use messengers for reasons of convenience, speed, and privacy.

Keywords: Journalism · Public relations · Mobile internet Messengers · Internet communication

1 Introduction

Modern media continues to change rapidly due to technical factors and especially due to the development of the mobile Internet. Unconditionally, the main gadget of our time is a smartphone. The young persons started the process of migration from computers to mobile gadgets [25]. After that, as it was predicted by M. Castells, new mobile technologies have been rapidly adopted by business and media [7]. In 2016 the number of mobile users exceeded the number of Internet users, and the number of connections to Internet sites from smartphones and tablets around the world exceeded the use of the Internet from computers and

© Springer Nature Switzerland AG 2018
S. S. Bodrunova (Ed.): INSCI 2018, LNCS 11193, pp. 257–269, 2018.
https://doi.org/10.1007/978-3-030-01437-7_20

laptops [8]. Here is an unstoppable process of integration of electronic devices into the life of a human being.

The most important trend in the modern media landscape deals with the growing use of instant messaging. Initially, instant messaging services, such as Facebook Messenger, Skype, Telegram, Viber, WhatsApp, etc., were used mainly for the exchange of messages for personal purposes. However, instant messengers have started to act as platforms for the distribution of mass media content [3]. In particular, we are talking about channels and chat-bots in Telegram [17]. Media penetration into this sphere was the result of an adaptation of media to new conditions and going to the place where the audience is located. Studying the processes of optimizing the media system in the context of adapting it to new technological realities is an urgent task of scientific research. Taking into account a large number of works by both domestic and foreign researchers in the field of social media, it should be noted, however, that today there is a lack of works in which the opinion of journalists and public relations specialists about instant messaging was clarified. This work aims to fill this gap.

2   Research Background

There are several starting points of our research which one must keep in mind before proceeding to the research design. First of all, our study relies heavily on the previous studies of social media in journalism and PR. On the one hand, there are many publications about networked journalism or web-journalism [11, 12,18,21,26,28]. They focus on the developments of new forms of journalism such as citizen journalism or web-journalism. Also, they trace the dynamics of the mass media audiences, predicting a decline of printed media. On the other hand, existing special literature about PR usually emphasizes benefits of social media marketing [1,9,13,19,20,24]. The main bonus for social media marketing is considered to be the level of engagement with clients and customers. The other important bonus deals with the "electronic word of mouth" with means that social media could be very effective and efficient tool to disseminate information [20].

However, some skeptical voices about risks and eventual costs of social media marketing in PR are almost invisible [2,27]. In all these publications technical factors dictate an evolution of PR and journalism facilitating the formation of new activities and corrupting existence of old-school journalism and PR. Thus, the Internet, social media, and now messenger applications attract the attention of researchers all around the world. However, there is a research gap in the field of new forms of communications and their applications in mass communication, especially, if we are talking about regional specifications and political/legal limitations across the globe.

The second starting issue deals with the co-evolution of journalism and PR. These two communication professions always influenced each other, but still, there are not so many publications on the issue. For example, in 2016 Schonhagen and Meissner claimed to be the first who produced "the first contribution of its systematic review" [23]. His historical analysis shows that "PR emerged due to biased reporting or the neglect of certain interests in media coverage" [23, 755]. PR and journalism have always been two sides of the "mass communication coin". They exchange personal and technologies back and forward, constructing the system of rational social communication.

Schonhagen and Meissner use a historical approach to construct a general theory of PR and journalism development. Due to the high level of abstraction this approach is less useful at the empirical level. Apart from the pioneering study of P. Schonhagen and M. Meissner, however, there are two publications in the topic with empirical research by A. Verchich with colleagues [30,31]. These publications actually use the approach we would like to apply in our study. Verchich with colleagues conducted two surveys among public relations practitioners and journalists in Serbia and Croatia. They used a membership list of PR and journalists associations in order to collect data. The surveys of 2016 and 2017 have collected opinions of over 600 journalists and PR practitioners about the occupational status and working conditions of the opposite profession. Verchich with colleagues calls this "coorientational research" aimed to explore the relationship between public relations practitioners and journalists.

Our study focuses on even less empirical level dealing with one the tools of professional communication - messenger applications. Journalists and PR practitioners have to work on-the-go, so instant communication is a part of their everyday job. We believe that communication studies must include journalism and PR as the most important parts of mass communication in today's world.

The concluding starting point actualizes the problems of PR and journalism developments in the post-soviet states. This includes common and specific transformations in the media, journalism, PR and propaganda activities. There are many publications on the issue [4,10,14,15,29]. Mass media and mass communication in post-soviet countries demonstrate high rates of the developments. For example, in Russia they have the impressive size and diversity of the current industry in terms of numbers and their growth rate, especially for advertising, which, during the first decade of the new millennium, has reached the level of the Western industrial countries (typically 1 per cent of the gross domestic product) [29]. Also, it is typical for post-soviet countries to have a situation of hybridization of mass media which became partially print, partially electronic, and partially Internet-media [4]. In terms of Internet penetration these four countries looks quite similar: in 2017 Russia has 76.1% of the population using the Internet, Belarus - 71.1, Kazakhstan - 76.4, and Kyrgystan - 40.7 [16]. However, the Internet still is not dominating news vehicle in Post-Soviet Kyrgyzstan and Kazakhstan [14].

Also, there is a lack of empirical studies of messenger applications [22]. We were able to find only one statistical research of the instant messaging about Telegram. This study showed that 77% of Telegram' users are persons of 18–34 years old, and, in terms of geography, Telegram is mostly Russian messenger application [29]. The countries of the Eurasian Economic Union have common patterns in mass media development, having noticeable influence from Russian mass media and IT companies and forming a new, united media market [5]. However, Belarus became a visible part of IT-business been able to develop such successful projects like Viber messenger application. Unfortunately, there is a huge gap between academic studies and recent developments in messengers in all four countries. The social network services have been in focus of empirical researches, but not of the messengers' applications and their use in mass communication.

3   Research Design

The main goal of the research was to determine the place and role of messengers in the professional communications of journalists and public relations specialists in the post-Soviet space. The research project has united four researchers from four countries currently affiliated with the research and teaching institutions in Belarus, Kazakhstan, Kyrgyzstan, and Russia. These countries constitute the core of the Eurasian Economic Union. The work was performed as a research initiative to invite attention to the messenger applications as a tool of professional communication for journalists and public relations specialists. This research project could be treated as a pilot study. The authors from Belarus, Kazakhstan, Kyrgyzstan, and Russia have united their efforts to track down recent developments in mass communication practices in the post-Soviet region.

Empirical data were obtained by the authors in four countries of the Eurasian Economic Union: Belarus, Kazakhstan, Kyrgyzstan, and Russia (see Fig. 1). The survey involved 256 experts in journalism and PR, who have both at least three years of experience in the field and the experience of using instant messengers in professional communication. Thus, our experts, the journalists and the PR-practitioners, have had solid job records and expertise in instant messaging. An expert poll, in this case, is one of the few methods that allow conducting an effective study that has both qualitative and quantitative indicators [6]. We also should mention a great deal of interest from our experts who participated in the research.

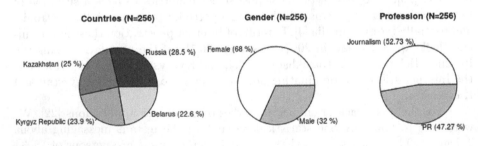

Fig. 1. Poll of experts: overview, N = 256, December 2017.

Since the subject has not been really investigated in the scientific literature, the study has to have an exploratory design, aiming to draw a general picture. This leads to the formation of several research questions:

1. What messenger applications do the journalists and the public relations specialists use in professional communication?
2. Why do they use messengers?
3. How widely stickers and gifs are used to express emotions?
4. Is there a noticeable automation of professional communications with the help of bots?
5. How widely used audio and video messages in instant messengers?
6. What is the role of the messengers in professional communication: basic, auxiliary, or insignificant?
7. What about the prospects for using instant messengers in journalism and PR?

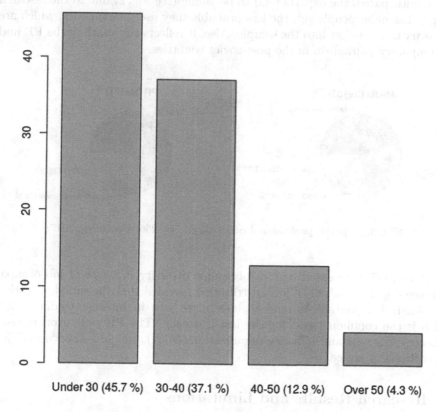

Fig. 2. Experts' age distribution, N = 256, December 2017

In December 2017 we conducted interviews with experts. The questionnaire included 19 questions. The first part of the questionnaire (Q1–Q7) intended to find traditional socio-demographic parameters of the sample. It included questions about age, gender, etc. The second part of the questionnaire (Q8–Q19) was created in order to answer the research questions. It included open-ended questions, closed-ended questions, and semi-closed questions, which allowed experts to contribute new information to the research. Not all questions from the questionnaire were actually asked in face-to-face or telephone interviews. For example, Q1 "Country of residence" was obvious and was marked by researchers automatically. The same reason applied for Q2 ("Gender"). The Q14 was about bots' usage in PR and journalism and was asked only if experts mentioned in the previous Q13 that he or she "is actually familiar with cases of bots usage in professional communication". That allowed us to keep the timing of interviews in the period of 15–20 min.

The analysis of the poll of experts shows that all four countries have almost equal representation at the level of one-fourth of the sample. Female experts constitute 68% of the sample which is normal for the field of journalism and PR. As we anticipated, the experts tend to be young (see Fig. 2) due to the research design. The older people get, the less probable they use smartphones, which are necessary to use to get into the sample. Also, it reflects the youth of the PR and contemporary journalism in the post-soviet countries.

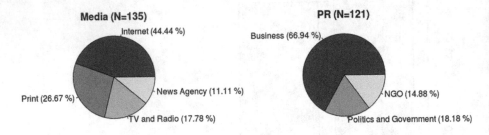

Fig. 3. Experts' professional occupation, N = 256, December 2017

Q6 and Q7 were asked to control sample diversity in terms of job occupation (see Fig. 3). Analysis of job' distribution revealed that the sample is rather diversified. The journalists tend to have more jobs in Internet media (44%), which is the common trend for the last 2 decade. The PR practitioners tend to occupy business and industry organizations (67%), which is also "usual" for international practice.

4   Research Results and Limitations

According to our data the most popular messenger application among our experts is the Facebook messenger (see Fig. 4). The second most popular is WhatsApp, which make the Facebook with two messengers to look like a winner. In order to verify that information we asked an open-ended question about the

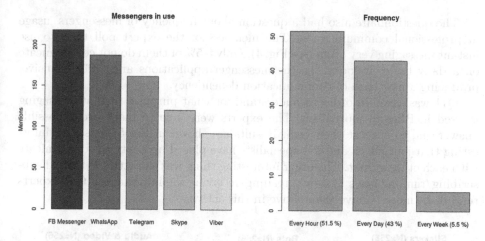

Fig. 4. Messengers in use and frequency of usage by the experts, N = 256, December 2017

best messenger application, not the most used, but preferred by the experts personally. 231 answers had been recorded on the Q9, 25 experts refused to answer. The answers have revealed that Telegram earned 85 voices, WhatsApp - 82, FB - 37, Viber - 21, Skype - 5, and Signal had 1. Obviously, PR practitioners and journalists have to use messengers applications which their clients are using. That is why FB Messenger and WhatsApp, having the biggest number of users in the world, are more popular. At the same time, in terms of perspective, the Telegram has chances to become more popular as Skype has more chances to be even less popular than today.

Purpose of use	Number of mentions
To communicate with journalists/PR specialists	223
To communicate with the sources of information	202
To subscribe to the news-feeds	136
To invite people to the special events	96
To run a news channel or to spread the information	86
To demonstrate personal ability to handle the gadgets	11
To communicate with colleagues at work	11

Fig. 5. Purposes to use messengers in professional communication by the experts, N = 256, December 2017

The questionnaire also had a question about frequency of messengers' usage in professional communication. The members of the expert poll tend to use instant messaging very often (see Fig. 4). Only 5.5% of them do not communicate on a daily bases. It looks like the messenger applications are really inclusive, producing a new form of communication dependency.

Q11 was asked in order to understand for what purposes instant messaging is used in PR and journalism. The experts were able to mark every possible answer and to suggest their own. Results are shown in Fig. 5. It is very interesting that journalists and PR specialists have placed necessity to communicate with each other at first. The other interesting thing was the attitude toward subscribing/running news feed or spreading/receiving the information. Our experts tend to be more passive than active in this activity.

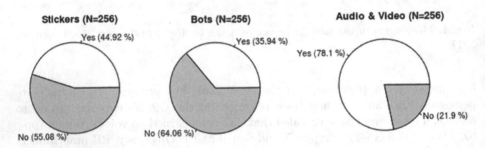

Fig. 6. Usage of stickers, bots, video- and audio-files by the experts, $N = 256$, December 2017

Next questions (Q12–Q15) were about practical features of instant messaging: stickers, bots, audio- and video-files (see Fig. 6). Only 44.92% of the experts are using stickers, 35.94% actually noted bots in PR and journalism. That numbers are not so high as it could be expected. However, our experts are using audio- and video-files transmission at the level of 78.1%.

One of the most important results of our study deals with the experts' opinion about the current role of the instant messaging in PR and journalism. 67.18% of the experts think that "messengers have practically replaced telephones and SMS-messages as a tool of professional communication" (Fig. 7). This reflects an opinion about the important role of messengers as a tool for professional communication. Also, these data underline the importance of instant messengers studies and immediate necessary to include the topic in teaching courses.

However, when we asked about the future of messengers comparing to the social media, the experts were not so sure (Fig. 8). Less than 50% thought that "Messengers will be more important than social media in PR and journalism in a short future". The number of unconfident experts rose from 5.86% to 23.44%. That tells us about difficulties to predict the development of the situation or about conservativeness of the experts.

The last question we asked (Q19) was about the future of instant messaging in PR and journalism. It was an open-ended question. The experts were supposed

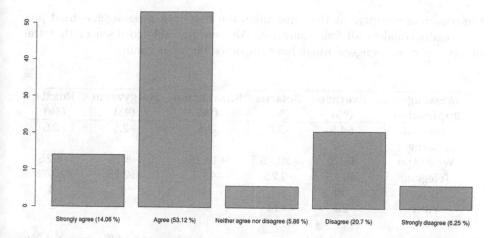

Fig. 7. "Messengers have practically replaced telephones and SMS-messages as a tool of professional communication" (Q16), N = 256, December 2017

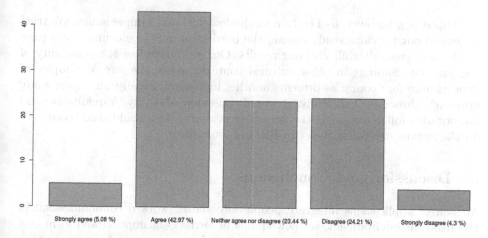

Fig. 8. "Messengers will be more important than social media in PR and journalism in a short future" (Q18), N = 256, December 2017

to express their opinions freely. Almost all experts expressed an opinion that "messenger applications will be more applied in a short future" due to their usability, mobility, privacy, and security.

According to our data, the most popular messenger application among respondents is the Facebook messenger, and the second most popular is WhatsApp, but most of the respondents personally would prefer Telegram. However, it must be mentioned that there is a significant country difference in messengers popularity (See Fig. 9). Belarus has the most peculiar situation: the WhatsApp is relatively less popular there, as the Viber is being used significantly. In Russia, the Telegram messenger is the most popular application, presumably, for the reason of security. At the same time, the Facebook messenger is used proportionally equal in all four countries. We were not able to discover that this differences of messengers' usage have impacted on other results.

Messenger application	Average (%)	Belarus (%)	Kazakhstan (%)	Kyrgyzstan (%)	Russia (%)
Facebook messenger	54.5	-3.5	-2.5	+2.5	+3.5
WhatsApp	46.75	-30.75	+14.25	+8.25	+8.25
Telegram	40.25	-9.25	-4.25	-12.25	+25.75
Skype	30	+3	+1	0	-4
Viber	23	+32	-16	-14	-2

Fig. 9. Messengers in use by the experts: average and country difference, $N = 256$, December 2017

This study, however, had certain methodological and sample issues. We tried to extend our previous study among the borders of only one country and raise the level of generalizability of our results. Our study reduces the possibility of applying our findings in other cultural contexts. Also, the size of samples of experts from four countries presents another limitation. Finally, an expert study approach, chosen for this study, gives only one view of reality. A qualitative and quantitative follows up seem the necessary next-step and would shed more light on the instant messaging usage in PR and journalism.

5   Discussion and Conclusions

Messenger applications integrate people into the networked communication in the real-time environment, set new trends in media consumption and form new directions for media development in the digital environment. A smartphone is already a universal media device and takes the most important place in the system of multi-platform news consumption. Mobile technologies influence the work of journalists and PR specialists. The data obtained show that journalists and PR specialists in four counties choose similar strategies for using instant messengers. In any case, it is obvious that modern technologies significantly change the creative activity of journalists and PR specialist. In particular, the respondents noted that instant messaging and mobile Internet require constant training of new technologies in multi-platform communication. Technological changes demand new tools for creating content in the digital environment. However, we come to the conclusion that many media and PR companies have not yet developed a clear strategy of presence in messengers, acting more by trial and error, which is confirmed by empirical data. In any case, there is a new challenge, accelerated by the digital transformation, to present content in modern mobile formats. Today, the editorial offices of traditional media and PR agencies follow the audience which sets the agenda.

The study has its controversial issues. For example, it is unclear how far will go a tendency then Internet media sites are replaced by social platforms and messenger applications such as Facebook, VKontakte, YouTube, Instagram, Viber, Telegram, etc. Social network services are dominating the Internet. However, messenger applications already compete with them. So, the academic community will have to discuss and study the next big competition between social networks and messengers. Some experts today consider Telegram and Viber as "new social networks". It is unclear how the audience will prefer to receive information: from the media or from other sources like social network services and messenger applications. A promising direction of research also includes the bots as one of the kind of robotic journalism and PR communication. The typological characteristic of channels in instant messengers deserves the attention of scientists. So far, the question remains unsolved, what is the reliability of the information in the channels in Telegram and the criteria for its verification. The advertising capabilities of instant messengers have also not been studied here. A separate block of research can be devoted to the psychological aspects of the use of instant messengers, in particular, the formation of dependence on these services. Also, the linguistic features of communications in messengers can become an object of empirical research. Interesting data could also be provided by a survey of adolescents and young people in order to study how they use instant messaging and mobile internet.

Acknowledgment. The work was performed as a research initiative to invite attention to the problem, to map up possible collaborative study and project granting. The authors would like to express their deepest gratitude to all the experts who took part in the study.

References

1. Allagui, I., Breslow, H.: Social media for public relations: lessons from four effective cases. Public Relat. Rev. **42**, 20–30 (2016). https://doi.org/10.1016/j.pubrev.2015.12.001
2. Assaad, W., Gomez, J.M., Ossietzky, C.: Social network in marketing (social media marketing): opportunities and risks. Int. J. Manag. Public Sect. Inf. Commun. Technol. **1**, 13–22 (2011). https://doi.org/10.5121/ijmpict.2011.2102
3. Barot, T.: Instant messaging: BBC news on chat apps. http://www.bbc.co.uk/academy/journalism/article/art20150408142840687. Accessed 4 Jan 2018
4. Bodrunova, S.S., Litvinenko, A.A.: Hybridization of the media system in Russia: technological and political aspects. World Med. J. Russ. Med. Journalism Stud. **3**, 37–49 (2013)
5. Bykov, I., Cherkashchenko, T., Dorskii, A., Kaverina, E.: Government regulation of advertising in the eurasian economic union: contradictions of public policy and advertising ethics. Int. J. Econ. Financ. Issues **5**, 116–120 (2015)
6. Bykov, I., Pobedinskiy, I., Achkasova, V., Kuzmin, A.: Managing governmental public relations in Russia: evidences from St. Petersburg. Int. Rev. Manag. Mark. **6**, 126–142 (2016)

7. Castells, M., Fernández-Ardèvol, M., Qiu, J.L., Sey, A.: Mobile Communication and Society: A Global Perspective. MIT Press, Cambridge (2009)
8. Digital in 2017: Global Overview. https://wearesocial.com/special-reports/digital-in-2017-global-overview. Accessed 4 Jan 2018
9. Evans, D.: Social Media Marketing: The Next Generation of Business Engagement. Wiley, New York (2010)
10. Freedman, E., Shafer, R. (eds.): After the Czars and Commissars: Journalism in Authoritarian Post-Soviet Central Asia. Michigan State University Press, East Lansing (2011)
11. Grueskin, B., Seave, A., Graves, L.: The Story So Far: What We Know About the Business of Digital Journalism. Columbia Journalism Review Books, New York (2011)
12. Hradziushka, A.A.: Contemporary Web-Journalism in Belarus. Belarusian State University Press, Minsk (2013)
13. Jansen, B.J., Zhang, M., Sobel, K., Chowdury, A.: Twitter power: tweets as electronic word of mouth. J. Am. Soc. Inf. Sci. Technol. 60, 2169–2188 (2009)
14. Junisbai, B., Junisbai, A., Fry, N.Y.: Mass media consumption in post-Soviet Kyrgyzstan and Kazakhstan: the view from below. Demokr. J. Post-Sov. 233, 233–256 (2015)
15. Ibrayeva, G., Myssayeva, K., Alzhanova, A.: Development of radio in Kazakhstan. J. Radio Audio Media. 19, 303–311 (2012). https://doi.org/10.1080/19376529.2012.722488
16. Internet World Stats. https://www.internetworldstats.com/. Accessed 4 Jan 2018
17. Ivanov, A.D.: Chatbot in telegram and Vkontakte as the new channel of news distribution. Vestnik Volga Univ. 3, 126–132 (2016)
18. McChesney, R., Nichols, J.: The Death and Life of American Journalism: The Media Revolution that will Begin the World Again. Nation Books, Philadelphia (2010)
19. Moreno, A., Navarro, C., Tench, R., Zerfass, A.: Does social media usage matter? An analysis of online practices and digital media perceptions of communication practitioners in Europe. Public Relat. Rev. 41, 242–253 (2015). https://doi.org/10.1016/j.pubrev.2014.12.006
20. Neti, S.: Social media and its role in marketing. Int. J. Enterp. Comput. Bus. Syst. 1, 13–29 (2011)
21. Pitt, L.F., Parent, M., Steyn, P.G., Berthon, P., Money, A.: The social media release as a corporate communication tool for bloggers. IEEE Trans. Prof. Commun. 54, 122–132 (2011)
22. Rahmanova, V.: Portate of the telegram most active audience in Russia. https://vc.ru/25614-audience-of-telegram. Accessed 4 Jan 2018
23. Schonhagen, P., Meissner, M.: The co-evolution of public relations and journalism: a first contribution to its systematic review. Public Relat. Rev. 42, 748–758 (2016). https://doi.org/10.1016/j.pubrev.2016.08.003
24. Scott, D.M.: The New Rules of Marketing and PR: How to Use News Releases, Blogs, Podcasting, Viral Marketing and Online Media to Reach Buyers Directly. Wiley, New York (2009)
25. Teenagers Say Goodbye to Facebook and Hello to Messenger Apps. https://www.theguardian.com/technology/2013/nov/10/. Accessed 4 Jan 2018
26. Toktagazin, M.B., Turysbek, R.S., Ussen, A.A., Nurtazina, R.A., Korganbekov, B.S., Hradziushka, A.A.: Modern internet epistolary in information and media discourse. IEJME-Math. Educ. 11, 1305–1319 (2016)

27. Toledano, M., Avidar, R.: Public relations, ethics, and social media: a cross-national study of PR practitioners. Public Relat. Rev. **42**, 161–169 (2016). https://doi.org/10.1016/j.pubrev.2015.11.012
28. Van der Haak, B., Parks, M., Castells, M.: The future of journalism: networked journalism. Int. J. Commun. **6**, 2923–2938 (2012)
29. Vartanova, E., Smirnov, S.: Contemporary structure of the Russian media industry. In: Rosenholm, A., Nordenstreng, K., Trubina, E. (eds.) 2010 Russian Mass Media and Changing Values, pp. 21–40. Routledge (2010)
30. Vercic, A.T., Colic, V.: Journalists and public relations specialists: a coorientational analysis. Public Relat. Rev. **42**, 522–529 (2016). https://doi.org/10.1016/j.pubrev.2016.03.007
31. Vercic, A.T., Lalic, D., Vujicic, D.: Journalists and public relations practitioners: comparing two countries. Public Relat. Rev. **43**, 527–536 (2017). https://doi.org/10.1016/j.pubrev.2017.04.006

Ensure Citizen-Oriented Data for 'Co-production' of Public Policy: Russian Case of 'Budget for Citizens'

Leonid Smorgunov[✉]

St. Petersburg State University,
Universitetskaya nab., 7/9, St. Petersburg 199034, Russia
l.smorgunov@spbu.ru

Abstract. Modern budgeting based on cooperation transforms designs of budgetary policy, accountability systems, processes of identifying public values and others. Ensure citizen-oriented data relating to the budget gets particular importance and shared learning of citizens and government for inclusive budget process becomes main requisite for successful collaboration. There is the difference in using 'co-production' between democratic and mixed political regimes with statist direction. The paper analyzes the Russian practice of "budget for the citizens" in the mixed (hybrid) regimes, introduced in 2013 at the federal and regional levels. Imitative institutions of "budget for the citizens" inure for legitimating regimes, but also they are good factors for mutual learning for cooperation. Transparency of budgetary data, its transformation for the citizens, and budgeting, initiated by citizens, effects on the character of Russian designs for inclusive budgeting. As shown in the article, citizens-oriented data do not directly influence the participation in budgeting. They are one of the causes in a complex set of influencing conditions. However, they are organically related to the inclusive model of citizen budget implementation. To study this complexity, a configurative method of comparative analysis (QCA) was used.

Keywords: Budget for citizens · Inclusive capacities · Co-production
Citizen-oriented data · Mixed regime

1 Introduction

One of the forms of involving citizens in public policy is participatory budgeting. The first experience of such budgeting we find in the 1980s in Brazil [20]. Then participatory budgeting was seized by many countries and regions. The study of budgeting for citizens, as a rule, refers to the internal mechanism of citizens' participation in the development of the budget at various levels of public policy [1], the process of discussing budget data and the development of a deliberative democracy [4], and the effectiveness of spending the budget in terms of civic participation [17]. A number of researchers agree that participatory budgeting is a form of inclusive institutions [6] that contribute to raising the overall justification for budget spending and forming a new cohort of citizens interested in participating in the affairs of the municipalities, regional authorities and the government of the country.

© Springer Nature Switzerland AG 2018
S. S. Bodrunova (Ed.): INSCI 2018, LNCS 11193, pp. 270–285, 2018.
https://doi.org/10.1007/978-3-030-01437-7_21

In the study of participatory budgeting, one can find the publications that describe the conditions for its emergence, the contextual factors that influence its inclusion in the overall design of public policy, which determine its integrity and effectiveness [16]. Part of the works clarify the specifics of the diffusion of the experience in the country's participatory budgeting, highlighting here such forms as learning, competition, pressure, and imitation [9]. In our paper, we follow this line of study of the budget for citizens, drawing attention to the basic requisites that contribute to the formation of the opportunity and willingness of citizens to participate in budgeting. These opportunities and readiness are associated with the use of conditions and the construction of institutions that determine the participatory capacity of citizens. In the previous article [19], we analyzed the general conditions that determine the possibility of forming citizen participation. This article analyzes not general conditions, but the place and role of citizen-oriented data in the overall system of inclusive conditions. Consequently, core point here is a *citizen-oriented data* which are included in the system of opportunities for participatory budgeting. What is the role of this point in the structure of opportunities? How is a citizen-oriented data used in a mixed political regime? Is it only served for legitimacy? Or a participatory budgeting is an important factor of mutual learning the citizens and the authorities for democratic collaboration?

For these purposes, in the paper a special method of qualitative comparative analysis – QCA/fs [8, 12] is used, which allows not only to study the complex diversity of the conditions of an event, process or object, but also to formulate certain ideas about the causal mechanism involved in order to achieve some result. As an object of research, 22 regions of Russia were taken, which received the highest ratings in the process of monitoring the openness of budget data and the formation of a "budget for citizens".

2 Co-production in Democratic and Mixed Political Regimes

Recently, the concepts of 'co-creation' and 'co-production' were actively used in political science, public administration, sociology as an innovation. Initially, this concept has fixed a new attitude to the provision of public services and was directed against the market-based approach to the organization of this activity [2]. New breath of this concept has acquired in the development of the movement for digital governance. In recent years, the concept of 'co-production' has become widely used in the study of public policy in general [10, 21]. Compared with the categories of "collaboration", "public involvement" this concept has expanded understanding of the cycle of public policies affecting the problem of political designs, governance of public policies, the joint formulation and implementation of public values and others. Co-production is new stance for democratic public policy in the world of uncertainty and complexity. Many scholars focused on the presentation of research materials relating to 'governance through collaboration', 'co-creation', and 'co-production' of public policy, not only in above aspects of the theme, but also in relation to the effect of collaboration on public policy, which would have corresponded with sustainable and inclusive development [18, 22]. Collaboration's and co-production's orientations in democratic public policy means: (1) policy design with a focus on the citizens, rather than the office;

(2) collaboration in public policy process rather than making agreement; expand public arenas for collaboration; (3) pay attention to the deliberation on public values and real needs; govern rather by shared judgments than norms; (4) take into account the real context of life of the public policy stakeholders (desire, space and time); (5) contextualize public policy process instead of typing; (6) ensure transparency, citizen-generated data and Internet resources for public policy.

There is the difference in using 'co-production' between democratic and mixed political regimes with statist direction. In Russia there is the same mixed regime with some specific characteristics: (1) party system, elections with a forceful governance of electoral processes; (2) superpresidential central power with the system of governance through presidential instructions; (3) multilevel governance (central, regional, municipal) with centralization; (4) constitutional rule of law with a bureaucratic mechanism of rule by law; (5) civil society with limited and controlled involvement of citizens in policy. Co-production is a new stance for democratic public policy, but in statist regimes with weak civil society co-production can be used more instrumentally for legitimizing political regimes. But here, the co-production institutions have a dual effect. The Russian practice of "budget for the citizens" in the mixed (hybrid) regimes, introduced in 2013 at the federal and regional levels, demonstrates this dual effect if we compare regional systems of budgeting. Imitative institutions of "budget for the citizens" inure for legitimating regimes in general, but also they are good factors for mutual learning for cooperation. Some regions use "budget for citizens" formally, but some of them try to initiate citizens for discussion and co-production of regional budget in direct or indirect senses. Transparency of budgetary data, its transformation for the citizens, and budgeting, initiated by citizens, affects on the complex character of Russian designs for inclusive budgeting. In the budget system for citizens, it is very important to form a co-set of budget data, which will be the basis for interaction between citizens and the government. The data, oriented not to specialists, but to citizens, also allows increasing the level of confidence in the system of public budgeting itself.

3 Ensure Citizen-Oriented Data Through Russian 'Budget for Citizens'

In Russia, the policy of involving citizens in the budget process began in 2013. In July, the Minister of Finance of the Russian Federation approved the Working Group on "Budget for Citizens". The joint order of the Ministry of Finance, the Ministry of Regional Development and the Ministry of Economic Development on August 22, 2013 approved the Methodological recommendations on the submission of budgets of the constituent entities of the Russian Federation, local budgets, and reports on their implementation in an accessible form for citizens. The Budget Message of the President of the Russian Federation on Budget Policy in 2014–2016 stated that "from 2013 onwards, at all levels of the administration, a brochure "Budget for Citizens" should be published (posted on the Internet). This will make it possible to inform the population in an accessible form about the relevant budgets, planned and achieved results of using budget funds" [3]. In October, a model of the first in the Russian Federation federal

"Budget for Citizens" was published. And in December the updated version of the "Budget for Citizens" to the Federal Law of December 2, 2013 No. 349-FZ "On the Federal Budget for 2014 and for the Planning Period of 2015 and 2016" was presented. This addition to the law was recommended by the State Duma and the Federation Council of the Federal Assembly of the Russian Federation. On the portal of the open government, a specialized website "Budget for Citizens" (http://budget.open.gov.ru/) was created, which became the organizing start for the dissemination of the practice of the open budget in the regions and municipalities of Russia. Currently, all 85 regions have open budgets for citizens and hundreds of municipalities use the practice of civil budgeting.

The budget for citizens in Russia is a simplified version of the budget document that uses informal language and accessible formats to make it easier for citizens to understand the budget, explain to them the plans and actions of the government during the budget year and show their forms of possible interaction with the government on issues of public expenditure finance. But this is not only simplified budget document. 'Budget for citizens' is a system of government-citizens relations around a simplified budget document.

There are three different languages, which ordinary are used during government-citizens communications: *managerial* (technocratic understanding public interest); *pluralistic* (political conflict); *communitarian* (ethos of public good) [7, 23]. Participatory budgeting is obviously must be oriented to using an ethos of public goods. Sometimes the scholars use the term 'just good enough data' for discussing the ways in which citizen data gives rise to alternative ways of creating, valuing and interpreting datasets [2, 5]. The International Monetary Fund mobilizes a definition of fiscal transparency as the clarity, reliability, frequency, timeliness, and relevance of public fiscal reporting and the openness to the public of the government's fiscal policy-making process [16, 547].

The general requirements for reporting data for the civil budget are defined in the "Methodological Recommendations" of the Russian Ministry of Communication, in which we could find some steps for using citizen-oriented approach to budget data. The following sections are usually included in the budget for citizens: a glossary explaining the basic concepts used in the budget process; general description of the region; the main indicators of the socio-economic development of the region in accordance with the forecast of its socio-economic development; the main tasks and priority directions of the budgetary policy of the region for the next financial year and planning period; the main characteristics of the budget (in absolute and relative terms), including information on incomes and expenditures, intergovernmental transfers planned to be received from the federal budget (budget of the constituent entity of the Russian Federation, local budget), as well as budget deficit/surplus; basic information on the intergovernmental fiscal relations of the region, including information on transfers to be received from the federal budget (the budget of the constituent entity of the Russian Federation) sent to local budgets planned to be received from local budgets; level of debt burden on the regional budget, including the structure of its debt; information on the position of the region in the ratings of the openness of budget data, the quality of management of regional finance; information on the holding and participation of the region in the competitions of projects on the presentation of budgets for citizens, on the implementation of projects of proactive budgeting, as well as projects aimed at increasing the budget literacy of the population.

At the same time, information must correspond to a number of criteria: (1) sufficiency, (2) clarity, (3) relevance, (4) reliability, (5) accessibility, (6) timeliness. General recommendations for budgeting for citizens include the following requirements, based on the general principles outlined above. First, the budget prepared for citizens should be an independent and self-sufficient document. Secondly, he must use a simple language without specialized jargons, understandable for ordinary citizens. Thirdly, the document should provide quick and easy access of citizens to information on the budget. Fourthly, it is specially emphasized that the budget for citizens should not be drawn up taking into account the needs of representatives of legislative or executive authorities. Fifthly, it should be a technical and "objective" document, not biased towards any one-party position and written in a neutral way. Sixthly, the budget should be focused on the goals and content of the budget, and not on the characteristics of the budget process. Seventh, the data must be accurate, reliable and trustworthy. Eighth, the budget for citizens should contain simple and effective schedules and diagrams, include comparative data for the previous fiscal year. Ninthly, the electronic budget page for citizens should not consist of a list of references to the initial budget, developed or adopted by public authorities; it must be an independent document. In the tenth place, it should be oriented towards the state of current knowledge of citizens about the budget. At the request of the Ministry of Communications in 2015 a study was made of the state of registration of budget data for citizens in accordance with these criteria. In the future, we will use these data to form the index of citizen-oriented data (*corient*).

The budget for citizens is targeted at certain target groups of citizens. The target group and its composition may be determined by the criteria for assigning citizens and/or organizations receiving support (or other forms of payment) from the budget to a particular target group. Such criteria can include qualitative characteristics of representatives of target groups, the number of representatives of the target group and its social significance, the amount of budgetary allocations directed to support the target group. The target group can be a group of citizens and/or organizations to which the activities of the governmental program of the subject of the Russian Federation (municipal program) are directed.

Beginning in 2015, the Research and Development Financial Institute (NIFI), commissioned by the Ministry of Finance of the Russian Federation, is rating the regions of Russia according to the criteria for open budgets. The methodology for assessing the regions establishes benchmarks for best practices on the content and accessibility of budget documents, as well as the use of mechanisms for public participation in the budget process. For our study, we used the results of ranking regions for 2015, which were compiled in the following main areas: characteristics of the originally approved budget, annual performance report, amendments to the law on the budget, interim reporting on budget execution and analytical data, draft budget and materials for it, financial control, public information on the activities of state institutions of the subject of the Russian Federation (planned and actual performance indicators), budget for citizens (the law on the budget, the annual report on the budget execution, the draft budget), and public participation (quarterly).

4 Research Hypotheses

In practice, the level of openness of budget data in the regions and the implementation of the "Budget for Citizens" program were to a certain extent determined by the activity of regional authorities in fulfilling the tasks assigned to them by the federal government. At the same time, it should be noted that the differentiation of regional development in its various dimensions - economic, social, and digital - did not affect the pace and intensity of introducing new approaches to budgeting. In the rating table, regions with different degrees of social and economic development (in Table 1) fell into list of the regions with very high level of open budget data.

Statistical analysis of the correlation between the openness of budget data and the level of socio-economic development (expressed in regional GDP per capita) shows low results. What is the unifying factor of influence on citizen participation in budgeting using the regional context? In our opinion, this complex factor will be such an indicator of regional development as the capacity for "inclusiveness". Under the capacity for inclusiveness we shell understand a quality of region in which citizens have the opportunities for participation, that is, public authorities are open to participation, *budget data is oriented on the citizens*, electronic infrastructure is well, and citizens have some practical skills for using electronic devises. *The main hypothesis of the study*, therefore, is that the higher the level of inclusive capacity of the region, the higher the openness of budget data and citizen participating in budgeting. Of course, to a certain extent, the open budget itself is a factor of inclusiveness, that is, can act as an independent variable. However, in this case, we take into account the time period when the open budget was a goal, rather than a means of achieving any result. At least, with respect to the policy of budgeting for citizens, we can say that it is still a task that needs to be addressed effectively.

As outcomes in our study we took (*open*) general rating data on the state of openness of budget data in the regions of Russia and (*cit*) general characteristics of the rating relative to the development of the "participation in budgeting" [15]. The outcome "open" allowed to talk about the general state of the region regarding the implementation of the principle of openness of budget data for citizens, which was wider than the budget for citizens, but covered the basic level of the region's readiness for initiative budgeting. The outcome "*cit*" characterized the level of development of the special program "Budget for Citizens" at the regional level concerning infrastructure and participation in budgeting.

Four characteristics of the inclusive capacity of the region in the aspect of the topic under study are, in our opinion, significant. First, inclusivity implies a high level of opportunities for citizens to use information. This level is determined, on the one hand, by the development of new means of communication and information, on the other, by the prevalence and acceptance of the idea of obtaining public services through the Internet. To this end, we formulated two conditions: *inf* - the level of development of the information society in the region and *serv* – share of the citizens, which are ready to use the e-services.

Table 1. 22nd high positions in the Rating of the Russian regions on open budgeting in 2015

Region	Place	Total marks, including:	Quality of data	Citizen participation	GRP per capita, thousand rub.	The share of households with a personal computer
Max of possible marks		*210,0*	*39*	*40*		
Krasnodar Kray	1	185,00	28	29	355,0	67,5
Orenburg Oblast	2	184,00	25	31	387,8	70,1
Omsk Oblast	3	182,50	26,5	31	312,0	71,7
Krasnoyarsk Kray	4	178,00	28	23	565,3	72,0
Murmansk Oblast	5	164,00	22	24	510,8	88,6
Adyghe Republic (Adygea)	6	162,00	28	18	183,4	59,8
Hanty-Mansiysky Autonomy Okrug - Yugra	7	157,50	28	8,5	1937,0	84,6
Moscow Oblast	8	154,00	27	21	441,8	78,6
Stavropol Kray	9	153,00	18	27	217,6	65,9
Vladimir Oblast	10	147,00	27	11	255,4	71,5
Udmurt Republic	11	132,00	24	10	328,0	68,8
Irkutsk Oblast	12	130,00	21	19	419,9	76,0
Bashkortostan Republic	13	119,50	25,5	10	323,6	70,6
Astrakhan Oblast	14	114,00	20,0	2	314,5	77,4
Penza Oblast	15	111,00	19	9	248,9	67,8
Kirov Oblast	16	109,00	14	3	212,5	66,5
Vologda Oblast	17	108,00	23	5	394,1	64,0
Ulyanovsk Oblast	18	104,50	17	16	239,2	63,0
Arkhangelsk Oblast	19	104,00	20	7	352,0	78,5
Altai Kray	20	102,50	13	17	206,7	67,8
Voronezh Oblast	21/22	102,00	20	1,5	352,9	73,7
Tambov Oblast	21/22	102,00	26	10	326,5	68,1

Secondly, inclusive ability is provided by the state of the middle class in the region (*income*) and the quality of life (*life*). Thirdly, proceeding from the research objectives, it is interesting to look at the role of citizens -oriented data in their stimulation of participation in public budgeting. For this purpose, an indicator *corient* was developed that captures the level of compliance of regional budgets for citizens-oriented data. The operationalization of these conditions, and therefore their metric values, are taken from various sources. The development of the information society (inf) is determined by the data of the Ministry of Communications of the Russian Federation [13]. Share of citizens registered in the Unified Register of Public Services (URPS) (*serv*) is also determined according to the data of the Ministry of Communications [11]. The state of the middle class in the region (*income*) is calculated by the median income per capita according to Rosstat. The quality of life (*life*) is measured according to the quality of life rating in the Russian regions on the Riarating portal [14]. And finally, an indicator *corient* is taken from the data of the Ministry of Communications on the correlation between requirements and practices of budget for citizens.

If we try to compare a citizen-oriented data and participation in budgeting, then it is difficult to unambiguously answer the character of the mutual connection. Figure 1 shows that there are large discrepancies between the data relating to these two variables. The participation variable in many cases is not related to variable citizens-oriented data. The level of the relationship, calculated as the Pearson coefficient, is 0.33, i.e. the connection is rather weak. That is why a more complex analysis of the conditions is necessary, determining the participation of citizens in the budgeting.

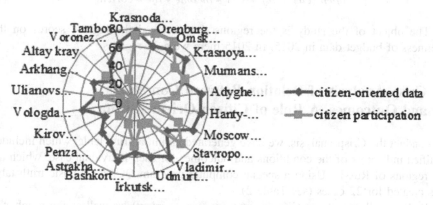

Fig. 1. Citizen-oriented data and participation (Russian regions 2015)

There is a problem of choosing boundary criteria. In our case, we use the principle of relativity, subordinating the choice of criteria to situational conditions. The study assumes that the entire volume of studied cases breaks up into two relatively equal sets of developed and insufficiently or undeveloped cases, taking into account the hypothesis of a normal distribution. For analysis purposes, the metric data for the conditiona and outcomes were recorded according to the QCA analysis, where one means quality, zero - no quality. The boundary criteria for the availability of quality were determined by the average values, i.e. among the values above ones characterized the presence of quality (1), below the average values indicated by the lack of quality (0). It was hypothetically assumed that there is a normal distribution of metric data. In this case, the designation of conditions and outcomes with a lowercase letter indicates the presence of quality, i.e. 1; a sign $\sim$ indicate a lack of quality (0).

The general hypothesis of the research is expressed by the following model, if we use QCA operators - qualitative comparative analysis:

$$open\ (cit) = inf + serv + income + life + corient \tag{1}$$

The openness of budgetary data (and citizen participation) in the region is determined by a combination of four conditions: the information development of the region *or* the share of citizens registered in the URPS *or* the availability of the middle class *or* the quality of life of the population *or* citizen-oriented data. What is the role of citizen-oriented data in the complex of these conditions?

In the previous study [19], we identified three models of budget implementation for citizens, based on the resulting combination of the conditions. *Technocratic model*, where the main were information and use of services. *Evolutionary model*, where the basic conditions were income and satisfaction with life. *Inclusive model*, which includes all the basic conditions. Consequently, the accompanying hypothesis in current study is the organic implementation of citizen-oriented data in the inclusive model of civic budgeting.

$$open\ (cit) = inf * serv * income * life * corient \tag{2}$$

The object of the study is the regions that received the highest scores on the openness of budget data in 2015. In 2015 there were 22 regions.

5   Crisp-Analysis of Relation Between Conditions and Outcomes. A Role of Citizen-Oriented Data

To conduct the Crisp-analysis, we have generated an initial truth table, which included codified indicators of the conditions and outcomes for each individual case, which are the regions of Russia. Using a special computer program QCA/fs, a basic truth table was created for 22 cases (see Table 2).

It shows all conditions (*life, income, inf, serv, corient*), as well as the number of cases that correspond to a particular configuration of the requisites. A separate column shows the values of the outcome (*open*). In this case, all configurations of the requisites are represented by the presence of the result. This is evidenced by 1 in this column and the raw consistency parameters, which for all rows are the same 1.000000. Consistency indicates that all the cases examined fall under the corresponding configuration; there are no contradictory results. According to the table, there are ten conditional configurations that satisfy the result. This complex configuration can be simplified using qualitative comparative analysis techniques (crisp-analysis). This simplification does not deprive the conclusion of the justification, but only allows to create a picture of the regular configurations of causes.

This crisp-analysis is important for us in two aspects. First, in essence, this approach starts with the premise of maximizing causal complexity, whereas the statistical method begins with the premise of the simplicity of the relationship. Secondly, the Boolean analysis technique contributes simultaneously to research in the integrity of the causes and effects of the phenomenon being studied, as well as to study the individual components of this integrity. In this respect, it includes an orientation toward holism and inductive analysis.

Table 2. Truthtable for relations between open budget and its requisites, 22 Russian regions in 2015

Life	Income	Inf	Serv	Corient	Number of cases	Open (QCA characteristics of outcomes)	Raw consistency
1	0	1	1	1	6	1	1.000000
1	1	1	1	1	3	1	1.000000
0	0	0	1	0	2	1	1.000000
0	0	1	0	1	2	1	1.000000
1	0	0	0	1	2	1	1.000000
1	0	1	0	0	2	1	1.000000
0	0	1	1	1	1	1	1.000000
0	1	1	1	1	1	1	1.000000
1	0	1	1	0	1	1	1.000000
1	1	0	0	1	1	1	1.000000
1	1	1	0	1	1	1	1.000000
1	0	1	1	1	6	1	1.000000

Analysis of the truth table using the Quinn-McCluskey algorithm yields the following result of the configuration of the conditions (3) that determine the presence of high openness of budget data in the regions of Russia.

$$Open = inf * serv * corient + life * \sim inc * inf * \sim corient + life * \sim inf$$
$$* \sim serv * corient + \sim life * \sim inc * inf * corient + \sim life * \sim inc$$
$$* \sim inf * serv * \sim corient + life * inc * \sim serv * corient + life * inc$$
$$* inf * corient$$

$$(3)$$

As can be seen from the eleven possible configurations of reasons for the openness of budget data, six configurations are natural for 22 regions. Note that the configuration of causes should be considered in the integrity of the presence and absence of quality, although the presence of a condition indicates its generating power. Thus, from the logical proposition (1), it can be concluded that the openness of budget data (*open*) is the result of complex solutions which consists from different present and absent conditions. For example, first solution (*inf * serv * corient*) means that the openness of budget data (*open*) in Russian regions is dependent of information society in region, citizen readiness for using electronic public service and citizen-oriented data. As can be seen from this complex solution, citizen-oriented data is a prerequisite for five combinations of conditions.

Using the factorization of Boolean expressions, we can obtain an even more economical formula and show this result (3).

$$Open = corient * (inf * serv * + life * \sim inf * \sim serv + \sim life * \sim inc * inf$$
$$+ life * inc * \sim serv + life * inc * inf) + \sim corient$$
$$* (life * \sim inc * inf + \sim life * \sim inc * \sim inf * serv *)$$

$$(4)$$

It (4) shows that an open budget requires some basic requisites. First, the high development of the citizen-oriented data is necessary conditionally; second, lack of these data is combined with a high level of satisfaction with life, a relatively developed information society and the willingness to use the Internet to obtain public services. True, all these requisites are necessary conditionally, but insufficient reasons, because we see their combination with other factors (their presence or absence).

However, more important are the conclusions from the formula 4, which confirm the concomitant hypothesis that *only an inclusive model necessarily requires data oriented to citizens*. The first part of the formula with the presence of the condition (data oriented to citizens) indicate that all models include this condition. However, the second part says that the lack of data oriented to citizens is characteristic only of the technocratic and evolutionary models.

The same procedure for working with the truth table for 22 regions will be conducted, using as a result the development of the "budget for citizens" program using the evaluation of citizen participation in budgeting. From the truth table (Table 3), you can see that the configuration of the conditions is the same as for the budget openness. However, there are contradictory results encoded by the letter C in the sixth column, when this configuration generates the result and does not generate it. This is also obvious when we look at the raw consistency.

Contradictory results require specific work with them. Charles Ragin says that their use is determined by theoretical considerations, which should be justified. It is clear that if we take into account that all the contradictory configurations give a positive result and include them in the analysis, then we will get the same final conclusion as in the case with the study of the openness of budget data. In this respect, formulas (3) and (5) could be similar. But we must first remove those assumptions in which there is no result. Then we get the following general solution (5) for this truth table.

Table 3. Truthtable for relations between participation in budgeting and its requisites, 22 Russian regions in 2015

Life	Incom	Inf	Serv	Corient	Number of cases	Cit (QCA characteristics of outcomes)	Raw consistency
1	0	1	1	1	6	C	0.333333
1	1	1	1	1	3	C	0.666667
1	0	1	0	0	2	C	0.500000
0	0	0	1	0	2	C	0.500000
1	0	0	0	1	2	1	1.000000
0	0	1	0	1	2	1	1.000000
1	0	1	1	0	1	1	1.000000
1	1	0	0	1	1	0	0.000000
1	1	1	0	1	1	0	0.000000
0	0	1	1	1	1	0	0.000000
0	1	1	1	1	1	0	0.000000
1	0	1	1	1	6	C	0.333333

$$Cit = life * \sim inc * inf * \sim corient + life * \sim inf * \sim serv * corient + life * inf$$
$$* serv * corient + \sim life * \sim inc * \sim inf * serv * \sim corient + \sim life$$
$$* \sim inc * inf * \sim serv * corient$$

$$(5)$$

The relevance of the corresponding contradictory configurations to obtain the result (participation in budgeting) is not obvious. Using the logic of experimental analysis, we can say that these configurations are not necessary and sufficient for a "participation in budgeting", so we can neglect part of them with low consistency 0.333333. Then the result of the investigation will be formula (6), which gives a definite new result: in the configuration of conditions, a significant 'Corient' condition appears as important factor of participation in budgeting.

$$Cit = life * \sim inc * inf * \sim corient + life * \sim inf * \sim serv * corient$$
$$+ \sim life * \sim inc * \sim inf * serv * \sim corient + \sim life * \sim inc * inf \quad (6)$$
$$* \sim serv * corient + life * inc * inf * serv * corient$$

$$Cit = corient * (life * \sim inf * \sim serv + life * inc * inf * serv + \sim life * \sim inc$$
$$* inf * \sim serv) + \sim corient (life * \sim inc * inf + \sim life * \sim inc * \sim inf * serv)$$

$$(7)$$

In formula (7), using factorization, the '*corient*' variable is singled out, which along with other conditions also becomes neither necessary nor sufficient. But here again the accompanying hypothesis is confirmed. If these citizens-oriented data are combined with all citizen participation models in budgeting (the first part of the formula), then the absence of this condition is not characteristic of the inclusive model.

6   Discussion and Further Perspectives

As the study showed, citizen-oriented data are an important condition for the development of "budget for citizens". However, they are not necessary, but only sufficient requisites for the development of citizen's participation, if we say on the all models of introducing open budget. In this regard, consideration of the factors of the development of "citizen's budgeting" should be accompanied by an analysis of the complex set of conditions defined in the paper as a structure of inclusive capacities. The latter includes social, economic, political, and infrastructure components that provide the opportunity and willingness to participate in budgeting. Under the capacity for inclusiveness we understand a quality of region in which citizens have the opportunities for participation, that is, public authorities are open to participation, budget data is oriented on the citizens, electronic infrastructure is well, and citizens have some practical skills for using electronic devises. It is also necessary to add qualities that characterize the satisfaction with life and the social state of participants who have material opportunities for free time, which is an important requisite for participation.

Although all conditions are important, however, these citizens-oriented data are most closely related to the inclusive model of the implementation of open data and the budget for citizens. Our study confirmed that this condition is organic for the system of opportunities that determines a more productive model of the policy of civil budgeting. At the same time, the inclusive model of implementation stumbles upon the limitations of a mixed political regime.

The effectiveness and efficiency of the structure of inclusive opportunities is largely determined by the nature of the political regime. In a democracy, this structure creates additional guarantees for the realization of human rights to participate in the decision of public affairs. It creates an important impetus for the democratic search for new forms of governance based on cooperation and co-production. In mixed modes, the structure of inclusive opportunities is intended first to demonstrate the willingness of the regime to follow new requests for participation and to legitimize the existing order. That is, it has limitations imposed by the system on development. Although the logic of the "budget for citizens" involves the search for innovations, they are implemented within the commands coming from the power agents. It is interesting, for example, that public opinion polls about the "budget for citizens" that are regularly conducted through relevant sites in Russian regions are, as a rule, truncated by a set of questionnaires, often formal, and the questions are closed. Of course, they fix the understanding of the situation primarily by authoritative agents and are more orientational rather than search engines. So, on the site of the "budget for citizens" of the Irkutsk Oblast only 6% of respondents, answering the question "For what purposes can you benefit from the Irkutsk region's open budget website?" chose the answer option "for building a dialogue with the authorities" (*openbudget.gfu.ru*). Only 14% of respondents in the Krasnoyarsk Kray are ready to submit their proposals on the articles of spending the budget (*minfin.krskstate.ru/openbudget*). This is, of course, a reflection of the gap between citizens and state authorities in the region. It should also be noted that the "budget for citizens" in the federal center is limited to information goals and does not involve detailed feedback from citizens. Although there are public councils and the Public Chamber of the Russian Federation, which take part in the discussion of budgetary matters, but in comparison with the regions and municipalities, the federal budget for citizens is limited for cooperation.

Imitative institutions of "budget for the citizens" inure for legitimating regimes in general, but also they are good factors for mutual learning for cooperation. Some regions use "budget for citizens" formally, but some of them try to initiate citizens for discussion and co-production of regional budget in direct or indirect senses. Transparency of budgetary data, its transformation for the citizens, and budgeting, initiated by citizens, affects on the complex character of Russian designs for inclusive budgeting. Residents of the regions as a whole are sympathetic to the new system of participation. So, 52% of respondents in Bashkortostan are ready to participate in the implementation of projects of proactive budgeting on the territory of the republic (*gas. bashkortostan.ru/budget*). They are even ready to take part in co-financing regional and municipal projects. To increase financial literacy in Russia, a system of training is being created that includes lessons in schools, seminars and webinars on relevant sites, an answer system for questions organized via the Internet and mobile applications, exhibitions and forums, etc.

7 Conclusion

In the paper an influence of citizen-oriented data on the participation in budgeting has been studied. However a direct influence of this variable is not obvious in all models of implementation. The main hypothesis that these factors have a direct impact on the process of formation of participatory budgeting was corrected in the sense that each factor generated a certain configurational link with other requisites of the studied processes. In its pure form, none of the factors has shown its effectiveness. But, more importantly, all conditions are organically related to the inclusive model of implementation of citizen budgeting. To analyze the dependency configuration, a qualitative comparative analysis method (QCA) was used. Of course, further studies of a greater variety of conditions and cases may lead to a refinement of these findings and the formation of new conceptual approaches.

The Russian practice of "budget for the citizens" in the mixed (hybrid) regimes, introduced in 2013 at the federal and regional levels, demonstrates this dual effect if we compare regional systems of budgeting. Imitative institutions of "budget for the citizens" inure for legitimating regimes in general, but also they are good factors for mutual learning for cooperation, collaboration and co-production. Although there is a mutual distrust between citizens and civil servants about the effectiveness of civil budgeting, however, it is overcome by the practice of cooperation. In 2017, in the regions of Russia, a policy is launched to develop initiative budgeting, which stimulates co-production in such an important sector of public policy as the formation and implementation of public budgets.

Funding. This work was supported with a grant from the Russian Foundation for Basic Research (Grant 18-011-00756 A "Study of citizens participation and building digital government").

References

1. Boukhis, I., Ayachi, R., Eloedi, Z., Mellouli, S., Amor, N.B.: Decision model for policy makers in the context of citizens engagement: application on participatory budgeting. Soc. Sci. Comput. Rev. **34**(6), 740–756 (2015)
2. Bovaird, T., Loffler, E.: From engagement to co-production: how users and communities contribute to public services. In: Pestoff, V., Brandsen, T., Verschuere, B. (eds.) New Public Governance, the Third Sector and Co-production. Sage, New York (2012)
3. Budzetnoe Poslanie Presidenta Rossiyskoy Federatsii o Budgetnoy Politike v 2014–2016 godah 13 Iyunia 2013 http://kremlin.ru/acts/news/18332. Accessed 20 Apr 2017
4. Cabannes, Y.: Participatory budgeting: a significant contribution to participatory democracy. Environ. Urban. **16**(1), 27–31 (2004)
5. Gabrys, J., Pritchard, H., Barratt, B.: Just good enough data: figuring data citizenships through air pollution sensing and data stories. In: Big Data and Society. July–December 1–14 (2016). https://doi.org/10.1177/2053951716679677
6. Ganuza, E., Frances, F.: The deliberative turn in participation: the problem of inclusion and deliberative opportunities in participatory budgeting. Eur. Polit. Sci. Rev. **4**(2), 283–302 (2012)
7. Eckerd, A.: Citizen language and administrative response: participation in environmental impact assessment. Adm. Soc. **49**(3), 348–373 (2017). https://doi.org/10.1177/0095399714548272
8. Rihoux, B., Grimm, H. (eds.): Innovative Comparative Methods for Policy Analysis. Beyond Quantitative-Qualitative Divide. Springer, Heidelberg (2006). https://doi.org/10.1007/0-387-28829-5
9. Krenjova, J., Raudla, R.: Policy diffusion at the local level: participatory budgeting in Estonia. Urban Aff. Rev. **3**(4), 1–29 (2017)
10. Lloyd, E.: Co-producing early years policy in England under the Coalition Government. Manag. Educ. **28**(4), 130–137 (2014)
11. Po raschetam Rosstata. d-russia.ru/rosstat-zafiksiroval-perevypolnenie-plana-dostich-v-2016-g-50-dlya-pokazatelya-dolya-grazhdanispolzuyushhih-elektronnye-gosuslugi.html. Accessed 19 Apr 2017
12. Ragin, Ch.: The Comparative Method: Moving Beyond Qualitative and Quantitative Strategies. University of California Press, Berkeley (1987)
13. Rating po urovniu razvitia informatsionnogo obschestva za 2015 god. http://minsvyaz.ru/ru/events/35027/. Accessed 21 Apr 2017
14. Rating rossiyskyh regionov po kachestvu szizni-2015. http://riarating.ru/regions_rankings/20160225/630011011.html. Accessed 10 Apr 2017
15. Rating sub'ektov Rossiyskoy Federatsii po urovniu otkrytosty budgetnyh dannyh za 2015. https://www.nifi.ru/ru/rating/2015/rezultaty-rejtinga-2015.html. Accessed 21 Apr 2017

16. Rios, A.-M., Bastida, F., Benito, B.: Budget transparency and legislative budgetary oversight: an international approach. Am. Rev. Public Adm. **46**(5), 546–568 (2014)
17. Rocker, A.: Framing Citizen Participation: Participatory Budgeting in France, Germany and the United Kingdom. Palgrave Macmillan, Basingstoke (2014)
18. Sicilia, M., Guarini, E., Sancino, A., Andreani, M., Ruffini, R.: Public services management and co-production in multi-level governance settings. Int. Rev. Adm. Sci. **82**(1), 8–27 (2016). https://doi.org/10.1177/0020852314566008
19. Smorgunov, L.: Requisites for open budgeting: a comparison of the 'Budget for Citizens' in Russian regions using QCA. In: Alexandrov, D.A., Boukhanovsky, A.V., Chugunov, A.V., Kabanov, Y., Koltsova, O. (eds.) DTGS 2017. CCIS, vol. 745, pp. 243–256. Springer, Cham (2017). https://doi.org/10.1007/978-3-319-69784-0_21
20. Souza, C.: Participatory budgeting in Brazilian cities: limits and possibilities in building democratic institutions. Environ. Urban. **13**(1), 159–184 (2001)
21. Van Eijk, C.: Trui, St.: Why engage in co-production of public services? Mixing theory and empirical evidence. Int. Rev. Admin. Sci. **82**(1), 28–46 (2016)
22. Walker, P., Shannon, P.: Participatory governance: towards a strategic model. Commun. Dev. J. **46**(2), ii63–ii82 (2011)
23. Williams, B., Matheny, A.: Democracy, Dialogue, and Environmental Disputes: The Languages of Social Regulation. Yale University Press, New Haven (1995)

Hacking the Knowledge of Maker Communities in Support of 21st Century Education

Christian Voigt[✉][iD], Sebastian Mair, and Elisabeth Unterfrauner

Centre for Social Innovation, 1150 Vienna, Austria
{voigt,mair,unterfrauner}@zsi.at

Abstract. The paper addresses the need to rethink education to be effective in a changing environment. More concretely we look at the intersection of craft-based learning, digital fabrication technologies and schools' capacities to absorb educational innovations. Although making and hacking are known activities within constructionist learning settings, they are not yet widespread at a school level. An explorative study of maker education across European countries has shown that a major impediment to innovations, such as digital fabrication in schools, were the perceived complexity of the process, the technical skills required and the lack of easily accessible resources for getting started or being able to troubleshoot if needed. The aim of this paper is to test the possibilities of referencing existing knowledge embedded in platforms such as instructables.com. Using the available API, we created a network graph of 225,681 instructables authored by 74,824 authors. The potential of that knowledge base is analysed in two steps: first, we describe the available content on the platform in terms of topics, structure and licenses and second, we explore the value of topic networks, as one specific possibility to make platform knowledge more accessible to educators and learners themselves. A first prototype has been implemented and evaluated, showing the importance of discussing the value and limitations of resources external to educational systems, learning by doing, accountability and the right to tinker in technology-embedded teaching.

Keywords: Digital fabrication · Education · Knowledge · Network
Platform hacking · Communities

1 Introduction

Looking back in history, every society over the different centuries had its specific demands in terms of skills requirements at the workplace and as a result in terms of education. Thus, broader societal developments tend to influence pedagogy, in terms of teaching methods as well as in terms of educational goals associated with specific skills and competences, required to enter the workforce [14]. With ever more fluid demands on educational systems comes the challenge of adapting

© Springer Nature Switzerland AG 2018
S. S. Bodrunova (Ed.): INSCI 2018, LNCS 11193, pp. 286–299, 2018.
https://doi.org/10.1007/978-3-030-01437-7_22

curricula, educational technologies and resources. Our aim is to open up existing resources by testing the possibilities of using content from platforms such as instructables.com. More concretely, two questions will be addressed:

(a) Given that emerging or relatively small communities might not yet have a seizable stock of resources related to technology enhanced learning topics, is it possible to use knowledge from more established communities as a starting point, being aware that communities such as instructables.com cultivate a much more informal learning dimension than what would be typical for schools.

(b) Content on established maker platforms goes into the hundred thousand and more. Therefore, when using content from established maker platforms, can we establish a transparent and effective way to select content that fits users' needs and results in resources being perceived as useful to learners and teachers?

The paper starts with analysing the potential of Instructables.com's knowledge base in two steps: first, we describe the available content on the platform in terms of topics, structure and collaboration behaviour (Sect. 4) and second, we explore the value of topic networks, as one specific possibility to make platform knowledge more accessible to educators and learners themselves (Sect. 5). A first prototype is then described in Sect. 6, followed by a brief evaluation section. The paper concludes by discussing the value and limitations of resources external to educational systems, learning by doing, accountability and the right to tinker in technology-embedded teaching.

2   The Demands of 21st Century Education

The 21st century is characterised by a shift of the workplace towards automation, globalisation and demographic change [17]. Computerisation and automation are seen as drivers for "routine" tasks and "lower skilled" jobs becoming obsolete in a near future. Areas where human workers are not yet easily replaced by automation include solving unpredictable problems and maintaining complex interactions with other humans [17,29]. Globalisation has led to a situation where services such as the ones offered by call centres are outsourced to countries with lower wages and where workers compete on global scale for jobs [12]. Spurring creativity and innovation is seen as key to compete in a globalised job market. Demographic change has an impact on the employment market in many ways: in terms of superannuation of the population, which will require more jobs in health and foster care; and in respect to diversity of the society [4,18].

Furthermore, most of the workplaces are characterised by less hierarchy and supervision and allow for more autonomy and responsibility and require working in teams. Workers are asked to continuously adapt to new challenges and demands and train themselves in new skills. Thus, one of the requirements in the current and near future employment market is the skill to know how to learn [7,13].

3   Maker Pedagogy

We can observe that the pedagogy in schools is already paying attention to these changed circumstances to a big extend. Learner centred teaching methods, constructive learning approaches, project based and collaborative learning have at least partly replaced ex-cathedra teaching, so that learners of the 21st century are encouraged to become creative, critical thinkers, skilled in communication and team work [3].

The so-called 21st century skills comprise a vast set of skills and competences complementing traditional skills. Frequently mentioned skills include [10]: critical thinking and problem solving; creativity and innovation; communication and collaboration; digital literacy consisting of information, media and ICT literacy; and finally interpersonal skills such as flexibility and adaptability, initiative and self-direction. One of the conclusions of the report by Jerald [17] is, that these "new" skills have become more important, but that they should complement rather than replace the skills pursued in traditional school subjects such as mathematics, grammar, and so forth. Hence, 'novel skills' must be trained not detached from the traditional school curriculum but as part of "traditional subjects". Many of the skills that are associated with 21st century skills are supported by the maker pedagogy, often integrated in project-based settings.

3.1   Tinkering Versus Instruction

As put forward by Resnick and Rosenbaum [27]: "The tinkering approach is characterized by a playful, experimental, iterative style of engagement, in which makers are continually reassessing their goals, exploring new paths, and imagining new possibilities. Tinkering is undervalued (and even discouraged) in many educational settings today, but it is well aligned with the goals and spirit of the progressive-constructionist tradition—and, in our view, it is exactly what is needed to help young people prepare for life in today's society". The quote shows how existing preferences in the educational system, e.g. emphasizing content delivery and quantitative assessment, run counter to a pluralism of learning paths including the bottom up experiences of creating tangible objects, the notion of adapting solutions to changing conditions and an essentially different way of accessing STEM problems.

The pedagogy of making builds on pedagogical schools of thoughts ranging from reform pedagogues to constructivists, from Montessori [24] to Piaget and Papert [1], who emphasized the value of self-regulated learning [16], empowering learners to decide on their learning goals and the ways to achieve them. In such learning settings teachers see their own role primarily in assisting the learner in their learning paths. The focus on instructional interactions in traditional teacher-learner relationships is therefore obsolete.

Learning through making is hands-on learning, where makers learn from observing others, recognising the value of trial and error, and taking part of interdisciplinary and collaborative teams [6,9,19]. In this, making is similar to problem solving and project-based learning approaches. Making includes a desire to produce things more collaboratively by improving design suggestions of others or by simply copying, mashing or personalising existing design elements [31]. Making is thus theoretically and historically founded on "learning by doing" principles [25, 26]. According to the Horizon report, which anticipates technological trends having an impact on educational settings, maker education will have an increasing impact on education in the following years [5].

3.2 Implications for Educational Systems

A recent study of innovations related to making and digital fabrication in schools [32] identified a number of barriers to innovating teaching practices, including a lack of knowledge about how to run the technology or how to integrate the use of maker technologies with curricular topics to be covered. Those barriers, in combination with cumbersome decision-making processes and restrictive funding options, could seriously hamper the use of novel technologies in schools. In order to overcome these limitations, educators mentioned several measures such as the use of sharing platforms or groups of like-minded people sharing their experience. From an innovation management perspective, technologies that enabled networking between innovative teachers were largely preferred over knowledge-banking strategies such as best practice collections or 'go-to experts' [32].

In itself, referring to networking and community building as promotional devices of educational purposes is not new. Innovation networks in education can be seen as an amalgamate of Wenger's communities of practice [34] and Kazmer's idea that knowledge is shaped by learners' membership in multiple overlapping communities [21]. The benefit that comes with considering communities is primarily based on their purpose giving nature, even though we must be aware of overstating the homogeneity of communities [33]. Wenger argues that throughout life, communities motivate our learning by defining the relevancy of problems and providing orientation in terms of where answers can be found or where previous attempts to find solutions have been unsuccessful. On a more practical level, however, we do not yet fully understand what makes collaboration in communities work [28]. Kaptelinin [20] argues that collective activities are structured, directed and motivated by objects, which capture the purpose of networking. Hence, objects in networks help individuals to express themselves in a cognitive as well as affective way – a process Knorr Cetina refers to as "object-centred sociality" [22]. Taking project descriptions as objects' enabling the shaping of knowledge and communities, the following section describes activities related to those objects.

4   Platform Activities on Instructables.com

Instructables.com is a platform enabling users to upload and share their do-it-yourself projects, which are commented upon and rated by other users for their quality. The website was launched in August 2005 and obtained by Autodesk in 2011. Figure 1 shows a relatively moderate start during the first 5 years, but since then monthly uploads have been overall on the rise. Instructables.com promotes a specific format for writing instructables - e.g. project descriptions -, including a step-by-step description and images for in-between results. Data on authors and their projects can be accessed via an Application Programming Interface (API). By October 2017, users had published roughly 250,000 projects, from which we obtained a dataset of 225,681 projects, published and shared by 74,824 distinct first-authors.

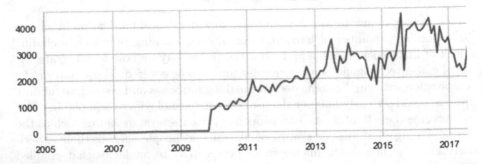

Fig. 1. Project uploads per month.

If we look at the distribution of published projects per platform user we see a long-tail distribution, fitting best a log-normal distribution (Fig. 2). Figure 2 shows two density functions, with the continuous line indicating the actual distribution of projects per user and the dotted line shows a lognormal distribution. The long-tailed distribution has been tested as described in [8] using the power law python package [2]. A practical interpretation of a long-tailed distributions is to see it as an indicator for a slow or maybe not too intuitive start, representing the large majority of users having just one project published. Figure 2 shows that only a few active users, namely the top 20 users by the time of analysis, had more than 200 projects. The most prolific user had about 500 projects, mostly in the crafts, gardening and food categories. However, projects tend to be mixed and in another case of a user with 179 projects, we can see a variety of themes including minimalist LED clocks, photography and chickpea meals. Furthermore, screening the top 20 users, it seemed that they had professional incentives to produce instructables, either as teachers, small businesses, makers or managers of makerspaces.

Early on we discarded the idea of selecting authors based on their project profiles, this would go against our intention to identify technology projects embedded in other areas such as gardening or art. We also looked into the self-descriptions of users in order to see whether there was a discernible education community. Without claiming that such an approach could not be promising, a first frequency count of keywords generated rather low numbers: student (1226), maker (961), school (790), teacher (299), company (255), fab (253), education (185) and 'instructor' appeared 66 times.

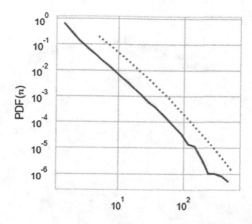

Fig. 2. Probability distribution of projects per single author.

Lastly, platform activities can be described in terms of ongoing collabora-tions, i.e. visible by the connectedness of an author. Connectedness refers to the number of people, an author has collaborated with. The rationale behind this measurement is that authors who contributed to more projects are more experienced and that project descriptions that were generated in collaboration with others, most likely have had an internal peer review process increasing the quality of the descriptions.

Figure 3 shows the largest component of the instructables network with 116 authors collaborating with, on average, 2.15 other authors. For example, the highlighted author 'tjaap' in Fig. 3, collaborated with 19 other authors and pro-duced multiple project descriptions in collaboration with user 'Roosch'.

5   Content: Types, Categories, Channels and Tags

Instructable.com content can be separated into two types: projects (97%) and guides (3%). Guides contain themed collections of projects around topics such as micro-boards or magnetism. Each project is allocated to one out of eight cat-egories, with technology, craft and workshop being the most popular categories (see Fig. 4, left). Originally content focused mostly on projects such as building electronic or mechanical devices to solve common problems around the home. The scope of the project has then expanded to include less technical categories, including Food, Living, Outside or Play.

Over time, the category 'play' was used less and, as expected, the category 'costumes' shows seasonal dependencies. At a more detailed level projects are organized into channels and can be described with key-words. Arduino is both the most frequently used channel (see Fig. 4, right) and the most frequently issued keyword, which again highlights the community's technical affinity.

So far, we analysed options to filter content on instructables.com by cate-gories and channels, which is a useful first step to narrow it down but does not

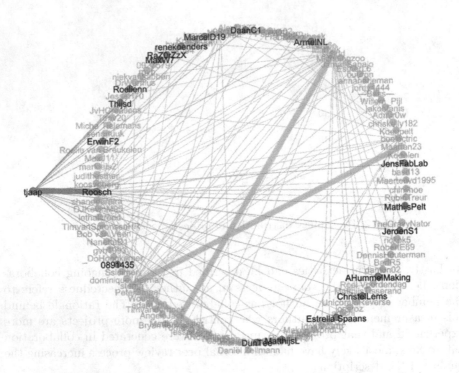

Fig. 3. Number of collaborations with other users. (Color figure online)

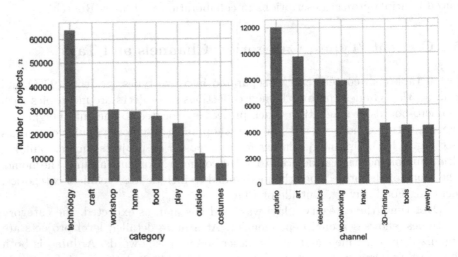

Fig. 4. Number of projects for the top eight categories and channels. (Color figure online)

leave many additional options for finding projects beyond pre-established categories. For the next step we generated a network graph based on user-allocated tags (Fig. 5).

The size of each node reflects the frequency of the 'tag' and if two tags are connected then this means that at least on project uses both tags. This way, for example, it will be possible to find projects that use the tags 'solar', 'lego' and 'iPhone'- tags that could be relevant in a school context - leading to a project that describes building a USB charger in a casing made by Lego bricks.

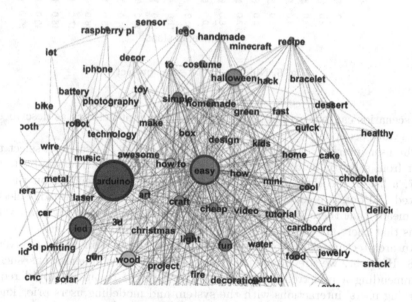

Fig. 5. Tag-based content network.

Another characteristic of project descriptions is 'step count', i.e. the number of steps used to describe the process of producing a specific outcome. Figure 6 shows a histogram of steps per project.

An interesting question would be whether 'step count' is positively related with pedagogical quality. 18% of all projects have only a single step, otherwise most project use five or six steps to break down instructions within project descriptions.

6   A Tag-Based Recommender Prototype

Providing the tag-based content network to end-users is close to providing a first prototype of a recommender systems as discussed in [23]. Manouselis et al. distinguish different recommendation goals, including recommending 'content related to a learner's current interest' and 'content related to specific topics',

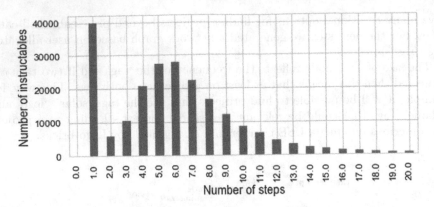

Fig. 6. Number of steps per project.

both scenarios can be covered with a tag-based content network as described in the previous section.

The user interface of the prototype is shown in Fig. 7. Users can select tags either from a list or by directly clicking on a node. As shown at the bottom of Fig. 7, a list of projects, ranked by likes, is generated, depending on the tags selected. All dots are color-coded: orange means that a tag is already selected, grey means that there is no project using the already selected tags and yellow means that there are projects using this specific combination of tags.

An architecture sketch of the system behind the user interface is given in Fig. 8. However, we are aware that more complex recommendations such as recommending a preferred pathway through a list of resources would require observing users' interactions with the system and modelling users prior knowledge about a given topic.

At the moment our prototype can filter resources by topics but does not take into account yet the importance of selecting materials with an adequate level of complexity so that users are neither over - nor underchallenged [15].

7   First Evaluation Results

The first objectives to be achieved with the prototype were related to makers' or teachers' needs to find resources which addressed the functioning of specific technical components (e.g. LED, DC motor, micro-boards) or tools for designing and programming (e.g. tinkercad.com or create.arduino.cc) in an applied context (water, garden, green, reuse etc.). At this point, it is important to be aware that the tags are attached to concrete objects and projects, hence more abstract tags such as 'sustainability', 'geography' or 'equity' are less frequently used.

Based on Manouselis et al.'s [23] overview of recommender systems in technologically enhanced learning settings, we established the following evaluation criteria:

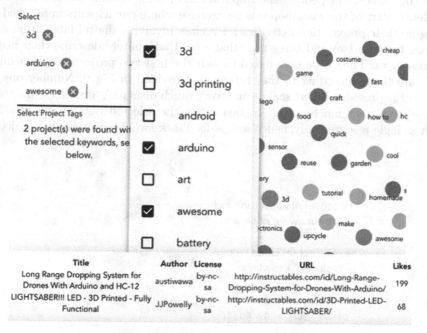

Browse about 40,000 projects on instructables.com via the top 100 assigned keywords.

Select at least two keywords, either via the dropdown on the left or by clicking directly on the keyword-circles. Selected keywords are marked orange, related keywords yellow and unrelated keywords grey. Projects that were assigned all selected keywords will be listed below.

Title	Author	License	URL	Likes
Long Range Dropping System for Drones With Arduino and HC-12	austiwawa	by-nc-sa	http://instructables.com/id/Long-Range-Dropping-System-for-Drones-With-Arduino/	199
LIGHTSABER!!! LED - 3D Printed - Fully Functional	JJPowelly	by-nc-sa	http://instructables.com/id/3D-Printed-LED-LIGHTSABER/	68

Fig. 7. User interface of tag-based recommender prototype. (Color figure online)

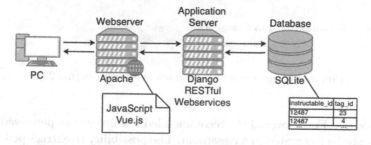

Fig. 8. Architecture sketch of tag-based recommender prototype.

- degree to which a recommended source uncovered hidden aspects of a topic,
- degree to which a recommended source included technical as well as pedagogically useful ideas and explanations,
- likelihood that the recommended source would actually be used and
- likelihood that the recommended source would need considerable reworking before it could be used.

In order to support the data collection for these evaluation criteria, a workshop with 12 teachers and tutors was organized. During that workshop we discussed the need for diverse types of resources helping teachers not only with the technical aspects of digital fabrication technologies in classrooms but also with the logistical or pedagogical implications of using specific technologies with students. Part of the workshop was an exercise where participants were asked to imagine their preparation activities for a class involving digital fabrication and choose between two and three tags that would adequately describe their needs for resources. They were then asked to visit the first two projects recommended and rate them according to the statements provided in Fig. 9. Number one to five on the provided Likert scale equal 'very much disagree', 'disagree', 'neutral', 'agree' and 'very much agree'. In two cases, the selected tags produced a list with a single resource only, hence we got feedback for 22 recommended projects.

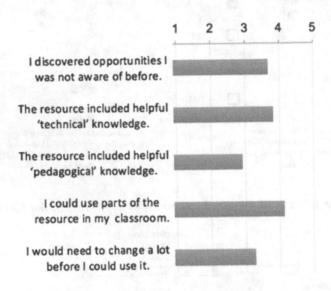

Fig. 9. Average score of recommended resources (n = 22).

As shown in Fig. 9, overall the recommended resources were perceived as useful enough to be integrated in a classroom. The possibility to extract pedagogical knowledge from projects on instructable.com was rated the least favourable, with a majority of respondents disagreeing with the statement 'The resource included helpful pedagogical knowledge'. However, that was to be expected since users of instructables.com see themselves first and foremost as technical experts or tinkerers and less as educators. Nonetheless, the pedagogical value of step-wise explanations, including the necessary details to also replicate a project step is a frequent topic in comments. With 50% of the resources, workshop participants agreed with 'I discovered opportunities I was not aware of before.'We also see this as one of the main benefits of looking into existing project descriptions, the chances that a project matches a specific user problem are rather small but providing inspiration to a teacher in search for a meaningful example or application area is a reasonable expectation. One common question was whether querying the tag-based network and searching through instructable.com's search engine would provide the same results. Indeed, finding resources is the main business of search engines. However, preliminary tests indicate that whereas instructable.com works fine for frequently used combinations such as 'arduino' and 'water', leading to similar results of automatic plant watering systems, less frequently used combinations such as 'arduino' and 'jewellery' are better served by relying on 'tags' provided by users.

8   Conclusion

At this stage it is still early for a final verdict on the overall value of hacking community knowledge to empower educational communities on their path to more hands-on learning, including digital fabrication tools. The current evaluation happened in a workshop, however, the final recommendation tool is planned to be integrated into a larger support system together with links to open educational resources, tool recommendations for learners and the possibility to support learning analytics running in the background. In such a context, feedback can be given online and larger numbers of users are addressable.

Revisiting the research questions posed in the first section, we would conclude that tapping into resources generated by relevant communities such as instructables.com is a valuable endeavour. The inspiration these resources can provide for teachers and learners as well as the technical details included in project descriptions was mentioned positively during the evaluation workshop described in the previous section.

Concerning the second question about a transparent and effective way to filter external resources for their use in an educational context, we would say that there are some promising options, but most likely direct feedback given by users integrating resources into their teaching and learning practices is needed to produce more accurate recommendations. For the moment, the list of recommended resources is ranked by likes. However, in the future we can also provide the option to rank resources by the connectedness of their authors (cf. Sect. 4) or the number of steps featured in a project (cf. Sect. 5), or a combination of multiple measurements.

To conclude, repurposing the effort from the instructable.com community to benefit education is an effective way to avoid reinventing the wheel. What is left to do, however, is opening up platforms and proactively supporting the reuse of materials [30]. This is not limited to choosing creative commons licenses, which is already encouraged, but also includes supporting rich APIs and giving sufficient visibility to the information contained within project descriptions (e.g. project collaborations and descriptive tags are currently not visible on published instructables).

Last but not least, education and technology are not necessarily an easy match [11]. Teachers, who are traditionally seen as domain experts need to embrace a diversity of knowledge sources, skills acquisition and learning by doing are equally valid approaches and education systems need to encourage individuals to take on more responsibility for their own learning. These are changes that happen outside technical systems, however, are critical conditions for technical innovations to unfold as envisioned.

Acknowledgement. This research was supported by the eCraft2Learn project (H2020) funded under Grant Agreement No 731345.

References

1. Ackermann, E.: Piaget's constructivism, papert's constructionism: what's the difference? Future Learn. Group Publ. **5**(3), 438 (2001)
2. Alstott, J., Bullmore, E., Plenz, D.: powerlaw: a python package for analysis of heavy-tailed distributions. PLoS One **9**(1), e85777 (2014). https://doi.org/10.1371/journal.pone.0085777
3. Ananiadou, K., Claro, M.: 21st century skills and competences for new millennium learners in OECD countries. Technical report, OECD (2009). https://doi.org/10.1787/218525261154
4. Barak, M.E.M.: Managing Diversity: Toward a Globally Inclusive Workplace. Sage Publications, Thousand Oaks (2016)
5. Becker, S.A., Cummins, M., Davis, A., Freeman, A., Hall, C.G., Ananthanarayanan, V.: NMC horizon report: 2017 higher, education edition. Technical report, The New Media Consortium (2017)
6. Bell, S.: Project-based learning for the 21st century: skills for the future. Clear. House **83**(2), 39–43 (2010). https://doi.org/10.1080/00098650903505415
7. Billett, S.: Learning in the Workplace: Strategies for Effective Practice. ERIC (2001)
8. Broido, A.D., Clauset, A.: Scale-free networks are rare. arXiv preprint arXiv:1801.03400 (2018)
9. Bruffee, K.A.: Collaborative Education, Interdependence, and the Authority of Knowledge. Johns Hopkins University Press, Baltimore (1993)
10. Budhai, S.S., Taddei, L.M.: Teaching the 4Cs with Technology: How do I Use 21st Century Tools to Teach 21st Century Skills? (ASCD Arias). ASCD (2015)
11. Collins, A., Halverson, R.: Rethinking Education in the Age of Technology: The Digital Revolution and Schooling in America. Teachers College Press, New York (2018)
12. Edwards, R., Usher, R.: Globalisation & Pedagogy: Space, Place and Identity. Routledge, Abingdon (2007)
13. Evans, K.: Learning, Work and Social Responsibility: Challenges for Lifelong Learning in a Global Age, vol. 13. Springer, Dordrecht (2009). https://doi.org/10.1007/978-1-4020-9759-1
14. Ezewu, E.: Sociology of Education. Longman, Lagos (1983)
15. Hedegaard, M.: The zone of proximal development as basis for instruction. In: Moll, L.C. (ed.) Vygotsky and Education: Instructional Implications and Applications of Sociohistorical Psychology, pp. 349–371. Cambridge University, Cambridge (1992)
16. van Hout-Wolters, B., Simons, R.J., Volet, S.: Active learning: self-directed learning and independent work. In: Simons, R.J., van der Linden, J., Duffy, T. (eds.) New Learning, pp. 21–36. Springer, Dordrecht (2000). https://doi.org/10.1007/0-306-47614-2_2

17. Jerald, C.: Defining a 21st century education. Center Pub. Educ. **16** (2009)
18. Jorgensen, B.: The ageing population and knowledge work: a context for action. Foresight **7**(1), 61–76 (2005). https://doi.org/10.1108/14636680510581321
19. Kaltman, G.S.: Hands-on learning. Child. Educ. **87**(2), S7–S7 (2010)
20. Kaptelinin, V.: The object of activity: making sense of the sense-maker. Mind Cult. Act. **12**(1), 4–18 (2005)
21. Kazmer, M.M.: Community-embedded learning. In: Andrews, R., Haythornthwaite, C. (eds.) The Sage Handbook of E-learning Research, pp. 311–327. Sage Publications, Thousand Oaks (2007)
22. Knorr Cetina, K.: Sociality with objects: social relations in postsocial knowledge societies. Theory Cult. Soc. **14**(4), 1–30 (1997). https://doi.org/10.1177/026327697014004001
23. Manouselis, N., Drachsler, H., Vuorikari, R., Hummel, H., Koper, R.: Recommender systems in technology enhanced learning. In: Ricci, F., Rokach, L., Shapira, B., Kantor, P.B. (eds.) Recommender Systems Handbook, pp. 387–415. Springer, Boston (2011). https://doi.org/10.1007/978-0-387-85820-3_12
24. Montessori, M.: The Montessori Method. Transaction Publishers, Piscataway (2013)
25. Papert, S., Harel, I.: Situating constructionism. Constructionism **36**(2), 1–11 (1991)
26. Papert, S.: The Children's Machine: Rethinking School in the Computer Age. Basic Books, New York (1993)
27. Resnick, M., Rosenbaum, E.: Designing for tinkerability. In: Honey, M., Kanter, D.E. (eds.) Design, Make, Play: Growing the Next Generation of STEM Innovators, pp. 163–181. CRC Press, Boca Raton (2013)
28. Stoll, L., Louis, K.S.: Professional learning communities: elaborating new approaches, pp. 1–13 (2007)
29. Unterfrauner, E., Voigt, C., Schön, S.: Towards a model of early entrepreneurial education: appreciation, facilitation and evaluation. In: 8th International Conference in Methodologies and Intelligent Systems for Technology Enhanced Learning (2018)
30. Voigt, C.: Not every remix is an innovation: a network perspective on the 3D-printing community. In: 10th ACM Web Science Conference, pp. 153–161 (2018). https://doi.org/10.1145/3201064.3201070
31. Voigt, C., Montero, C.S., Menichinelli, M.: An empirically informed taxonomy for the maker movement. In: Bagnoli, F., et al. (eds.) INSCI 2016. LNCS, vol. 9934, pp. 189–204. Springer, Cham (2016). https://doi.org/10.1007/978-3-319-45982-0_17
32. Voigt, C., Schön, S., Hofer, M.: Innovation management in schools: barriers and enablers to making as educative practice. In: Multikonferenz Wirtschaftsinformatik (MKWI) (2018)
33. Voigt, C., Unterfrauner, E., Stelzer, R.: Diversity in FabLabs: culture, role models and the gendering of making. In: Kompatsiaris, I., et al. (eds.) INSCI 2017. LNCS, vol. 10673, pp. 52–68. Springer, Cham (2017). https://doi.org/10.1007/978-3-319-70284-1_5
34. Wenger, E.: Communities of practice and social learning systems. In: Nicolini, D., Gherardi, S., Yanow, D. (eds.) Knowing in Organizations: A Practice-Based Approach, pp. 76–99. ME Sharpe Inc. (2003)

Cybersport Community: Social Structures Transformation as a Basis for Intercultural Dialogue

Vera Boguslavskaya[1] , Ekaterina Budnik[1] , Alyona Azizulova[1] ,
and Larisa V. Sharakhina[2(✉)]

[1] The Pushkin State Russian Language Institute, Moscow, Russia
{vvboguslavskaya, eabudnik}@pushkin.institute,
azizla.swiftwind@mail.ru
[2] Saint Petersburg Electrotechnical University "LETI"/ETU,
St. Petersburg, Russia
lvkolganova@gmail.com

Abstract. The existence of the cybersport community as a special Information society social structure whose members are united by common interests and have their own communication infrastructure is reviewed in the article. ESport Mass Media features as an element of eSport media scene constituting cybersport community are represented. The potential of e-sports as a platform for creating a tolerant attitude to representatives of other countries and cultures, intercultural and interethnic dialogue is demonstrated. Social dialect development as a marker of recognition in the society of gamers also analysed.

Keywords: ESport · ESport media · Social structures
Intercultural communication · Information society

1 Introduction

If to conceptualize the cybersport (esport) and cybersport media in the modern society we should stress that their existence became possible only in Information society as far as esport is the result of information technologies development itself. Review of e-sport community as media communication community phenomenon in the global intercultural communication scene should be considered as a primary objective of the analysis, the appearance and development of the phenomenon (as an extralinguistic factor) forms the tendency of e-sport sociolect evolution.

Post-industrial and Information society scholars considered globalization as one of the key features of it (David Harvey, Anthony Giddens, Manuel Castells, Saskia Sassen, and others) and the focus of their researches was made on social communication and structure transformation rather than on economic impact. According to their points of views globalization can't be viewed only as successful business models' global replication, but mostly social structures, human mentalities and language practices transformation.

© Springer Nature Switzerland AG 2018
S. S. Bodrunova (Ed.): INSCI 2018, LNCS 11193, pp. 300–311, 2018.
https://doi.org/10.1007/978-3-030-01437-7_23

Moreover, information technologies influence on globalization processes lead to rethinking of "social structure" concept. A British sociologist Anthony Giddens, e.g., defines structures as consisting of rules and resources involving human action: the rules constrain the actions, the resources make it possible, and system can be understood through the application of generative rules and resources is produced and reproduced in social interaction [1].

Thus, we may state the reality of virtual social structures.

As a matter of interest, we may note that 2 or 3 decades ago the most of researchers considered virtual reality and online communication as supplements to direct inter-personal communication [2, 3]. The modern reality shows the different situation: lots of people replace direct interpersonal communication by online interaction with no travel costs and extended communication geography [4].

Internet allowed uniting in one communication system different nations, cultures, and subcultures representatives, who are different in mass-communication interactions due to their priorities. And these complex priorities intercommunication represents the system of values, which can lead to nationally specific values model creation, illus-trating individual liberty in mass communication [5]. In this case the main feature separating "e-sports from casual play in living rooms is <its> the ability to attract audiences, but game audiences have expanded beyond just competitions" [6], thus e-sport forms a communication community, unites participants and the audience (ob-servers, fans, third parties) in one cybersport community with different roles in it.

Modern Internet communication can be viewed as a global self-actualization arena [7]. The Article 19 of The Universal Declaration of Human Rights states: "Everyone has the right to freedom of opinion and expression; this right includes freedom to hold opinions without interference and to seek, receive and impart information and ideas through any media and regardless of frontiers" (the Declaration was proclaimed by the United Nations General Assembly in Paris on 10 December 1948 [8].

But at the same time, it is becoming obvious that "Internet is a little more to reproduce frontiers of users' mentalities and a bit less than destroy boundaries" [9]. And here is the case of interest for our and further investigation the book by T.L. Taylor "Raising the Stakes: E-Sports and the Professionalization of Computer Gam-ing": "one of the interesting things about e-sports is the way it is constructed across national lines but still quite rooted and shaped by local contexts" [10].

As the result, information technologies development made different countries cit-izens with different physical abilities union real (based on their common interests, lifestyles, traditions, possibly thinking patterns), and these are quite closed commu-nities. Cybersport constitutes the corroboration as far as an esport community exists beyond borders but has its rituals, forms its common language, which can't be understood by other people.

Computer video games have become the object of a research discipline "Game Studies" regarded to begin its history in 2001 by "Game Studies. The International Journal of Computer Game Research" foundation by IT University of Copenhagen (http://www.gamestudies.org/). MIT Game Lab often considered as a world renown authority in the field of game industry and the research "E-Sports Broadcasting" by Sell [11] is of interest for us as a prerequisite for our study.

These provisions will be acknowledged by researches represented in the article. Mediatexts (127 articles, news, comments) from Dota 2, Counter-Strike: Global Offensive (CS:GO), and Hearthstone: Heroes of Warcraft games mediascene, provided by Russian e-sport Mass media such as Cybersport.ru, Cyber.Sports.ru and e-sport Internet streaming records by RuHub and StarLadder on Twitch and Youtube in November 2016 - May 2018 (with the focus on texts in April – May 2018) composed the empirical basis of the research. Traditional methods of linguistic analysis (semantic-syntactic and stylistic methods), discourse analysis, elements of praxiological-linguistic and linguoculturological analysis designed the methodology.

2   Esport Media Scene

ESport, or cybersport is a form of virtual competition using videogames. These contestants are organised in teams or represented by individuals and their computers serve as sports equipments, while the game creates a virtual space and determines rules of the competition. And e-sport gained its own media scene and formed its international virtual community in a relatively short period of time.

Lots of countries as well as Russia officially recognized eSports as an official real sport and supported by governments (Order No 470 Ministry of Sport of the Russian Federation, issued 29.04.2016). E-sport Federation of Russia singles out the following cybersport disciplines based on e-sport games genres: "Battle Arena", "Real Time Strategy" (RTS), "Shooter", "Fighting", "Contention-Based Puzzles", "Technical Simulator Games", and "Sport Simulator Games". But at the same time such classification is still used for official documents, because e-sport games Dota 2, League of Legends, and Heroes of the Storm are considered as RTS games, but these games created their own information and media scenes. Gamers and journalists interested in these games use different term systems and slangs and are likely to be confused by fragments of other game discourses. In this case football and cyberfootball have much more similarities in comparison with these games assertedly considered to belong to one e-sport discipline.

At the same time there are only about 20 e-sport games with tournaments corresponding to contention-based elements presence, absence of plot, short game sessions and primary equal treatment of all gamers, that's why e-sport community tend to view definite games as definite e-sport disciplines. The most popular it the world are still "Counter-Strike: Global Offensive" (about 12 million players, the most popular in USA – 17,81% of the whole world number of gamers) and "Dota 2 (about 8 million players, the most popular in Russia – 18,13% gamers) [12].

Today we may state that local computer games are moving towards global multiplayer contests with millions of gamers competing to each other rather than to machine intelligence. And for the present time every mobile casual game for every age and gender has its league table for gamers results cross-checking. Esport has become a scope of gamers' activity where their contention-based interests could become a profession, a lifestyle forming their interest areas and system of values.

Thus, computer videogames have become a factor of a new social reality formation and a new network social communication space creation which is possible to managing and modeling as any other media scene [13]. Analysing computer game phenomenon V. Goudimov already in 2005 considered it as a factor of social reality and civil morality formation [14]. According to researches broadcasting of major eSports competitions draw bigger audiences than the Stanley Cup final and the National Hockey League contests; the Juniper Research and Adobe forecast the NBA and Formula One rates hitting in coming years [15].

ESport media scene created in a short period of time meets the esport community members needs and interests, forms their information channels to broadcast professional cybersport contests [16].

A lot of traditional mass media in Russia try to include topics related to e-sport events (Match.TV can serve as an example), reprinting content from specialized e-sport Mass Media, but this content is quite specific and can't be perceived with much interest by the audience of such Mass Media. Thus, specialized e-sport Mass Media are still should be considered as main "tools" for e-sport media discourse. Cybersport.ru and Cyber.sports.ru, special sections of Championat.com and Sports.ru, Mid.tv niche TV channel may serve as examples in Russia. Other media mostly reprint the information. Unlike the printed and electronic Mass Media, devoted to computer games novelties reviews the esport media content based on analytics and news of the cybersport competitions, teams and gamers, different tournaments results, etc. [17].

Mostly Russian esport articles are accompanied by high quality visual content such as videonews, tournament recordings and highlights. If to analyse the philological part of these materials we are mostly interested in the visualization which serves as an esthetic part of it and functions as a tool of influense on auditorium minds: photos and illustrations, official symbols and infographics used in eSport media publications.

Besides eSport information portals niche Twitch-channels broadcasting such tournaments with professional commenting, analytics are to review as an examples of cybersport Mass Media. RuHub and StarLadder accompanied by Youtube channels introducing tournaments broadcasts are considered as the most popular of them [16].

ESport tournaments broadcasts are viewed by millions of people worldwide and 24/7: the most popular and vital contests are aired through streaming platforms offered by the above mentioned Twitch.tv, Youtube, and Facebook, VKontakte.

The statistics represented by Newzoo (https://newzoo.com) states the 2012-2015 audience gain from 134 mln. to 226 mln. of viewers, and 350 mln. of viewers are forecasted by 2019. And the quantity of eSport competitions viewers who observe such tournaments twice per a month (that is to say on a regular basis) exceeded the half of the total number. Dota 2 Tournament pay-off (The International 2017 with US$25 million in prize money) between the European Team Liquid and the Chinese LGD Forever Young was viewed by 11 mln. of people eventhough for the most of CIS countries and China it was in the dead of night.

2.1 ESport Media Interactivity

ESport Mass Media can be characterized by stressed interactivity expressed in the following features: good feedback, blogosphere, interactive embedding, eSport broadcasts interactivity.

1. Feedback

Every eSport mediaplatform has a tool for evaluating and commenting on the materials. And the users' comments of the article very often exceed the volume of it by 10 or more times. The discussion of the article is followed by the discussion of the comments and the exchange of opinions or additional information. Thus, the process of reading is not finished within the official material and followed by the comments reading. It creates a possibility to communicate with journalists and analyst who also read the content.

Users are let to demonstrate their attitude to any comment, like or dislike it with one mouse click. Users' points number gained this way is represented in their profiles and is ranked accordingly, thus, article commenting is transformed to a game with a profile evolution.

Special moderators are responsible to organize a discussion, to delete coarse language and abusive comments. Within the commenting sector users apply gamers slang and no miscommunications could be observed as far as they are the members of one media scene.

And it is a very frequent case when article authors or bloggers are the most active commentators of their materials.

2. Blogosphere

As far as eSport media are developing and the industrial information volumes are rising constantly lots of eSport media adapted to the readers initiative to write their own stories instead of content reading only. For example, the biggest Russian eSport media Cybersport.ru has a special rubric for users' blogs and some of the stories after moderation process can be represented on its frontpage.

Special eSprot column of a popular Russian Sport.ru is comprised of cybersport journalists' blogs.

Blog entries as well as official material include not only texts but also photo and TV materials, and infographics. Users do not find themselves limited by tight terminology and are in habbit to use slangisms, broadcasting quotations and internet-mems. But this feature can be observed as a basic difference of Cybersport.ru and Cyber.Sports.ru articles: the first one mostly represents official journalistic materials, and the second one is comprised of blogers' entries and has a reputation of entertaining news media.

3. Interactive embedding

Such materials include polls, tests, and contests mostly with entertainment content. We can find these embeddings both on official Mass Media web-pages and social media. Thanks to these users do not only perceive news but test their consciousness and expertise, vote for their favourite teams, and gain virtual and sometimes real prizes for their activities.

4. ESport broadcasts interactivity

Online eSport broadcasting tournaments and other events have a higher level of interactivity in comparison to news media.

The basic communication platform of official commentators with their spectators is represented by online chats of streaming platforms (Twitch, Youtube). These chats are used during broadcasts for interactions to ask questions and feedbacks in case of video or sound troubles. Observers can also express their emotions with a help of special smiles.

Since there are lots of users who would like to leave their message in a chat, chat moderators are forced to impose restrictions on the quantity of messages by one user per a minute and other. Such restrictions help normal chat functioning and in the period of wide broadcasts with a number of 200,000 viewers and more a message ribbon is updating with a very high frequency and reading it becomes challenging.

There are other chat restrictions can be noted: automatic moderation does not let to occur words with lots of upper cases and ban for a period of time users overdoing unreadable symbols. These symbols are used rather often to create special graphic images directly in such chats. And in case of interest other users can start to copy such combinations and repeat this image again and again. One of the first of such images was a picture of a goose and as a result of it an idiomatic phrase in Russian "Let the goose, workies!". Nevertheless, such behavior can be punished by a temporal ban.

Unfortunately, automatic chat moderation during broadcasts is not applied to coarse language. Russian speaking viewers are often to use this interdiction absence to transform a broadcasting chat into creative offence area. Need to notice that international chats (mostly in English) are more tolerant and welcoming to other viewers, commentators, and teams rather than Russian ones.

Besides interactive chat broadcasts are very often have embedded communication with social media users, e.g. Twitter. Aired anchors and commentators invite viewers to publish their questions, photos, etc. with special hashtags. Then editors choose the most interesting publications to represent them during the broadcast pauses, analysts are let to answer these questions or to comment on photos. Moreover, random giveaways are very widespread during such broadcasts.

Thus, we represented main features on eSport media scene as a communication platform of cybersport community, our further focus will be made on intercultural communication as a feature of eSport community.

3 Intercultural Communication in the Cybersports Community

Despite the fact that in the scientific environment the debates about the benefits and dangers of hobby for computer games still persist, Massive Multiplayer Online Role Playing Games (MMORPGs), and in particular the relation between computer-mediated-communication (CMC) on the emergence of specific group cultures in virtual groups created in the game context, provide an opportunity to make intercultural communication an integral part of everyday life.

Today, the creators of computer games and the organizers of cybersport tournaments initially focus on the international audience. Servers for online games are located in various parts of the world. Team leaders recruit players of different origins. It is rather difficult to determine cultural aspects (the nationality or ethnicity of the players) as important for most of the teams, and usually their policy of recruitment is based on much more practical issues (knowledge of language for a better communication and cooperation when gaming). For the e-sports community, there are no political boundaries and fans of all countries of the region form their community. Also, team leaders are in charge of many social roles: they support group actions, regulate group attitudes and help solving group conflicts. As such, they constitute a fundamental element of group cohesion.

Adherence to any cybersport discipline automatically means engaging in the global gaming community. Since a very large number of international tournaments take place annually, where players from all over the world are invited, tournament qualifications are constantly played on the Internet: relating to server locality, these qualifications are divided according to the regions (for ex., in the discipline Dota 2: North and South America, Europe, CIS, China and South-East Asia). Since at the main part of the competition the team represents not a specific country, but a whole region, political barriers are automatically removed. This is obvious on the CIS saturation coverage of events: tournaments are broadcasted and commented on in Russian, regardless of whether in Russia, Ukraine or Kazakhstan there is broadcasting studio. Mixed compounds are often formed within the region, but cases of the formation of multinational teams from all points of the world are frequent - it all depends on the possibility of communication and the level of the game.

One of the unspoken laws of the functioning in the e-sports community is tolerance which is one of the consequences of globalization. According to some studies, pro-e-sports youth is more tolerant and predisposed to inter-ethnic communication [18]. In this regard, e-sports events can be exploited as an effective way of forming interethnic and intercultural communication in the youth environment.

Virtus.pro team called "The Legendary Golden five" success in Dota 2 2016 Boston Major tournament had representatives from Russia and Ukraine and their success in qualification tournaments led to their superiority image formation (by visual and verbal content) by e-sport media regardless to political discourse of Russian-Ukrainian relations [19, 20].

Many players have found political correctness to be the best method of avoiding conflicts resulting in a team breakdown, which caused professional e-sport managers to create strict regulations as regards sanctions to people who insult others because of their race, sex, beliefs, etc. For ex., the Valve company, the creator of Dota2, has also an in-game policy of banning outraging players and even teams from the game for different periods according to the amount of reports from other players.

Overwatch World Cup can serve us as an example of tolerance promotion for younger generation mentalities as far as this tournament is open to unexperienced gamers. It is a team shooter game plotted in future with such game characters as scientists, military men, inventors from different countries of the world (Russia, GB, Switzerland, Brasilia, Namibia, China, etc.); they work together to combat terrorism [21].

Despite the fact that the subject of military battles in computer games is practically materialized (compared to traditional sports, where appealing to such images is a kind of detailed thematic metaphor), the unifying power of e-sports cannot be overemphasized. In virtual reality, political differences lose their validity. Moreover, thanks to universal vocabulary and a large number of English wordloans, in-game communication, that is essential for teamwork, is being established between representatives of various nations [22]. Given that this communication occurs between representatives of young generations of different countries, it is easy to guess what a beneficial effect such an association has on strengthening minds - an influence that would be difficult to provide by any other special means. In the context of our political situation, this is best seen in the relationship between Russian and Ukrainian players. Within the framework of the cybersport industry, Russia, Ukraine, Belarus, Kazakhstan and other CIS countries are considered to be a single region (this is important at the level of regional qualifications for various tournaments, where a specific number of seats is allocated for each of the world regions). And, despite recent conflicts between countries, the CIS region has not lost its integrity either in the global plan or in terms of the attitude of the players of the organizations and the community towards this. Most of the teams from the CIS continue to be mixed in the sense of nationality, fans from Russia support teams from Ukraine, and vice versa.

In this regard, it can be assumed that, under some conditions, such as regularity and focus on cooperation, e-sports activities can be an effective way of creating inter-ethnic and intercultural communication among young people.

As in many other spheres of human activity, English is the international language of communication, which is the original language in most video games. This causes a huge flow of English loanwords, which form the professional language of cybersport media, and it, in turn, is the basis for the slang, used by e-sports fans for communication. To understand this social dialect, the elementary English skills are not enough – one needs to remember the names of the game objects and understand the system of their interaction. That is why former professionals mostly become journalists, commentators, editors of cybersport media.

But large volumes of situational international communication also have side effects: Russian-speaking young people outside the gaming environment continue to communicate in a mixture of Russian and English, distorting both simultaneously, supplying their speech with in-game slang. One, who is not immersed in the informational field of e-sports, will not be able to understand anything from such a communication. This kind of social dialect is partly used by commentators during cybersport broadcasts, and it also serves as a marker for belonging to the gaming community.

4   The Language of Cybersport

In the studies of sports journalism, the question of the justification of using a large number of special terminology in journalism has already been a subject of research [23]. The question, then, arises as to how much sports journalism and eSport media take into account the interests of the unprepared reader. Identification of key elements in the discourse of e-sports news determines the degree of availability of such content for the mass recipient, helps to create recommendations on the choice of the form of submission of information [24].

In order to answer the aforesaid question, it is necessary to touch on the following problem – the delineation of special terminology that has much to do with cybersport discourse and gaming slang. Its frequent usage is a sign of journalists' unprofessionalism and their unwillingness to work for a wider audience.

In modern reality, there are sublingual systems, the dynamics of which do not allow one to unequivocally distinguish between the terminology and slang. Such systems include, for example, computer language (or Internet slang), as well as the language of some sports, including the terminology of extreme sportsmen and cyber sportsmen.

Like any other new sports terminology, e-sports came into Russian society with its formed English loanwords. Since the dynamics of the distribution of virtual competitions is extremely high and the flow of loanwords is great, e-journalists often come up with the question: should one or another unit of vocabulary be considered a term or a jargon and in what cases the loanword is worth being substituted with a Russian analog, and when it is impractical.

Traditional sport, which appeared in Russia long before the information age, has its own terminology systems. Within these systems, there is a division into terms proper, informal terms (professionalism) and slang (from the first to the third, the degree of expressiveness, saving of speech resources and unofficial communication situations in which they are used increase). In those sports spheres that have not yet become professional (skateboarding, parkour, kiting, extreme sports), the character of communication is informal in any situation, the style of vocabulary differentiation is virtually minimal. Despite the fact that due to the general availability of virtual competitions, professional athletes, journalists and spectators/gamers use the same terminology system; in this linguistic environment it is often possible to distinguish the term and jargon.

And most often this line has to be carried out exactly to journalists - creators of content on cybersport portals and social networks, analysts and commentators of tournament broadcasts. As we have already mentioned, the basis for the professional slang of cyber sportsmen are English wordloans, which adopt to the Russian language system and even begin to form their own family of words. The emergence of such loanwords depends largely on (1) the emergence of new games;(2) the award to a particular game of the status of cybersport discipline; (3) the release of updates and patches to existing disciplines.

As in other similar cases, the borrowed terms differ in their compactness and capacity. Attempts to express their content by means of the Russian language lead to the creation of cumbersome constructions. Such constructions slow down the speech of the journalist and make it difficult to understand.

The fact that these lexical units are borrowed is confirmed by the peculiarities of using these units by Russian-speaking journalists, particularly during cybersport broadcasts - which characterizes the formation of linguocultural features of virtual communication [25, 26]. Usually, even those terms that are never found in printed materials either in translated or in transliterated form (for example, the names of "artefacts' in Dota 2 – Aeon Disk, Nullifier, Bloodthorn), in Russian oral speech are declining according to Russian grammar rules. As for those terms that have already received their transliterated word form in the game and media texts, their "morphological and derivational adaptation <...> indicate a complete and unconditional entry into the terminology of new professional language" [27]: to force - "to push", in

Russian interpretation the verb is transliterated as [fors] and changed according to Russian grammar rules.

The grammatical gender of such loanwords is determined, in addition to their genus in the English language, (1) by their sound appearance (for example, anglicisms on a hard consonant "plant", "spawned" according to the masculine nouns with a solid base and zero ending), (2) their gender and aspect correlation (Healing Salve is treated as a "bottle with a healing drink," which gives the female gender of declension – "-a" at the end: "drank salv**a**", "left without salv**a**").

How does modern cyber journalism deal with the loanwords? Since the virtual competitions is tied to games and gaming clients (special software for connecting to on-line games), official translations or localization help to adapt borrowed terms into the Russian language. Due to russification, some lexical units become the official terms (compare *tower - "taver"* (colloq.) in Russian version, without translation).

The analysis of the Russian e-sport media scene can give as examples of other languages expressions to transform into the world spread proverbial phrases. "Que ota?" (the correct variant will be "quer outra") should be translated from Portuguese as "Do you want some more?" in the meaning of "Do you want to take one more bullet?", and it is a world spread battle-cry in Counter-Strike media space regardless to the level of Portuguese language knowledge.

Dota 2 game developers significantly contributed to some commentators' expressions popularization by embedding then into the game scene as shouted slogans: the cosmopolitan diffusion got the Ukranian commentators' Vitaly Volochai ("Ай-яй-яй-яй-яй, что сейчас произошло!") and Roman Lepekhin ("Это! Просто! Нечто!") and other expressions in Russian.

The e-sportsmen's nicknames are the case of cross-cultural mixture interest too. The most of them use Latin alphabet and it makes the work of international commentators easier during tournaments broadcastings, but there are lots of other examples: Alexander "XBOCT" Dashkevich nickname is comprised of Latin symbols, but English-speaking commentators pronounce it like "Huvoss", imitating the Russian sounding; Singapore gamer Daryl Koh 冰冰冰 Pei Xiang has 3 Chinese characters meaning "ice" in his nickname and the international e-sport community recognize him as "iceiceice".

E-sport words of new literacy, speech etiquette and the active development of methods and channels for replenishing vocabulary are seeking their ways to become a part of a special terminology system.

Summarizing all the above mentioned, it should be noted that the problem of distinguishing terminology and jargon, which in turn is closely connected with the issues of borrowing and adapting the English language lexicon, is very acute within the framework of the eSport media discourse and needs further and deeper research.

5 Conclusion

Thus, the glimpses of our review of e-sport community as media communication community phenomenon in the global intercultural communication scene represented in the article makes the possibility to state the existence of the cybersport community as a special social structure whose members are united by common interests and have their own communication infrastructure. For e-sports' media is characterized by a high degree of interactivity, which manifests itself in the following characteristics: feedback, blogging, interactive inclusion, interactivity of cybersport broadcasts. Today in the world of computer games there is a tendency of transition from local cyberspace to global, covering millions of players, which naturally forms situations for intercultural communication. Interaction between the members of the e-sports community is limited to a greater extent by language barriers (if any), rather than by geographic or cultural differences, which demonstrates the potential of e-sports as a platform for creating a tolerant attitude to representatives of other countries and cultures, intercultural and interethnic dialogue. Nevertheless, a large number of borrowings, mainly from the English language, allows us to talk about the formation of social dialect, the possession of which serves as a marker of recognition in the society of gamers. The above characteristics of the cybersport community form it into a separate flexible social system, which is capable of self-development and self-regulation, regardless of external events.

References

1. Bryant, C., Jary, D.: The Blackwell companion to major contemporary social theorists. Blackwell, Oxford (2003). https://doi.org/10.1002/9780470999912.ch11. / Accessed 11 June 2018
2. Dutton, W.H.: Society on the Line: Information Politics in the Digital Age. Oxford University Press, Oxford (1999)
3. Woolgar, S.: Virtual Society? Technology, Cyberbole, Reality. Oxford University Press, Oxford (2002)
4. Dutton, W.H.: Social Transformation in an Information Society: Rethinking Access to You and the World. http://www.unesco.org/new/en/communication-and-information/resources/publications-and-communication-materials/publications/full-list/social-transformation-in-an-information-society-rethinking-access-to-you-and-the-world/. Accessed 09 June 2018
5. Korkonosenko, S.G., Kudryavtseva, M.E., Slutskiy, P.A.: Individual Liberty in Mass Communication. ETU Publishing House, St. Petersburg (2010)
6. Anderson, S.L.: Watching people is not a game: interactive online corporeality, twitch.tv and videogame streams. Game Stud. **17**(1) (2017). http://gamestudies.org/1701/articles/anderson. Accessed 17 July 2018
7. Sharakhina, L.V.: Splinternet in individual's social inequality formation. In: XIV Whole Russian Scientific Conference Proceedings of Information-Communication-Society, pp. 298–301. ETU Publishing House, St. Petersburg (2017)
8. General Assembly resolution 217 A. http://www.un.org/en/universal-declaration-human-rights/. Accessed 09 June 2018
9. Epple, N.: Virtual kitchens. Vedomosti 4211, 25 November 2016
10. Taylor, T.L.: Raising the Stakes: E-Sports and the Professionalization of Computer Gaming. First MIT Press Paperback edition (2015)
11. Sell, J.: E-sports broadcasting. Thesis for Masters of Science in Comparative Media Studies. Massachusetts Institute of Technology (2015), http://gamelab.mit.edu/research/e-sports-broadcasting/. Accessed 09 June 2018

12. Kiryukin, A.: «FUki»: Geography of Games: Russians Like Dota2 while Americans – CS: GO, Cybersport.ru (2015/04/05), https://www.cybersport.ru/news/geografiya-igr-rossiyane-lyubyat-dota-2-a-amerikantsy-cs-go. Accessed 14 July 2018
13. Boguslavskaya, V.V.: Methodology features of journalistic texts lingvosociocultural modeling. accents. New Mass Commun. 5–6(26–27), 97–102 (2001)
14. Goudimov, V.V.: Video Games Psychology and Gamers Fantasies. http://www.medicin form.net/comp/comp_psych23.htm. Accessed 10 June 2018
15. Meshalkin, Y.: To win by gaming. ESport Industry Landscape: Money, Brands, the Biggest Tournaments. Sport Marketing in Russia 1, 36–39 (2018). https://marspo.ru/files/D_ MarSpo_2018.pdf. Accessed 10 June 2018
16. Zaripov, A.R.: Sport internet media: structural semiotic analyses. Res. Prior. 20, 2 (2015)
17. Terpelets, Zh.A.: Linguistic and genres peculiarities of sport discourse as a mass media discourse variant. In: Kuban State Sport and Tourism University Academic Staff Scientific and Methodical Conference Proceedings, Krasnodar (2015)
18. Afonina, I.S., Alieva, M.G.: Psychological characteristics of the personality of gamers and cyber sportsmen. In: A Compilation of Articles of the 14th International Scientific and Research Competition, Part 4, pp. 202–204. MCSN "Science and Education", Penza (2018). Best Student Article 2018
19. Medvedeva, Y.: The key hope of CIS in Boston, Cyber.sports.ru., 28 Nov 2016. https:// cyber.sports.ru/tribuna/blogs/valvemajor/1118985.html. Accessed 14 July 2018
20. Naumov, M.: «Leko»: The New CIS Kings: Virtus.pro – the main favourite of The Boston Major, Cybersport.ru, 12 Mar 2016. Accessed 14 July 2018
21. https://playoverwatch.com/ru-ru/. Accessed 17 July 2018
22. Gerasimenko, T.L., Budnik, E.A.: Experience of using Skype technology as an effective means of forming and improving communicative language competence. Internet-J. "NAUKOVEDENIE" 7(3) (2015). http://naukovedenie.ru/PDF/46PVN315.pdf. Accessed 14 June 2018
23. Khromov, S.S., Boguslavskaya, V.V.: Russian language in modern intercultural commu-nication: some issues and problems. Transl. Ind. 1(1), 372–376 (2013)
24. Pokalyukhin, S.Yu.: Linguistic analysis of sports commentary. Ling. Mobil. 4(43), 83–86 (2013)
25. Boguslavskaya, V.V., Boguslavsky, I.V.: Mediatext and hashtags: digital media transfor-mation. Humanit. Vector 12(5), 51–58 (2017)
26. Erofeeva, I.V., Boguslavskaya, V.V., Teplyashina, A.N., Tolstokulakova, Yu.V.: Linguistic and cultural modeling of the media text. ZabSU, Chita (2017)
27. Panevina, O.S., Trofimova, Yu.A.: The problem of translation and interpretation computer lexicon. Actual Probl. Humanit. Nat. Sci. 1-2(97), 38–40 (2017)

Author Index

Printed in the United States
By Bookmasters

Printed in the United States
By Bookmasters